hands-on
science

Grade Seven

Jennifer Lawson

Kevin Chambers

Janine Donovan

Richard Hechter

Jennifer Janzen

Nancy Josephson

Sean Levenson

PORTAGE & MAIN PRESS

Winnipeg • Manitoba • Canada

Portage & Main Press acknowledges the financial support of the Government of Canada through the Book Publishing Industry Development Program (BPIDP) for our publishing activities.

Printed and bound in Canada by
The Prolific Group

**National Library of Canada
Cataloguing in Publication**

Lawson, Jennifer E. (Jennifer Elizabeth), 1959-
   Hands-on science: grade 7/Jennifer Lawson.

Includes bibliographical references.

For use with the Manitoba grade 7 curriculum.

ISBN 10: 1-55379-025-1
ISBN 13: 978-1-55379-025-9

1. Science – Study and teaching
   (Elementary)
   I. Title.

Q161.2.L397 2004 372.35'044 C2004-902744-1

ISBN-10: 1-55379-025-1
ISBN-13: 978-1-55379-025-9

Series Editor: Jill Condra
Assistant Editor: Leigh Hambly

Book and Cover Design: Relish Design Ltd.
Illustrations: Jess Dixon

PORTAGE & MAIN PRESS

100-318 McDermot Avenue
Winnipeg, Manitoba, Canada R3A 0A2

E-mail: books@portageandmainpress.com
Tel: 204-987-3500
Toll Free: 1-800-667-9673
Fax: 1-866-734-8477

Contents

Introduction to *Hands-On Science*

Program Introduction

Hands-On Science develops students' scientific literacy through active inquiry, problem solving, and decision making. With each activity in the program, students are encouraged to explore, investigate, and ask questions as a means of heightening their own curiosity about the world around them. Students solve problems through firsthand experiences, and by observing and examining objects within their environment. In order for students to develop scientific literacy, hands-on experience is of utmost importance – in fact, it is essential.

The Foundations of Scientific Literacy

Hands-On Science focuses on the four foundation statements for scientific literacy in Canada, as established in the Pan-Canadian Protocol.* These foundation statements are the bases for the learning outcomes identified in ***Hands-On Science***.

Foundation 1: Science, Technology, Society, and the Environment (STSE)

Students will develop an understanding of the nature of science and technology, of the relationships between science and technology, and of the social and environmental contexts of science and technology.

Foundation 2: Skills

Students will develop the skills required for scientific and technological inquiry, for solving problems, for communicating scientific ideas and results, for working collaboratively, and for making informed decisions.

Foundation 3: Knowledge

Students will construct knowledge and understandings of concepts in life science, physical science, and earth and space science, and apply these understandings to interpret, integrate, and extend their knowledge.

Foundation 4: Attitudes

Students will be encouraged to develop attitudes that support responsible acquisition and application of scientific and technological knowledge to the mutual benefit of self, society, and the environment.

Common Framework of Science Learning Outcomes K-12: Pan-Canadian Protocol for Collaboration on School Curriculum (1997).

▶

Unit 1: Interactions Within Ecosystems

- ☐ Use appropriate vocabulary related to their investigations of interactions within ecosystems.

  Include: ecosystem, biosphere, abiotic, biotic, organisms, ecological succession, photosynthesis, cellular respiration, ecological pyramid, bioaccumulation, scavengers, decomposers, micro-organisms

- ☐ Define ecosystem, and describe various examples that range from the microscopic to the entire biosphere.

  Include: a place on Earth where living things interact with other living things as well as non-living things

- ☐ Identify abiotic and biotic components of ecosystems that allow particular organisms to survive.

- ☐ Describe ecological succession and identify signs of succession in a variety of ecosystems.

  Include: the natural process whereby some species are replaced by other species in a predictable pattern

- ☐ Identify and describe positive and negative examples of human interventions that have an impact on ecological succession or the makeup of ecosystems.

  Examples: positive - protecting habitats, reintroducing species; negative - preventing natural fires, introducing non-indigenous species, draining wetlands for agriculture or housing

- ☐ Identify environmental, social, and economic factors that should be considered in the management and preservation of ecosystems.

  Examples: habitat preservation, recreation, employment, industrial growth, resource development

- ☐ Propose a course of action to protect the habitat of a particular organism within an ecosystem.

  Examples: protect the nesting habitat of a given bird in a local wetland

- ☐ Compare photosynthesis to cellular respiration, and explain how both are part of the cycling of matter and the transfer of energy in ecosystems.

  Include: photosynthesis: water + carbon dioxide + light energy = sugar + oxygen in the presence of chlorophyll; cellular respiration: sugar + oxygen = water + carbon dioxide + energy

- ☐ Analyze food webs, using ecological pyramids, to show energy gained or lost at various consumer levels.

  Include: producers; primary, secondary, and tertiary consumers

- ☐ Analyze, using ecological pyramids, the implications of the loss of producers and consumers to the transfer of energy within an ecosystem.

- ☐ Explain, using ecological pyramids, the potential for bioaccumulation within an ecosystem.

- ☐ Provide examples of scavengers and decomposers, and describe their role in cycling matter in an ecosystem.

  Include: micro-organisms

- ☐ Demonstrate proper use and care of the microscope to observe micro-organisms.

  Include: preparing wet mounts beginning with the least powerful lens; focussing; drawing specimens; indicating magnification

- ☐ Identify benefical and harmful roles played by micro-organisms.

  Examples: benefical - aids in digestion, composting, food and vaccine production; harmful - causes disease, food spoilage

- ☐ Research and describe human food production or preservation techniques that apply a knowledge of micro-organisms.

  Examples: bread and yogurt making, food drying, sterilization, refrigeration

Unit 2: Particle Theory of Matter

- ☐ Use appropriate vocabulary related to their investigations of the particle theory of matter.

  Include: boiling and melting points, pure substance, scientific theory, particle theory of matter, temperature, heat, conduction, convection, radiation, mixture, solution, mechanical mixture, homogeneous heterogeneous, solutes, solvents, solubility, concentration, dilute, concentrated, saturated, unsaturated, terms related to forms of energy

- ☐ Evaluate different types of thermometers using the design process.

Examples: materials used, range, sensitivity, durability, scale, cost

- ☐ Demonstrate the effects of heating and cooling on the volume of solids, liquids, and gases, and give examples from daily life.
- ☐ Compare the boiling and melting points of a variety of substances and recognize that boiling and melting points are properties of pure substances.

  Include: water

- ☐ Explain what scientific theories are, and provide some examples.

  Include: a scientific theory helps to explain an observation; when this explanation has been repeatedly tested and shown to be consistent it is generally accepted in the scientific world

- ☐ Describe the particle theory of matter and use it to explain changes of state.
- ☐ Differentiate between the concept of temperature and the concept of heat.
- ☐ Demonstrate how heat can be transmitted through solids, liquids, and gases.

  Include: conduction, convection, radiation

- ☐ Plan an experiment to identify materials that are good heat insulators and good heat conductors, and describe some uses of these materials.
- ☐ Use the design process to construct a prototype that controls the transfer of heat energy.

  Examples: insulated lunch bag, solar oven, home insulation

- ☐ Recognize that heat energy is the most common by-product of energy transformations, and describe some examples.

  Examples: thermal pollution, body heat, friction

- ☐ Identify different forms of energy that can be transformed into heat energy.

  Include: mechanical, chemical, nuclear, electrical

- ☐ Differentiate between pure substances and mixtures by using the particle theory of matter.

  Include: a pure substance is made up of one type of particle; a mixture is made up of two or more types of particles

- ☐ Differentiate between the two types of mixtures, solutions and mechanical mixtures.

  Include: solutions - homogeneous; mechanical mixtures - heterogeneous mixtures

- ☐ Classify a variety of substances used in daily life as pure substances, solutions, or mechanical mixtures.

  Examples: distilled water paint thinner, mouthwash, peanut butter, liquid soap, medicines, sunscreens

- ☐ dentify solutes and solvents in common solid, liquid, and gaseous solutions.
- ☐ Describe solutions by using the particle theory of matter.

  Include: particles have an attraction for each other; the attraction between the particles of solute and solvent keeps them in solution

- ☐ Demonstrate different methods of separating the components of both solutions and mechanical mixtures.

  Examples: distillation, chromatography, evaporation, sieving, dissolving, filtration, decanting, magnetism, sedimentation

- ☐ Identify a separation technique used in industry, and explain why it is appropriate.
- ☐ Experiment to determine factors that affect solubility.

  Include: agitation, surface area, temperature

- ☐ Describe the concentration of a solution in qualitative and quantitative terms, and give examples from daily life when the concentration of a solution influences its usefulness.

  Include: dilute, concentrated, grams of solute per 100 mL

- ☐ Demonstrate the difference between saturated and unsaturated solutions.
- ☐ Discuss the potential harmful effects of some substances on the environment, and identify methods to ensure their safe use and disposal.

  Examples: pollution of groundwater from improper disposal of paints and solvents; pollution of the atmosphere by car exhaust

Unit 3: Heat

Overall Expectations

- ☐ Use appropriate vocabulary related to their investigations of forces and structures.

  Include: frame, shell, solid, centre of gravity, stability, compression, tension, shear, torsion, internal and external forces, stress, structural

▶

---

fatigue, structural failure, load, magnitude, point and plane of application, efficiency.

- ☐ Classify natural and human-built structures found locally and around the world.

  Include: frame, shell, solid

- ☐ dentify the centre of gravity in a model structure, and demonstrate that changes in the location of a structure's centre of gravity affect its stability.

- ☐ dentify internal forces acting on a structure, and describe them using diagrams

  Examples: compression, tension, shear, torsion

- ☐ Identify external forces acting of a structure, and describe them using diagrams

  Examples: snow on a rooftop, wind on a tent, water against a beaver dam

- ☐ Recognize that internal and external forces apply stress to structures, and describe examples in which this stress has led to structual fatigue or structural failure.

- ☐ Investigate to determine that the effect of a force on a structure depends on its magnitude, direction, and point and plane of application.

- ☐ Describe, using diagrams, how common structural shapes and components can increase the strength and stability of a structure.

  Examples: a triangle distributes the downward force of a load evenly between its two vertices

- ☐ Describe and demonstrate methods to increase the strength of materials

  Examples: corrugation of surfaces, lamination of adjacent members, alteration of the shape of components

- ☐ Determine the efficiency of a structure by comparing its mass with the mass of the load it supports.

- ☐ Evaluate a structure to determine the appropriateness of its design, using the design process.

  Examples: jacket, foot stool, local building

- ☐ Use the design process to construct a structure that will withstand the application of an external force.

  Examples: a tower that will remain standing during a simulated earthquake

Unit 4: Forces and Structures

- ☐ Use appropriate vocabulary related to their investigations of the Earth's crust.

  Include: crust, mantle, outer core, inner core, weathering (physical, biological and chemical), erosion, rock cycle, fossil fuel, geothermal energy, continental drift theory, theory of plate tectonics

- ☐ Describe the Earth's structure.

  Include: crust, mantle, outer core, inner core

- ☐ Describe the geological processes involved in rock and mineral formation, and classify rocks and minerals by their method of formation.

- ☐ Investigate and describe the processes of weathering and erosion, and recognize that they cause changes in the landscape over time.

  Include: physical, biological, and chemical weathering

- ☐ Explain how rocks on the Earth constantly undergo a slow process of change through the rock cycle.

- ☐ Identify geologic resources that are used by humans as sources of energy, and describe their method of formation.

  Include: fossil fuels, geothermal energy

- ☐ Identify geologic resources that are present in Manitoba and Canada, and describe the processes involved in their location, extraction, processing, and recycling.

  Include: fossil fuels, minerals

- ☐ Identify environmental impacts of geological resource extraction, and describe techniques used to address these.

- ☐ Recognize that soil is a natural resource, and explain how the characteristics of soil determine its use.

- ☐ Describe methods used to control soil erosion, and recognize the importance of soil conservation.

  Examples: economically important to the agri-food industry, important for controlling the flow of water, necessary for plant growth.

- ☐ Identify environmental, social, and economic factors that should be considered in making informed decisions about land use.

- ☐ Describe evidence used to support the continental drift theory and explain why this theory was not generally accepted by scientists.

▶

☐ Describe evidence used to support the theory of
plate tectonics, the role technology has played in
the development of this theory, and reasons why it
is generally accepted by scientists.

☐ Explain geological processes and events using the
theory of plate tectonics.

Include: mountain formation, earthquakes,
volcanoes

☐ Identify specialized careers involving the study
of the Earth's crust or the utilization of geological
resources, and give examples of technologies used
in each.

Examples: geophysicist, seismologist,
volcanologist, farmer

▶

Program Principles

1. Effective science programs involve hands-on inquiry, problem solving, and decision making.

2. The development of students' skills, attitudes, knowledge, and understanding of STSE issues forms the foundation of the science program.

3. Students have a natural curiosity about science and the world around them. This curiosity must be maintained, fostered, and enhanced through active learning.

4. Science activities must be meaningful, worthwhile, and relate to real-life experiences.

5. The teacher's role in science education is to facilitate activities and encourage critical thinking and reflection. Students learn best by doing, rather than by just listening. The teacher, therefore, should focus on formulating and asking questions rather than simply telling.

6. Science should be taught in correlation with other school subjects. Themes and topics of study should integrate ideas and skills from several core areas whenever possible.

7. The science program should encompass, and draw on, a wide range of educational resources, including literature, nonfiction research material, audio-visual resources, technology, as well as people and places in the local community.

8. Assessment of student learning in science should be designed to focus on performance and understanding, and should be conducted through meaningful assessment techniques carried on throughout the unit of study.

Program Implementation

Program Resources

Hands-On Science is arranged in a format that makes it easy for teachers to plan and implement.

Units are the selected topics of study for the grade level. The units relate directly to the outcomes, which complement those established in the Pan-Canadian Protocol and the Manitoba Curriculum Document for grades 5 to 8 science. The units are organized into several activities. Each unit also includes books for students, a list of annotated web sites, and references for teachers.

The introduction to each unit summarizes the general goals for the unit. The introduction provides an overview of the unit, planning suggestions for teachers, and a list of science vocabulary that should be introduced and focused upon during lessons.

Each unit is organized into topics, based on the outcomes. The topics are arranged in the following format:

Science Background Information for Teachers: Some topics provide teachers with the basic scientific knowledge they will need to present the activities. This information is offered in a clear, concise format, and focuses specifically on the topic of study.

Materials: A complete list of materials required to conduct the main activity is given. The quantity of materials required will depend on how you conduct activities. If students are working individually, you will need enough materials for each student. If students are working in groups, the materials required will be significantly reduced. Many of the identified items are for the teacher to use for display purposes, or for making charts for recording students' ideas.

Hands-On Science • Grade 7

In some cases, visual materials – large pictures, sample charts, and diagrams – have been included with the activity to assist the teacher in presenting ideas and questions, and to encourage discussion. You may wish to reproduce these visuals, mount them on sturdy paper, and laminate them so they can be used for years to come.

Activity: This section details a step-by-step procedure, including higher-level questioning techniques, and suggestions for encouraging exploration and investigation.

Activity Sheet: The reproducible activity sheets are designed to correlate with the outcomes of the activity. Often, the activity sheets are to be used during the activity to record results of investigations. At other times, the sheets are to be used as a follow-up to the activities. Students may work independently on the sheets, in small groups, or you may choose to read through the sheets together and complete them in a large group setting. Activity sheets can also be made into overheads or large experience charts. Since it is important for students to learn to construct their own charts and recording formats, you may want to use the activity sheets as examples of ways to record and communicate ideas about an activity. Students can then create their own sheets rather than use the ones provided.

Note: Activity sheets are meant to be used only in conjunction with, or as a follow-up to, the hands-on activities. The activity sheets are not intended to be the science lesson itself or the sole assessment for the lesson.

Extension: Included are optional activities to extend, enrich, and reinforce the outcomes.

Activity Centre: Included are independent student activities that focus on the outcomes.

Assessment Suggestions: Often, suggestions are made for assessing student learning. These assessment strategies focus specifically on the outcomes of a particular activity topic (assessment is dealt with in detail on page 14). Keep in mind that the suggestions made within the activities are merely ideas to consider – you may use your own assessment techniques, or refer to the other assessment strategies on pages 16-26.

Classroom Environment

The classroom setting is an important aspect of any learning process. An active environment, one that gently hums with the purposeful conversations and activities of students, indicates that meaningful learning is taking place. When studying a specific topic, you should display related objects and materials, student work, pictures and posters, graphs and charts made during activities, and summary charts of important concepts taught and learned. An active environment reinforces concepts and skills that have been stressed during science activities.

Time Lines

No two groups of students will cover topics and material at the same rate. Planning the duration of units is the responsibility of the teacher. In some cases, the activities will not be completed during one block of time and will have to be carried over. In other cases, students may be especially interested in one topic and may want to expand upon it. The individual needs of the students should be considered; there are no strict time lines involved in *Hands-On Science*. It is important, however, to spend time on every unit in the program so that students focus on all of the curriculum outcomes established for their grade level.

▶

Classroom Management

Although hands-on activities are emphasized throughout this program, the manner in which these experiences are handled is up to you.

In some cases, you may have all students manipulating materials individually; in others, you may choose to use small group settings. Small groups encourage the development of social skills, enable all students to be active in the learning process, and mean less cost in terms of materials and equipment.

Occasionally, especially when safety concerns are an issue, you may decide to demonstrate an activity, while still encouraging as much student interaction as possible. Again, classroom management is up to you, since it is the teacher who ultimately determines how the students in his or her care function best in the learning environment.

Science Skills: Guidelines for Teachers

While involved in the activities of **Hands-On Science**, students will use a variety of skills as they answer questions, solve problems, and make decisions. These skills are not unique to science, but they are integral to students' acquisition of scientific literacy.

The skills include initiating and planning, performing and recording, analyzing and interpreting, as well as communicating and the ability to work in teams. Although the wide variety of skills are not all presented here, the following guidelines provide a framework to use to encourage students' skill development in specific areas.

Observing

Students learn to perceive characteristics and changes through the use of all five senses. Students are encouraged to use sight, smell, touch, hearing, and taste (when safe) to gain information about objects and events. Observations may be qualitative (by properties such as texture or colour), or quantitative (such as size or number), or both. Observing includes:

- gaining information through the senses
- identifying similarities and differences, and making comparisons
- sequencing events or objects

Note: For safety reasons, stress to students that substances should never be tasted, smelled, or even touched without teacher permission.

Exploring

Students need ample opportunities to manipulate materials and equipment in order to discover and learn new ideas and concepts. During exploration, students need to be encouraged to use their observation skills. Discussion is also an integral component of exploration; it allows students to communicate their discoveries.

Classifying

This skill is used to group or sort objects and events. Classification is based on observable properties. For example, changes in matter can be classified as physical or chemical. In the same way, organisms can be classified as single-cell and multicellular. One of the strategies used for sorting involves the use of Venn diagrams (either a double Venn or a triple Venn). Venn diagrams can involve distinct groups, or can intersect to show similar characteristics.

Venn Diagram With Distinctive Groups:

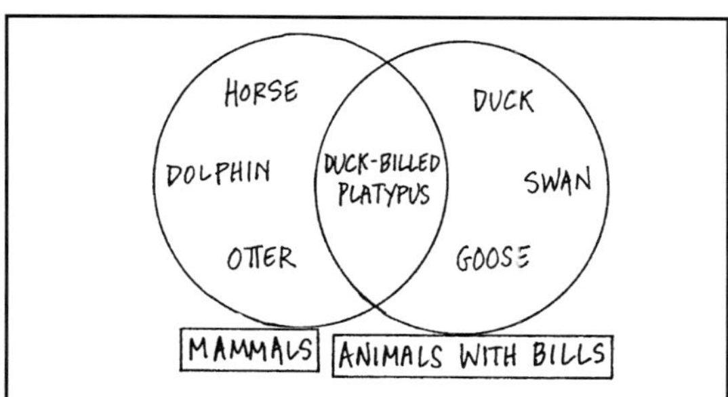

Measuring

This is a process of discovering the dimensions or quantity of objects or events and usually involves the use of standards of length, area, mass, volume, capacity, temperature, time, and speed. Measuring skills also include the ability to choose appropriate measuring devices, and using proper terms for direction and position.

An essential skill of measurement is estimating. Regularly, students should be encouraged to estimate before they measure. Estimation allows students opportunities to take risks, use background knowledge, and learn from the process.

The metric system is the foundation of measuring activities. Teachers should be familiar with, and regularly use, these basic measurement units.

Length: Length is measured in metres, portions of a metre, or multiples of a metre. The most commonly used units are:

- millimetre (mm): about the thickness of a paper match
- centimetre (cm): about the width of your index fingernail
- metre (m): about the length of a man's stride
- kilometre (km): 1000 metres

Mass: Mass, or weight, is measured in grams, portions of a gram, or multiples of a gram.

The most commonly used units are:

- gram (g): about the weight of a paper clip
- kilogram (kg): a cordless telephone weighs about 2 kilograms
- tonne (t): about the weight of a compact car

Note: When measuring to determine the heaviness of an object, the term mass is more scientifically accurate than the term weight. As a result, teachers should use the term mass and encourage students to do so as well.

Capacity: Capacity refers to the amount of fluid a container holds, and is measured in litres, portions of a litre, and multiples of a litre. The most commonly used units are:

- millilitre (ml): a soup spoon holds about 15 millilitres
- litre (l): milk comes in litre containers, or portions and multiples of a litre

Volume: Volume refers to the amount of space taken up by an object and is measured in cubic units, generally cubic centimetres (cm^3) and cubic metres (m^3).

Note: Volume and capacity are often used interchangeably. However, a teacher should use the terms correctly in context, referring to liquid measure as capacity and space taken up as volume. Students should also be encouraged to use these terms correctly.

Area: Area is measured in square centimetres, or portions and multiples thereof. By becoming familiar with the units of length, the teacher can understand area measurements by thinking of that unit in a two-dimensional form, such as square centimetres (cm^2) and square metres (m^2).

Temperature: Temperature is measured in degrees Celsius (°C). Normal room temperature is 21 °C; water freezes at 0 °C and boils at 100 °C.

►

Communicating

In science, one communicates by means of diagrams, graphs, charts, maps, models, symbols, as well as with written and spoken languages. Communicating includes:

- reading and interpreting data from tables and charts
- making tables and charts
- reading and interpreting data from graphs
- making graphs
- making labelled diagrams
- making models
- using oral and written language

When presenting students with charts and graphs, or when students make their own as part of a specific activity, there are guidelines that should be followed.

- A *bar graph* is a common form of scientific communication. Bar graphs should always be titled so that the information communicated is easily understood. These titles should be capitalized in the same manner as one would title a story. Both axes of the graph should also be titled and capitalized in the same way. In most cases, graduated markings are noted on one axis and the objects or events being compared are noted on the other. On a bar graph, the bars must be separate, as each bar represents a distinct piece of data.

- A *double bar graph* can also be used to communicate scientific results. This type of graph is commonly used when comparing similar attributes in different objects. For example, an investigation in flight may have students constructing a model airplane with and without flaps, from different types of paper. The resulting double bar graph may look as follows:

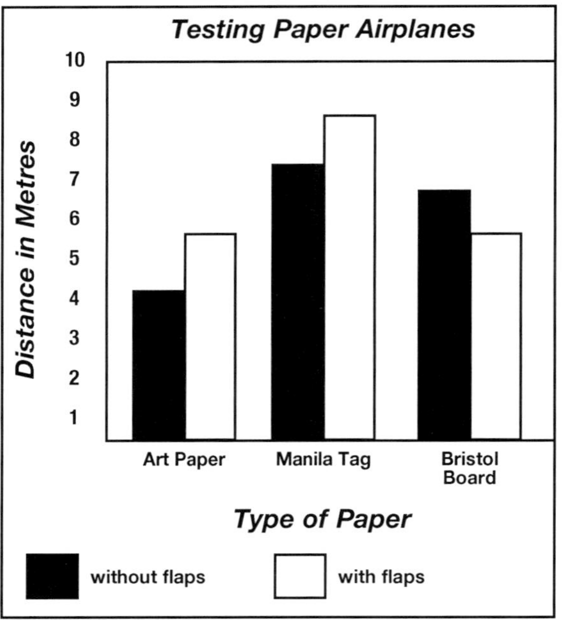

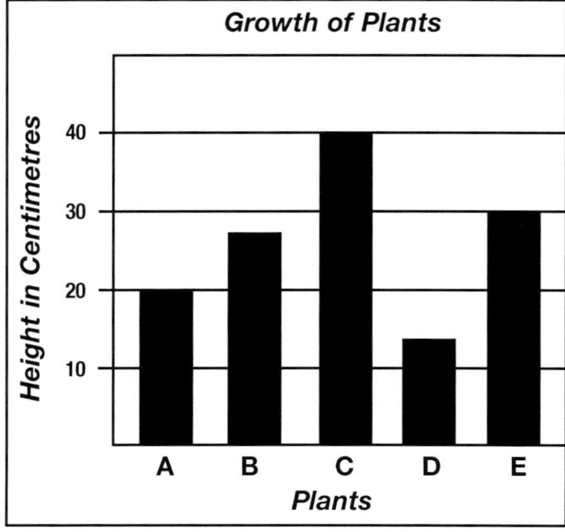

- A *broken line graph* is used to communicate data when measuring an object or event over a period of time. For example, a broken line graph may be used to present daily outdoor high temperatures over a period of one week.

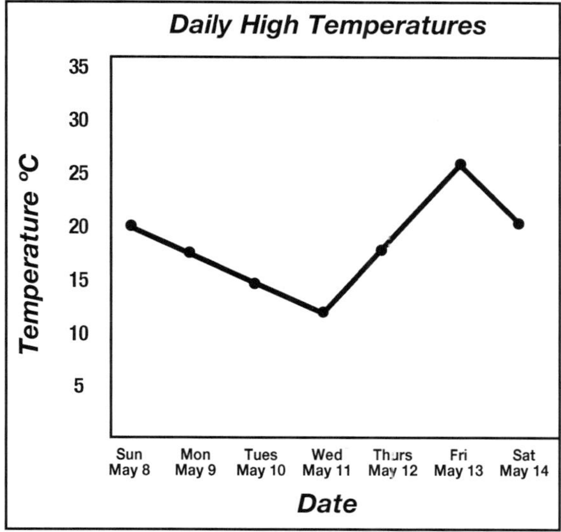

In the same way, *double broken line graph* can be used to compare two sets of data, such as the daily high temperatures in two cities.

- A *pie graph* is used to present information about one specific object or event. For example, a pie graph can be used to indicate energy consumption in Canada.

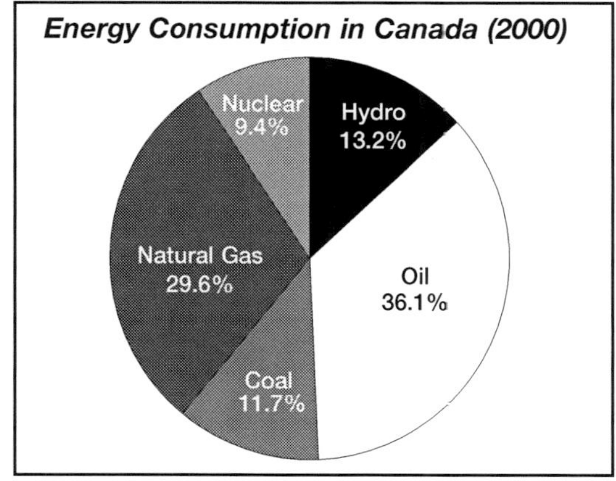

- *Charts* also require appropriate titles, and both columns and rows need specific headings. Again, all of these titles and headings require capitalization as in titles of a story. Charts can be made in the form of checklists or can include room for additional written information, data, and diagrams.

Flying Devices		
Device	Air Craft	Space Craft
Space Shuttle		✓
Helicopter	✓	
Jet Airplane	✓	

Animal Tracks		
Animal	Location of Tracks	Diagram
Rabbit	backyard	
Deer	open field near school	

Measuring Length		
Object	Estimate (cm)	Length (cm)
book	30 cm	27 cm
pencil	10 cm	16 cm

- A *frequency table* presents data as a tally or count of how often an event occurs. Examples include the frequency of traffic at a given corner, at different times of the day, or, in the example below, the frequency of black bear sightings in different months in a provincial park.

Frequency Table:

Black Bear Sightings		
Month	Tally	Frequency
July	‖‖‖ ‖‖	8
August	‖‖‖ ‖‖‖ ‖	11
September	‖‖‖ ‖‖‖ ‖‖‖	15

Data from a frequency table can be displayed on a histogram to show the frequency of events. Making a histogram is similar to making a bar graph, except there are no spaces between bars.

Histogram:

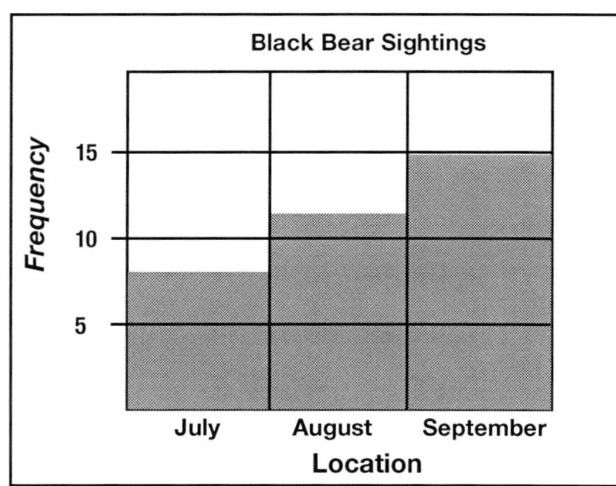

- *Stem-and-Leaf plots* show trends in data. For example, a group of students kept track of the amount of television they watched in one week (in hours). The results were: 5, 7, 9, 11, 12, 14, 18, 21, 23, 24, 24, 26, 28, 28, 35, 35, 35, 38, 38, 42, 42

To make a stem-and-leaf plot, the tens values are placed on the left of the 'stem' line, and the ones digits are on the right of the 'stem' line. See the example below:

Stem	Leaf
0	5 7 9
1	1 2 4 4 4 8
2	1 3 4 4 6 8 8
3	5 5 5 8 8 8
4	2 2

- A *flow chart* is a diagram of the movement or action of things engaged in a complete activity. Examples include the human digestive process, or as in the example below, the food cycle.

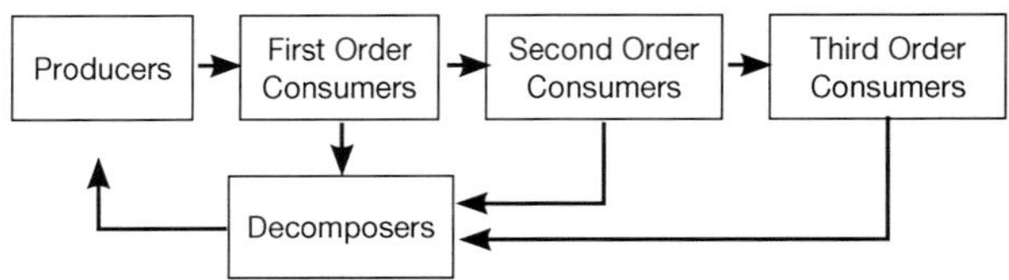

Communicating also involves using the language and terminology of science. Students should be encouraged to use the appropriate vocabulary related to their investigations; for example, protist, molecule, thermal, geology, structure, radiation, environment, conductive. The language of science also includes terms like predict, infer, estimate, measure, design, construct, experiment, and hypothesize. Teachers should use this vocabulary regularly throughout all activities and encourage their students to do the same. Students should also be encouraged to use the vocabulary and terminology in written form. Consider developing whole-class or individual glossaries so students can record the terms learned and define them in their own words. Unit glossary black line masters are included throughout ***Hands-on Science***.

Predicting

A prediction refers to the question: What do you think will happen? For example, when a balloon is blown up, ask students to predict what they think will happen when the balloon is placed in a basin of ice cold water. It is important to provide opportunities for students to make predictions and for them to feel safe doing so.

Inferring

When students are asked to make an inference, it generally means that they are being asked to explain why something occurs. For example, after placing an inflated balloon in a basin of ice cold water, ask students to infer why the balloon appeared to shrink. Again, it is important to encourage students to take risks when making such inferences. Before explaining scientific phenomena to students, they should be given opportunities to infer for themselves.

Investigating and Experimenting

When investigations and experiments are done in the classroom, planning and recording the process and the results are essential. There are standard guidelines for writing up experiments:

- Purpose: what we want to find out
- Hypothesis: what we think will happen
- Materials: what we used
- Method: what we did
- Results: what we observed
- Conclusion: what we found out
- Application: how we can use what we learned

Researching

Many opportunities should be provided for students to research topics studied in class. Research skills involve finding, organizing, and presenting information. For best results, teachers should always provide a structure for the research, indicating questions to be answered, as well as a format for conducting the research. Suggestions for research guidelines are presented regularly throughout *Hands-On Science*.

Using the Design Process

Throughout *Hands-On Science*, students are given opportunities to use the design process to design and construct objects. There are specific steps in the design process:

1. Identify a need.
2. Create a plan.
3. Develop a product.
4. Communicate the results.

The design process also involves research and experimentation.

▶

Assessment Plan

The Hands-On Science Assessment Plan

Hands-On Science provides a variety of assessment tools that enable teachers to build a comprehensive and authentic daily assessment plan for students.

Embedded Assessment

Assess students as they work, by using the questions provided with each activity. These questions promote higher-level thinking skills, active inquiry, problem solving, and decision making. Anecdotal records and observations are examples of embedded assessment:

- **Anecdotal Records:** Recording observations during science activities is critical in having an authentic view of a student's progress. The anecdotal record sheet presented on page 16 provides the teacher with a format for recording individual or group observations.

- **Individual Student Observations:** During those activities when a teacher wishes to focus more on specific students, individual student observations sheets may be used (page 17). This black line master provides more space for comments and is especially useful during conferencing, interviews, or individual student presentations.

Performance Assessment

Performance assessment is a planned, systematic observation and is based on students actually doing a specific science activity.

- **Rubrics:** To assess students' performance on a specific task, rubrics are used in *Hands-On Science* to standardize and streamline scoring. A sample rubric and a black line master for teacher use are included on pages 18 and 19. For any specific

activity, the teacher selects four criteria that relate directly to the outcomes for the specific activity being assessed. Students are then given a check mark for each criterion accomplished, to determine a rubric score for the assessment from a total of four marks. These rubric scores can then be transferred to the rubric class record sheet on page 20.

Cooperative Skills

In order to assess students' ability to work effectively in a group, teachers must observe the interaction within these groups. A cooperative skills teacher assessment sheet is included on page 21 for teachers to use while conducting such observations.

Student Self-Assessment

It is important to encourage students to reflect on their own learning in science. For this purpose, teachers will find included a student self-assessment sheet on page 22, as well as a cooperative skills self-assessment sheet on page 23. Of course, students will also reflect on their own learning during class discussions and through other written assignments.

Science Portfolios

Select, with student input, work to include in a science portfolio. This can include activity sheets, research projects, photographs of projects, as well as other written material. Use the portfolio to reflect the student's growth in scientific literacy over the school year. Black line masters are included to organize the portfolio (science portfolio table of contents on page 24 and the science portfolio entry record on page 25).

End-of-Unit Assessment

To reflect on student's overall achievement in each unit of study, teachers need to consider

the knowledge and skills that form the bases
of the science program. The results of all
assessment strategies implemented throughout
the unit must be used to determine the
students' achievement. A black line master
is included on page 26, and can be used
to record information on individual student
achievement for each unit in the science
program. The chart can be used to record
specific results of achievement (percentage
marks, rubric scores, grades, and so on) as well
as anacdotal comments to support the results.

Note: The criteria listed on the chart focus on the
foundation of scientific literacy, as established in
the Pan Canadian Protocol.

Note: In each unit of *Hands-On Science*,
suggestions for assessment are provided for
several lessons. Keep in mind that these are merely
suggestions. Teachers are encouraged to use both
the assessment strategies presented here in a wide
variety of ways and their own valuable experience
as educators.

▶

Date: _______________________

Anecdotal Record

Purpose of Observation: _______________________

Student/Group	**Student/Group**
Comments	**Comments**
Student/Group	**Student/Group**
Comments	**Comments**
Student/Group	**Student/Group**
Comments	**Comments**

Date: _______________________

Individual Student Observations

Purpose of Observation: _________________________________

Student ____

Observations

Student ____

Observations

Student ____

Observations

Sample Rubric

Interactions Within Ecosystems

Science Unit: ___________________________

Science Activity: _______ Examining Microorganisms _______

Date: ___________________________

4 – Full Accomplishment
3 – Substantial Accomplishment
2 – Partial Accomplishment
1 – Little Accomplishment

Student	Criteria				Rubric Score /4
	Follows Directions	Uses Microscope Equipment Appropriately	Uses Resources to Identify Microorganisms	Records Detailed Observations	
Jesse	✓		✓	✓	3
Suon	✓	✓	✓	✓	4

Rubric

Science Unit: _______________________________

Science Activity: _______________________________

Date: _______________________________

4 – Full Accomplishment
3 – Substantial Accomplishment
2 – Partial Accomplishment
1 – Little Accomplishment

Student	Criteria				Rubric Score /4

Teacher: _______________________

Rubric Class Record

Student	Unit/Activity/Date									
					Rubric Scores /4					

Cooperative Skills
Teacher Assessment

Date: ____

Task: ____

____

Group Member	Cooperative Skills					
	Contributes ideas and participates in discussion	Respects and accepts contributions of others	Asks questions	Remains focused	Encourages others	Completes individual commitment to the group

Comments: ____

____

____

____

Student Self-Assessment
Reflecting on My Science Learning

1. Science Topic: ____

____

2. Science Activity: ____

____

____

3. What I learned: ____

____

____

4. Diagrams:

5. I would like to learn more about: _______________________

____

____

6. I would like to improve in: _______________________

____

____

Date: ________________________   Name: ________________________

Cooperative Skills Self-Assessment

Students in my group:

________________________   ________________________

________________________   ________________________

Group Work – How Did I Do Today?

Group Work	How I Did (✔)		
	Very Good	**Satisfactory**	**Needs Improvement**
I shared ideas and contributed to disussion.			
I listened to others and respected their ideas.			
I asked questions.			
I stayed on task.			
I encouraged others.			
I helped with the work.			

I did very well in ____

____

Date: _______________________   **Name:** _______________________

Science Portfolio Table of Contents

Entry	Date	Selection
1.	_______________	_______________________
2.	_______________	_______________________
3.	_______________	_______________________
4.	_______________	_______________________
5.	_______________	_______________________
6.	_______________	_______________________
7.	_______________	_______________________
8.	_______________	_______________________
9.	_______________	_______________________
10.	_______________	_______________________
11.	_______________	_______________________
12.	_______________	_______________________
13.	_______________	_______________________
14.	_______________	_______________________
15.	_______________	_______________________
16.	_______________	_______________________
17.	_______________	_______________________
18.	_______________	_______________________
19.	_______________	_______________________
20.	_______________	_______________________

Science Portfolio Entry Record

This work was chosen by _________________

This work is _________________

____

I chose this work because _________________

____

____

____

- ✂

Date: _________________ **Name:** _________________

Science Entry Record

This work was chosen by _________________

This work is _________________

____

I chose this work because _________________

____

____

End-of-Unit Assessment

Unit: _______________________________   Student: _______________________________

Foundations of Scientific Literacy	Achievement Results	Comments
STSE ■ science and technology connections ■ environmental issues		
Skills ■ inquiry, problem solving, decision making ■ design skills ■ use of equipment/materials		
Knowledge ■ understanding basic concepts ■ communicating ideas and explanations		
Attitudes ■ responsibility ■ curiosity ■ accuracy		
Summary		

Interactions within Ecosystems

Books for Students

Allaby, Michael. *How It Works: The Environment*. London: Horus Books, 1996.

George, Michael. *Tundra: The Barren Wilderness*. Manakato, MN: Creative Education, 2002.

Hickman, Pamela. *The Kids Canadian Tree Book*. Toronto: Kids Can Press, 1995. (also in series Bird Book, Bug Book, Plant Book).

Lovett, Sarah. *Extremely Weird Micro Monsters*. Santa Fe, NM: John Muir Publications, 1993.

Orr, Richard. *Nature's Cross Sections*. Richmond Hill, ON: Scholastic Canada, 1995.

Rotter, Charles. *The Prairie: An Enduring Spirit*. Mankato, MN: Creative Education, 2002.

Rotter, Charles. *Wetlands: A Vanishing Resource*. Mankato, MN: Creative Education, 2002.

Shell, Barry. *Great Canadian Scientists*. Victoria, BC: Polestar Books, 1997.

Vancleave, Janice. *Ecology for Every Kid*. New York: John Wiley and Sons, 1996.

Magazines

Owl: The Discovery Magazine for Kids (PO Box 726, Markham Station, Markham, ON L3P 7U9)

Web sites

- **www.mts.net/~gcg/index.html**

  Global Change Game. Manitoba-based group designed a simulation game that students play on a world map the size of a basketball court and deal with major problems in the world today.

- **www.skyfishproject.org**

  Kids Making A Difference: As a 12-year-old, Severn Cullis-Suzuki and a delegation of other young people spoke to world leaders at the "Rio" gathering on global issues. This web site is an arena for examining and questioning the sustainability of our world, and how we live our lives.

- **www.inac.gc.ca/ks**

  Kids Stop is a web site that has many classroom applications and contains information about First Nation, Inuit, and Métis peoples.

- **www.durable.gc.ca**

  This site gives ideas for lessons (based on Canadian curricula) from Agriculture and Agri-Food Canada, Environment Canada, Fisheries and Oceans Canada, Health Canada, and Natural Resources Canada. There are many connections to this unit teachers can consider/adapt.

- **www.earthday.ca**

  Keep up-to-date on initiatives and events related to celebrating Earth Day and Earth Month (April) annually.

- **www.ecokids.ca**

  Lots of ideas, activities, and event information on a variety of ecology-based issues.

- **www.davidsuzuki.org**

  For up-to-date information on habitat destruction, climate change, fossil fuels, air/water pollution, this web site is devoted to "wake-up calls." Click on *The Nature Challenge* for ideas on what individuals can do.

- **www.greenschools.ca/seeds**

  Society, Environment and Energy Development Site (SEEDS). Become an Environmental Green School and join the 4500+ schools across Canada currently registered with the program. SEEDS also has many other ecology-related programs, from pond ecology studies to bird counts to climate change that might be of interest/use. Check out the Writing Challenge that has free rewards (all grades).

- **www.natureconservancy.ca**

  An organization devoted to the protection of Canada's nature through the purchase of small to large pieces of precious/unique lands. Check out to see what's "for sale" in your neighbourhood – and why it is deemed worth saving.

- **www.ec.gc.ca/climate/**

  Environment Canada: Specific sites for many issues. Example: climate change for citizens: (www.ec.gc.ca, for general information).

- **www.eya.ca**

  Environmental Youth Alliance offers workshops on green energy and climate change.

■ **www.greenteacher.com**

Green Teacher magazine is an excellent resource on current issues, ideas for teaching, web sites, book reviews – a must for teachers!

■ **www.panda.org**

World Wildlife Fund offers a variety of ecologically based campaigns to save endangered species and habitats.

Introduction

The study of ecosystems is an introduction to the field of ecology. In this unit, students consider:

- how organisms interact with each other and their environment
- how energy is cycled in an environment
- how natural factors affect ecosystems
- how humans influence ecosystems
- how humans produce food and how microorganisms play a role in the entire production process

Students may be familiar with many ideas and concepts in this unit from studies in previous grades. To assess prior knowledge and introduce lessons, it may be beneficial to conduct informal discussions, brainstorming sessions, small-group sharing, and KWL activities (see Lesson 6 for a sample KWL chart).

It is highly recommended that this unit be done in the spring time, due to the use of immediate outdoor school spaces for activities supporting many outcomes, and for the relative ease of planning related field trips at this time of year.

Note: The micro-aquatic ecosystem or hay infusion activity conducted in lesson 5 requires 24 days of standing time. Consider starting this infusion prior to beginning the unit so it is ready for use in lesson 5. Please see p.53 for details in starting the infusion.

Science Vocabulary

Throughout this unit, teachers should use, and encourage students to use such as: *abiotic, biotic, ecology, organism, ecosystem, environment, biosphere, biome, species, culture, quadrat, population, microorganism, succession, climax community, producer, consumer, primary consumer, secondary consumer, tertiary consumer, herbivore, carnivore, decomposer, scavenger, food chain, food web, food pyramid, bioaccumulation, photosynthesis, chlorophyll, cellular respiration, carbon dioxide-oxygen cycle.*

▶

1 | Introduction to Ecology

Background Information for Teachers

Ecology: The study of how living things interact with each other and with the environment.

Organism: any individual living thing. An organism can be made of many cells (humans) or made of only one cell (some bacteria, members of the moneran kingdom. One-celled organisms are often called *microorganisms*).

Biotic: refers to the living organisms in the environment.

Abiotic: refers to the nonliving factors that influence living things, such as climate, sunlight, water, geology, and minerals.

Materials

- chart paper
- felt markers
- highlighter
- masking tape
- dictionaries (standard and biology-related ones for students)
- Information Sheet titled "Definition of Ecology" (included. Make an overhead copy of this sheet. (1.1.1)
- three-point-approach chart (included. Make an overhead copy of this sheet.) (1.2.1)
- nonpermanent overhead pens
- overhead projector

Activity: Part One

Introduce the term *ecology* first by asking students for their ideas. Display the overhead, "Definition of Ecology" (1.1.1). Ask:

- How would you describe ecology in your own words?
- Can you think of other words, ideas, or concepts that might relate to ecology?

Divide the class into working groups. Give each group a piece of chart paper and a few markers. Have them to write the word ecology in the middle and create a word splash of their ideas around it. Give them 5 to 7 minutes to come up with as many words as they can generate.

Note: A word splash is a means of recording words and short phrases in a free-style format, as in the following example:

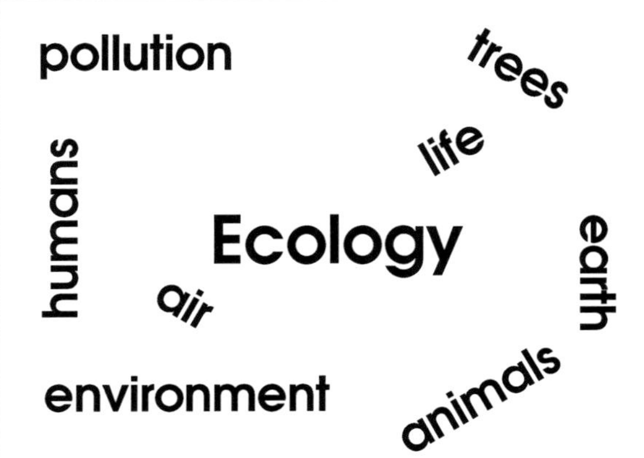

Display the word splashes around the room. Have students identify the words that appear most frequently. Highlight these words, and discuss what they have in common.

Focus now on the terms *biotic* and *abiotic*, as presented on the definition overhead. Ask:

- Can you describe these terms in your own words?
- What is an organism?
- Can the words on our word splashes be grouped as biotic and abiotic?

Have group members underline biotic words and abiotic words with different coloured markers.

Note: Not all words will be easily sorted as biotic and abiotic. The purpose here is to familiarize students with new vocabulary in an informal classification exercise.

   Hands-On Science • Grade 7

Activity: Part Two

Explain that students will become familiar with many new words and use them during activities. Hand out the activity sheet (three-point-approach chart) (1.1.2). Using the overhead copy of this sheet, model how to complete the chart using the term *ecology*, as in the example below:

Definition	Term	Diagram
The science that studies how living things interact with each other and with the enviroment	Ecology **Examples:** Ecologists, Environmentalists, Dr. Charles Krebs, David Suzuki	

Now have students complete the three-point-approach charts/activity sheet for the terms *ecology, organism, biotic,* and *abiotic*.

Note: This three-point-approach chart will be used throughout the unit to record new terms. It is an excellent way of encouraging students to formulate and clarify their ideas about a given term. The sheets can be bound together to form an "Eco-Dictionary" for each student.

Activity Sheet

Directions to students:

Note: Copy several sheets for each student.

Complete a three-point-approach chart for each new term (1.1.2). Continue with this process throughout the unit as new terms are introduced.

Extension

Share with students that the term *ecology* comes from the Greek word for "house." Challenge them by asking:

- How is "house" a fitting word to use in defining ecology?

Assessment Suggestion

Check students' three-point-approach charts/activity sheets for definitions of ecology, abiotic, and biotic. Focus on the clarity of the definition, how the diagram supports this, and the choice example. Use the Individual Student Observations sheet on page 17 to record results.

Definition of Ecology

Ecology is the science that studies how living things interact with each other and with the environment. The environment is both biotic and abiotic.

Biotic refers to the **living** organisms in the environment.

Abiotic refers to the **nonliving** factors that also influence living things, such as climate, sunlight, water, geology, and minerals.

Three-Point-Approach

Definition	Term	Diagram
	Examples	
Definition	Term	Diagram
	Examples	
Definition	Term	Diagram
	Examples	

2 | Ecosystems: Small Places to Big Spaces

Background Information for Teachers

Vocabulary terms students will use or teachers might need in this (and subsequent) lessons are:

Biosphere: the layers of the earth (crust, atmosphere, and hydrasphere) that is inhabited by living things.

Ecosystem: a specific area of the biosphere in which organisms interact with one another and with the abiotic environment.

Environment: collective term for the conditions in which an organism lives (e.g., temperature, light, water, other organisms).

Biome: a large geographical region that has a similar climate condition throughout its area.

Species: term used to describe each different kind of living thing. It is the smallest unit of classification used. For example, *Homo sapiens* is the notation for humans: *Homo* is the genus and *sapiens* is the species. The universal language of classification is Latin.

Materials

- large collection of pictures of natural and urban spaces (depicting examples of plant and animal life; natural components such as soil, rocks, clouds; as well as human-made objects such as vehicles, buildings, and highways. Collect such pictures from magazines and old calendars and include a variety of scenes such as mountain ranges, ponds, sunsets over lakes, parks, children splashing through puddles on a rainy day, a city, people walking down a busy street, forest scenes, prairie scenes, seasonal scenes, and so on.)
- masking tape
- chart paper
- markers
- globe
- map titled, "Biomes of the World" (included. Make a copy for each student.) (1.2.2)
- wall map of the world

Activity: Part One

Display the pictures of natural and urban spaces. Ask:

- How might you group these pictures into 2, 3, or 4 groups?
- Can you think of anything all these pictures have in common?

Relate back to the definition of *ecology*, and of how each picture shows in some way how living things survive in and relate to their surroundings. Point out that these surroundings are often referred to as the *environment*. The term for all the living things (organisms) interacting with each other and the environment is called an *ecosystem*. Record these terms on chart paper.

Activity: Part Two

Have pairs of students choose one picture from the display (or distribute randomly). Challenge them to identify all the parts of the picture that might be part of this ecosystem, even if some things cannot be seen in the picture.

Model by using one picture as an example and quickly listing (verbally and visually) all the parts you can think of. For example, with a picture of a wheat field:

wheat	weeds	mustard	mice	coyote
webs	spiders	worms	beetles	caterpillars
butterflies	rocks	soil	air	sunshine
bacteria	minerals	fertilizers	herbicides	tractor
farmer				

2

Have students record their ideas on the activity sheet and attach their completed sheet to the picture.

Note: Collect these for use in the next lesson.

Activity Sheet

Directions to students:

Examine your picture carefully. Identify all parts of this ecosystem, even those that cannot be seen but likely exist there. Record your ideas on your activity sheet (1.2.1).

Activity: Part Three

Display the globe. Ask:

- What is this called?

- What does a globe represent? (model of the earth)

- Where do living things exist on Earth?

Encourage students to think about where plants and animals live. Explain that the earth is made up of many layers. All life on Earth exists on just three of those layers: the atmosphere, the hydrosphere, and the crust. This is the *biosphere*.

As a class, examine the globe and have students identify the location of these layers. Focus now on Earth's crust. Ask:

- What types of vegetation are found on earth?

- Do all regions of the world have the same types of vegetation?

- In what geographical region would you find a desert?

- In what geographical region would you find tundra, forests, or grasslands?

Distribute copies of the map, "Biomes of the World" (1.2.2). Explain that a *biome* is a large region of similar climate conditions, for example, Tundra, in the Arctic. The biomes are named to reflect their dominant natural vegetation. Discuss the forms of vegetation listed on the legend.

Display the wall map of the world. Review the biomes, and encourage students to use the wall map to identify the geographical locations (continents, countries) of each biome.

Extensions

- Have students research the latin names for species. For example, the latin term for human species is *Homo sapiens*. The domestic cat is *Felis domesticus*. The climbing rose is *Rosa setigera*.

Note: The first word in the latin name (the genus) uses a capital letter. The second word (the species) uses a lower case.

- Continue to have students complete a three-point-approach chart for each new term (e.g., ecosystem, environment, biosphere, biome, species).

Identifying Components
of an Ecosystem

An ecosystem is a specific area where organisms interact with each other and with the abiotic environment.

Look at your picture. Think of a title that describes the ecosystem in this picture.

____

____

____

Identify all of the biotic and abiotic components of this ecosystem (even the ones you may not be able to see in the picture).

____

____

____

____

____

____

Biomes of the World

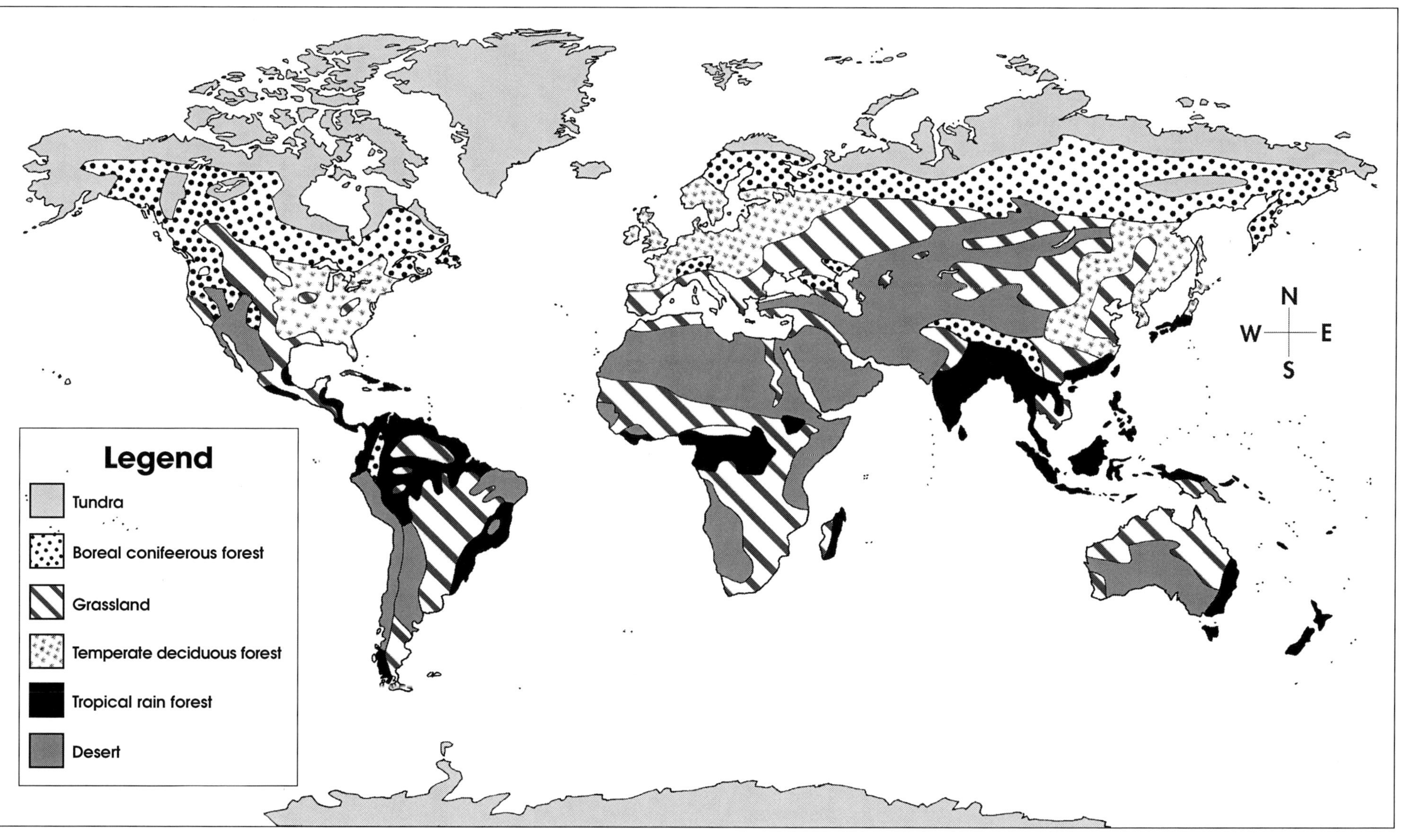

Abiotic and Biotic Elements of Ecosystems

3

Background Information for Teachers

This lesson will reinforce students' understanding of biotic and abiotic elements of an ecosystem.

Human-made objects such as vehicles, buildings, and roads could be considered abiotic (not living), but they are not the same as rocks, water, air, and clouds, which are non-living components of nature. Human-made objects are, therefore, referred to as *cultural*. *Culture* is what humans do, make, or say.

In the second part of this lesson, students will examine a small area of an ecosystem in order to study organisms in detail. A *quadrat* is a marked square chosen at random for population studies. Usually the standard size is 1m^2.

Students will use data from this study to construct charts on the populations in this ecosystem quadrat. The term *population* refers to a group of the same living organisms existing at the same time in an area.

Materials

- pictures and activity sheets from previous lesson
- chart paper
- markers
- poster board
- glue
- scissors
- string
- wire coat hangers
- hand magnifiers (one per student)

Activity: Part One

Have the same pairs of students refer to the pictures they chose in the prior lesson and to the completed activity sheet (1.1.2). Review that the scientific term for the living components of an ecosystem is *biotic*. Record this term on chart paper, along with the definition "living components of an ecosystem." Ask:

- Which words describe *biotic* components of your picture?

Have the students circle these words from activity sheet 1.2.1, and share their words with the class. On the chart, record all words suggested.

Now review that the scientific term for nonliving components of an ecosystem is *abiotic*. Record this term on chart paper, along with the definition "nonliving components of an ecosystem." Ask:

- Which words describe abiotic components of your picture?

Have the students underline these words and share their words with the class. On the chart, record these words. Ask:

- Which components of your pictures are made by humans?

Have students place a check mark beside these words (even if they have already identified them as abiotic).

Note: It is optional to introduce the term *culture* here.

3

Now provide each pair of students with a sheet of poster board, glue, construction paper, scissors, and string. Have the pairs display their pictures by making labels (e.g., abiotic on rectangular pieces of paper, biotic on oval, culture on irregular shape – optional) and attaching string from the labels to appropriate areas of the picture. Two examples are provided:

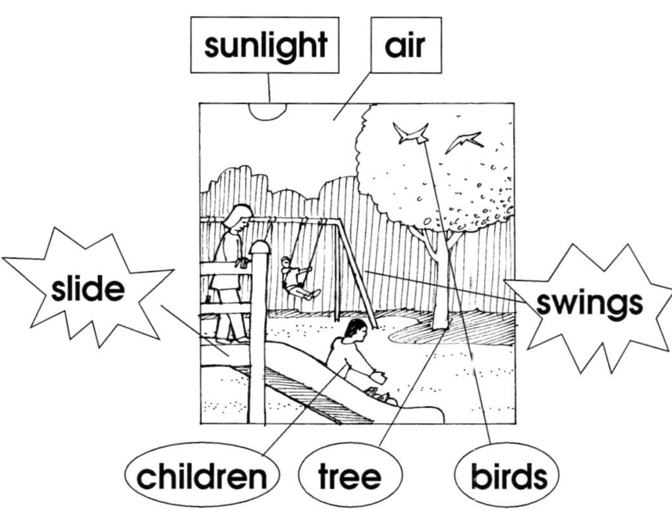

Activity: Part Two

Conduct a short schoolyard (or other immediate environment) field trip to reinforce vocabulary and concepts discussed so far and to provide some opportunities for "real life" experiences.

Explain that ecologists often study a few tiny pieces of an ecosystem to give them an idea about the "big picture." These small areas, called *quadrats*, are randomly selected within a particular ecosystem. One way to study in quadrats is by stretching a coat hanger into a square-shape and throwing it into a field. (This works best where there are no large trees or bushes!) The scientists then spend time watching the activity inside the space defined by the coat hanger quadrat.

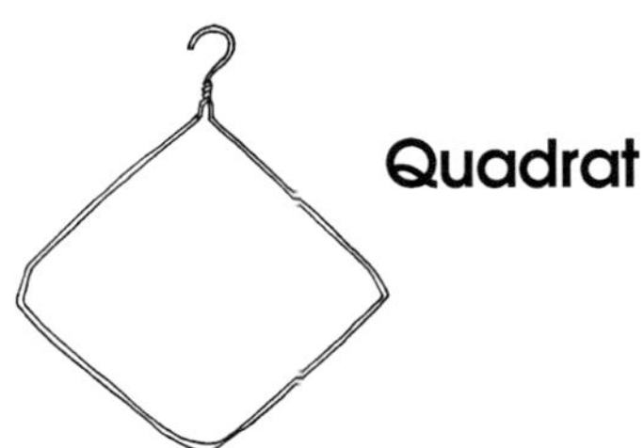

Explain to the class that during this study, the students will be looking at biotic and abiotic elements of the mini-ecosystem. They will also be counting *populations*. Ask:

- What is a population?

Explain that a population refers to a specific group of living things in a given area, such as earthworms or dandelions.

Divide the class into working groups. Provide each group with a wire coat hanger. Each student should have his/her own hand magnifier and the activity sheet (1.3.1). Have the students follow the directions on the activity sheet to complete the task.

Back in the classroom, have the students again classify abiotic and biotic (and cultural – optional) components of the ecosystem, using their tally results. This can be done using the t-chart on Activity Sheet B (1.3.2). For example:

Quadrat Study

Abiotic	Biotic
pebbles - 4	dandelions - 10
soil - NA	grass blades - 77
water (puddle) - NA	ants - 4
sunlight - NA	beetles - 2
	caterpillar - 1

The data collected will be approximate, but is useful to build on ideas of population change and interaction. Use the data to ask:

- Which of the biotic factors seems to be the greatest in the area we explore? (plants, grasses)

- Why do you think this might be so?

- Which abiotic factors might influence the plants being the greatest/most common of the biotic factors? (e.g., soil conditions)

- What might happen if one of the biotic factors (e.g., insects) was removed?

- How would other populations be affected?

- What might happen if one of the abiotic factors (e.g., water) was removed?

- How would other populations be affected?

Discuss other changes that may cause populations to increase or decrease, for example, extended increase or decrease in temperature, over-use of ecosystem by humans (playground use by students), environmental enhancement projects (proper care of grass in field, fertilizers, regular watering, planting of more indigenous species, and so on).

Activity Sheet A

Directions to students:

Follow the procedures to study the ecosystem quadrat.

Activity Sheet B

Directions to students:

Use the t-chart to classify abiotic and biotic components of the ecosystem (1.3.2).

Assessment Suggestions

- Observe students as they work together to study the ecosystem. Use the Cooperative Skills Teacher Assessment sheet on page 21 to record results.

- Have the students complete a Cooperative Skills Self-Assessment sheet on page 23 to reflect on their ability to work together in a group.

Ecosystem Study

The steps to follow are:

1. Once on-site within the ecosystem, stay in your group.
2. Spread out around the ecosystem, but stay within sight of the teacher.
3. Bend the coat hanger to make a square shape.
4. Observe and record everything inside the area defined by the coat hanger for 10-15 minutes.
5. Use the magnifiers respectfully.
6. Sketch and label what you observe.

Note: If there is more than one of something (pebbles, blades of grass, ants), use a tally to count them.

Date: _______________________   Name: _______________________

Quadrat Study

Abiotic	Biotic

4 | How to Use a Microscope

Background Information for Teachers

A diagram of a microscope (1.4.1), instructions for use (1.4.2), and procedures for preparing a wet mount slide (1.4.3) are included with this lesson.

Materials

- microscopes (Activities will prove most valuable when more powerful microscopes with electrical light sources can be obtained. If your school does not have these, try to borrow them from a local senior school.)
- tables
- light sources
- commercially prepared slides
- slides
- cover slips
- print samples (from magazines or recycled paper)
- hair samples
- eyedroppers
- water
- diagram of microscope (included. Make an overhead copy, as well as a photocopy for each student.) (1.4.1)
- information sheet titled, "Preparing a Wet-Mount Slide" (Included. Make an overhead copy of this sheet.) (1.4.3)

Activity: Part One

Divide the class into working groups, and provide each group with a microscope. Display the overhead diagram of the microscope, and guide students in identifying the components.

Stress the importance of proper care for microscopes:

Caring for a microscope

- Clean lenses using lens paper only.
- Handle microscopes with care. They are fragile and expensive.
- Carry microscopes with one hand under the base and one hand holding the arm, ensuring that the electrical cord is not dangling.
- When putting away the microscope, put the lowest power objective lens in place and cover the microscope with the dust cover.

Provide the students with commercially prepared slides. Guide them in positioning the slides, adjusting light, and focusing on the specimen. Provide plenty of time for students to work together on this activity, and to trade slides with other groups for additional practice.

Finally, provide the students with Activity Sheet A (1.4.2), and guide them in determining magnification.

Activity Sheet A

Directions to students:

Complete the chart for determining total magnification (1.4.2).

▶

4

Activity: Part Two

Display the overhead titled, "Preparing a Wet-Mount Slide" (1.4.3). Review the procedures and provide each group with the materials for making their own wet-mount slides. Also provide each student with a copy of Activity Sheet B (1.4.3). Have the students work in their groups to prepare slides and complete the activity sheet.

Activity Sheet B

Directions to students:

Prepare slides as directed, and complete the sheet with your observations (1.4.3).

Assessment Suggestion

Observe students as they work with the microscopes. Focus on their ability to demonstrate proper care and use of the equipment. Record results on the Anecdotal Record sheet on page 16.

Microscope

ocular lens (eye piece)
coarse adjustment knob
body tube
fine adjustment knob
medium power
objective lens
revolving nose piece
high power
objective lens
low power
objective lens
arm
clips
stage
diaphragm
mirror/light source
base

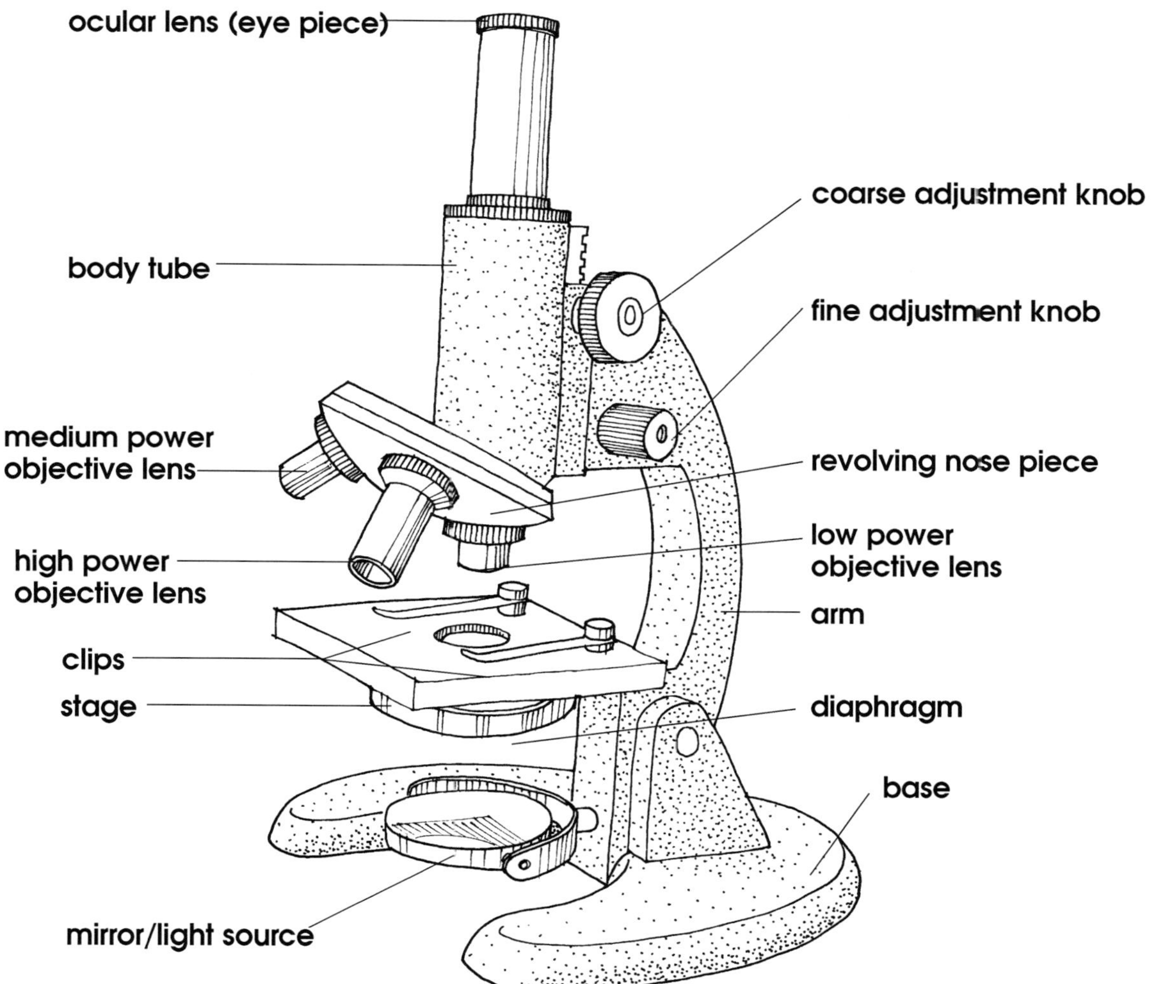

Date: _______________________   Name: _______________________

Determining Total Magnification on a Compound Microscope

Total Magnification = ocular lens power x objective lens power

The units used to indicate magnification are times (X)

For example, if the ocular lens power is 5X and the objective lens power is 4X, then:

5X x 4X = 20X

Complete the chart, determining the total magnification for each combination of ocular and objective lenses found on your microscope.

	Ocular Lens Power (X)	Objective Lens Power (X)	Total Magnification (X)
Low Power			
Medium Power			
High Power			

Does the highest total magnification always provide the best view of a specimen? Explain your answer.

____

____

____

Preparing a Wet-Mount Slide

1. Place a drop of water on the slide.

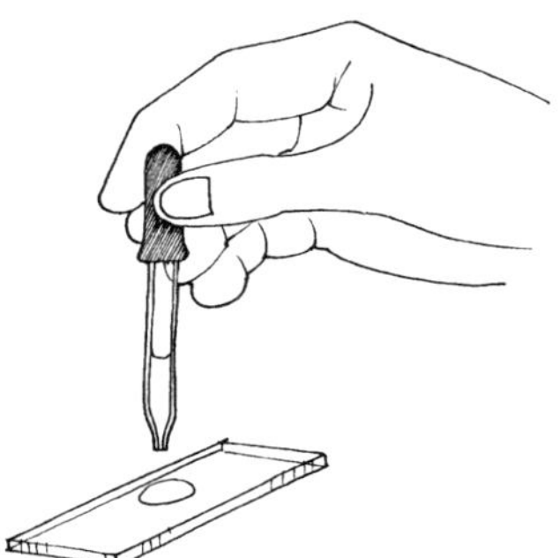

2. Place the specimen in the water.

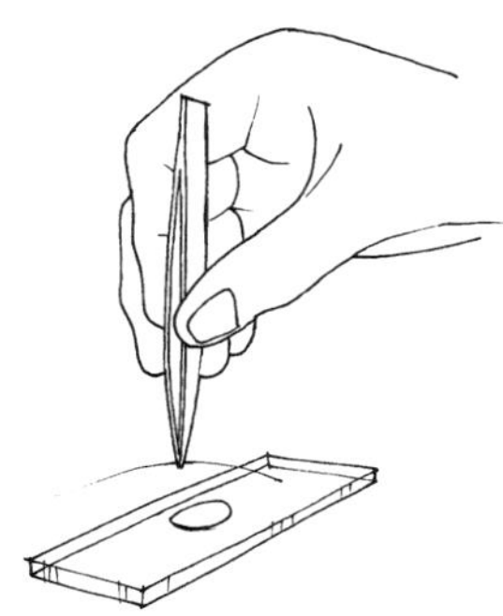

3. Hold the cover slip at a 45-degree angle, and then release. This will reduce air bubbles.

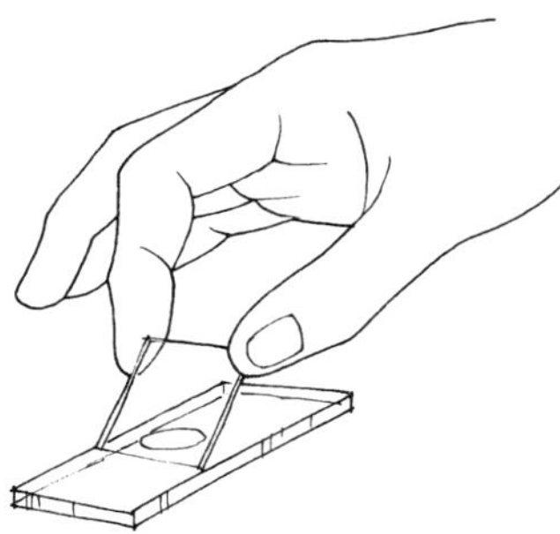

4. Gently tap on the cover slip to eliminate any remaining air bubbles.

Preparing Wet Mount Slides

1. From a print sample, locate a lower case *h*. Prepare a wet-mount slide of the letter. Draw the letter as it appears on the slide, without the aid of the microscope.

2. Place your slide on the microscope under low power. Draw the letter as it appears now.

3. Compare the two views. Describe the appearance of the letter *h*. Also describe what the paper and ink look like in each view.

4. Draw what you think each of the following letters below would look like through the microscope:

   k   g

   R   Q

5. Prepare a wet-mount slide of a hair sample. Beginning with low power, focus the hair as clearly as possible. Draw what the hair looks like, and record the total magnification.

5 | Succession: The Order of Things

Background Information for Teachers

Succession, although a straightforward concept, is comprised of a series of complex, interactive steps. It is the progressive, gradual change of the composition of a community of organisms. During succession, plant populations are constantly replaced by new species. One dominant species gives way to another. The final community in a succession is referred to as a *climax community*. This means that the community has changed to an end point where no other significant changes will occur – the climax community dominates. All being well (i.e., if there is no interference), the climax community will maintain itself over time. Each region follows a pattern of succession and climax depending on abiotic factors such as climate and soil condition. This pattern remains the same as long as the climate of the area does not change. A classic example of this in Canada is the Old Growth Forests of the West Coast. "Old Growth" refers to a climax community of evergreen trees (e.g., Douglas Fir, Yew) that have existed over decades – some for even five hundred years.

Places where succession can be observed easily include pond edges, borders between fields (undisturbed by cultivation) and tree stands, abandoned farm fields and abandoned orchards.

In some places, succession is impacted by natural disasters such as fire or flood. Without fires, for example, there would have been fewer prairie spaces. Hence, the term *fire ecology* is used to refer to the natural and significant role such events can play in maintaining certain communities and populations within these communities. (Think of the prairie bison.)

Today, humans often use this concept of fire ecology to maintain monocultures such as a wheat field; farmers burn stubble. This is a type of *artificial succession*. The use of pesticides and herbicides could also be considered artificial controls.

Here are some examples of succession and its stages:

(1) Succession in a freshwater pond ecosystem:

- The pond represents the first stage in a succession.
- Stream water running into pond carries soil particles.
- Soil particles accumulate over time.
- Pond plants grow and die.
- Soil and plants form a sort of "compost" in the pond.
- The pond becomes a bog.
- Over time a bog may become a meadow.
- As trees grow, the meadow might become a forest (the climax community).

(2) Succession in an asper forest ecosystem:

- Aspens represent a stage in the succession.
- Over time, aspens will be replaced with different dominant species such as spruce and pine, oak, and hickory, depending on location and climate. These are new climax communities.
- If a fire occurs, the aspens could be replaced by many grasses and shrubs such as wolf willow or blueberries, as well as by new aspen seedlings. The succession then begins again
- This type of succession is often seen on the edge of fields where grasses give way to shrubs, which give way to trees in an observable linear pattern.

(3) Succession in a field of wheat:

- Through the human activity of ploughing, new "pioneer" organisms (wheat seeds) are introduced.
- Wheat plants are established immediately as the dominant climax community.

5

- Wheat plant dominance can be maintained through the use of herbicides and/or pesticides.
- Due to the artificiality of this succession, over time, the field must be supplemented with fertilizers (mineral supplements).

In this lesson, students will learn about succession through visuals and text, then through their own study an a micro-ecosystem. In this activity, they will study *microorganisms*, which are microscopic organisms usually viewed best with the aid of a powerful microscope. Microorganisms include monerans, protists, and some fungi.

Note: Microorganisms will be dealt with in further detail in lesson 9.

Materials

- Activity Sheets A and B (1.3.1 and 1.3.2) from Lesson 3 (quadrat study)
- information sheet titled, "Succession in a Freshwater Pond Ecosystem" (Included. Make a copy for each student.) (1.5.1)
- chart paper
- markers
- large jar
- hay or dried grass
- few grains cooked rice
- pond water
- microscopes
- eyedroppers
  slides
- slip covers
- pipettes or straws
- paper towels
- cotton balls
- information sheet titled, "The Water Drop Zoo" (Included. Make a copy for each student.) (1.5.5)

- microorganism diagrams titled, "The Moneran Kingdom," (1.5.3) and "The Protist Kingdom" (1.5.4) (Included. Make one copy of each, mount on sturdy tag board, and laminate.)
- lab coats (optional)
- scissors
- three-point-approach chart (1.1.2)

Activity: Part One

Use the activity sheet (1.3.1) and t-chart (1.3.2) from lesson 3 as a springboard for opening discussion. Ask:

- If nothing interfered with the schoolyard field (or other area) we examined, how do you think it would look by the end of June, October, or in 2 years or more?
- Which species might stay as a part of the ecosystem over time? (e.g., microorganisms or small insects). Why? (e.g., food source remains)
- Which species might disappear from the field ecosystem? (e.g., dandelions).
- Why? (e.g., Field might be sprayed for weeds, inhibiting the growth of dandelions and increasing the growth of grasses.)
- What other species might increase? (e.g., wild flower seeds might spread from neighbouring gardens.)

After discussing students' ideas, introduce the term *succession* and explain that it refers to the natural (or human-made) changes in an ecosystem over time.

Hand out the information sheet titled, "Succession in a Freshwater Pond Ecosystem" (1.5.1). Discuss the illustrations and text, focusing on how the ecosystem changes over time. Discuss the *climax community* as a term used to describe the final stage in succession.

    Hands-On Science • Grade 7

Focus once again on the schoolyard field. Ask:

- Do you think the field always looked the way it does now?
- What do you think it might a have looked like 200 years ago?
- What changes might have occurred?
- What might have caused these changes?

Try to establish the steps in the process of succession in the schoolyard field that more-or-less parallel those in the "Freshwater Pond Ecosystem" example. Have students brainstorm the steps. Record ideas on chart paper, using illustrations and text.

Discuss other examples of succession, using the Background Information for Teachers, as well as ideas suggested by students. In their lab books or on blank paper, have students complete an illustrated example of succession.

Close by, have students complete a three-point-approach chart for *succession* (1.1.2).

Activity: Part Two

Start a *micro-aquatic ecosystem* or *hay infusion* to allow students an opportunity to examine microorganisms and learn more about succession. Involve students in the process by following these steps:

1. Collect a handful of hay or dried grass/plant material. Chop into small pieces.
2. Add it to 1 litre of water in a pot. Bring to boil and simmer 5 minutes. This makes a "grass" soup for microscopic protozoa to feed on.
3. Let cool.
4. Place in a large jar that will leave some air space (about $1/4$ of the jar) at the top.
5. Add a few grains of cooked rice (potential food). Cover.
6. Let stand 24 days in a warm room.
7. Add some pond water or 5-10 ml of soil and tiny bits of dead leaves (protozoa will come from these).

Note: If desired, add some small aquatic plants such as duckweed.

Note: One jar is sufficient for a whole-class study.

Students are now ready to begin examining this ecosystem. Explain that they will be using a microscope to examine organisms in the micro-ecosystem. Ask:

- Why do you think this is called a micro-ecosystem?
- What organisms might you find?
- What is the name for microscopic living things? (microorganisms)

As a class, discuss the process for this study. The activity may be best conducted at a centre, where students work independently over a period of time. This will also allow them to observe more changes in the ecosystem over time.

Set up the centre with a display of the microorganism diagrams (1.5.3 and 1.5.4), microscopes, lab coats, slides, cover slips, pipettes, eyedroppers, and paper towel.

Establish lab rules with students. Here are a couple of points to consider:

- Limit number of students at the centre at a given time.
- Centre must be left tidy. (Consider daily or weekly "lab assistants" to help monitor tidiness. Some students will enjoy doing this. Provide old lab coats, if possible!)
- Remind students they are dealing with living organisms – even the microscopic deserve respect.

▶

5

Encourage students to make wet-mount slides from different locations in the jar, using pipettes to access water samples (e.g., water surface, side of jar, mid-level, bottom of jar).

Note: To slow down the movement of microorganisms and make them easier to examine, have students place a very tiny piece of a cotton ball (a few fibres only) on the slide first and squeeze a drop of water onto this. Then, position the cover slip.

At the centre have enough copies of the information sheet, "The Water Drop Zoo" (1.5.5), Activity Sheet A (1.5.6), and Activity Sheet B (1.5.7). Students will use the information sheets to guide their exploration of microorganisms, and to assist them in identifying these creatures. They may also refer to the microorganism diagrams for assistance.

Have students visit the centre and complete several copies of these activity sheets over a period of time to observe how the ecosystem changes. After several days, students will notice changes in the organisms they are finding. Even in a micro-aquarium we can see the concept of succession working! Have students predict and record which organisms (or type of organisms) they think will end up as the *dominant* species. Other questions to ask include:

- How can you tell where in the jar you might find certain of these microorganisms? (e.g., hydra attaches to debris or uses an air bubble).

- Can you see how the design of a microorganism helps its movement or lifestyle? (e.g., paramecium has many hairs that move.)

- Can you see how the design of aquatic plants is helpful? (e.g., duckweed)

Activity Sheet A

Directions to students:

Complete the activity sheet (1.5.6) as you observe microorganisms under the microscope.

Activity Sheet B

Directions to students:

Complete the data chart as you observe microorganisms under the microscope.

Activity: Part Three

Make a class tally based on the data charts students completed during activity centre time. Notice the dates of observations and the changes in populations of certain microorganisms. Review how *succession* occurs in this ecosystem. Compare to other succession examples studied (freshwater pond, school yard, field, forest). Now, ask the students:

- What might happen if we put the jar in bright sunlight?

Discuss ideas, then test students' predictions and observe what happens. Increasing the amount of sunlight exposure to small green plants (especially duckweed) can cause a dramatic "population explosion" to occur. Have students infer what this will do to this ecosystem in the long-term.

Note: The positive and negative effects of human action on ecosystems are dealt with in subsequent lessons.

Activity: Part Four

Have students graph the compiled class data from the micro-ecosystem (hay infusion) activity centre. Criteria to ask for/solicit from students could include:

- title
- legend (choose minimum of 2 microorganisms to include in the graph)
- clear labelling of axes
- clear scale along axes
- graph neatly completed
- graph accurately reflects data
- could be either bar or line graph
- a paragraph of 3 to 4 sentences describing what the graph means

Here is a sample of how a graph might look:

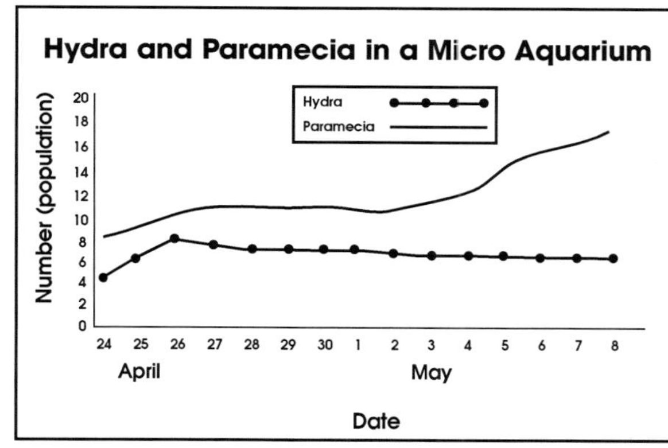

Extensions

- To focus more on aquatic plants and their adaptations, provide students with copies of the information sheet titled "Duckweed Duplication" (1.5.8). As a class, read through the information, discuss ideas and diagrams, and answer questions presented.

- Have students research the climax community of Canada's Old Growth Forest of the West Coast.

Assessment Suggestion

Identify criteria for behaviour at the activity centre. For example:

- care of microscope
- preparation of wet-mount slides
- completion of data sheets
- clean-up

List these criteria on the Rubric on page 19. Observe students as they work at the centre, and record results accordingly.

Succession in a Freshwater Pond Ecosystem

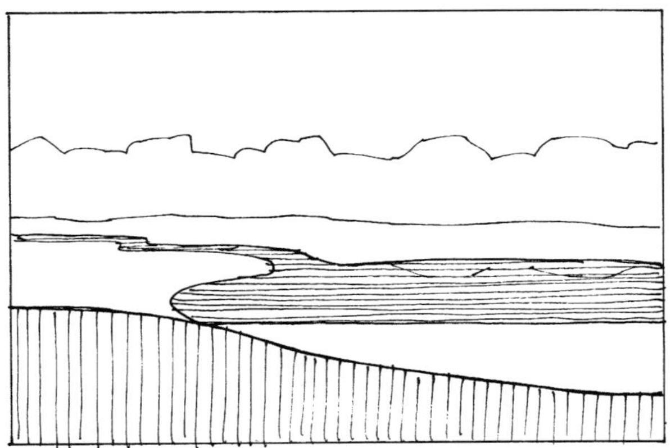

1. The pond represents the first stage in a succession.

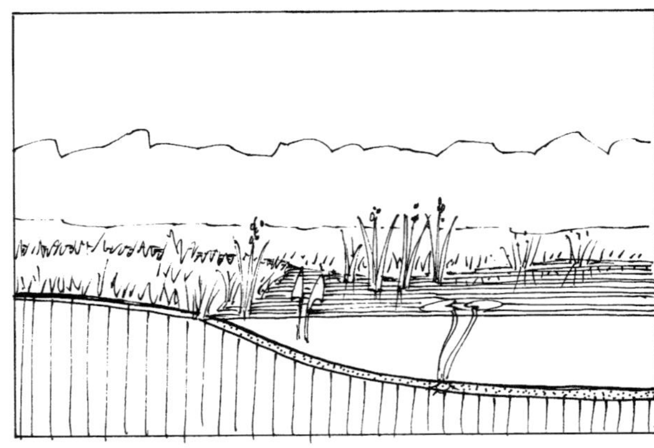

2. Stream water running into pond carries soil particles in which plants germinate in shallow areas.

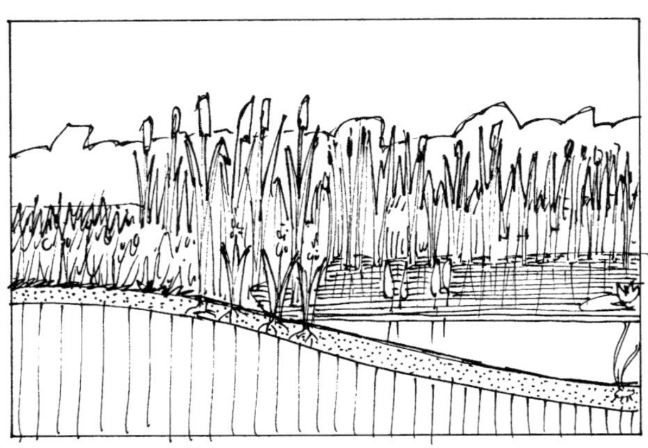

3. Soil particles accumulate over time and so do plants around the edge.

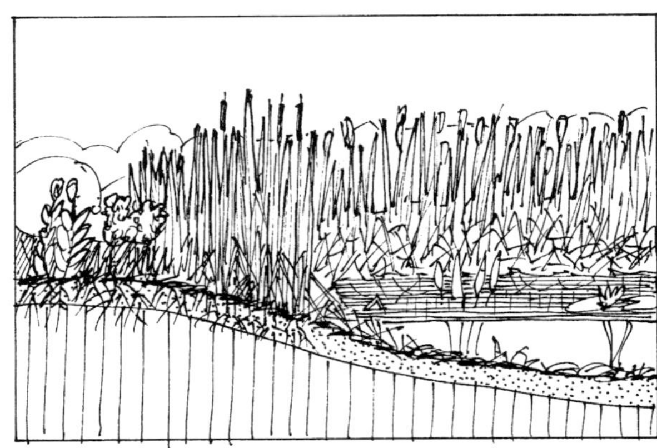

4. Pond plants grow and die, in doing so, they compost and build up soil.

5. Soil replaces water and other plants take the place of water plants.

6. The pond becomes a marsh. Willows and other pioneer trees grow at edge.

7. Over time a marsh may become a meadow with trees encroaching on the sides.

8. As trees grow, the meadow might become a forest (the climax community).

Protist Kingdom

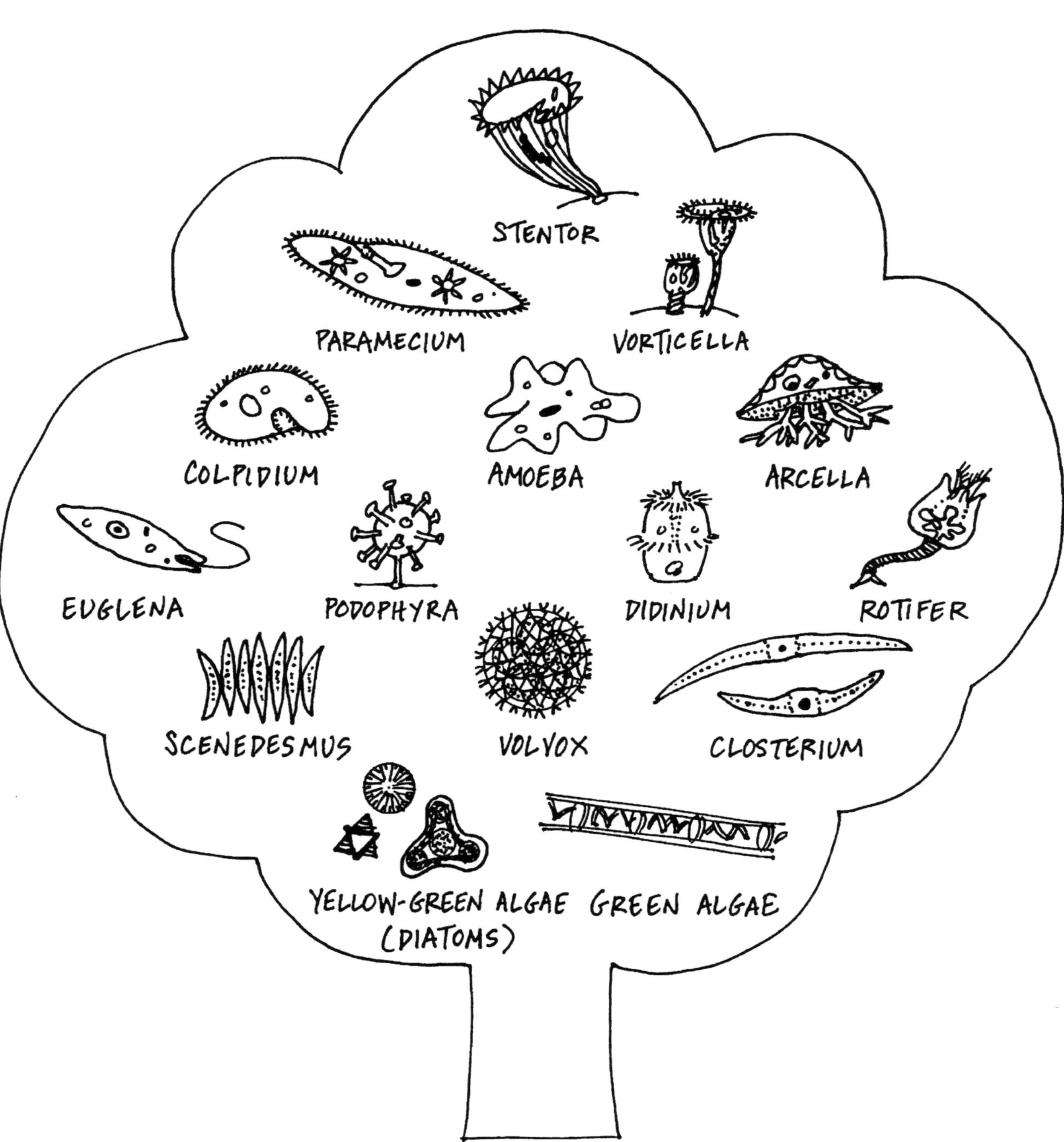

Monera Kingdom

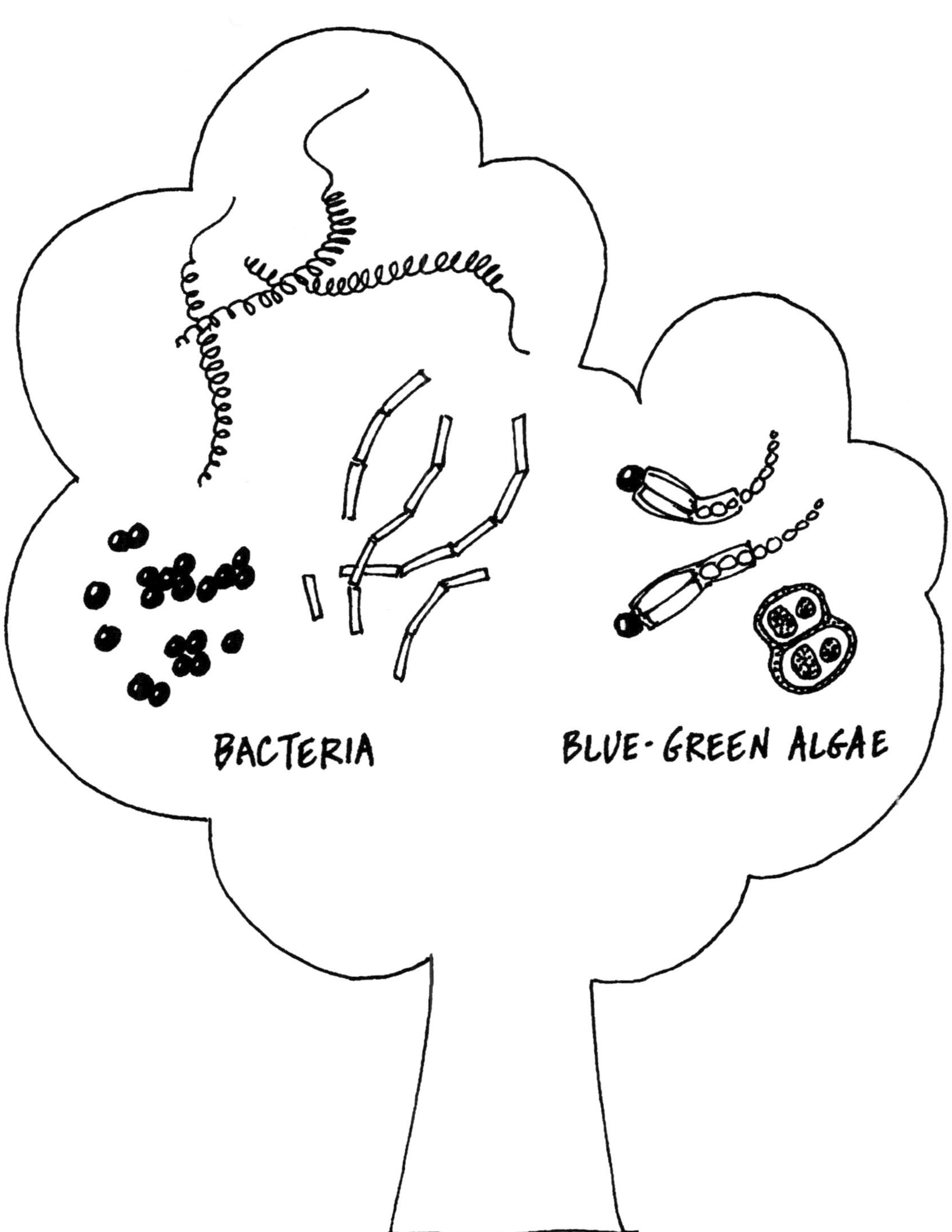

The Water Drop Zoo

Amoeba – are surface or bottom dwellers, but may attach to side of jars too. Use a gentle jet of water from a full eyedropper to move them.

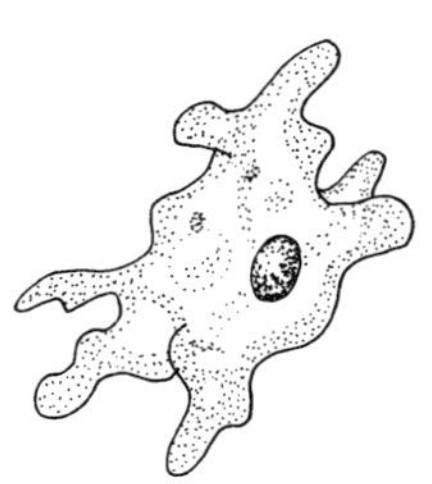

Spirostomum – freely moves through the infusion but will collect on the bottom when undistrubed.

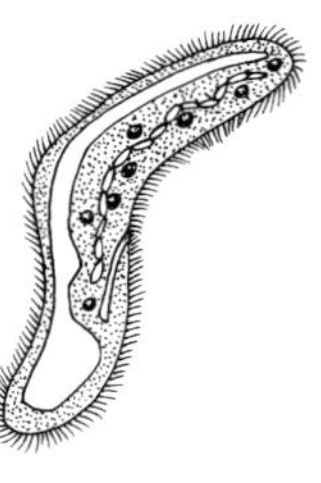

Stentor – is a surface or bottom dweller, like the amoeba

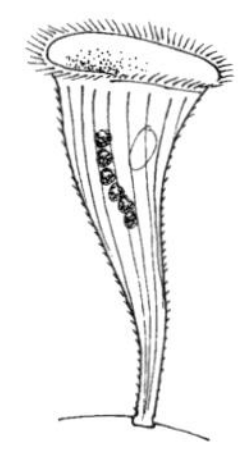

Volvox – like to collect in areas where there is moderate light (not direct sunlight, though!)

Vorticella – may fix itself to the bottom, attach to debris, or suspend on the water surface.

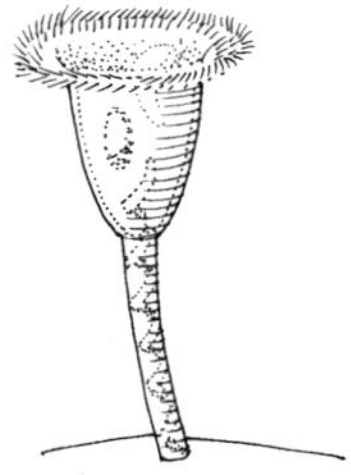

Paramecium – is a protozoa that moves fast through the infusion! Can you catch one under a wet-mount slide?

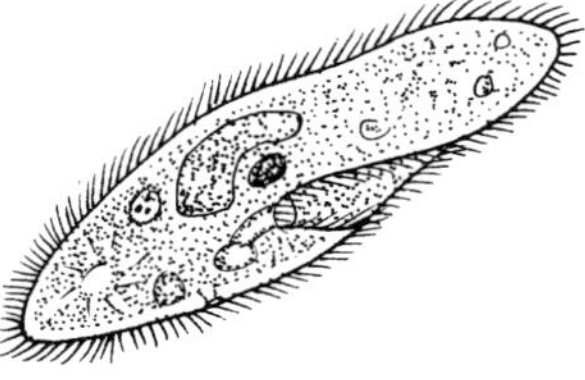

Euglena – is another fast-moving protozoa.

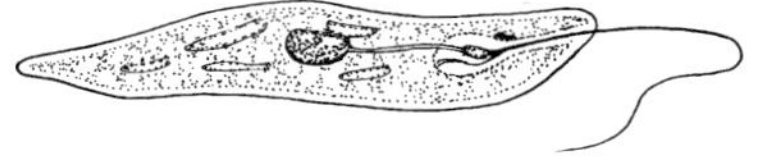

Rotifer – is a hardy little protozoa that can put up with a crowded space if it has to!

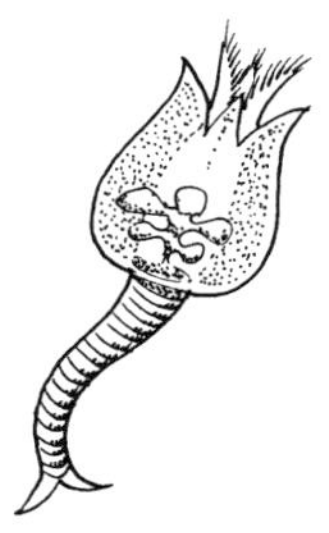

Elodea – (Canadian Pondweed) one of the easiest to grow.

Hydra – often suspend themselves from their bases by tiny air bubbles, but will also attach to other surfaces.

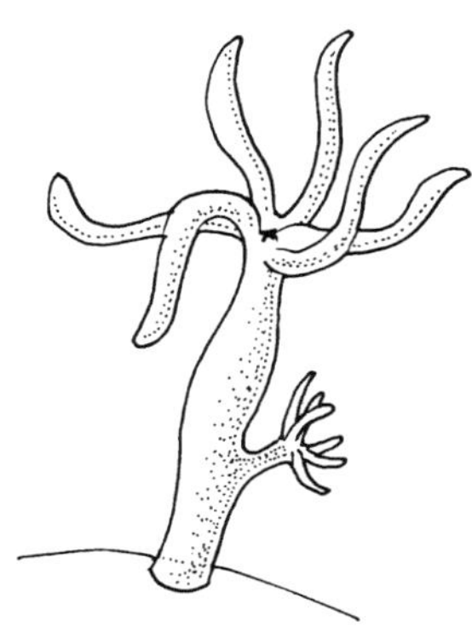

Duckweed – float on top of the water.

Elodea and duckweed provide shade, shelter and food for many of the infusion animals. Underwater plants act like an aquarium pump to make oxygen for them.

Algae – can be single or many celled. They like cooler temperatures and indirect light best. (Shade the jar with a piece of white paper.)

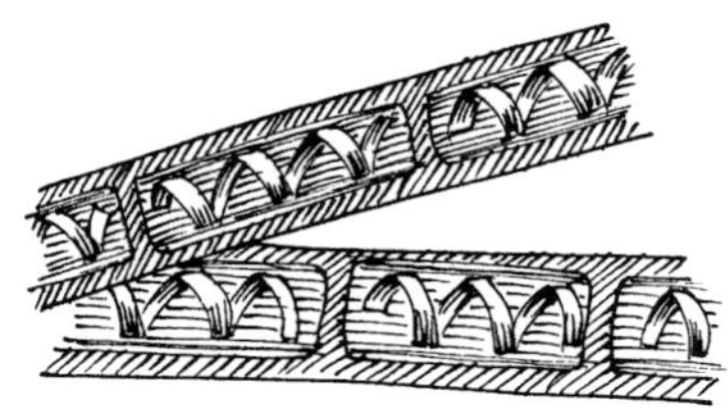

Date: ___________________   **Name:** _____________________________

Microorganisms

1. Draw a labelled diagram of what you observe under the microscope.

2. Label any microorganism that you can identify.

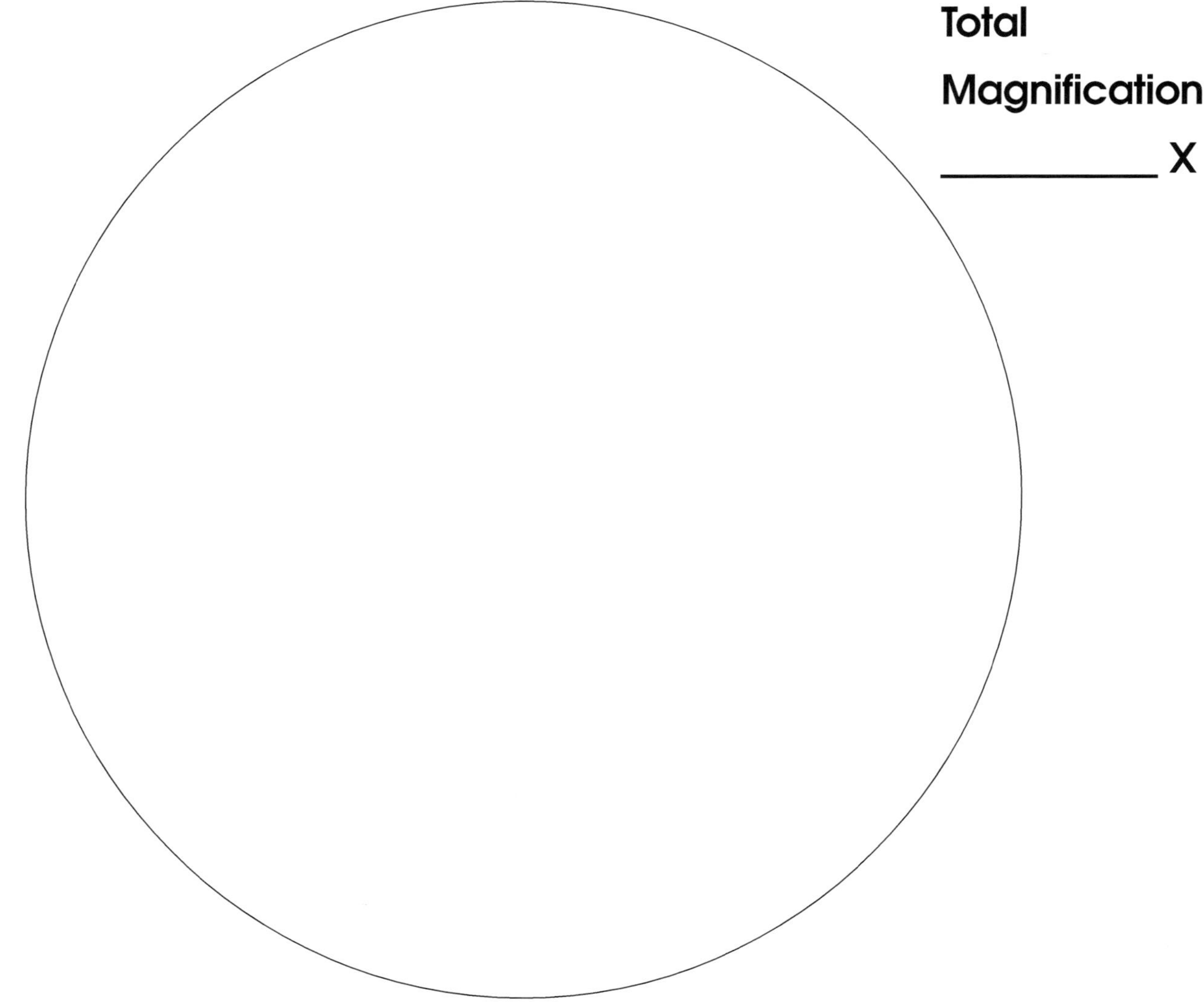

Total

Magnification:

___________ X

Which microorganism do you find most interesting? ___________

Why? ____

____

Date: _______________________   **Name:** __________________________

Data Chart: Water Drop Zoo

Date and Time	Microorganism (Name and Draw)	Location In Jar	Number Sighted	Movement

Duckweed Duplication

Duckweed is a small flat plant that floats on the surface of the water. It produces flowers, but has another, faster method of reproducing. Branches grow out from the sides of one parent plant. When they are big enough, the branches break off and float away to become a new and separate plant.

Duckweed is often found in clusters of ten or twenty plants of all different sizes and ages.

Why would it be an advantage for duckweed to reproduce so rapidly? When might this be a disadvatage?

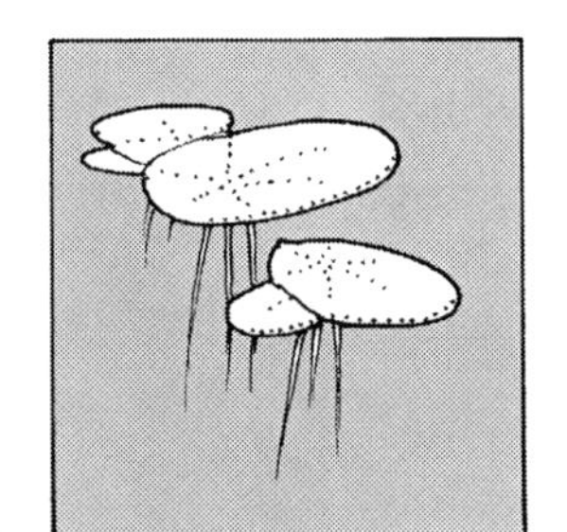

duck swimming through
duckweed

6 | Building Blocks in an Ecological Food Pyramid

Background Information for Teachers

Producers: organisms that make their own food (green plants). These are the beginning of the food chain. Producers are said to occupy the first trophic level of a food chain. Trophic level refers to a step in the flow of energy through an ecosystem where all species in that ecosystem have the same main nutritional sources.

Consumers: organisms such as *herbivores* (plant-eaters) and *carnivores* (meat-eaters). Herbivores are the second trophic level and carnivores the third trophic levels.

Note: With students, use the term *primary consumer, secondary consumer,* and *tertiary consumer.*

Decomposers: organisms that get energy from the chemical breakdown of animal or plant waste and dead organisms (e.g., earthworms, many bacteria and fungi). They break down organic material that is hard for other organisms to digest, returning it to the environment in inorganic form for re-use by plants.

Bacteria, fungi, and some **protozoa**: consumers that operate at all levels of the food chain. They are integral parts of many cycles (nitrogen cycle, carbon cycle).

Scavenger: decomposer/consumers that feed on animal carcasses, garbage. Hyenas and vultures are well-known examples but even some butterflies are scavengers. In Canada, crows are common scavengers.

Predator: carnivore that hunts another animal for food.

Prey: The animal hunted by a predator.

Food Chain: The order of organisms through which energy is transferred. Each link (trophic level) in the chain feeds on and gets energy from the one preceding it and in turn is eaten by the one following it, providing energy to the next level. Food chains are seldom more than three or four links, as the energy loss at each level is so great the links cannot be sustained beyond this.

Food Web: all the food chains in an ecosystem interacting together.

Food Pyramid: a stylized food chain or web representing the loss of energy throughout the trophic levels.

Note: Diagrams of food chains, food webs, and food pyramids are included in this lesson.

Materials

- chart paper
- markers
- KWL chart (included. Make copies for working groups of students.) (1.6.1)
- picture collection from Lesson 2
- large bowl of popcorn
- diagrams of food chains, food webs, and food pyramids (included. Make overhead transparencies of these sheets, as well as a copy for each student.)
- nonpermanent overhead pens

Activity: Part One

A food chain is a concept many students will have knowledge about from past studies in science. Assess prior knowledge to gage how to apply subsequent parts of this lesson by facilitating a KWL. Divide the class into working groups and provide each group with a KWL chart (1.6.1). Have the students complete the first two columns of the KWL chart, recording their definitions, examples, and background knowledge about food chains.

Following this group activity, provide an opportunity to share ideas. Ask:

■ What do you know about food chains?

Students will likely come up with terms such as producers and consumers. Ask:

■ If you know what a *producer* is and a *consumer* is, can you infer what a decomposer is? (a scavenger)

■ What other words do you know that are related to the food chain? (herbivore, carnivore, predator, and prey are likely answers)

■ What do consumers get from the food they eat? (energy)

On the chart paper make a list of all relevant vocabulary introduced during this activity, and discuss the definitions of each term. Have students complete a three-point-approach chart for these terms.

Activity: Part Two

Display the overhead diagram titled "A Food Chain – Example # 1" (1.6.2). As a class, discuss the cycle and identify each level in the chain. Ask:

■ Can you identify the producer?
■ Which are consumers?

Introduce the terms *primary*, *secondary*, and *tertiary* consumers. Record the terms on chart paper, identify examples on the food chain, and determine definitions for each term. Record these definitions on the chart.

Now ask:

■ Which animal is a herbivore (carnivore, predator, prey)?
■ Which organisms might act as decomposers in this food chain?
■ Which organisms might act as scavengers in this food chain?

Now focus on the structure of the diagram itself. Ask:

■ In which direction do the arrows on the food chain always point?
■ Why do you think the arrows point in this direction?
■ What do these consumers get from their food? (energy)

Remind students that the arrows on a food chain always point toward the "eaters" to show the energy transfer.

Now have the class work in their groups again. Provide each group with a scene from the picture collection from lesson 2. Have the groups discuss the plants and animals in their scene and identify a possible food chain in a scene (e.g., alpine meadow with a grizzly bear in it). Provide time for each group to describe their food chain for the class. Ask:

■ You will not see these in any of our pictures, but where do you think the microorganisms would be found? (Microorganisms are what make any food chain a cycle.)
■ What might happen if human beings were introduced into your scene/picture (if none are there already)?
■ How do you think the living organisms would react if some abiotic factor changed, like an increased temperature for several months?

Encourage students to share their ideas, opinions, and knowledge informally.

Divide the class into working groups. Provide all students with their own copies of the diagram titled, "A Food Chain – Example # 2" (1.6.3), as well as Activity Sheet A (1.6.4). Have the groups discuss the diagram and complete their activity sheets.

Once students have completed the task, display the overhead transparency of this food chain, and have the groups share their ideas. Discuss findings as a class.

Activity Sheet A

Directions to students:

Complete the activity sheet by referring to the food chain diagram.

Activity: Part Three

Display the overhead diagram titled, "A Food Web – Example # 1" (1.6.5). As a class, examine the diagram and discuss the differences between a food chain and a food web. Emphasize that a food web shows the inter-relationship between several food chains

Use the diagram to reinforce vocabulary and familiarize students with the dynamics of energy flow through an ecosystem. Remind students that a food web shows energy flow from one organism to another.

Maintain the students in their working groups. Provide all students with a copy of the diagram titled, "A Food Web – Example # 2" (1.6.6). Distribute a copy of Activity Sheet B (1.6.7) to each student. Have the groups discuss the food cycle and complete their activity sheets.

Once students have completed the task, display the overhead transparency of this food web, and have the groups share their ideas. Discuss findings as a class.

Activity Sheet B

Directions to students:

Complete the sheet by referring to the food web diagram.

Activity: Part Four

Safety Note: Consider all possible food allergies prior to conducting an activities involving food products (e.g., popcorn, oil).

Display the overhead titled, "The Food Pyramid – Example # 1" (1.6.8). Ask:

- What does this diagram show?
- How is this food cycle different from the others we have looked at?

Explain to the class that this is a *food pyramid*. It shows differences in the size and numbers of different organisms in the various levels of a food chain. Ask:

- Why do you think it is called a *pyramid*?

Using a nonpermanent overhead pen, draw a triangle around the outside of the diagram to exemplify the pyramidal shape. Explain that the base of a food pyramid is the largest and is made up of green plants. Ask:

- What is another name for a green plant? (producer)
- What comes next on the pyramid? (primary consumers, planteaters)
- Are there less or more of these?

Continue this procedure, discussing each level of the food pyramid. Further explain that a food pyramid also shows how energy is lost and gained. Animals gain energy from what they eat. At the same time, as energy moves from the sun, to plants, and on to animals, much of it is lost. For example, an animal gains only about 10% of the energy of the plant it eats. The other 90% is lost to heat or is never digested.

Demonstrate this concept with a bowl of popcorn. One student is the Sun, twelve students are producers, six students are primary consumers, three students are secondary consumers, and one student is a tertiary consumer. Have the producers stand in a line

facing the Sun. The primary consumers stand in a line facing the Sun. The primary consumers stand in a line behind the producers, the secondary consumers behind them, and finally the tertiary consumer. Have the students note the triangular/pyramidal shape of the group (excluding the Sun). Also note that the plants are the closest to the Sun because they get their energy from the Sun.

The student acting as the sun holds the bowl of popcorn, which represents energy. Each plant gets a handful of popcorn, eats some, and passes it back to a primary consumer. Each primary consumer gets popcorn from two plants. They eat some, and pass it back to the secondary consumers. Each secondary consumer gets popcorn from three primary consumers. They eat some, then pass it back to the tertiary consumer.

Following this demonstration, discuss the activity. Ask:

- Why do plants pass back some of their popcorn?
- Why do primary consumers get popcorn from two plants?
- Why do secondary consumers eat some popcorn before passing it back?
- How much of the original bowl of popcorn does the tertiary consumer get?
- How does this activity show energy gain?
- How does it show energy loss?

Now divide the class into working groups and provide each student with a copy of the diagram titled, "A Food Pyramid – Example # 2," (1.6.9) along with Activity Sheet C (1.6.10). Have the students work together in their groups to discuss the pyramid and complete the sheet.

Once students have completed this activity, discuss their results. Be sure to clarify questions and conceptions about food pyramids and energy.

Students should be keeping up with their three-point-approach charts for all new vocabulary.

Activity Sheet C

Directions to students:

Examine the diagram of the food pyramid to complete the activity sheet (1.6.10).

Activity: Part Five

Have students complete the last column of the KWL chart, reflecting on what they have learned about food chains.

Extensions

To practice using vocabulary and concepts learned, and to provide some skills in the compilation and analysis of qualitative and quantitative data, involve students in a predator-prey game (1.6.11). Use the game instructions provided to help review the game with students.

Divide the class into pairs. Each pair needs a copy of the game instructions, 60 red beans, 60 white beans (have these ready in a baggie ahead of time), recording paper (or lab book), and graph paper (for final assignment). A working area of two desks pushed together or small tables is helpful.

Provide plenty of time for students to review the game instructions, play the game, record ideas, and collect data.

Following the game, have each pair of students use their data to:

(1) graph the changes from one line (generation) to the next.
(2) write a report on what the graph tells about the population dynamics of these organisms. Students must draw conclusions (infer) from the graph and decide what has happened.

Some reasons for changes in organisms might be: over-hunting, changes in producers, or harsh winters.

- Teachers may provide information on the work of actual Canadian ecologists who have contributed to the field through their research. A recommended resource for this purpose is *Great Canadian Scientists* by Barry Shell (see Books for Students). For each scientist, Shell tells the story of the research in an engaging manner, gives some background about the young scientist and explains the science behind the research. Activities are also suggested. Some profiles relevant to his unit are:
- Birute Galdikas (studies orangutans)
- Charles Krebs (Zoologist and ecologist who studies rodent population cycles)
- Walter Lewis and Memory Elvin-Lewis (Ethno-botanists famous for research on the medicinal plants of the tropical rainforest)
- William Ricker (Fisheries biologist, inventor of the "Ricker Curve" for describing fish population dynamics)

Note: This is also an appropriate time to discuss contributions of Aboriginal peoples to the practice of sound ecological principles.

Assessment Suggestions

Set criteria for the predator-prey game assignment with the students. For example:

- clear, complete graph
- report uses complete sentences, paragraphs
- correct spelling
- conclusions or inferences about what the graph shows are logical and relevant to current issues discussed in class (or elsewhere).

Date: ___________________   Name: ___________________

KWL

Topic: ____

We know...	We Want to Know...	We Learned...

A Food Chain:
Example #1

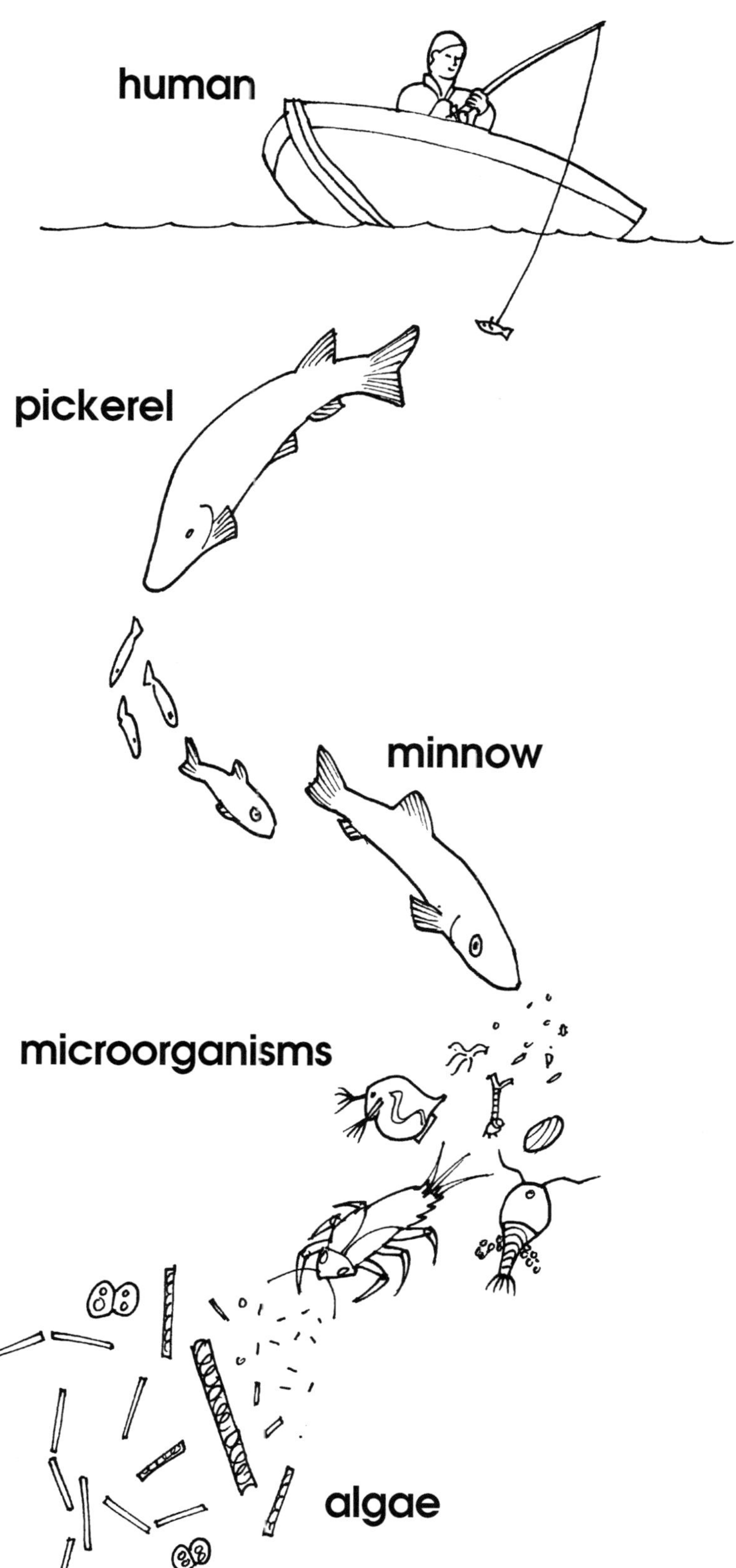

A Food Chain:
Example #2

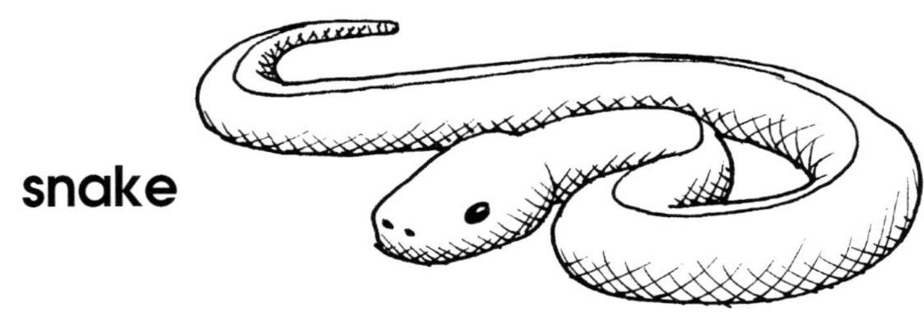

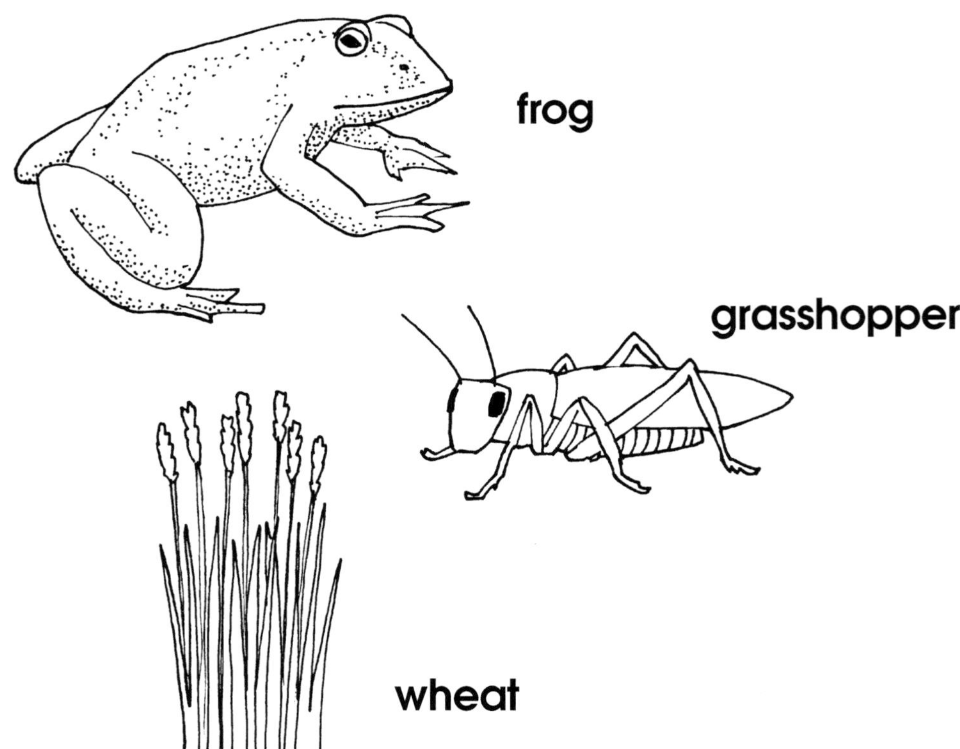

A Food Chain

1. In what ecosystem might this chain be found?

    ____

2. Label producers and consumers (primary, secondary, tertiary).

3. What would happen if one of the organisms of the chain was over-hunted or exterminated by a pesticide or herbicide?

    ____

    ____

    ____

    ____

    ____

4. Draw and label a food chain using different organisms. Include a scavenger in your food chain?

A Food Web:

Example #1

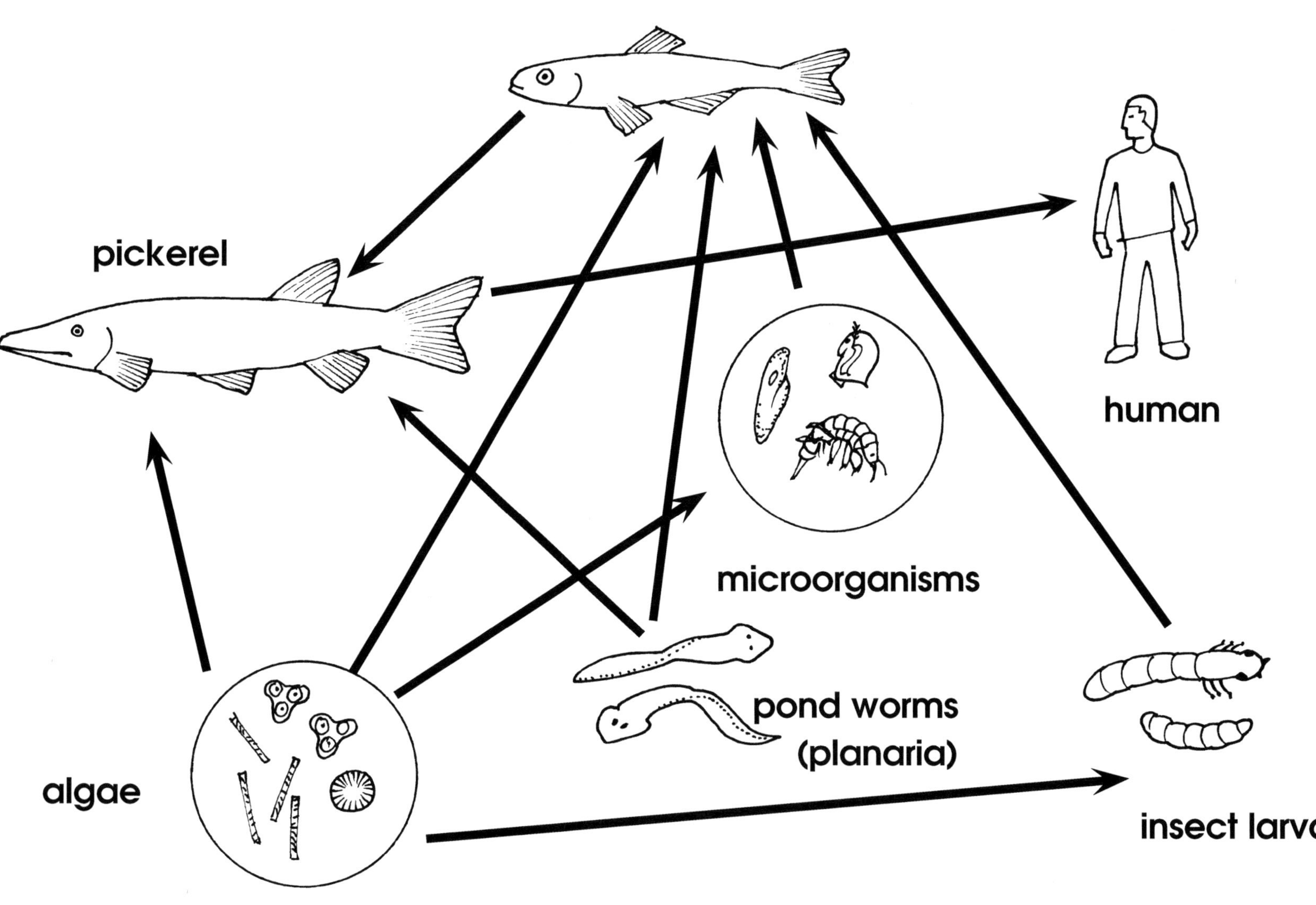

A Food Web:
Example #2

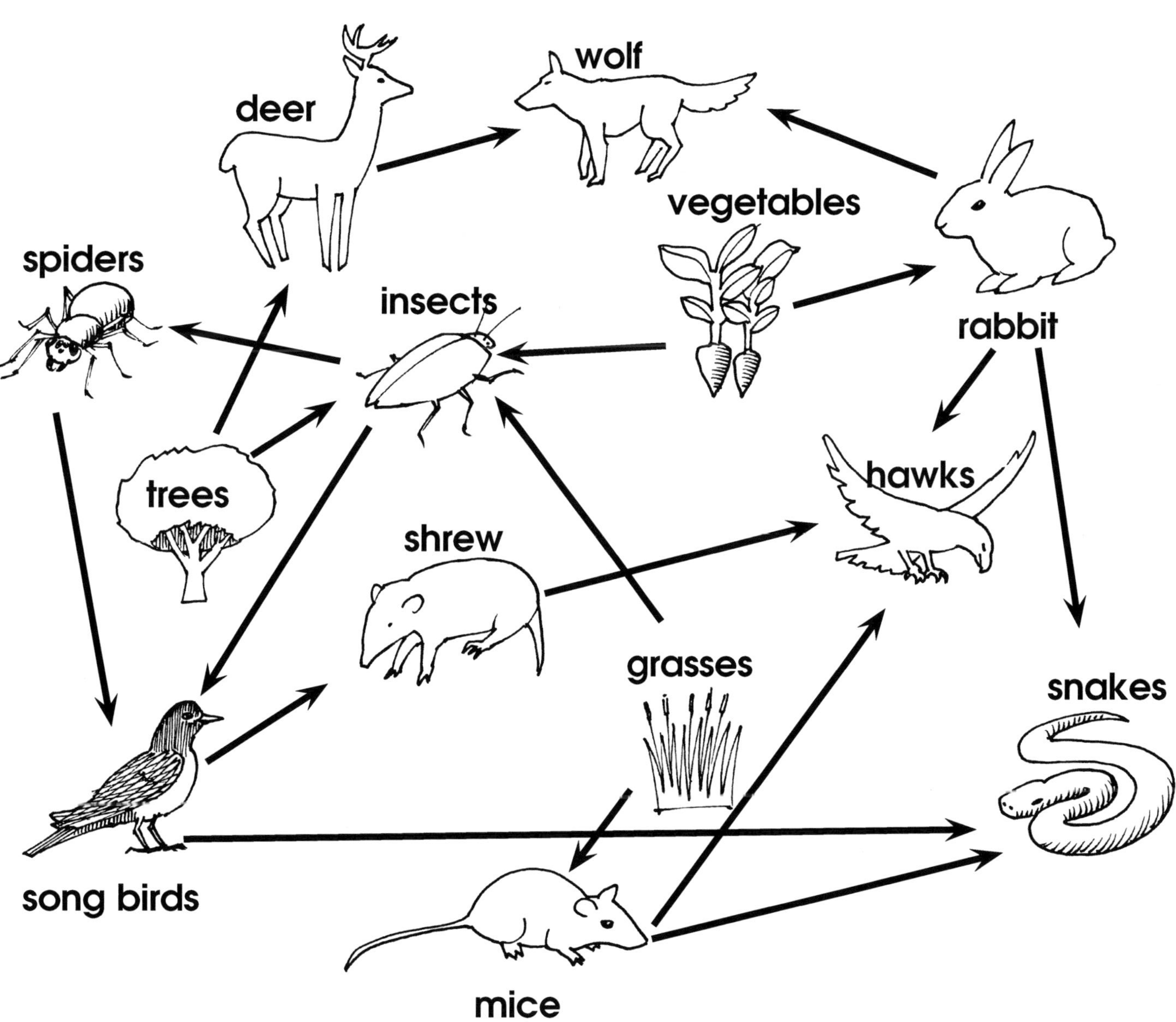

A Food Web

Date: _________________________   Name: _____________________________

1. In what ecosystem might this food web be found?

   ____

2. How many simple food chains can you find in this food web?
   Record these.

   ____

   ____

   ____

   ____

3. Label the producers, consumers (primary, secondary, and tertiary).

4. Are there any scavengers or decomposers in this food web? Label any that appear. Where might they be found if you could put them into this food chain? Add these to the food web.

5. Redraw the food web removing one of the consumers.

6. What might the loss of this consumer do to the food web and the ecosystem over time?

   ____

   ____

A Food Pyramid:

Example #1

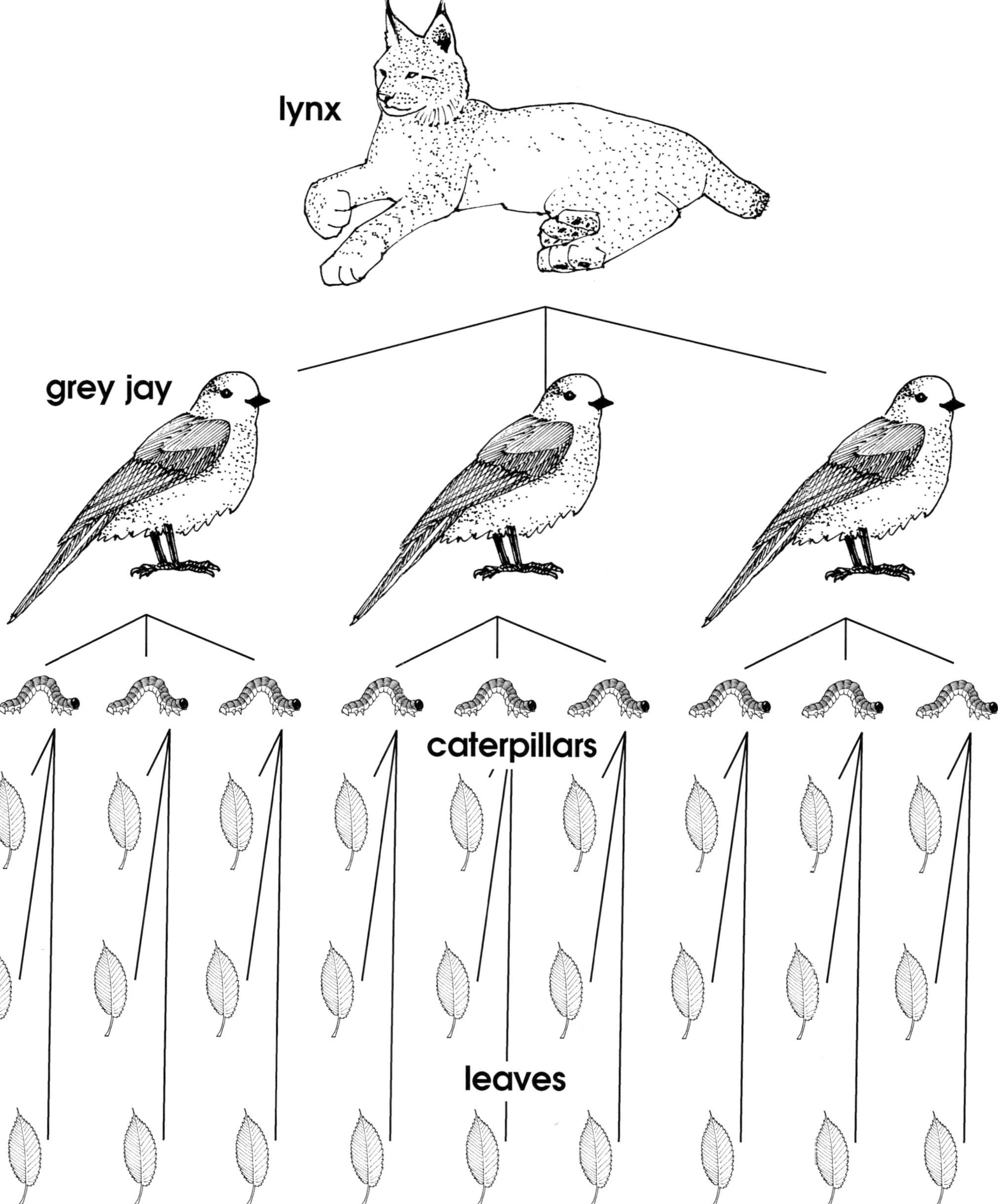

A Food Pyramid:

Example #2

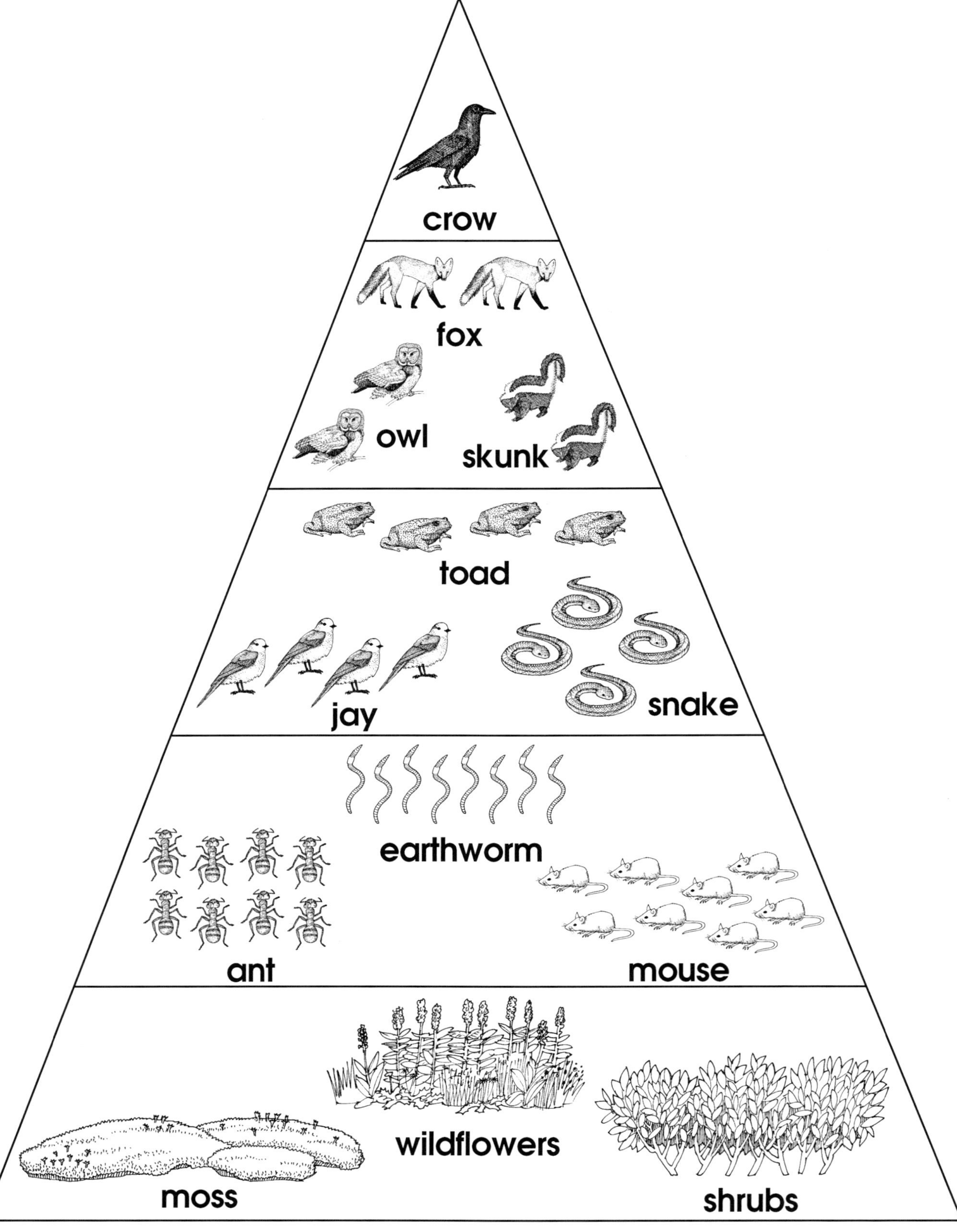

A Food Pyramid

1. How is a food pyramid different from a food chain?

____

____

2. In what ecosystem might this pyramid be found?

____

3. Label all the members of this pyramid (e.g., producer, all levels of consumer, scavenger, decomposer).

4. Use this food pyramid to explain energy gain and loss.

____

____

____

____

____

____

Predator-Prey Relationship Game

1. Mix the bag of red and white beans well.

2. Carefully pour them onto your desk.

3. Line up all the beans randomly single file; there should be 50 of each.

4. Put extra ones back into the baggie.

5. The red beans are *predators* and the white beans are *prey*. Name your predator and prey according to species familiar to you. (e.g., predator-coyote; prey-mole).

6. Start at one end. Add or subtract red or white beans from the population using these rules:

Rule #1: red-white or white-red means the predatory (red) has captured prey (white). Since the predator will eat the prey and then be able to reproduce, take the white one out of the line and add an extra red one from the baggie, making 2 red. Put the white one back in the baggie.

Rule #2: red-red means 2 predators. There is too much competition so both starve and die. Remove both and put them in the baggie.

Rule #3: white-white means 2 prey. This means they have not been eaten so are able to reproduce. Add one white from the bag.

7. When you finish going through the whole line this way (looking at pairs of beans), count how many red and how many white are left. Make a chart to record this data.

8. Count out another line of 50 red and 50 white beans mix up and repeat using the 3 rules.

9. Do this until time runs out or you run out of one colour of bean.

7 Human Action and Ecosystems

Background Information for Teachers

In this lesson, the concept of *bioaccumulation* is introduced. The term refers to the collection or increasing incidence of something in a food chain or pyramid. For example, a pesticide applied to organisms that are primary consumers (e.g., grasshoppers in a grain field) will collect in organisms that eat these (secondary consumers), and so on. So, snakes that eat grasshoppers collect more of the pesticide in their systems. A hawk (tertiary consumer) that catches a snake gets an even bigger dose of the pesticide. Probably one of the most well-known examples of bioaccumulation is DDT, which is now banned from use in the environment.

The ecological principle, called The Law of Unexpected Consequences (or LUC for short) may well be of interest to grade-seven students. This law is about what happens when we do something without thinking about it, such as skateboarding without a helmet, burning leaves on a windy day, or (the classic) playing baseball too close to the neighbour's picture window! Many thoughtless actions have resulted in serious ecological effects. LUC is cited in this lesson when dealing with the issue of pesticide use and bioaccumulation

The topic of human action and ecosystems is extensive and complex. To make it manageable for both teacher and students, two short articles are included with the lesson. The purposes of these articles are to provide:

- springboards for whole- and small-group debate.
- opportunities to use vocabulary and other learning in a relevant context
- a change of pace from the rather heavy curriculum content expected in this unit.
- opportunities to use skills in other subject areas and to make connections to these subject areas (language arts; social studies.).

Both stories are written in a generic manner but refer to actual documented environmental occurrences.

Materials

- stories titled, "When the Pesticide Becomes the Pest" (1.7.1) and "No Sporting Chance" (1.7.2) (included. Make a copy for each student.)
- chart paper
- markers
- related articles from newspapers, journals, and books
- reference material on endangered species

About the stories:

"When The Pesticide Becomes the Pest": This scenario outlines the use of the pesticide DDT used during the 1950s, by the Government of Canada. In time, it was found that good insects were exterminated (pesticides are not selective), and producers such as phytoplankton (tiny algae that produce a large portion of the earth's oxygen and are a vital source of food for many other microorganisms) actually absorbed the DDT. The DDT was eaten and collected in minnows, larger fish, and in other organisms, such as bears and in birds, that ate fish. Many birds suffered drastic declines in their populations as the DDT collected in their systems to a point where it interfered with the production of strong, protective eggshells. One well-known example is the peregrine falcon population that declined to fewer than 200 birds. It took special efforts to save the species, but the peregrine falcon was removed from the Endangered Species List in 1999.

▶

"No Sporting Chance": Although this occured in Lake Victoria, Africa's largest freshwater lake, in the 1960's it could happen in Canada. The hunter fish was the Nile Perch, and the food fish was the tilapia.

Activity: Part One

Provide students with the story titled, "When the Pesticide Becomes the Pest" (1.7.1). Have them read the story independently, then share ideas and summaries in pairs (Think-Pair-Share strategy). As a class, discuss the article. Ask:

- What do you think was happening in this ecosystem?
- How do you think the lumber mill manager would react if the government had done nothing?
- Do you think the government had alternatives it could use? What might the alternatives be?

Explain to the students that what happened in this ecosystem is an example of bioaccumulation. Record this term on chart paper. Explain that bioaccumulation occurs when something, such as a chemical, is introduced into an ecosystem food chain. In this case, a pesticide was used to kill budworms. These primary consumers, and other insects killed by the pesticide, were eaten by secondary consumers. The secondary consumers collected pesticide in their systems from each insect they ate. The pesticide, therefore, *accumulated* in the organisms, killing some and adversely affecting others. Ask:

- What would a food chain look like that shows the effects of the pesticide?

Encourage students to share their ideas about what the chain might look like. Have each student draw a rough sketch of this food chain, then share their sketches in working groups. Have each group design and complete a food chain, showing bioaccumulation and the effects of the pesticide. Invite each group to share their food chain with the class.

Ask:

- What does the title of the story mean? Why is it appropriate?
- Is it possible for something similar to happen today? Think of examples.
- Optional: How does this story show the Law of Unexpected Consequences (LUC) principle?

Activity: Part Two

Provide each student with a copy of the story, "No Sporting Chance" (1.7.2). Have the students read the article independently then complete the activity sheet (1.7.3).

Once students have completed the activity sheets, discuss the article. Ask:

- What are some other examples where an ecosystem's balance has been upset?
- Have you any personal experiences you can share?
- What would a food web look like before the introduction and after the introduction of the hunter fish? (Draw the before and after food webs as students make suggestions, or have students do the drawing.)
- How does this story show the importance of having many different organisms living in balance? (This is called *biodiversity*.)
- What actions might the Aboriginal peoples take in this situation?
- How might this situation have been prevented from happening in the first place?
- If you owned a cottage on this lake, what would your reaction be? How would you help the future of the lake? The future of the Aboriginal peoples? Would you be willing to give up your cottage to ensure the health of the lake?

7

- Optional: How does this story show the Law of Unexpected Circumstances (LUC)?

Activity Sheet A

Directions to students:

Complete the Story Analysis sheet (1.7.3) for the story titled, "No Sporting Chance" (1.7.2).

Activity: Part Three

Have students complete a mini-research report on an endangered or extinct species, using Activity Sheet B or C (1.7.4 or 1.7.5) as a guideline. Provide reference material (books, web sites), and have students access information to complete the sheet. Display these sheets on a bulletin board with photographs, illustrations, or computer-printed pictures of the species.

Note: Two sheets are included here; one for researching an endangered species and one for researching an extinct species. Have each student select a topic, or assign topics.

Activity Sheet B

Directions to students:

Use the sheet as a guide to researching an endangered species.

Activity Sheet C

Directions to students:

Use the sheet as a guide to researching an extinct species.

Extension

Other articles based on similar issues are readily available in newspapers, magazines, and online (see Web Sites). Collect several articles to supplement the two articles provided. Look for topics such as:

- hazardous waste mishaps (oil spills/industrial pollution)
- medical discoveries (microorganisms/genetics)
- pesticide issues (as related to human health-allergies)
- recycling initiatives
- global warming (natural vs. manufactured changes already being observed; debates on fossil fuel consumption)

When the Pesticide Becomes the Pest

The evergreen trees were being attacked! The manager at the lumber mill looked out of his office window and frowned. What would happen to his job and the jobs of all his workers if all the trees were destroyed?

The trees were being attacked by the spruce budworm. The insects ate the young, soft new leaf shoots at the tips of the tree branches. The trees, therefore, were not able to grow. If the attacks continued, the trees would die in three to five years.

Fortunately, help was available. The spruce budworm infestation was causing such a huge problem for the evergreen forest in the country (and the lumber industry) that the government stepped in to help. It sent crop dusters to spray large areas of forest with a chemical that killed the budworms. The chemical – a pesticide – destroyed unwanted pests.It was already used to kill grasshoppers, which ate grain crops, and weevils, which ate cotton crops. The pesticide killed may other insects too.

At the lumber mill, the manager was relieved to have government scientists to help solve the budworm problem. Of course, getting rid of the pests took time, but in a few years the forests seemed normal again and jobs at the mill looked secure. The manger could enjoy fishing on the weekend without worrying about his future.

But a strange thing was happening. The streams in the forest where he often fished were full of dead fish. The manager was still catching live fish, but he started to wonder if they were safe to eat.

One day, he mentioned his concern to a friend. His friend was a volunteer with a bird studies organization and was banding opsreys in the area. The friend told him that they were finding smashed eggs in the osprey nests. It seemed that the birds were accidentally breaking their own eggs. Something was strange, but no one knew what it was.

No Sporting Chance

The large, beautiful lake had something for everyone. People came from all over to fish, canoe, and watch birds and sunsets. The lake, home to many species of fish, provided the local Aboriginal communities with healthy fresh food. The aboriginal people also worked as fishing guides.

One year, a man who had a summer cottage on the lake decided another sport fish would be a good addition to the lake.

The new species of fish was a fighter. It was so mean that it went after the other fish in the lake, and killed many of them. The best food fish were able to escape the hunter fish by diving too deep for the new fish to follow. Still, the hunter fish ate many other types of fish in the lake. Over time, however, the algae population grew in the water. The algae died from overpopulation and sank to the bottom of the lake and eventually destroyed the deep water safety of the best food fish.

But the hunter fish caused even more damage. These fish ate snail-eating fish. Can you guess what happened next? The snails overpopulated! To make matters worse the snails carried parasites that could give the people who ate them diseases. The food fish population decreased without enough fish to control the snail and algae populations.

The aboriginal people, who ate the majority of the food fish, tried to adjust to the changes in their food supply. For example, when they realized the new fish did not sun-dry well enough for storage, they decided to roast the fish. Roasting worked well, but required fire, and fire required wood from the trees that surrounded the village and lake.

In time, the forests became bare and damaged. Birds left. The fish supply dwindled and people stopped visiting the lake to fish, canoe, and watch birds and sunsets. The aboriginal people could no longer make a living as fishing guides. They no longer had a healthy abundant food source. All this happened because of one man's wish for better sport fishing!

Date: _______________________   Name: _______________________

Article Analysis

Article Title: ____

Summary:

Illustration:

The Author's Message:

**Application –
Relevance to Today:**

Facts About an Endangered Species

Date: _________________________ **Name:** _________________________

Species: _________________________________

Physical Description: _____________________________

____

____

____

Habitat: ____

Food: ____

Enemies: ____

Draw a food chain that includes this species:

What occurred that resulted in this species becoming endangered? _______________________

____

____

____

What could be done now to improve the fate of this living thing?

____

____

Facts About an Extinct Species

Species: ____

Physical Description: ___________________________________

____

____

Habitat: ____

Food: ____

Enemies: ____

Draw a food chain that includes this species:

What occurred that resulted in this species becoming extinct?

____

____

____

____

What could be done now to improve the fate of this living thing?

____

____

Energy Cycles in Ecosystems and the Importance of Plants

Background Information for Teachers

There is a good reason why plants are called producers. Plants can make food for other organisms (consumers). They use inorganic (nonliving or abiotic) matter to do this – water and minerals. They need carbon dioxide (another abiotic factor). They not only make food but oxygen too, which is something else organisms need to live! It is estimated that plants produce almost 100 billion tonnes of oxygen per year.

Plants cannot do any of this without light energy from the Sun, or an artificial source as in a greenhouse, with a special electric grow-bulb.

Light energy is trapped by *chlorophyll*, which is found in the leaves or other green parts of the plants. (The cactus has no leaves – only spines – so photosynthesis takes place in the main body of the plant.) It is the leaf that is the "power producer" of a green plant.

When the chlorophyll molecules absorb energy from the Sun, it is converted to more usable *chemical energy*. This is a complicated process. Carbon dioxide and water from the cell and its surroundings are changed into *carbohydrates* (mainly *glucose*) and *oxygen*. Oxygen could be called a "waste product" in this case.

Plants can use glucose energy immediately, but it is usually changed and moved to other parts of the plant for storage. This storage can take three forms.

(1) sugar (sucrose): stored in some plants such as sugar beets and sugar cane
(2) cellulose: makes up the walls of plant cells. It is found in some algae and fungi
(3) starch: stored in leaves and stems. Starch, as a stored energy, can be changed back to glucose

Plants provide us with many nutrients other than sugar, fibre, and starch. They can change glucose into fat, protein (peanuts, soybeans), or combine glucose with other materials to form vitamins (vitamin C). Vitamins help plants grow and repair themselves in the same way vitamins do in consumers (e.g., humans).

The minerals that plants get from the soil can often be found in other parts of the plant as well. This is where consumers get the important minerals they need to be healthy.

Glucose is dissolved in water to be carried to all parts of the plant. In trees, this mixture is called *sap*.

Sap is stored as a starch in trunks and roots of trees during the winter; if it stayed in leaves it would be lost when the leaves drop in autumn. In spring, heat (light) energy turns the starch back into sugar, which begins flowing to all parts of the tree again. Buds open and leaves unfurl. In some species, such as the sugar maple (*Acer saccharun*), the sap is "tapped" by humans and made into maple sugar and syrup.

Cellular Respiration: Both plants and animals need oxygen to release energy from their food. The energy is released by a chemical change called *cellular respiration*. This name is used because the process takes place only inside living cells. Cellular respiration requires glucose and oxygen. It produces carbon dioxide, water, and energy that cells use.

Photosynthesis and respiration are complementary processes. This eternal cycle is a key feature of ecosystems.

Carbon Dioxide-Oxygen Cycle: carbon from carbon dioxide is built up into complex organic compounds in plants during photosynthesis.

▶

8

These are broken down in 2 ways:

(1) back to carbon dioxide in cellular respiration

(2) back to carbon dioxide in the decomposing process carried out by bacteria and fungi after the plant dies. Composting is an example.

When consumers eat plants and other animals, carbon is broken down into carbon dioxide (and other nutrients in other cycles like the nitrogen cycle) by the same two processes, cellular respiration and decay.

Materials

- chart paper
- markers
- overhead projector
- overhead pens
- diagram titled, "Photosynthesis" (included. Make an overhead copy, as well as a copy for each student.) (1.8.1)
- diagram titled, "Cellular Respiration" (included. Make an overhead copy, as well as a copy for each student.) (1.8.2)
- a few potted houseplants
- black construction paper
- tape
- limewater (a saturated solution of calcium hydroxide can be obtained from scientific supply companies, but try your local high school science department first. You do not need much.)
- large plastic bags (fairly thick and rigid)
- plastic straw
- small funnel that will fit into one end of straw
- diagram titled, "The Carbon Dioxide-Oxygen Cycle" (included. Make an overhead copy of this sheet, as well as a copy for each student.) (1.8.3)

Activity: Part One

Write the term *Producers* on chart paper. Call attention to one of the plants in the classroom. Ask:

- Why are plants called *producers*? (Stress that plants are able to *produce* their own food.

Now record the term *Photosynthesis*. Explain to students that this is the process that green plants use to make food. The plants are producers. Ask:

- What words or parts of words do you see in *photosynthesis*?
- Can you infer what it might mean given what you know about these other words? "Photo" refers to light; "synthesis" refers to making something.

Display the overhead diagram "Photosynthesis" (1.8.1). Have students examine the diagram and read the descriptive definition. Lead students through the process of photosynthesis in more detail, using the Background Information for Teachers. Clarify their understanding of this process through guided questions. Ask:

- What role does the Sun play in photosynthesis? (light energy)
- Where is the Sun's energy trapped? (in chlorophyll found in green parts of plants)
- What happens when the chlorophyll absorbs this energy? (it is converted to glucose/sugar and oxygen)
- What happens to the glucose energy? (some of the energy is used immediately, some is used for plant growth, and some is stored)

Now display the overhead diagram "Cellular Respiration" (1.8.2). Discuss the diagram and the definition provided. Add detail, using the Background Information for Teachers.

Lead a discussion to compare/contrast photosynthesis and cellular respiration. Ask:

- How are these two processes the same?
- How are they different?
- How do the two processes work together in a cycle?

Activity: Part Two

Extend students' understanding of photosynthesis and cellular respiration by doing the following investigations on light and the role of chlorophyll on the production of carbon dioxide at night (using houseplants):

1. What happens when a leaf is blocked from sunlight?
   - Tape a few small pieces of black construction paper to leaves on one plant.
   - Have the students predict what will happen.
   - Wait 4 to7 days. Remove the paper. Observe.

Students will notice that leaves will have become much paler. Ask:

- Why do you think this happened? (Infer that photosynthesis is not taking place because the chlorophyll needs sunlight to do this.)

2. What happens when plants "sleep"
   - Place a plastic bag (a thick bag is best, not the produce bags from a grocery store) over another houseplant. Tape the edge of the bag to the sides of the pot.
   - Leave the plant in a completely dark place overnight.
   - Have students predict what will be observed the next day.
   - The next day, remove the plastic bag from the plant. Observe and discuss.

Students will notice that there is evidence of condensation. Ask:

- What else might be in the bag?

Remove the bag as quickly and as carefully as possible. Seal the bag immediately. Insert one end of the straw into a small opening in the bag and one end of the funnel into the straw. Carefully add limewater through a funnel and straw. Observe. Ask:

- What happens to the limewater? (It turns milky or cloudy.)

Explain to the students that limewater is used in laboratory tests to detect the presence of carbon dioxide gas. If it turns cloudy, the gas is present. Ask:

- How does this investigation help us understand cellular respiration?

Remind students that animals also go through the process of cellular respiration, taking in food, oxygen, and water. This makes energy and releases carbon dioxide and water. Ask:

- What do you think might happen if I exhale into the jar of limewater?

Once students share their ideas, test their predictions. The cloudy liquid will indicate the presence of carbon dioxide in your exhaled breath.

Activity: Part Three

Extend students' understanding of energy cycles by introducing the carbon dioxide/oxygen cycle, which makes further connections between photosynthesis and cellular respiration. Display the overhead titled, "The Carbon Dioxide – Oxygen Cycle" (1.8.3). Conduct a think-pair-share activity. First, have students individually examine the diagram and reflect on what the diagram represents. Then, divide the class into pairs of students and have students share their

ideas with their partners. Have students share their thoughts as a class. Discuss the carbon cycle and its relationship to photosynthesis and cellular respiration.

Finally, have students complete Activity Sheet A and B (1.8.4 and 1.8.5) to show their understanding of the cycle processes of photosynthesis and cellular respiration.

Note: Students should continue to complete three-point-approach charts for all new vocabulary.

Activity Sheet A

Directions to students:

Complete the compare/contrast frame for the processes of photosynthesis and cellular respiration.

Activity Sheet B

Directions to students:

Use the information from your compare/contrast frame to complete the Venn diagram.

Extensions

- Give each student a leaf from a plant or tree. Have the students tear the leaf in two parts. Using a hand lens, they should be able to see the waxy layer on the underside of the leaf. This is the *cuticle*. It is waterproof but transparent. Ask:

  - What might the function of the cuticle be? (Keeps in moisture but lets in sunlight). Separate a piece of the cuticle, and put it on a slide. Examine this under a microscope. Students should be able to see the "mouths" (stomata) through which the plants "breathe." Just as we breathe out water vapour and gases, so do they.

- To reinforce the process of photosynthesis, present students with an analogy of a plant being like a food processing plant. Use the extension diagram "A Green Plant: Nature's Food Factory" (1.8.5) as a springboard for discussion.

Photosynthesis

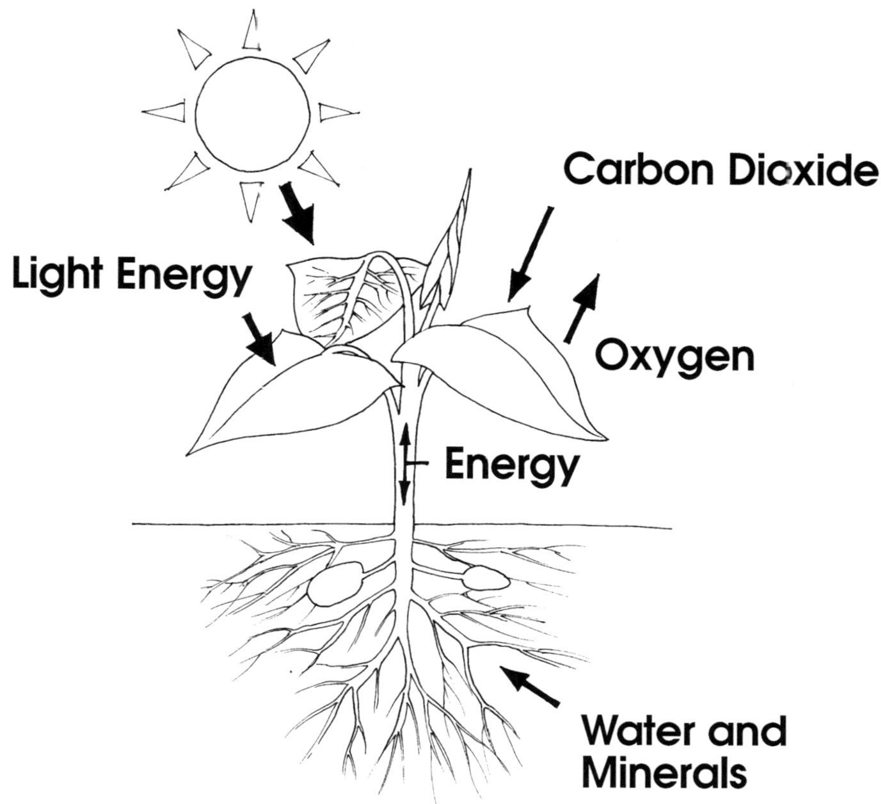

Green plants use energy from the Sun, water, nutrients from the soil, carbon dioxide from the air, and chlorophyll (the green colouring matter in leaves) to produce food that is made of sugars and starches. The food then circulates throughout the plant in the form of sap. Some of the food is used immediately by the plant for energy. Some is sent off to the roots for storage, and some is used to make more of the plant through growth. This food manufacturing process is called photosynthesis – *photo* means "light" and "synthesis" means *putting together*.

---

light energy + carbon dioxide + water and minerals

(with the help of chlorophyll)

make

sugar + oxygen

Cellular Respiration

In animals, cellular respiration is ongoing.

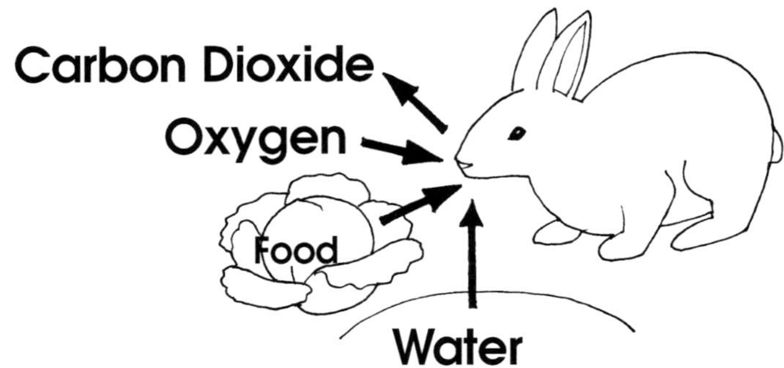

In plants, cellular respiration occurs at night when there is no light energy and photosynthesis cannot take place. Plants then release carbon dioxide.

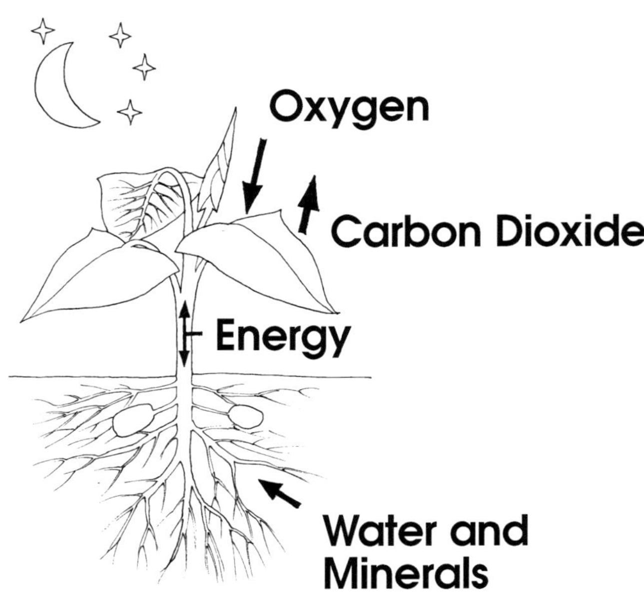

Both plants and animals need oxygen to release energy from their food. The energy is released by a chemical change called *cellular respiration*. This name is used because the process takes place only inside living cells. Cellular respiration requires glucose and oxygen. It produces carbon dioxide, water, and energy that cells use.

> **sugar + oxygen**
>
> **make**
>
> **energy + carbon dioxide + water and minerals**

Carbon Dioxide - Oxygen Cycle

Living things release larger carbon-containing molecules into the environment through their body's waste, and through decomposition after death.

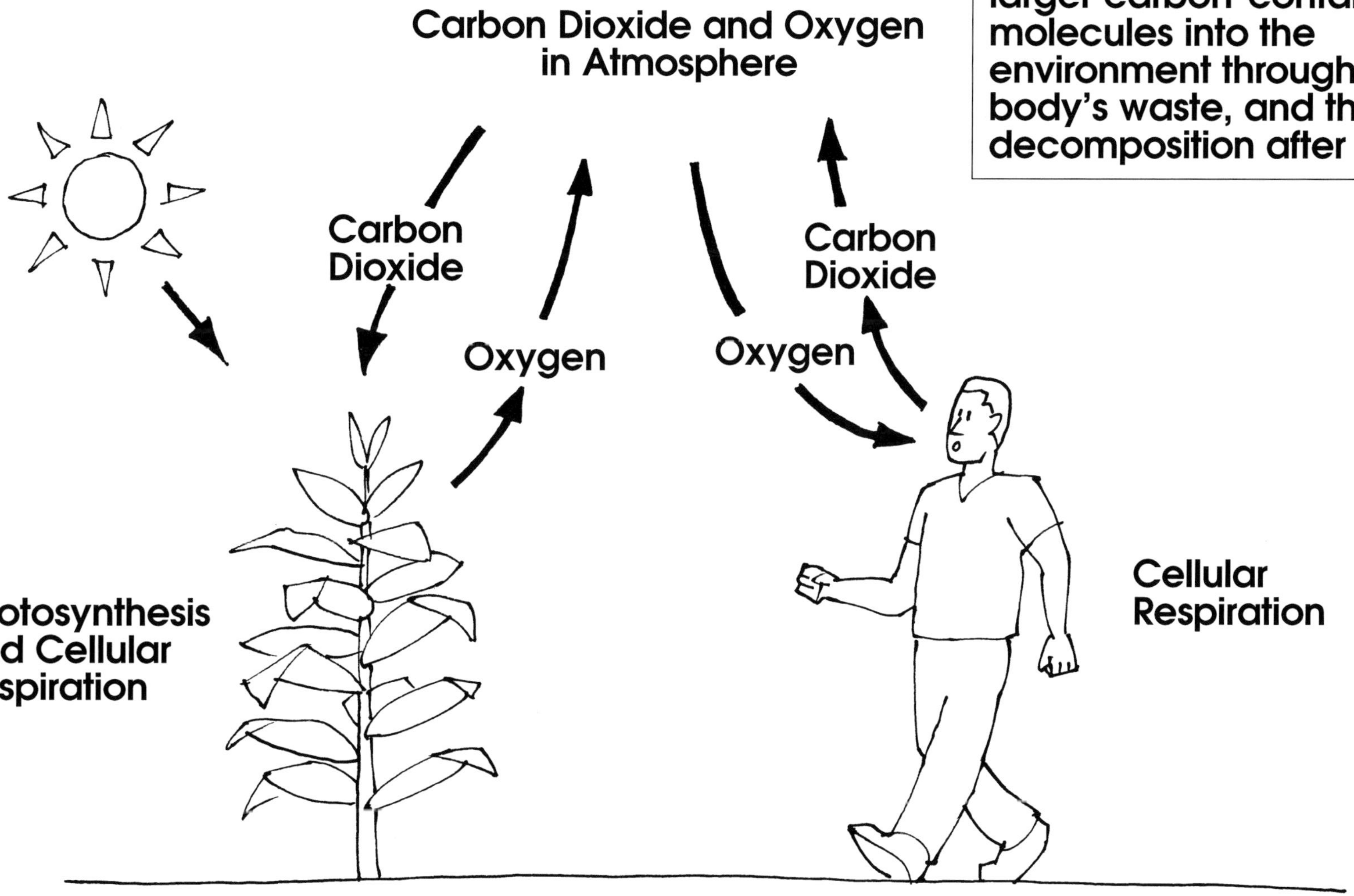

Date: ___________________   Name: ___________________________

Compare/Contrast Frame

COMPARE

How are photosynthesis and cellular respiration alike?

CONTRAST

How are photosynthesis and cellular respiration different?

Write a statement to compare and contrast the two processes.

Venn Diagram

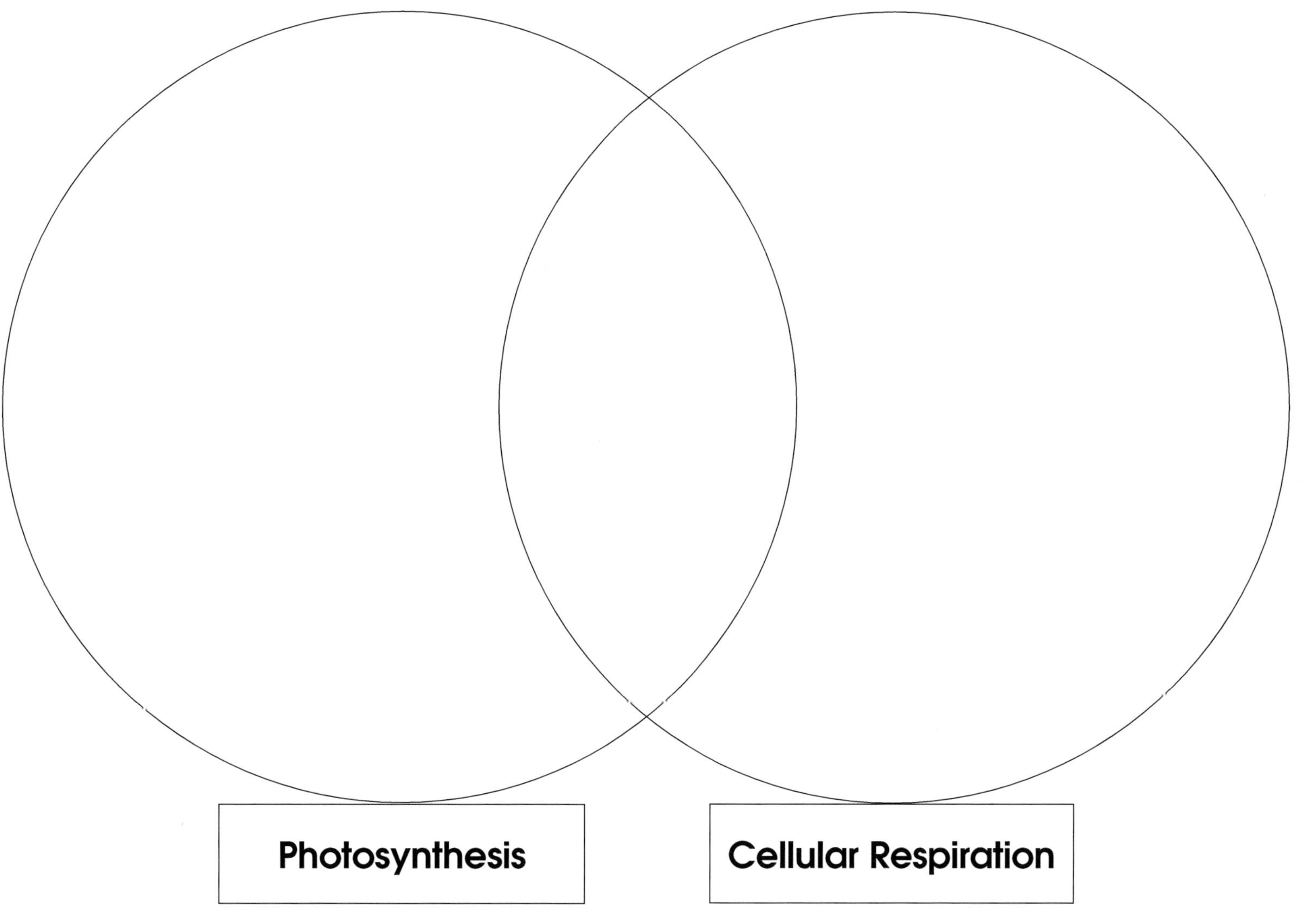

A Green Plant: Nature's Food Factory

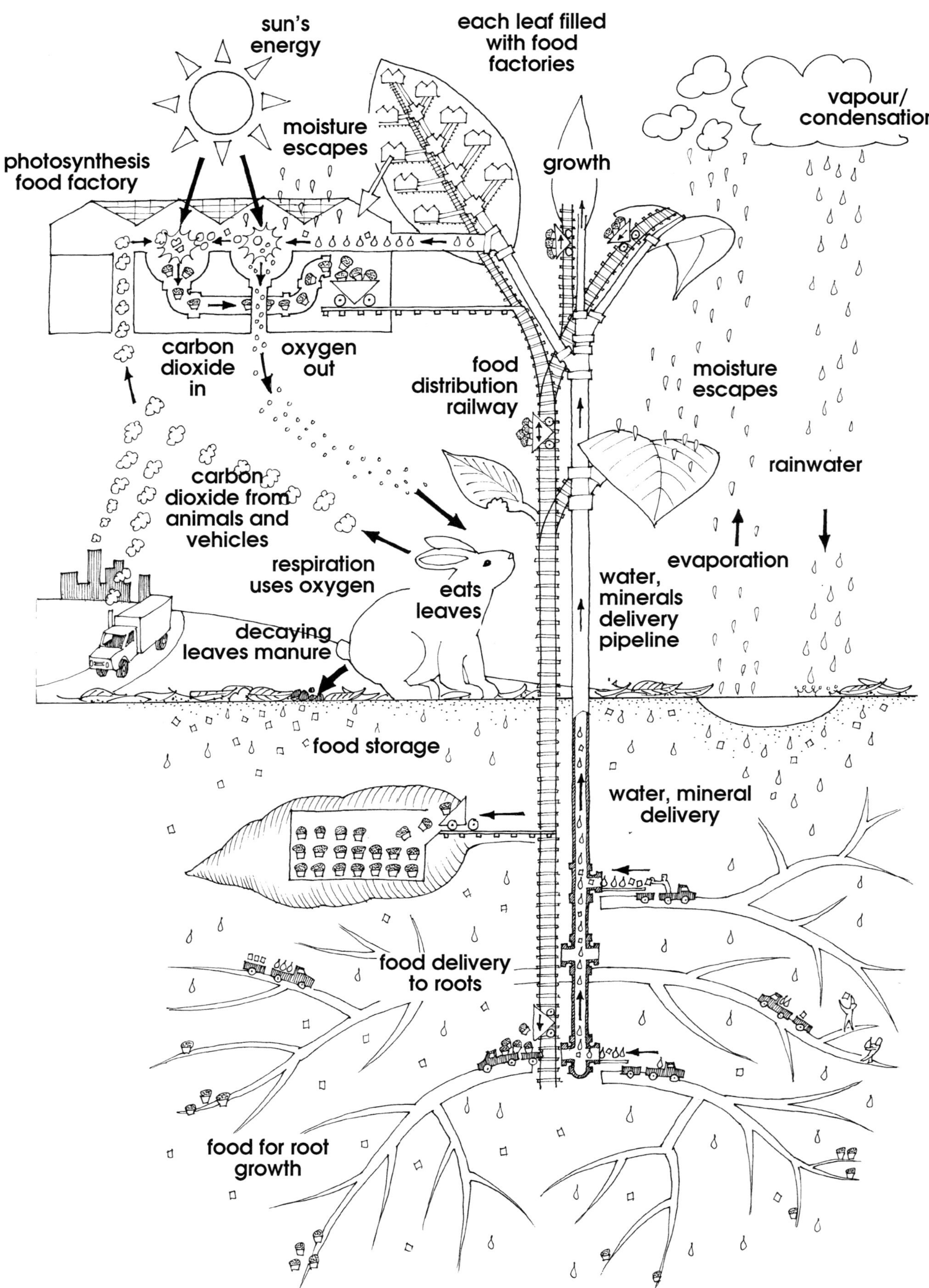

9 | Examining Organisms in Soil

Background Information for Teachers

This lesson begins with a study of a soil ecosystem and the importance of decomposers. The soil ecosystem can include organisms from every classification (except fish), as well as plant root systems. (You may wish to review the animal kingdom focused upon in the Grade 6 science program.) Invertebrates are especially abundant in soil ecosystems. The most common are:

Nematodes: thread-like animals such as roundworms, pinworms, and threadworms. These are not really worms. They are found in soil and as parasites in other animals.

Annelids: segmented worms, such as earthworms and leeches

Arthropods: animals with jointed legs and segmented bodies, such as centipedes (2 legs per body section), spiders (8 legs and 2 body parts), insects (6 legs and 3 body parts), and crustacean such as crabs and p tt bugs

Among the soil organisms are bi lions of microscopic organisms – bacteria, algae, and fungi. These decomposers play a crucial role in the decomposition of organic material. They return nutrients to the soil where they become available again to the foundation of any ecological food pyramid, the plants.

Materials

- diagram titled, "A Soil Ecosystem" (included. Make an overhead copy of th s sheet. You may also wish to colour the diagram to make objects more visible.) (1.9.1)
- chart paper
- markers

- soil samples (from the edge of a compost heap or from some other location where there is an abundance of decaying plant material. This is essertial in order to see a variety of organisms.)
- small clear plastic cortainers with lids, such as those used for food storage
- magnifiers
- tweezers
- small strainers
- plastic spoons
- wax paper

Activity: Part One

Use the overhead titled, "A Soil Ecosystem" (1.9.1) to focus a whole-class discussion. Ask:

- What evidence of plant life can you see? (dandelion, grass, leaves, acorn, algae)
- What animals live here?
- What is a *decomposer*?

Review that a decompose is an organism that breaks down plant parts, returning nutrients to the soil. Ask:

- Which organisms in this soil ecosystem might be decomposers?
- What might be a possible food chain within this ecosystem?

As students share their ideas, sketch a food chain on chart paper. Ask:

- How do the plants use soil?
- How do the animals use soil?
- What is the importance of a soil ecosystem to all other ecosystems? (Think back to photosynthesis.)

Focus students' attention cn the magnified section of the soil ecosystem. Ask:

- What do you think these are?
- What is a *microorganism*?
- What kinds of microorganisms do you know about?

▶

Explain that there are billions of microscopic organisms, such as bacteria, algae, and fungi, that are part of a soil ecosystem. These microorganisms decompose organic material such as plants, and return nutrients.

Divide the class into working groups, and provide the groups with chart paper and markers. Have them construct a concept web describing the soil ecosystem:

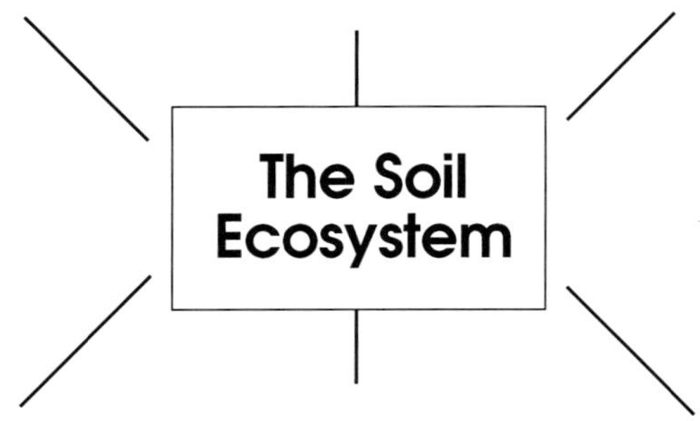

Encourage students to describe soil organisms and abiotic components of the ecosystem, and to outline the importance of soil (e.g., nourish plants/crops, provide habitats, and so on).

Have students share their webs by doing an informal "Gallery Walk" (students display their work for others to view, discuss, and learn from, just like in an art gallery).

Activity: Part Two

Explain to the students that they are now going to have an opportunity to examine a soil ecosystem firsthand. Provide each student with a copy of the activity sheet (1.9.2). Discuss the organisms and information presented, and challenge the students to look for these organisms in their soil samples.

Divide the class into working groups. Provide each group with a soil sample in a clear plastic container, tweezers, plastic spoons, strainers, and magnifiers. Have the students cover their workspace with wax paper. This allows for better visibility of small creatures. Challenge the students to be soil ecologists: their task is to examine the soil sample for living organisms. Encourage the students to examine closely, and treat all organisms with respect (keep them alive!)

Provide plenty of time for the groups to examine samples, locate organisms, identify these using the classification key, and tally those found. Following this hands-on investigation, discuss students' observations. Ask:

- Which was the most common organism you found?
- Why do you think there was an abundance of this organism?

Encourage students to infer about the easiest organism to spot, ideal living conditions, population explosion, and so on. Ask:

- Do you think your sample is an example of a healthy or rich soil ecosystem? Why? Why not?
- Is there an abundance of living organisms in the soil?
- Why are organisms important for healthy, or rich, soil?
- How can we ensure that gardens and fields have healthy soil?

Discuss environmentally sound actions such as leaving plant material to decay naturally, avoid the use of herbicide that may kill decomposers, establishing composting piles, fallowing fields, and so on.

Activity Sheet

Note: This is a three-page activity sheet.

Directions to students:

Use the classification key to keep a tally of the soil organisms you observe. (1.9.2)

9

Extensions

- Debate: Adding ferilizer to soil is a beneficial (harmful) practice. Have students research, take a stand on the issue, and debate with classmates.

- Conduct a long-term vermicomposting project in the classroom. Earthworms are easy to see, easy to maintain on vegetable matter, odourless, and vital contributors to a soil's health. Commercial vermicomposters are readily available from several retail sources.

A Soil Ecosystem

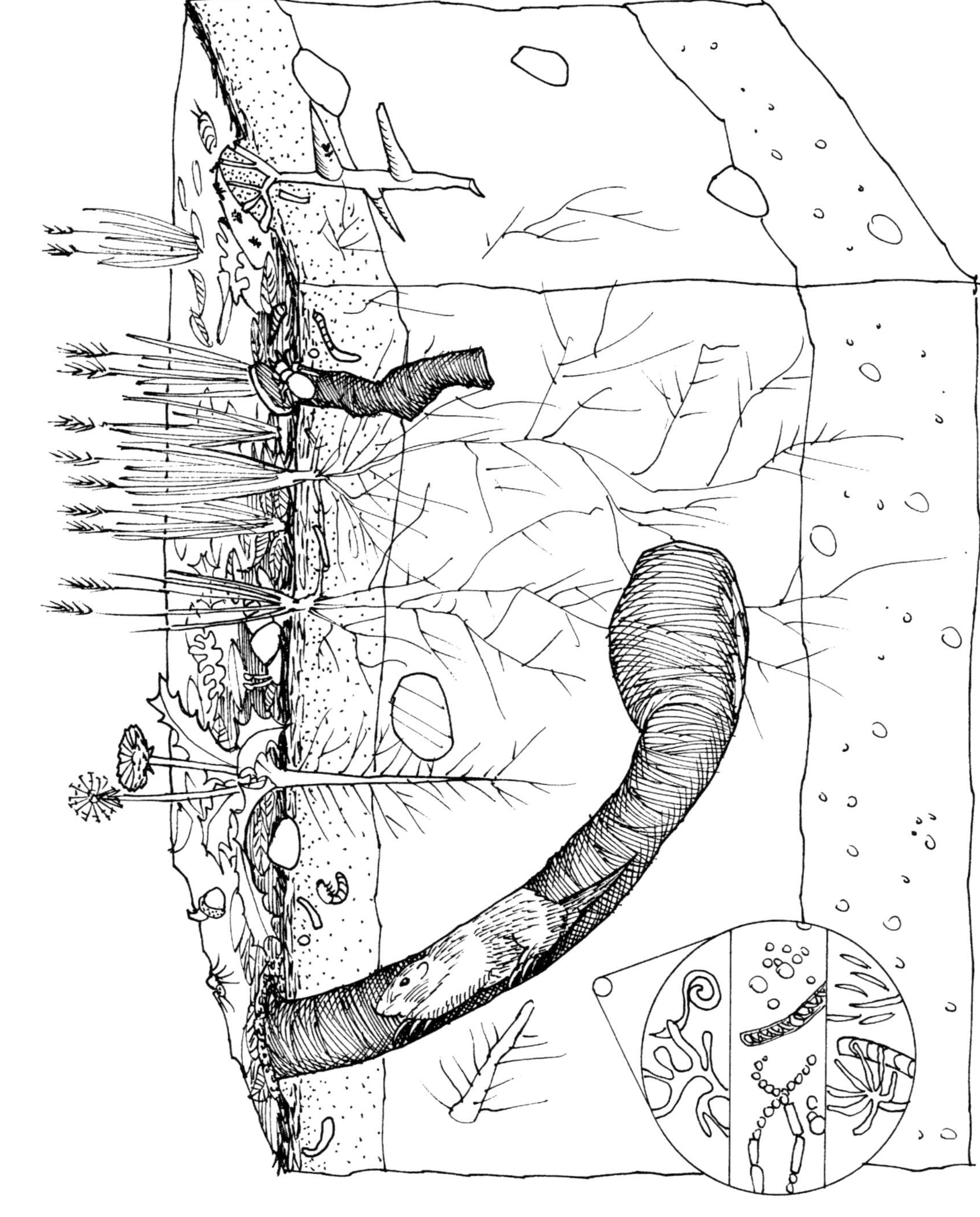

Classification Key: Soil Organisms

Earthworm

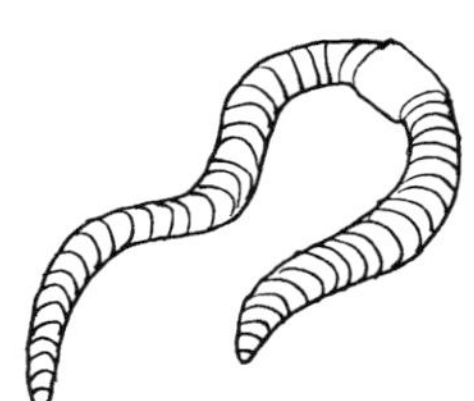

Food: decaying plants

tally:

Pit Bug

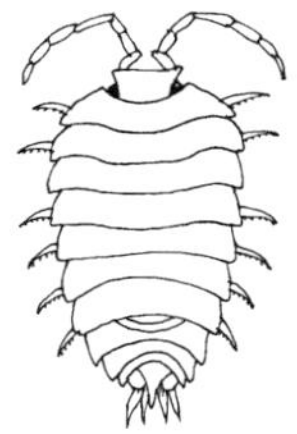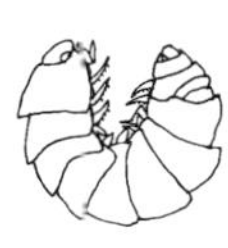

Food: decaying plants

tally:

Centipede

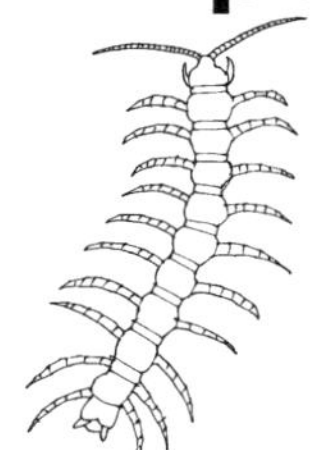

Food: small animals in the soil

tally:

Millipede

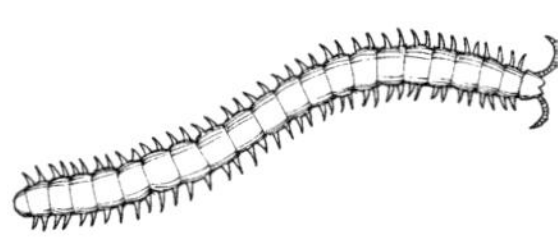

Food: plant material

tally:

Roundworm

Food: bacteria, fungi, decaying plants, roots of plants, and other small animals

tally:

Snail

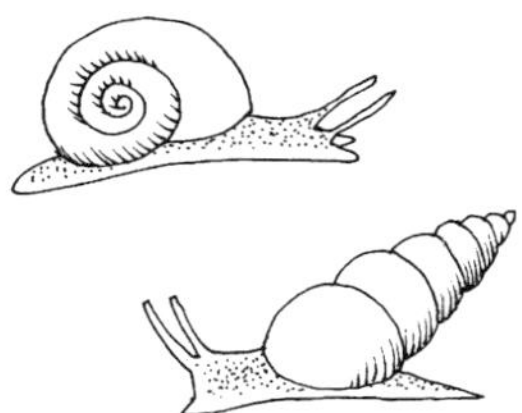

Food: leaf litter, plants

tally:

Slug

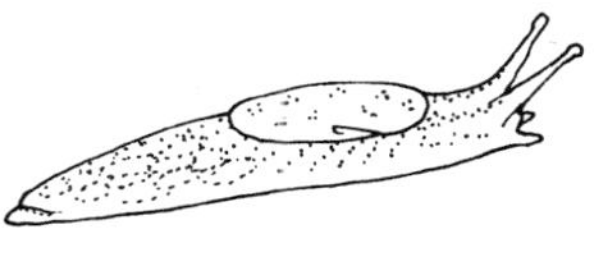

Food: leaf litter, plants

tally:

Spidermite

Food: roundworm, annelid worms, other mites

tally:

Oribateid Mite

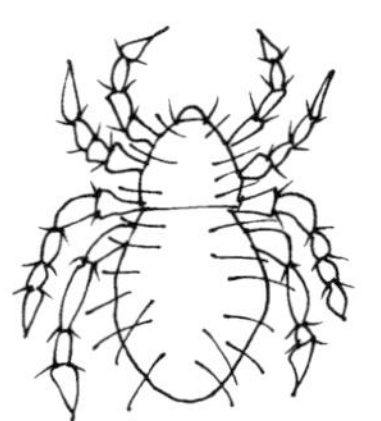

Food: plant material, fungi, collembola

tally:

Mesostigmatid Mite

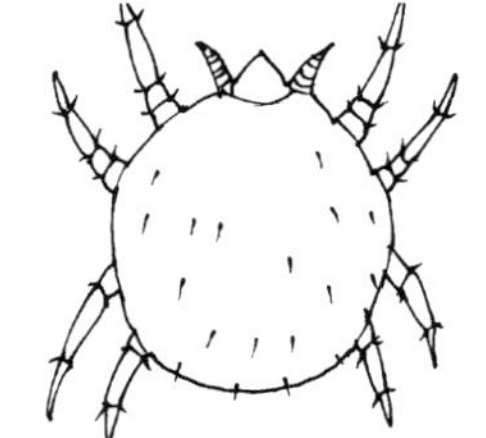

Food: roundworm, annelid worms, other mites

tally:

Wolf Spider

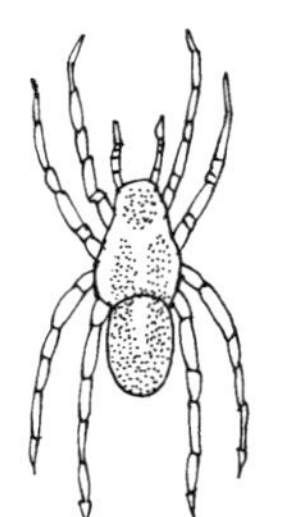

Food: insects and other small animals

tally:

Crab Spider

Food: insects and other small animals

tally:

Beetle

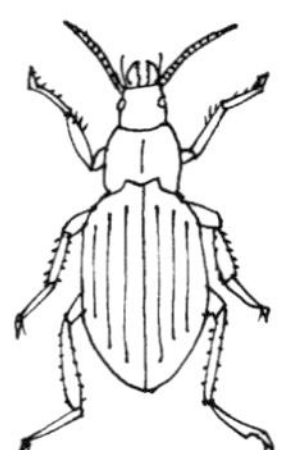

Food: plant material or soil animals

tally:

Earwig

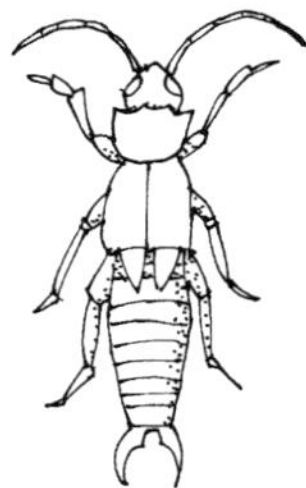

Food: plant material

tally:

Springtails

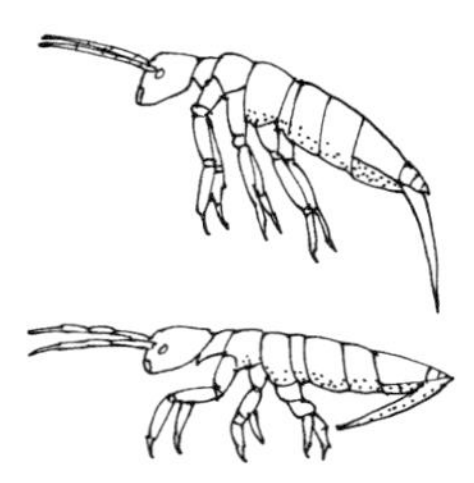

Food: plant material, fungi

tally:

Beetle larva

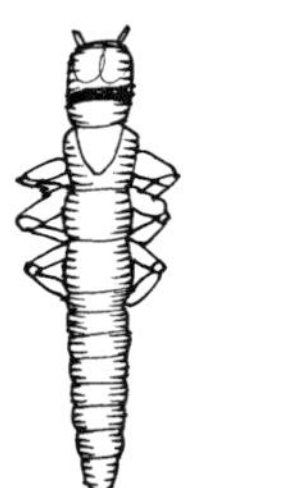

Food: plant material or soil animals

tally:

Fly larva

Food: decaying plants

tally:

Lacewing larva

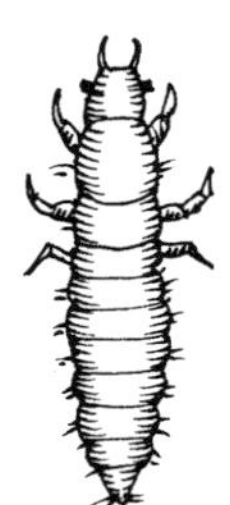

Food: decaying plants

tally:

Moth larva

Food: plant material

tally:

Moth pupa

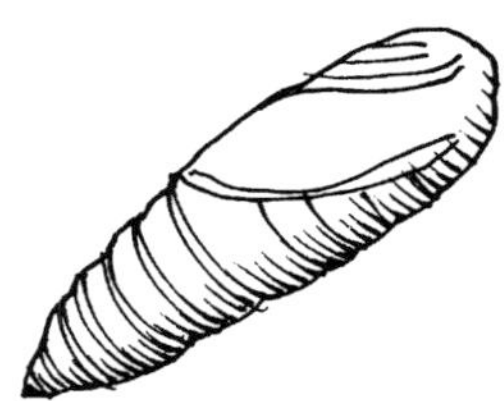

Do not feed

tally:

10 | Bacteria

Background Information for Teachers

In this lesson, emphasis in placed on the Monera kingdom, as students research bacteria. The Monera kingdom is made up of single-celled microorganisms, mainly bacteria. Blue-green algae are also in the Monera kingdom. The algae are similar to bacteria in their structure and behaviours: both, for example, are killed by drugs such as antibiotics.

Bacteria have both a negative and positive impact on other living things. Some are parasites that live in the bodies of other organisms, and cause diseases. In humans, food poisoning and diseases such as strep throat, tonsillitis, and tuberculosis are caused by bacteria. However, bacteria also help the cycle of life by decomposing material and returning it to the soil. Bacteria are also used in treating sewage. Other forms of bacteria are used in making dairy products such as cheese, yogurt, and sour cream.

Materials

- diagram titled, "Monera Kingdom" (used in lesson 5. Make an overhead copy of this sheet.) (1.10.1)
- reference material on bacteria (books, magazines, web sites, and so on)
- poster board
- chart paper
- markers

Activity

Begin this lesson by reviewing students' knowledge of microorganisms. Remind them of their investigation of microorganisms in the hay infusion and the soil ecosystem. In pairs, have students share what they remember about microorganisms, then discuss the microorganisms observed in these ecosystems. Ask:

- What is a microorganism?
- Which microorganisms have you learned about?

List students' descriptions and examples on chart paper. Focus now on the Monera kingdom (1.10.1). Display the overhead and have students examine the diagram. Ask:

- Which microorganisms belong to the Monera kingdom?
- What do you know about bacteria?
- Are these organisms beneficial or harmful?

Record students' ideas on chart paper. Explain that, in partners, students are going to conduct research on bacteria to find out more about these microorganisms. Explain that research projects are to include:

- a written report
- a descriptive and illustrated poster
- an oral presentation

Divide the class into pairs of students and provide each pair with reference material and Activity Sheets A (1.10.2), B (1.10.3), and C (1.10.4). Review the activity sheets, and clarify any questions that students may have about the assignment. Allow plenty of time for students to work on their projects, prepare their final report, design the poster, and practice their oral presentation.

10

Activity Sheet A

Directions to students:

Review the expectations for this research assignment. Check off each item as you accomplish the task on the activity sheet (1.10.2).

Activity Sheet B

Directions to students:

Keep track of your progress on the project by completing the chart each time you work on the research (1.10.3).

Activity Sheet C

Note: Make several copies of this sheet for students to use with each resource from which they obtain information.

Directions to students:

Use this sheet to record information (1.10.4). Use one sheet for each resource (book, web site, encyclopedia, magazine, and so on).

Assessment Suggestion

During oral presentations, have students provide peer feedback using the sheet titled, "Research Presentation: Peer Feedback" (1.10.5), included with this lesson. As a class, identify criteria that students might consider when providing feedback. For example:

- What I learned: (Record brief notes on new ideas)
- What I liked:
    - clear voice
    - eye contact
    - neat, descriptive poster
    - accurate information
    - answered questions
    - both students shared in the presentation

Monera Kingdom

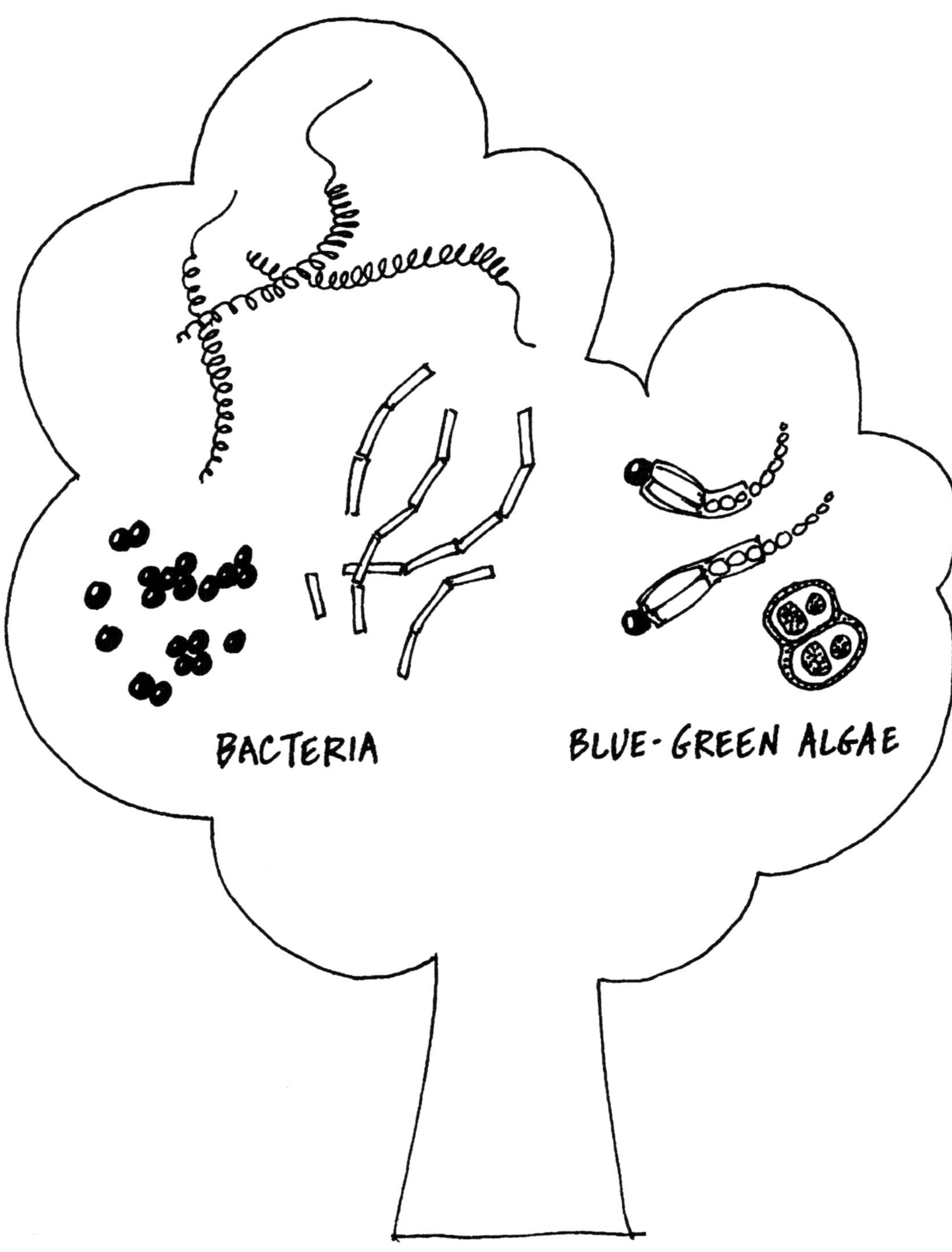

Research Checklist

Date: _____________________ **Names:** _____________________

____

Our research includes:

1. A written report, including:

   - a definition of bacteria ☐

   - examples ☐

   - harmful roles played by bacteria ☐

   - beneficial roles played by bacteria ☐

   - bibliography of references used ☐

2. A poster including:

   - visuals (e.g., illustrations, charts, graphs, photos) ☐

3. An oral report:

   - presented by both partners ☐

4. Time Management Record ☐

5. Information Gathering sheets ☐

Date: _______________________   Names: _________________________________

____

Keeping Our Research On Track

Research Topic: ____

Time-Management Record

Date	Length Of Time	What We Accomplished

Date: ___________________   **Names:** _______________________

____

Information Gathering

Research Topic: ____

Resources Used:

Research Presentation:
Peer Feedback

Presenters: ____

What I Learned	What I Liked

Presenters: ____

What I Learned	What I Liked

Presenters: ____

What I Learned	What I Liked

11 | Microorganisms and Food

Background Information for Teachers

This lesson will extend students' understanding of the role of microorganisms in human food production and preservation techniques. For example, *yeast* – a single celled fungi – is used as a leavening agent to make bread rise. *Bacteria* is used in the production of dairy products such as cheese, yogurt, and sour cream.

Food preservation techniques focus on limiting the growth of bacteria. Such techniques include refrigeration, freezing, drying, dehydrating, canning, salting, smoking, pickling, and pasteurizing.

Biotechnology involves the use of living things, such as microorganisms, in the manufacturing of products. This is an ever-expanding field of science.

Materials

- chart paper
- markers
- information sheet titled, "Microorganisms and Food Preservation" (included. Make copies for each student.) (1.11.2)
- reference material on microorganisms, foods production, and biotechnology

Activity: Part One

Begin with a class brainstorming activity on "food." Ask students to contribute as many ideas as they can about food. Encourage thoughtful responses through some questioning. Ask:

- Where does our food come from?
- How is food made?

When a sufficient list has been generated, ask students:

- Which food words are related to animals? (underline)
- Which food words are related to plants? (circle)

Distribute copies of Activity Sheet A (1.11.1). Have students complete the task at home and return the completed sheet the next day.

Activity Sheet A

Directions to students:

Use the chart to record information about food items in your home. (1.11.1)

Activity: Part Two

Once students have returned Activity Sheet A (1.11.1), discuss their results. In working groups, have students examine and organize their data as a compare/contrast classification tree. Have them record the following tree diagram onto chart paper:

FOOD

Refrigerator　　　Cupboard

Plants	Others		Plants	Others

- The groups now use the tree diagram to classify each food item on their sheets. Display the completed charts and discuss the results.

11

Activity: Part Three

As a class, use the classification tree diagrams to conduct a discussion about why certain foods are refrigerated. Ask:

- Which items require refrigeration?
- Which do not?
- Why do you think some items need to be refrigerated, and other items do not?
- What would happen if a food item, such as milk, was not refrigerated?
- What causes the milk to go sour?
- What other methods do humans use to preserve their food? (freezing, drying, pasteurizing, canning)
- How are microorganisms used in the production of food?

Distribute copies of the information sheet titled, "Microorganisms and Food Preservation" (1.11.2). Read and discuss the information presented.

Activity: Part Four

Discuss as a class how, in food preservation, microorganisms play a negative role and cause food spoilage. Ask:

- Do you know of any positive uses of microorganisms?
- Can you identify examples of microorganisms used in food production?

Explain to the class that biotechnology is a field of science that involves the use of living things, such as microorganisms, in the manufacturing food products.

Distribute copies of Activity Sheet B (1.11.3), and provide students with reference material on food production, microorganisms, and biotechnology. Have the students conduct research to complete the activity sheet and share results as a class.

Activity Sheet B

Directions to students:

Research and record facts on how microorganisms are used in food production.

Extensions

- Plan a field trip to a local food processing plant (bakery, cannery, wild rice cooperative).
- Invite speakers, such as Aboriginal community elders or hunters, to share their knowledge of and experiences with traditional Aboriginal food gathering and processing.
- Have students make bread or yogurt in the classroom. The yeast can be examined under the microscope.

End-Of-Unit Assessment

Reflect on the tasks undertaken by each student throughout the unit to complete the End-Of-Unit Assessment chart on page 26. Consider all assessment tools, investigations, and activities when identifying and commenting on individual student achievement.

Looking at Foods

1. Examine foods found in your home.

2. Identify ten food items in the refrigerator.

3. Indicate whether they are plant or animal products.

4. Identify ten foods found in the cupboard.

5. Indicate whether they are plant or animal products.

6. Note where each food item is manufactured (geographic location).

7. Design a chart for this information

Microorganisms and Food Preservation

Microorganisms are present in all foods. If microorganisms, are allowed to grow uncontrolled, food will spoil. Microorganisms thrive in warm, moist habitats, where there is ample food, and space to multiply. Many methods are used to preserve food by controlling the growth of microorganisms. These include:

Refrigerating and freezing foods, such as meat, limit the growth of bacteria by keeping meat cool, and inhospitable to bacterial growth. Microorganisms need warmth to thrive.

Drying foods, such as fruit, removes the water that bacteria needs to grow.

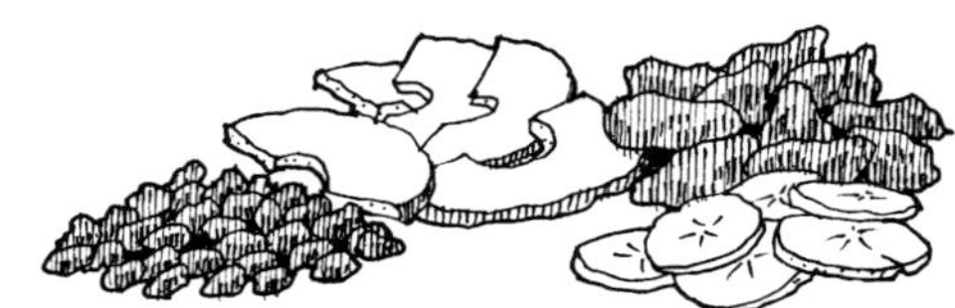

Pasteurizing is often used to help preserve dairy foods, such as milk. In this process the milk is heated very quickly and then cooled. The process kills bacteria that is present in the food.

Canning is often used to preserve fruits and vegetables. The food is heated under sterile conditions to kill the bacteria. The food is then sealed in an airtight container, which limits outside sources of bacteria from contaminating it.

Microorganisms and Food Production

Microorganisms are sometimes used to produce certain foods. Find out how microorganisms are used in the production of these foods. Use sentences and labelled diagrams to describe these methods of food production.

1. Bread (using yeast):

2. Dairy products such as sour cream, yogurt, and cheese (using bacteria):

References for Teachers

Books

Abercrombie, M., C. J. Hickman, and M. J. Johnson. *The Penguin Dictionary of Biology*. New York: Viking Press, 1977.

Bosack, Susan. *Science Is*. Richmond Hill, ON: Scholastic Canada, 1991.

Brennan, Richard P. *Dictionary of Scientific Literacy*. New York: John Wiley & Sons, 1992.

Cadieux, Charles L. *Wildlife Extinction*. Washington, DC: Stone Wall Press, 1991. **Note:** The appendix in Cadieux's book has a list of endangered species.

Glass, Don (Ed.) *How Can You Tell If a Spider Is Dead? And More Moments of Science*. Bloomington: Indian University Press, 1996.

Hazen, Robert M., and James Trefil. *Science Matters: Achieving Scientific Literacy*. New York: Doubleday, 1991.

Hoyt, Enrich. *The Whales of Canada: An Equinox Wildlife Book*. Camden, ON: Camden House, 1984.

Karstad, Aleta. *Canadian Nature Notebook*. Toronto: McGraw-Hill Ryerson, 1970.

Pendergrass, W. R., and R. H. Whether. *Care of Lower Invertebrates*. Burlington, NC: Caroline Biological Supply Company, 1997.

Pruitt, William O., Jr. *Wild Harmony – The Cycle of Life in the Northern Fores*t. Saskatoon, SK: Western Producer Prairie Books, 1983.

Shell, Barry. *Great Canadian Scientists*. Victoria, BC: Polestar Books, 1996.

Magazines

Canadian Geographic. (The Royal Canadian Geographic Society, 39 McArthur Ave. Ottawa, ON K1L 8L9)

Equinox – Canada's Magazine of Discovery. (Malcolm Publishing, 11450 Albert-Hudon Blvd. Montreal North, QC H1G 3J9)

Particle Theory of Matter

Books for Students

Ardley, Neil. *The Science Book of Energy*. New York: Dorling Kindersley, 1992.

Bell, J,L. *Soap Science: A Science Book Bubbling With 36 Experiments*. Reading, Mass: Addison-Wesley, 1993.

Bosak, Susan. *Science Is...* Richmond Hill, ON: Scholastic Canada, 1991.

Bridgman, Roger. *Technology.* Eyewitness Science Series. New York: Dorling Kindersley, 1995.

Challoner, Jack. *Energy.* Eyewitness Science Series. New York: Dorling Kindersley, 1993.

Fullick, Ann. *Chemicals in Action*. Des Plaines, IL: Heinemann Library, 2000.

Fullick, Ann. *Matter*. Des Plaines, IL: Heinemann Library, 2000.

Gardner, Robert. *Science Around the House*. New York: Julian Messner,1989.

Gardner, Robert. *Kitchen Chemistry*. Engelwood Cliffs, NJ: Silver Burdett, 1988.

Griffin, Margaret, and Griffin, R. *It's a Gas!*. Toronto: Kids Can Press,1993.

Macaulay, David. *The New Way Things Work*. Boston: Houghton Mifflin, 1998.

Martin, Theresa. *Flat Earth? Round Earth?* New York: Prometheus Books, 2002.

Mebane, Robert. *Plastics and Polymers*. New York: Twenty-First Century Books,1995.

Nowakowski, Sharon (ed) *How and Why Science at Home*. Chicago: World Book Encyclopedia, 1998.

Nowakowski, Sharon (ed.). *How and Why Science in the Air*. Chicago: World Book Encyclopedia,1998.

Nowakowski, Sharon (ed.). *How and Why Science in the Water*. Chicago: World Book Encyclopedia,1998.

Nye, Bill. *Bill Nye the Science Guy's Big Blast of Science*. Reading, MA: Addison-Wesley Publishing, 1993.

Rising, Trudy. *Light Magic and Other Science Activities about Energy*. Toronto: Greey de Pencier Books, 1994.

Rogers, Kirsteen. *The Useborne Internet-Linked Library Science Encyclopedia*. London: Useborne Publishing, 2001.

Smith, Alaistar (et. Al), *The Useborne Internet Linked Library of Science Mixtures and Compounds*. London: Useborne Publishing, 2001.

Verstraete, Larry. *Extreme Science: Science in the Danger Zone*. Richmond Hill, ON: Scholastic Canada, 2000.

Wyatt, Valerie. *The Science Book for Girls and Other Intelligent Beings*. Toronto: Kids Can Press, 1993.

Web Sites

- **www.chem4kids.com**

  Maintained by Andrew Rader Studios, this site contains information on a wide range of chemistry topics. The site is well organized and most text is at a reading level appropriate for grade 7 students.

- **http://lorien.ncl.ac.uk/ming/distil/distil0.htm**

  University of Newcastle-Upon-Tyme Chemical and Process Engineering Department. This distillation page is sponsored by R.C. Costello and Associates, Inc.

- **http://asloley.home.mindspring.com/dis00001.html**

  Andrew Soley's Distillation Page provides a good explanation of continuous and batch distillation.

- **www.epa.gov/globalwarming/kids/greenhouse.html**

  This EPA site includes information about global warming, greenhouse gases, weather systems, and so on. It also includes an excellent animation describing the effects of global warming on the water cycle.

- **www.discovery.panasonic.co.jp/en/library/lib09heat/**

  The Wonders of Heat: contains information about what heat is and how it affects us.

- **www.nrc.gov/reading-rm/basic-ref/students.html**

  U.S. Nuclear Regulatory Commission Kids Site: contains information about how nuclear power plants are used to create heat, which is converted into electricity.

- **www.brainpop.com/**

  The Science section of this web site contains dozens of animated movie clips. Two of the clips are "Heat" and "Temperature."

- **www.infoplease.com**

  Infoplease.com contains a wide variety of dictionary and encyclopaedia entries on a wide range of topics. For the purposes of this unit, try the search word "heat."

- **www.unidata.ucar.edu/staff/blynds/tmp.html**

  This site contains a description of what temperature is and a brief history of the development of thermometers and temperature scales.

- **www.fsis.usda.gov/oa/thermy/kitchen.htm**

  U.S. Food Safety and Inspection Service: contains descriptions of many types of kitchen thermometers (meat, candy, fridge, oven, and so on.).

- **http://inventors.about.com/gi/dynamic/offsite.htm?site=http://**

  About.com: this site contains information about several types of thermometers found around the home.

- **http://inventors.about.com/library/inventors/blthermometer.htm**

  Includes a brief history of the development of thermometers and temperature scales as well as links to other useful sites.

- **http://home.howstuffworks.com**

  Information on thermometers, thermostats, thermoses, refrigerators, heat pumps, and much more. Use the "search" tool to select a topic.

Introduction

Matter is anything that takes up space and has mass (weight). In this unit students will learn to recognize the differences in matter, and will come to understand how matter is used and how important it is in our daily life. Students will use the Particle Theory of Matter to explain and describe changes of state, differences between pure substances and mixtures, and the characteristics of solutions.

Students will also learn what heat is and what the difference is between heat and temperature. They will investigate how heat travels and how insulators and conductors affect the process of heat transfer.

The progression from understanding concrete observations and concepts (e.g., the temperature of boiling water), to abstract ones (e.g., chemical bonding or heat transfer by radiation), requires that students apply scientific theories to everyday situations. The activities presented in this unit provide opportunities for the application of concepts, and include a design challenge. As the unit progresses, students should be encouraged to link their understanding of the concepts to the Particle Theory of Matter. In this way, new understandings will fit into an existing framework.

Throughout this unit, there are many opportunities for hands-on activities as they are outlined in the lessons. Teachers can use several quick and easy demonstrations to help students understand key points. All the activities and demonstrations can be completed with easily obtained items found in households and classrooms.

Safety Note: It is important that students understand that they are not to taste any substance presented to them in the teaching of this unit, unless directed to do so by the instructor. Students should also exercise care in handling substances used in this unit. Hands should be washed thoroughly after each "hands-on" activity. Substances used in experiments should be viewed as potentially hazardous, and handled accordingly. When in doubt, err on the side of caution.

Appropriate care must be taken when dealing with hot substances. Take the time to familiarize students with safe procedures for heating and handling substances, and for operating equipment. It is also important to ensure that no mercury thermometers are used in classrooms.

The last lesson in this unit provides students with an opportunity to use what they have learned to deal with a 'real life' situation. They will be asked to apply what they now understand about solvents, solutions, mixtures, separation methods, water quality, and pollutants. They will be asked to develop a plan to minimize the environmental impact of different groups on the quality of a small lake. This activity should help the teacher to assess how well students are transferring their theoretical understanding of concepts, to real applications of those concepts.

Science and Technology Vocabulary

Throughout this unit, teachers should use, and encourage students to use, accurate scientific vocabulary including: *mixture, mechanical mixture, solution, solute, solvent, mass, concentration, dissolve, soluble, insoluble, saturated, unsaturated, supersaturated, dilute, heterogeneous, homogeneous, concentration, boiling and melting points, particle theory of matter, temperature, heat, conduction, convection, radiation, kinetic, heat transfer, molecule, energy,*

1 | Scientific Theories

Background Information for Teachers

Scientific theories are statements that explain observations. For example, most people would agree that a flat sheet of paper will fall more slowly than a similarly sized sheet of paper that has been crumpled into a ball. In the past, if enough people agreed on an observation and a corresponding statement of what was observed, then it was said to be a scientific theory. Centuries ago, this process led to the belief that Earth was flat. We now understand that this scientific theory is incorrect. It was based on faulty information, or incorrect interpretation of observable facts.

Humans believed the Flat Earth theory for hundreds of years. It was also commonly believed that Earth was the centre of the solar system. Aristotle believed that heavier objects fell faster than lighter objects. As we know now, these theories are not true. They have been disproved through experimentation and accurate observation. Scientific theories are accepted as true if they can be fairly tested by many different people in many different places and consistently result in the same outcome.

This initial lesson is designed to introduce students to the concept of scientific theories, and the Particle Theory of Matter. It is from understanding the principles of the Particle Theory of Matter that students can better understand the activities and results that they will obtain in the subsequent lessons in this unit.

The lesson begins with an introduction to scientific theories, as introduced through the book *Flat Earth? Round Earth?* by Theresa Martin. Next, students investigate the Theory of Gravity. This will lead them to understand the need to test theories through careful experimentation. Finally, students will be exposed to the Particle Theory of Matter. This activity includes several demonstrations that support the observations of the theory. Students will begin a learning log that they can use to record and classify their findings throughout this unit. As students come to understand the concepts in this unit, they will enter them into their learning log and make the connections between the particle Theory of Matter and their observations.

The Particle Theory of Matter states:

1. All matter is composed of very small particles called atoms and molecules that are too small to be seen.

2. All the particles of matter are in constant motion because they have energy. Particles in solids are held tightly in place, but do move. Particles in liquids move more freely, and particles in gasses move much more freely yet. In solids, liquids, and gases alike, the particles are held together by forces of attraction between the particles.

3. There are spaces between the particles. The size of the spaces varies with the type of matter, (e.g., solid, liquid, or gas).

4. The addition of heat energy causes particles to move faster, stretching their bonds.

Materials

- book titled, *Flat Earth? Round Earth?* by Theresa Martin
- chart paper
- small plastic pop bottles with lids
- water
- graph paper
- metre sticks
- safety goggles
- markers
- recycled notepaper (scrap paper of the same size/type)

- information sheet titled, "The Particle Theory of Matter" (included: make an overhead copy of this sheet.) (2.1.2)
- overhead projector

Activity: Part One

Begin this lesson by reading the book titled, *Flat Earth? Round Earth?*, by Theresa Martin. The book tells the story of a student trying to convince a friend that Earth is round. The story sets the stage for a discussion on scientific theories.

Note: You may wish to read the story to the class over a few days, or you might have access to multiple copies so each student can read the book independently.

Once the class has finished reading the book, discuss the events of the story, focussing on Nathan's investigations to prove Earth is round. Ask:

- In what ways did Nathan attempt to convince Stan that Earth is round?
- Did Nathan conduct tests?
- Did the results of his tests support his belief that Earth is round?

Now record the term "Scientific Theory" on chart paper, and have students share their understanding of this term. Record their ideas, definitions, and examples on the chart paper.

Following this brainstorming session, explain that a scientific theory is an agreed-upon explanation for an observed event. It is a hypothesis that has been tested, is supported by scientific fact, and continues to explain all new observations. Scientific theories come to be accepted slowly as a result of repeated instances where they explain observations.

Focus on the story *Flat Earth? Round Earth?* once again. Explain to the class that long ago, people believed that Earth was flat. Scientific theories have been used over the past centuries to prove that Earth is, in fact, round.

Explain to students that they will conduct an experiment that concerns gravity. Ask:

- What is gravity?
- What do you know about gravitational force?
- Do you know any scientific theories related to gravity?

Introduce students to Aristotle's theory that heavier objects fall faster than lighter objects. For many hundreds of years this theory was accepted as fact.

Divide the class into working groups. Hand out Activity Sheet A (2.1.1). Allow students (in working groups) sufficient time to complete the activity and record their observations.

Following the activity, have the groups share their results. As you discuss their results, it will become apparent that the pop bottles fell to the floor at the same rate (they took the same time to fall the same distance). Ask:

- What does this tell us about Aristotle's Theory of Gravitational Pull?

Explain that this disproves Aristotle's Theory of Gravitational Pull. Galileo was the first person to disprove Aristotle's theory. He did so by using the scientific method and carefully recording his observations.

Activity Sheet A

Note: This is a two-page activity sheet.

Directions to students:

Follow the instructions on the activity sheet to test Aristotle's theory that heavier objects fall faster than lighter objects. Start by developing an hypothesis (a prediction) about what will happen when you drop the bottles from the

▶

---

same height. Record your hypothesis, then carry out the experiment. Record your results in the table provided (2.1.1).

Activity: Part Two

In this activity, students will discover that matter is made up of particles. This is the first, and key, principle of the Particle Theory of Matter.

Hand each student a piece of notepaper. Direct the students to follow you in your actions. Explain to the students that the piece of paper can be used to demonstrate one of the key principles that describes the properties and behaviour of matter. Ask:

- Does the paper have weight or mass? (yes)
- Does paper take up space or have volume? (yes)

Direct the students to tear their paper in half and hold the pieces in the same hand. Ask:

- Does the paper continue to have the same mass and the same volume? (yes)

Direct the students to tear the pieces of paper in half again, and ask the same questions. Have students continue to tear the pieces of paper into smaller and smaller pieces. As the pieces continue to get smaller, reinforce the idea that the mass and the volume have not changed (although the shape has). As long as none of the pieces has been lost, the total mass and volume of paper will remain the same from the start of this activity to the end.

Explain that around 400 B.C.E., a Greek scholar named Democritus formed an understanding of matter based on an experiment very much like this one. He concluded that all matter (solids, liquids, and gases) is made up of very tiny particles. This theory has been tested by thousands of experiments since then and is accepted as valid. Explain to the students

that today we call these *particles, atoms,* and *molecules.*

Activity: Part Three

Now that students understand that matter is made up of many smaller particles, it is appropriate to detail the rest of the Particle Theory of Matter, and set up the expectations for the completion of the learning log.

Display the information sheet titled, "The Particle Theory of Matter" (2.1.2). Hand out copies of Activity Sheet B (2.1.3) to the students. Have them copy these key principles of the Particle Theory of Matter onto their learning logs.

As the unit progresses, have the students keep their learning logs up to date by entering their information. Use these logs as a way to generate extension ideas and possible avenues for further inquiry. Make sure that students are able to clearly link the concepts presented in the activities in this unit to the key concepts as noted in the Particle Theory of Matter.

Activity Sheet B

Note: This is a two-page activity sheet. Make several copies of page two for each student.

Directions to students:

Use the learning log to keep track of the various experiments and demonstrations throughout this unit. For each experiment or demonstration, identify which part of the Particle Theory of Matter is being demonstrated (2.1.3).

Extensions

- Continue investigations with gravitational theory. Drop two pieces of notepaper at the same time from the same height. Make sure that one piece of paper is crumpled into a ball and the other one is flat. Students will observe that the crumpled ball falls much faster than the flat piece of paper.

Hands-On Science • Grade 7

Challenge students to explain why this is so in light of having just discovered that gravity acts equally on objects regardless of their weight. After having listened to the student responses, explain that the flat sheet of paper has a much larger surface area. This increases friction with air molecules and, therefore, the paper falls more slowly than the crumpled ball of paper.

- Conduct further studies on some of the Greek scholars and scientists mentioned in this unit. Describe some of the theories they developed, and identify which are still accepted theories today. Try to identify what observations or faulty premises might have led to theories that have since been disproved.

Assessment Suggestion

As students conduct the Falling Pop Bottles investigation, observe their ability to follow the steps of a basic experiment, conduct a fair test, observe an event, and reach a conclusion based on observations. Use the Anecdotal Record sheet on page 16 to record results.

Falling Pop Bottles

Overview:

You will perform an experiment to determine if heavy objects fall faster than lighter objects of the same size and shape. You will do this by dropping two pop bottles at the same time, from the same height. Each pop bottle will have a different amount of water in it, making one heavier than the other. One person in the group will drop the bottles at the same time, from the same height. The other group members will observe to determine which pop bottle hits the floor first.

Materials:

- 2 empty plastic pop bottles
- metre stick
- water
- marker
- safety goggles

Procedure:

1. Label one empty pop bottle "A," and the other empty pop bottle "B."

2. Fill bottle A half full of water, and screw the cap on tightly.

3. Fill bottle B full of water, and screw the cap on tightly.

4. Fill in the Hypothesis section of this sheet.

5. One group member will put on safety goggles and hold the two pop bottles 1 metre from the floor.

6. The other group members will put on safety goggles and get down to floor level to observe which bottle hits the floor first. (Be sure that all group members maintain a safe distance from where the bottles will hit the floor.)

7. Repeat this experiment 10 times from the same height, recording your results each time.

8. Now repeat this experiment again 5 times, each time changing the height at which you drop both bottles (e.g., drop both bottles from 0.5 m, 0.75m, 1.25m, 1.5m, 2.0m), and record your results.

Hypothesis: (Predict what will happen when you drop both bottles from the same height at the same time.)

Results: For each repetition, make a checkmark to show which bottle hits the ground first.

	Height	Bottle A	Bottle B	Same Time
1 m – Trial 1				
1 m – Trial 2				
1 m – Trial 3				
1 m – Trial 4				
1 m – Trial 5				
1 m – Trial 6				
1 m – Trial 7				
1 m – Trial 8				
1 m – Trial 9				
1 m – Trial 10				
Height #2 _____				
Height #3 _____				
Height #4 _____				
Height #5 _____				
Height #6 _____				

Conclusion: Based on your results, what statement can you make about your observations? Do heavier objects fall faster than lighter objects? Was Aristotle correct? If not, what observations might have led to Aristotle's belief that heavier objects fall faster than lighter objects?

____

____

____

____

The Particle Theory of Matter

1. All matter is composed of very small particles called *atoms* and *molecules* that are too small to be seen.

2. All of the particles of matter are in constant motion because they have energy. Particles in solids are held tightly in place but do move. Particles in liquids move more freely. Particles in gases move much more freely yet. The particles in solids, liquids, and gases are held together by forces of attraction between the particles.

3. There are spaces between the particles. The size of the spaces varies with the type of matter (e.g., a solid, liquid, or gas).

4. The addition of heat energy causes particles to move faster, stretching their bonds.

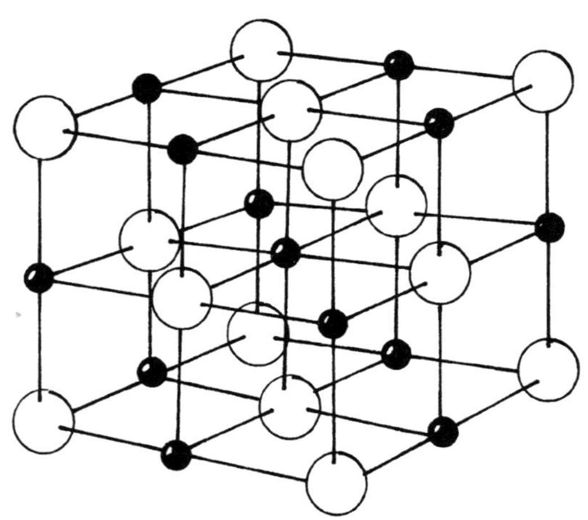

NaCl – salt

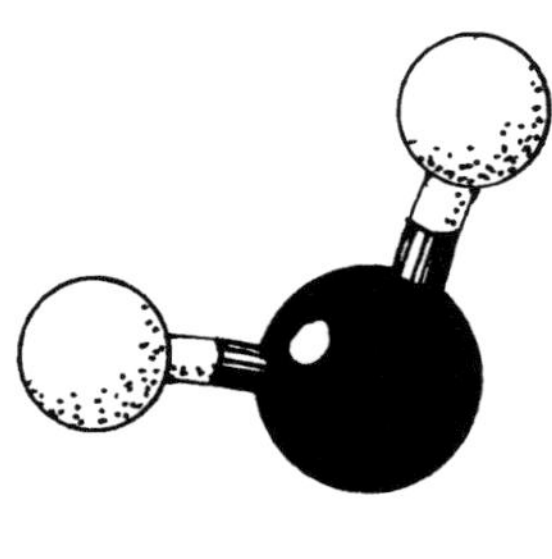

H_2O – water

Date: _________________________   Name: _____________________________

Particle Theory of Matter
Learning Log

Key Principles of the Particle Theory of Matter:

1. ____

   ____

   ____

2. ____

   ____

   ____

3. ____

   ____

   ____

4. ____

   ____

   ____

Directions: Use the table to keep track of your activities throughout this unit. Include your thoughts and understandings of the key concepts presented in the table. In each of your log entries, try to link what you have learned to the key concepts of the Particle Theory of Matter.

Name: ________________________________

Learning Log

Activity/Lesson	Key Concept	Link to Particle Theory	Reasoning/ Explanation/Ideas
Example: Tearing Paper	Paper is made up of many tiny particles called molecules.	Principle #1	The molecules did not change even when we tore up the paper.

2 | Pure Substances and Mixtures

Background Information for Teachers

This lesson introduces several new terms that have specific meaning regarding matter. Students will need to have a firm grasp of these terms if they are to understand the lessons that follow.

Pure Substance: matter consisting of only one type of particle (e.g., distilled water, refined sugar)

Mixture: matter consisting of more than one type of particle (e.g., air, tap water, granola). Mixtures can be divided into two categories: mechanical mixtures and solutions.

Mechanical Mixture: a mixture where individual particles can be identified (granola, concrete). Mechanical mixtures can be homogeneous or heterogeneous.

Homogeneous Mixture: a mixture where particles of each component substance are evenly dispersed

Heterogeneous Mixture: a mixture where particles of each component substance are not evenly dispersed

Solution: a mixture where individual particles are interspersed homogeneously. Individual particles cannot be identified (air, tap water).

Materials

- 8 glass jars or other transparent containers (at least 500 mL each)
- water
- granulated sugar
- breakfast cereal (such as granola that has different parts that can be viewed easily)
- index cards
- chart paper
- markers
- candle or wooden splint
- matches
- food colouring
- rice
- marbles or pebbles
- chicken noodle soup
- carbonated water or soda pop

Activity: Part One: Define and Illustrate

Place two glass jars (or other transparent containers) on the desktop. Fill one jar with granulated sugar. Fill the second jar with breakfast cereal. Label the jars A and B. Ask your students to describe the contents of each container. Record their responses on chart paper.

On two index cards, record the terms *pure substance* and *mixture*. Challenge students to place these cards in front of the appropriate jars. As a class, discuss definitions of a pure substance and of a mixture.

Individually, or in small groups, have students complete Activity Sheet A. Once they have completed this sheet, have them share their responses with the group.

Activity Sheet A

Directions to students:

Define the terms *pure substance,* and *mixture* in your own words. Draw a diagram that illustrates the difference between a pure substance and a mixture. List several examples of pure substances and mixtures in everyday life (2.2.1).

▶

Activity: Part Two: Classifying Pure Substances and Mixtures

Provide students with Activity Sheet B. Have them complete this sheet as they observe the following demonstration:

Place 6 glass jars (or other transparent containers) on the desktop. Label the jars #1 through #6.

Print the following labels on index cards:

gas + gas   liquid + liquid   solid + solid

solid + gas   solid + liquid   gas + liquid

Display these index cards where students can see them.

Explain to students that you will be combining substances to illustrate these six different types of mixtures. Fill the jars one at a time with the substances indicated below. As you fill each container, discuss what you are adding. For each mixture, challenge the students to identify the appropriate index card label. Encourage them to justify their answer. As each jar is discussed, introduce related vocabulary as described below. Record terms on chart paper, along with brief descriptors and examples suggested by students. Have students complete the activity sheet during this demonstration.

Jar #1: Half fill the jar with marbles (or marble-sized pebbles), then add a handful of uncooked rice. This is an example of a solid in solid mixture. It is a *mechanical mixture* because the individual substances (marbles and rice) are identifiable. Introduce the terms *heterogeneous* and *homogeneous mixtures*, explaining that this is an example of a *heterogeneous mixture* because the substances are not evenly distributed.

Jar #2: Fill the jar with water, then add a few drops of liquid food colouring. Stir to distribute food colouring. This is an example of a liquid in liquid mixture. It is a *solution*, which means that the individual particles of water and food colouring cannot be identified.

Jar #3: Fill the jar with carbonated water or soda pop. This is an example of a gas in liquid mixture. The CO_2 is dissolved in the liquid, therefore, this is an example of a gas in liquid solution. The bubbles are formed when the temperature of the solution rises and the CO_2 can no longer remain in solution. The bubbles are no longer part of the liquid/gas mixture.

Jar #4: Fill the jar with chicken noodle soup (or any other appropriate mixture, such as sand in water). This is a solid in liquid mixture. It is a mechanical mixture because the individual substances can be identified.

Jar #5: Light a match or wood splint. Hold a jar upside down over the flame to collect the fumes. When enough smoke particles have been collected, place the jar open side down on the table, trapping the fumes inside. This is an example of a solid in gas mixture. It is not a solution because the smoke particles are not dissolved in the air; they are solid particles suspended in the air.

Jar #6: Leave the jar open on the table. Simply state that it is filled with a solution. This is an example of a gas in gas mixture (air is a solution of nitrogen, oxygen, carbon dioxide, and traces of several other gases). The mixture is a solution.

▶

Activity Sheet B

Directions to students:

As you watch the demonstration, record your observations on the activity sheet. Match each mixture to the correct jar number, and record the contents of the mixture (2.2.2).

Extension

Have students keep a un t glossary of all important terms and vocabulary. Use the extension activity sheet (2.2.3).

Date: ___________________   **Name:** ___________________

Pure Substances and Mixtures

Define the following terms in your own words:

Pure substance:

____

____

Mixture:

____

____

Draw a diagram that illustrates the difference between pure substances and mixtures.

Pure Substance	Mixture

List some examples of pure substances and mixtures in everyday life.

Pure Substance	Mixture

Classifying Mixtures

2.2.2 – 137

Mixture of gas and gas Jar # _______ Substances: _______________ and _______________	**Mixture of solid and solid** Jar # _______ Substances: _______________ and _______________	**Mixture of solid and gas** Jar # _______ Substances: _______________ and _______________
Mixture of liquid and liquid Jar # _______ Substances: _______________ and _______________	**Mixture of gas and liquid** Jar # _______ Substances: _______________ and _______________	**Mixture of solid and liquid** Jar # _______ Substances: _______________ and _______________

Define homogeneous mixture, and give an example:

____

____

Define heterogeneous mixture, and give an example:

____

____

Name: ______________________________

Unit Glossary

Term:

→

Definition:

→

Diagrams and Examples:

Term:

→

Definition:

→

Diagrams and Examples:

Term:

→

Definition:

→

Diagrams and Examples:

3 | Solutions, Solutes, and Solvents

Key Terms:

Solute: a substance that is dissolved in a solvent

Solvent: the substance that the solute is dissolved in

Solubility: the amount of a solute that will dissolve in a solvent – usually measured in molarity (moles/litre)

Concentration: the ratio of solute to solvent in a solution

Diluted solution: a low concentration of a solute in a solvent

Concentrated solution: a high concentration of a solute in a solvent

Saturated solution: the highest possible concentration of a solute in a solvent (no more solute will dissolve without changing pressure or temperature)

Rate of Solution: how fast a solute will dissolve in a solvent. Rate of solution can be affected by such things as temperature and particle size.

Background Information For Teachers

This lesson further clarifies the concept of solutions as introduced in the previous lesson.

Solutions are mixtures in which the particles of each substance mix together so completely that it seems as if a whole new substance has been created, or that one of the substances has disappeared. All solutions are homogeneous, which means that the particles of each substance in the solution are spread evenly throughout. In a solution, you are not able to see the different particles anymore. For example, sugar is a solid that can be dissolved in water. When dissolved, the particles of sugar spread out evenly and fit between the particles of water.

The sugar is still present, but it is no longer visible as a separate substance.

Not all substances are soluble in water. Sand, for example, will not dissolve in water no matter how long you stir the mixture. Some substances that are not soluble in water are soluble in other substances. For example, gold is not soluble in water, but is soluble in mercury. It is important when discussing solubility to identify both the solute and solvent in question.

Solutions can be solid (alloys such as bronze or brass), liquid (carbonated water, nail polish remover), or gas (air, and so on).

Each particle of matter has a slight attraction for other particles. The attraction between these individual particles, not unlike magnetism, helps to hold the solution together, in an even distribution. This even distribution, or concentration can change if we alter the amount of solute, or the temperature or pressure of the solvent.

Several factors can affect the solubility of a substance. One of the main factors is temperature. Temperature affects the solubility of different types of substances in different ways. In general, as temperature of the solvent increases, the solubility of a solid will increase, but the solubility of a gas will decrease. The increased solubility of a solid in a liquid with increased temperature will be illustrated in the activities included in this lesson. The decreased solubility of gas in a liquid with increased temperature can be illustrated by pouring a glass of very cold tap water – from a tap with an aerator attachment works best – and setting it on the counter to warm. As the temperature rises, gases dissolved in the water begin to come out of the solution and form tiny bubbles on the inside of the glass. Another illustration of this process is the sudden "fizz" that occurs when you take a drink of soda

pop. The temperature of the solution is suddenly increased when it is inside the mouth, reducing the solubility of the CO_2 gas. The fizz is the CO_2 gas forming into bubbles as it comes out of solution.

Materials

- drawing paper
- granulated sugar in transparent container (labelled Substance 1)
- table salt in transparent container (labelled Substance 2)
- two clear plastic cups (per each pair or group of students)
- graduated cylinders (or other measuring devices) to measure 100 ml of water for each experiment
- two clear plastic or glass beakers for whole group demonstration (about 500 ml capacity)
- chart paper
- markers
- scales (that can measure grams)
- jug of ice water
- jug of room temperature water
- kettle of hot water
- thermometers (one per pair or group of students)
- spoons for stirring
- solubility table (Included. Make an overhead copy of this sheet.) (2.3.2)
- overhead projector
- nonpermanent overhead pens

Activity: Part One

On chart paper, draw a table that matches the one on the activity sheet.

Begin this lesson with a whole group demonstration of how to perform this experiment. Students can participate as assistants who stir the solutions, record the tallies, and so on. Provide the students with drawing paper and have them label a diagram of the investigation, while you perform the demonstration.

Place the two beakers at the front of the classroom where everyone can see them. Label the beakers "Beaker A" and "Beaker B." Pour 300 ml of room temperature water into each beaker. Place a thermometer in one of the beakers to determine the temperature. Record this temperature on your table. Show the students the two substances that will be used in this experiment (sugar and salt). Note that they are visually indistinguishable from each other. Ask students to predict what these substances might be (sugar and salt will probably be among the answers given). Do not confirm the identities of the substances. Ask:

- How could the identities of these substances be determined?

Safety Note: Stress that it is NEVER an acceptable practice to identify a substance by tasting it. Remind students that until a substance is identified, it should be handled as if it is potentially toxic.

Students may or may not suggest that substances can be identified by measuring how much will dissolve in water. Tell students to keep this problem in mind as they watch the demonstration.

Use the demonstration to model careful and precise measurement techniques using gram scales and accurate record keeping. Beginning with Substance 1, add the substance to the solvent in Beaker A in 10 g increments, and stir until the substance is dissolved. Explain to the students that a solution with a low concentration of a substance is called a *diluted solution*. This solution, with just a small amount of Substance 1 added to it, would be considered a diluted solution.

Place a tally mark on your table each time you add more of the substance to the solution. (Be patient! Depending on your room temperature, somewhat more than 600 g of sugar should dissolve in 300 ml of water! You may wish to speed up the process for the demonstration by adding the sugar in larger increments.)

After adding several increments of Substance 1, explain to the students that a solution with a high concentration of a substance is called a *concentrated solution*. This solution, with a large amount of Substance 1 added to it, would be considered a concentrated solution.

Describe your actions to students as you carry them out, and discuss why you are doing things in a particular way. For example:

"I'm measuring very carefully so that I will have an accurate measurement of how much solute I am adding."

"I am making sure that I have exactly 10 grams each time I measure."

"I am placing a tally mark on my table each time I add solute so that I don't lose track of how much I've added."

Draw students' attention to the fact that even though a large amount of Substance 1 is being added to the solution, the volume of the solution is not increasing substantially. Ask:

- How does the Particle Theory of Matter explain this phenomenon?

Explain that as the substance dissolves, the molecules of sugar fit between the molecules of water. The solution becomes denser, but does not increase substantially in volume.

Continue adding Substance 1 to Beaker A until no more will dissolve (crystals will be visible on the bottom even after stirring). Explain that the solution is now *saturated* (no more of Substance 1 will dissolve in the solution). Show students how to record solubility (___ grams of solute/ ___ ml of solvent at ___ °C).

Repeat the process for Substance 2 in Beaker B. This second solution should reach saturation at a much lower concentration than the first solution (see the Solubility Table, 2.3.2).

Divide the class into working groups. Each group will require two clear plastic drinking cups, 250 ml of Substance 1 (sugar), 250 ml of Substance 2 (salt), gram scales for measuring, spoons, a thermometer, and the activity sheet (2.3.1). Students will measure 100 ml of water into each of their cups.

Have one third of the groups use the ice water, one third use the room temperature water, and one third use the hot water.

Note: Students who use hot water may need more sugar.

Have students determine the solubility of each of their substances by following the directions on the activity sheet.

Following this investigation, draw a Class Summary Table on chart paper for groups to record their results, as in the example below:

Solubility of Two Substances in Water		
	Substance 1	Substance 2
Ice Water		
Room Temperature Water		
Hot Water		

▶

If some results are very far off, this will provide an opportunity to discuss the importance of accurate measurement and record keeping. Discuss the results and draw conclusions from this data. Ask:

- Which substance had a higher solubility rate?
- How did the water temperature affect solubility?
- What do you think these substances are?

Activity Sheet

Directions to students:

Determine the solubility of the two substances in water. Record your results on the activity sheet (2.3.1).

Activity: Part Two

Display the overhead copy of the Solubility Table (2.3.2). As a class, use the table to determine the identity of the two substances. Ask:

- If you were to assume that the substances we used were sugar and salt, how could you use this table and your results to determine which was which?

As a class, examine the Solubility Table along with the Class Summary Chart, and discuss how to use this data to identify the substances.

Use this data to challenge the students to determine diluted, concentrated, and saturated solutions, and complete the chart on the overhead.

Solubility

1. Measure 100 ml of water into each cup (your teacher will tell you to use ice water, room temperature water, or hot water). Label your cups "A" and "B."

2. Measure the temperature of the water in your cups with the thermometer.

3. Record this temperature on the table below.

4. Add 10 grams of Substance 1 to Cup A, using the scales to measure accurately. Stir until the substance is dissolved. Repeat this process, recording a tally mark on the chart below each time you add 10 grams.

5. Continue to add Substance 1 to Cup A until no more of the substance will dissolve. You now have a saturated solution. Determine the amount of Substance 1 that dissolved in your solution by counting your tally marks and multiplying by 10 g.

6. The solubility of Substance 1 is written as ___grams/100ml of water at ___ °C.

7. Repeat this process for Substance 2, first checking the temperature of the water in Cup B. If the temperature has changed very much, obtain new water at an appropriate temperature.

Solubility of Two Substances in Water
Temperature of water: _______
Substance 1 - Tally:
Solubility of Substance 1:
Substance 2 - Tally:
Solubility of Substance 2:

Solubility Table

Solubility of Sugar and Salt in 100ml of Water											
Temperature	0°C	10°C	20°C	30°C	40°C	50°C	60°C	70°C	80°C	90°C	100°C
$C_{12}H_{22}O_{11}$ Sucrose (cane or beet sugar)	179.2	190.5	203.9	219.5	238.1	260.4	287.3	320.5	362.1	415.7	487.2
NaCl sodium chloride (table salt)	35.7	35.8	36.0	36.3	36.6	37.0	37.3	37.8	38.4	39.0	39.8

Identify whether the following solutions are diluted, concentrated, or saturated:

	Diluted	Concentrated	Saturated
203.9 g sugar in 100 ml water at 20°C		✓	
67.2 g sugar in 100 ml water at 80°C	✓		
250.1 g sugar in 100 ml water at 50°C	✓		
13.2 g salt in 100 ml water at 90°C	✓		
36.4 g salt in 100 ml water at 40°C	✓		
381 g sugar in 200 ml water at 10°C			✓
72 g salt in 200 ml water at 20°C			✓

4 Rate of Solution

Background Information for Teachers

In order to conduct a fair test in a scientific experiment, certain variables must be controlled, while other variables are manipulated. *Controlled variables* are always kept the same. For example, in an experiment testing the effects of water type on plants, one would use the same type of seeds, the same soil, the same amount of light, and the same temperature. These are the controlled variables. The one factor that would change is the type of water used; tap water, or rainwater. This is the *manipulated variable.* These terms will be introduced and used as students experiment with rate of solution.

Materials

- granulated sugar
- clear plastic cups
- graduated cylinders
- scales (that can measure grams)
- timing devices (clock with second hand, stop watches, wrist watches)
- jug of ice water
- jug of room temperature water
- kettle of hot water
- thermometers
- spoons or stir sticks (for stirring)
- recycled photocopy paper (cut into quarters)
- centimetre graph paper (included. Make 2 copies for each student.) (2.4.3)
- measuring spoons
- rock sugar (large crystals of sugar. If you are unable to find large crystals of sugar, you can either make them ahead of time for yourself, as described in the Extension Activity, or you can use whole and crushed rock candy. If you use candy, check ahead of time to make sure it will completely dissolve – some candies have additives that will leave insoluble residue or will cloud the water.

Due to the nature of rock sugar, you will not be able to accurately measure 15 g by volume. You will require scales for accurate measurement. If you do not have access to scales, candy may be a better choice – use four whole candies to represent rock sugar and the same number of crushed candies to represent granulated sugar.)

Activity: Part One

Students will investigate the effect of temperature on the rate of solution of granulated sugar in water.

Divide the class into working groups of students. Provide each group with Activity Sheet A (2.4.1), 4 small pieces of paper, sugar, scales, spoons, and a timing device, 100 ml of ice water in one cup, and 100 ml of hot water in another cup.

As a class, read through Activity Sheet A (2.4.1) and ensure that students clearly understand the steps of the investigation. Review the following terms: *controlled variable* and *manipulated variable.*

Note: These terms should be added to the unit glossary.

Discuss these terms as they relate to this investigation. Have the groups follow the instructions on the activity sheet (2.4.1) to investigate solubility and temperature.

Activity Sheet A

Directions to students:

Investigate the rate of solution, using the activity sheet as a guide (2.4.1). Record your results.

Activity: Part Two

Students will investigate the effect of crystal size (particle size) on the rate of solution of sugar in water.

Provide groups with Activity Sheet B (2.4.2), rock sugar, granulated sugar, spoons, scales, and a timing device. Provide each group with two glasses of room temperature water, each measuring 100 ml. Have the students use the instructions on the activity sheet as a guide for this investigation.

Activity Sheet B

Directions to students:

Record the results of your experiment and answer the questions.

Activity: Part Three

Have students make bar graphs to represent the data they collected during each of the two investigations. As a class, review the requirements of a bar graph:

- appropriate title
- labelled axes
- separated bars
- accurate representation of data

Have students construct the graphs independently, using the graph paper included with this lesson (2.4.3).

Activity Centre

Set up a centre where students can further investigate solubility of various substances and the variables that can affect solubility and rate of solution. Include a variety of substances that are soluble in water, as well as substances that are insoluble in water. If possible, also include a variety of other liquids that students can use as solvents (e.g., mineral oil, vinegar, soda water. Students may investigate differences in solubility and rate of solution of individual substances in various solvents, and the effects of the presence of other solutes already in solution. For example, is the solubility and rate of solution of sugar the same in pure water and in mineral water, or in a water solution that is already saturated with salt?

Extension

For many substances, temperature of the solvent is a significant determining factor in t he solubility of the substance (for example, the solubility of cane sugar in water). What happens, then, if a saturated solution at a high temperature is cooled? Investigate this by making a saturated solution of sugar in boiling (or near boiling) water. Suspend a paper clip tied to a string into this solution and allow the solution to cool. As the solution cools, some of the sugar will come out of solution and crystallize on the paper clip. This process takes some time. Crystals will not be immediately apparent. Try leaving the solution in a cool place overnight or over a weekend.

Assessment Suggestion

Assess students' completed bar graphs. List the criteria (identified in Activity: Part Three) on the Rubric on page 19, and record results for each student.

Rate of Solution and Temperature

Dissolving sugar in hot water and in cold water:

Measure 100 ml each of hot water and ice water into 2 cups.

Measure 15 g of sugar onto four small pieces of paper.

Pour 15 g of sugar into each cup at the same time, and stir both cups at the same rate.

Carefully keep track of how long the sugar takes to dissolve in each cup. Have students record their results.

Repeat three more times.

Record results on the chart below.

Rate of Solution of Sugar in Hot and Cold Water		
	Time to Dissolve in Hot Water	Time to Dissolve in Cold Water
First 15 g of sugar		
Second 15 g of sugar		
Third 15 g of sugar		
Fourth 15 g of sugar		

What is the effect of temperature on the rate of solution of sugar in water?

____

What are the controlled variables in this investigation?

____

What is the manipulated variable?

____

Rate of Solution and Particle Size

Dissolving granulated sugar and rock sugar in room temperature water:

Measure 15 g of granulated sugar onto four small pieces of paper.

Measure 15 g of rock sugar onto another four small pieces of paper.

Pour the sugar into the 2 cups.

Stir both cups at the same rate, timing carefully to determine how long each substance takes to completely dissolve.

Repeat three more times.

Record results on the chart below.

Rate of Solution of Granulated and Rock Sugar in Room Temperature Water		
	Time for Granulated Sugar to Dissolve	Time for Rock Sugar to Dissolve
First 15 g sugar		
Second 15 g sugar		
Third 15 g sugar		
Fourth 15 g sugar		

What is the effect of crystal size on the rate of solution of sugar in water?

____

What are the controlled variables?

____

What is the manipulated variable?

____

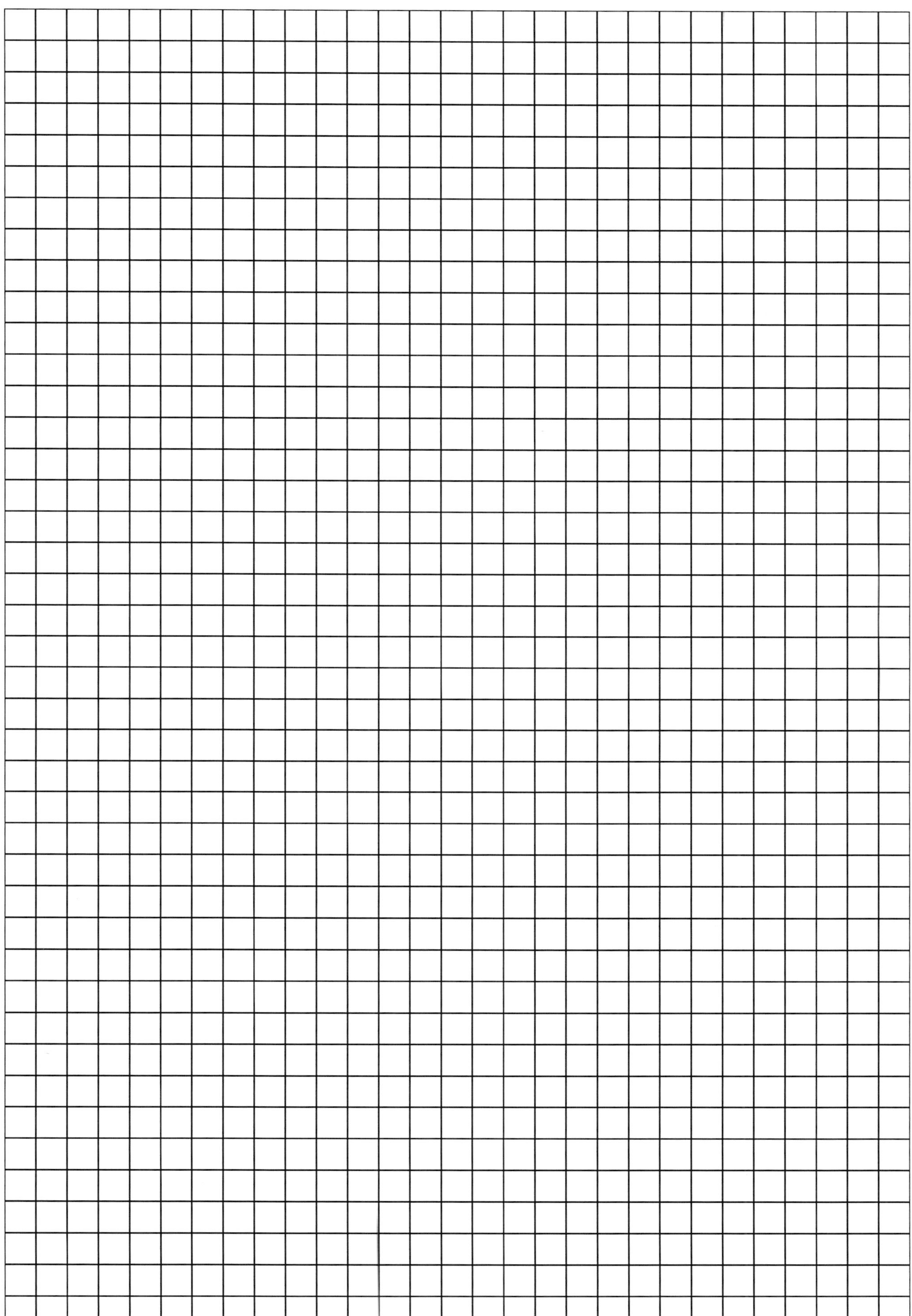

5 | Separating Mixtures and Solutions

Background Information For Teachers

The vast majority of the matter around us consists of either mixtures or solutions. Mixtures and solutions are composed of different substances and each has unique properties, such as different boiling points or different solubility. When different substances in mixtures combine, they do not chemically bond. This means that it is possible to separate the individual parts of mixtures and solutions. This is important in industry, as many raw materials, such as crude oil, need to be processed (separated) in order to isolate the desired substances (e.g., gasoline).

There are several different methods of separating mixtures. Each one is briefly described in Activity: Part One. Each separation technique
is followed by a suggestion for student involvement. The students can work in small groups to complete each activity, or you may choose to set up a jigsaw activity using cooperative learning. Groups are formed as "experts" and they conduct one activity and report their learning back to the whole class. The activity sheets can be kept together and after they are assessed, will form a valuable learning log for this lesson. The activity sheet is designed as black line master for all of the separation activities.

This activity will work well if it is set up as a series of stations around the classroom, with all materials and equipment organized prior to the lesson.

Materials

- activity centre cards (included. Copy and laminate the cards.) (2.5.1)

Note: Materials are identified as per each investigation.

Decantation:

- jars (or other clear containers) with lids
- water
- soil, sand, small rocks

Filtration:

- coffee filters, cloth, wire mesh screens, cotton balls, and any other filtering materials you can find
- large container of muddy water
- small containers for filtering muddy water

Chromatography:

- coffee filters
- water soluble markers
- eye droppers
- water

Evaporation:

- warming light (a desk lamp will do)
- water
- small containers for creating solutions
- water-soluble substances such as sugar, salt, lemon juice, and so on.
- spoons
- eye droppers
- wax paper
- magnifying glasses

Magnetism:

- mixture of iron fillings and sand
- magnets

Distillation:

- container of muddy water
- cookie sheet (chilled; filling it with ice or snow works)
- oven mitts
- empty container for collecting water
- hot plate or other heat source
- reference books and on-line resources related to separation methods

5

Activity: Part One

Set up the following activities as stations around the classroom. At each centre, display the activity cards, along with required materials.

Divide the class into working groups. Each group will require 6 copies of Activity Sheet A (2.5.2) (one for each investigation).

Note: It is suggested that the students conduct the first five seperation activities, but that the teacher demonstrate the process of distillation.

1. Decantation:

This activity involves allowing solid particles in a liquid to settle over a period of time, then decanting the liquid. This method can produce some very interesting results. Layering of the sediment will occur if a variety of particle sizes are represented in the material that is mixed into the water. This is a similar principle to the first stage of managing solid wastes at sewage treatment plants. This can also provide links to the understanding of weathering and erosion, sedimentary rock formation, and paleontology.

2. Filtration:

Filtration is another method used to separate solids from liquids. It consists of passing a solid/liquid mixture through a permeable material that the liquid can pass through, but the solids cannot.

3. Chromatography:

There are several different types of chromatography. All rely on the fact that different substances react differently as they pass through or around different media. It can be used to analyze the different components in a mixture, or to separate the components from each other.

A demonstration of the basic principles of chromatography can be achieved using coffee filters (white ones show the results best) and noncolourfast markers. The coloured inks in the markers are made up of various mixtures of substances. Use the marker to make a mark at the centre of the coffee fiter then drop a small amount of water onto the mark. The inks from the marker will begin to creep along the fibres of the filter. The substances in the solution that interact more strongly with the water will move the farthest along the filter. The substances that interact more strongly with the fibres in the filter will remain closest to the original mark. The resultant colour bands on the filters (called a *chromatogram*) can then be compared with known chromatograms to identify the substances (dyes).

In most cases, black markers will have the most variation in colour. Each brand of marker has its own unique chromatogram. If two black markers of different make were to be compared using chromatography, they would each have different chromatograms.

This investigation is a natural link to art, and the science of light and colour mixing.

4. Evaporation:

Evaporation is one method of extracting a solid solute from a solution. The solution is warmed and the liquid (solvent) evaporates. As the volume of the solvent is decreased by evaporation, the solute can no longer remain in solution. This process can be used to extract sea salt from sea water. Salt pans left in desert areas where lakes have evaporated are a natural instance of this process.

As students conduct this investigation, they will notice that the structure of the crystals from each solution is different. If lemon juice is used, the water in that solution is evaporated, and crystals of citric acid are left behind.

5. Magnetism:

This process can be used to separate magnetic from nonmagnetic substances. A magnet is dragged through the mixture, and the magnetic substances are attracted to the magnet.

The students will easily see the simplicity in this separation technique. They will appreciate how important this technique is in industry where thousands of tons of iron ore are removed from crushed rock. Of course, the mining industry uses gigantic electromagnets instead of small hand-held magnets.

6. Distillation:

This investigation is best done as a demonstration as opposed to student activity. Students can complete the activity sheet as you demonstrate the process of distillation.

Use the diagram below to assist in setting up your demonstration. Heat a container of muddy water to the boiling point, allow the steam to come into contact with a chilled cookie sheet (where it will condense), tilt the cookie sheet so that the droplets run to one end and collect the water in a second container.

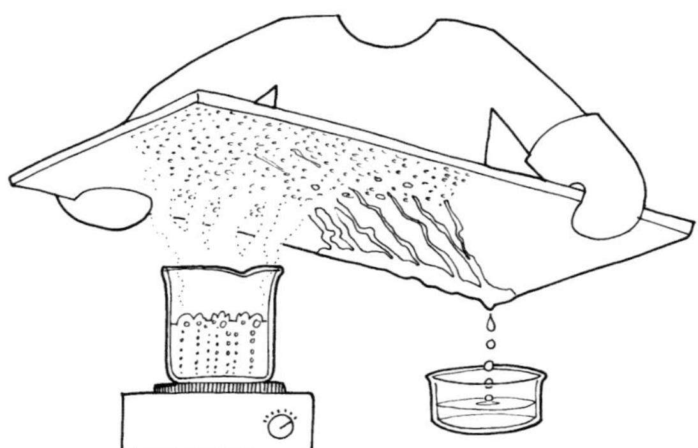

These droplets are pure water. Distillation is a basic process in the production of some brands of bottled water (distilled water). The process of distillation is based on the fact that different substances boil at different temperatures. A solution can be heated very slowly until the component with the lowest boiling point begins to vapourize. The vapour is collected and cooled in another container. This process can be repeated until each of the component substances has been separated.

Activity Sheet A

Directions to students:

For each station, fill out a copy of the activity sheet (2.5.2).

Activity: Part Two

After students have completed the activities at the stations, they can discuss their results. Use the information provided in Activity: Part Two to explain phenomena or answer students questions. Encourage students to apply these investigations to real life. Using Activity Sheet B, have students identify at least one real-life use of each separation method.

Note: Students may have adequate knowledge in order to complete this task independently, or may require related reference materials and teacher guidance.

5

Activity Sheet B

Directions to students:

Following your investigations, identify at least one real-life use of each separation method. Record your results on Activity Sheet B (2.5.3).

Assessment Suggestion

Have the students complete the Student Self-Assessment sheet on page 22 to reflect on what they learned about separating mixtures and solutions.

Activity Centre Cards

Decantation

Materials:

- jars (or other clear containers) with lids
- water
- soil, sand, small rocks

Procedures:

1. Pour various types of soil, sand, and small rocks into a jar half filled with water.

2. Place the lid on the jar and shake it vigorously.

3. Allow the mixture to settle for at least a school day.

4. Repeat this investigation with various rock and soil types, and compare the results.

Filtration

Materials:

- coffee filters, cloth, wire mesh screens, cotton balls, and other filtering materials
- container of muddy water
- small containers for filtering muddy water

Procedures:

1. Examine several different filtering materials.

2. Use these to filter the muddy water.

3. Investigate using these filters singly, or in various combinations, to determine the best way to filter muddy water.

Chromatography

Materials:

- coffee filters
- water soluble markers
- eye droppers
- water

Procedure:

1. Make a heavy mark of colour at the centre of a coffee filter.

2. Using an eyedropper, gently squeeze water onto the centre of the filter, and observe what happens.

3. Repeat this activity with different coloured markers or different brands of markers.

4. Compare two of the same colours from different brands of markers to determine if they have the same chromatogram.

Evaporation

Materials:

- warming light
- water
- small containers for creating solutions
- water soluble substances such as sugar, salt, lemon juice
- wax paper
- magnifying glasses
- eye droppers
- spoons

Procedure:

1. Mix different concentrated solutions. The solutions could be salt and water, sugar and water, lemon juice and water, or other substances provided.

2. Place drops of the solutions on pieces of wax paper, and heat them with the lamp, held close to the solution. The water will evaporate, leaving crystal structures.

3. Use magnifying glasses to observe differences in crystal structures.

Magnetism

Materials:

- mixture of iron fillings and sand
- magnets

Procedure:

1. Place a magnet in the mixture.

2. Drag a magnet through the mixture and observe.

3. Try different magnets and compare their strength.

Separation Methods:
Student Record Sheet

Complete this sheet for each investigation. Make sure you include all of the information possible for each section. Clearly label all of your drawings. Record your observations in point form.

Type of separation method being investigated: _______________

Diagram:	Observations:

Summary: (How did this activity work out for your group? Was there anything in this investigation that you would like to learn more about?)

Uses of Separation Methods:
Application

For each of the six separation methods presented in this lesson, identify at least one real-life use of the process.

1. Decantation:

____

____

____

2. Filtration:

____

____

____

3. Chromatography:

____

____

____

4. Evaporation:

____

____

____

5. Magnetism:

____

____

____

6. Distillation:

____

____

____

Dangerous Mixtures and Solutions and Their Effects on the Environment

Background Information for Teachers

Fresh water, although vital to human survival, is often put at risk by human activity. Water is constantly cycling through our environment. The waste products resulting from human activity can be detrimental to the quality of this resource.

Water pollution results from untreated household, industrial, and agricultural waste that runs into rivers and streams. Chemicals released into the air that then enter the water cycle when they are dissolved in rain water, pollutants leaching from solid waste sites into ground water, and a host of other sources also contribute to pollution. Water containing high concentrations of organic waste can provide a good growth medium for bacteria that use oxygen to break down organic matter. If the dissolved oxygen in water is depleted through this process, aquatic life that depends on oxygen for survival will be negatively impacted. Increased fertilizer concentrations in runoff can over stimulate plant growth in aquatic environments, resulting in a depletion of oxygen available for other aquatic organisms.

Not all water pollution results in over stimulation of plant growth or oxygen depletion. Other pollutants such as pesticides, lead, and mercury can all have toxic effects on organisms, which depend on water for survival. Over time, poisonous substances such as lead and mercury can become concentrated in the organ and muscle tissue of fish, and can be passed on to humans when the fish are eaten. Pesticides kill the tiniest creatures in aquatic environments, which can result in severe disruptions in the rest of the food chain.

Materials

- Samples of cleaned, empty comtainers from household cleaning products, including those with warning labels on the packaging
- hazard cards (included. Copy, cut out, and mount on sturdy tag board.) (2.6.1)
- chart paper
- markers
- Letter to Parents/Guardians (included. Make a copy for each student.) (2.6.4)

Activity

Display a common household cleaner. Survey the students to determine how many have products like this at home. Make a list of the ingredients from the package on chart paper. (If no ingredients are listed, then list the precautions and/or first-aid remedies.) Point out the caution symbol (if there is one), and have the students try to explain its meaning. Ask:

- How is this product used?
- How is this product disposed of once it is used? (Most cleaning products have disposal instructions on the labels.)
- Would you drink this product and the water it was in after it was used? Why not?
- Do you think that this product would harm the living organisms in a stream or pond? How?

Point out to students that when this product is disposed of, it can either go to a waste water treatment facility or directly back into the environment if it is not properly disposed of. Many household cleaners contain harmful substances. If the water that is combined with these substances is not treated, the substances can have a negative impact on water quality.

▶

6

Display the various hazard symbol cards (2.6.1) and have students infer the caution based on each symbol. Match these cards to the household cleaners with the same symbols.

Note: For reference, the hazard symbols identify the following cautions:

 Flammable and combustible material

 Oxidizing material

 Radiation warning

 Bioharzardous infectious material

 Material causing immediate and serious toxic effect

 Compressed gas

 Materials causing other toxic effects

 Corrosive material

Explain to students that they will examine the various cleaning products in their homes. Hand out copies of Activity Sheet A (2.6.2), and Activity Sheet B (2.6.3), and discuss them with students to ensure that they have a good understanding of the safety issues involved in handling the products they may find.

Safety Note: Students should be supervised when examining household cleaning products, as many of these are hazardous. Send home the Letter to Parents/Guardians (2.6.4), and stress to students that they should do their assignment with adult supervision at home.

Activity Sheet A

Directions to students:

Look through your kitchen and bathroom cupboards at home. On the activity sheet list several of the cleaning products that you find there. Include the brand name, manufacturer, warnings/first-aid instructions, and whether the product lists phosphates as one of its main ingredients.

Activity Sheet B

Directions to students:

Identify products in your home that display the warning symbols in the table. Describe the hazard that is indicated by the symbol. Note all first-aid instructions on the labels.

Extensions

- Have the students research safe alternatives to some commercial cleaning products. For example, vinegar and water is effective as a glass cleaner. Have the students produce a news item for the school newsletter, along with recipes for alternative cleaners.

- Invite your school's custodian to speak with your students about workplace health and safety.

Hazard Symbols

Hazard Symbols

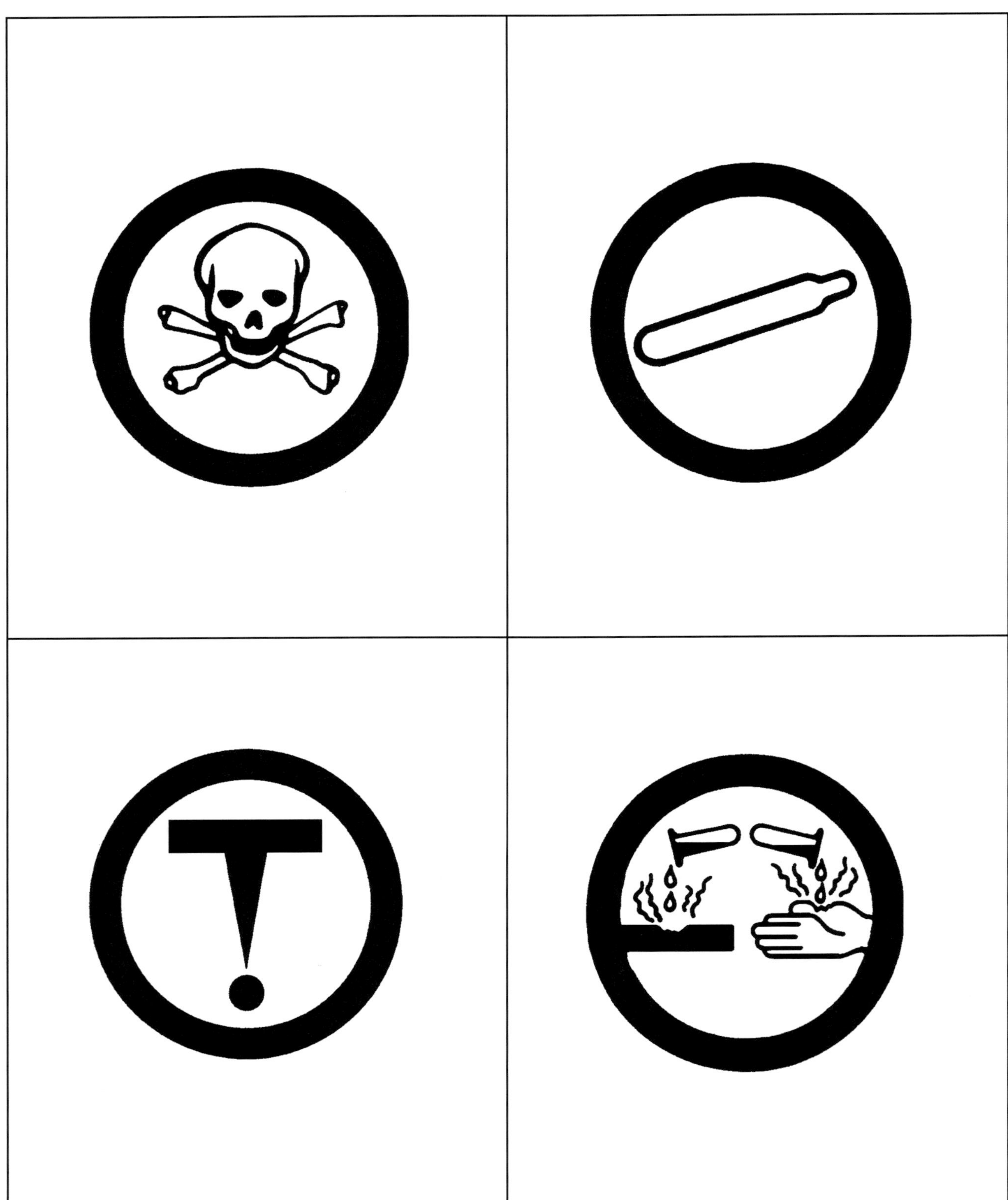

Date: ___________________________   **Name:** ___________________________

Household Chemical Survey

Look through your kitchen and bathroom cupboards at home. List all of the cleaning products you find including the product name, manufacturer, uses, and cautions or warnings (including first-aid treatments, if available).

Product Name	Manufacturer	Uses	Caution, Warning, First-Aid Treatment

Date: _________________________   **Name:** _____________________________

Find products in your home that have one or more of the symbols illustrated below on its packaging. Name the product, describe what the symbol means, and note any first-aid treatments listed on the label. Also note any disposal instructions that are included on the label.

Symbol	Product	Hazard

Letter to Parents/Guardians

Dear Parents/Guardians:

In science we are studying about The Particle Theory of Matter. Part of our unit involves learning about household mixtures and solutions. My assignment is to look through our kitchen and bathroom for cleaning products. I have to gather information from the labels on the cleaning products. For safety reasons, it is important that I do this activity with adult supervision.

Thanks for your help!

From,

____

Student's name

Safety Note: Cleaning products can be hazardous, so I am not to smell, taste, or touch any of these substances.

Assignment Due Date: ___________

7 | Heat and Temperature

Background Information for Teachers

As students progress through the next few investigations in this unit, they will discover that heat is a key component of change in matter. An important distinction must be made between temperature and heat. Temperature is a measure of how hot or cold something is. More specifically, temperature is a measure of the average kinetic energy (energy of motion) of the molecules of a substance at a given point. Heat is the thermal energy that flows from one substance to another substance, thus increasing the average kinetic energy of the molecules within the second substance and increasing its temperature. In other words, energy can be transferred between substances as thermal energy (heat) and can be stored within substances as kinetic energy, which can be measured at any specific point within the substance as temperature.

An example of the difference between heat and temperature is as follows. A bonfire gives off an enormous amount of heat into the cool night air. A burning match does not give off as much heat as a bonfire. However, if two thermometers were placed directly onto the burning wood (one in the bonfire and one on the match), they would read the same temperature.

Temperature is an accurate measure of the movement of molecules around a thermometer.

Heat is the transfer of the kinetic energy of those moving molecules from one substance to another.

Materials

- Styrofoam bowls (3 for each student)
- very warm water, tepid water, cold water
- paper towels
- chart paper
- markers
- thermometers
- glue sticks
- *National Geographic* magazines (or other outdoor magazines)
- dictionaries
- scissors
- rulers
- Learning Logs (Make additional copies of 2.1.3 for students.)

Note: In order to make conceptual connections, students will continue with their Learning Logs, describing their understanding of heat and the Particle Theory of Matter.

Activity: Part One

Provide each student with three Styrofoam bowls, and have them label the bowls "A," "B," and "C." Fill the first bowl with very warm water, the second bowl with tepid water, and the third bowl with cold water.

Have the students place one hand in the bowl of warm water and the other hand in the bowl of cold water. Students should keep their hands in the water for at least one minute. While this continues, ask the students to describe what each hand is sensing.

After one minute has passed, have the students place both hands in the tepid water. Ask:

- What are your hands sensing now? (The hand that was in the cold water should now feel very hot, and the hand that was in the warm water should now feel very cold.)
- Why do you think this occurs?
- What does the term *temperature* mean?
- How would you describe the temperature of the water in each bowl?
- What does the term *heat* mean?

7

Record the terms *temperature* and *heat* on chart paper, and determine a class definition for each. Students may wish to check dictionaries, as well as glossaries in related science texts or reference books. For example:

Temperature is a measure of the energy contained within a substance.

Heat is the energy that flows from a warmer substance to a cooler substance.

Have students dry their hands and touch several items in the classroom with both hands (items should feel warm with one hand and cool with the other hand). Have students record their observations on Activity Sheet A (2.7.1).

Explain to the students that within the skin of the human body, there are receptors for heat and cold that respond to temperatures above or below skin temperature. While the student's hands were in the warm/cold water, there would have been a *heat transfer* either from the water to the hand (warm water), or from the hand to the water (cold water). In both cases, the heat transfer resulted in changes in temperature in the hand and in the water. When the temperature of the water and the temperature of the hand equalized, the heat/cold receptors in the skin ceased to respond. However, when both hands were placed in tepid water, differences between skin temperature and water temperature again came into play. Receptors in the "warm" hand sent signals that were interpreted as "cold"; receptors in the "cold" hand sent signals that were interpreted as "warm."

Have students refill their bowls with warm, tepid, and cold water. Ask:

- What is your estimate of the temperature of the water in each bowl?

Encourage students to place a finger in each of the three bowls to assist them in estimating the temperature of each one. Have them place a thermometer into each bowl, observe the reading, and record this on their activity sheets.

Guide students in completing this activity sheet. Draw diagrams of this investigation on chart paper, modelling how to use arrows to indicate heat transfer.

Challenge students to explain the difference between the heat they felt on their hand, and the reading of the thermometer in the bowl with tepid water. Encourage students to differentiate between heat and temperature. Make note of the key words that are used in the explanations and add these to the chart paper.

Have the students make note of this activity in the Learning Logs they started in the previous unit. The concept of heat and temperature is closely related to the fourth point of the Particle Theory of Matter – the addition of heat energy causes particles to move faster, stretching their bonds. This connection will become more clear to students when heat transfer by conduction is discussed later in this unit.

Activity Sheet A

Note: This is a two-page activity sheet.

Directions to students:

Use the activity sheet to record your observations (2.7.1).

7

Activity: Part Two

Divide the class into working groups, and provide each group with a thermometer, chart paper, markers, rulers, glue sticks, and several magazines. Have the students examine the thermometer closely, then draw a large outline of a thermometer on the chart paper. On this diagram, have them indicate 0°C and draw graduations above and below this mark so that their thermometers can read up to 200°C and as low as –200°C. Graduations should be made in multiples of 5°C.

Now have the students look through the magazines for pictures that represent a variety of temperatures (hot summer day, autumn evening, molten iron, icicles, and so on). Have them glue the pictures around the thermometer. In groups, have the students estimate an approximate temperature represented in the pictures and link their pictures to their thermometer with lines pointing to the appropriate temperatures. Allow the students enough working time to collect and display a wide variety of pictures.

When students have completed this part of the activity, have each group explain the chart by describing two pictures that were difficult to place on the chart. For example, a group may have cut out a picture of molten iron being poured in a refinery. The students may have placed the picture at the top of the thermometer, but are not sure if 200°C was hot enough to indicate the temperature of molten iron.

Discuss challenges such as this as a class, and encourage students to modify their Experience Charts throughout this unit as they learn more about heat and temperature.

Have students continue to use the unit glossary to record new terms, definitions, and example.

Extensions

- Introduce your students to the Environment Canada web site. Use this resource to track temperature changes across the country over a period of time. Alternatively, have your students each select a city (local, national, international) and identify the highest and lowest temperatures on record for that location.
- Have your students take the three bowls of water experiment "on the road" to another classroom, and conduct the experiment with younger students.

Safety Note: Make sure the water is not too warm for safe use.

Water Temperature

1. Briefly describe what you felt when you placed your hands in the bowl with warm water and the bowl with cold water:

   ____

   ____

   ____

2. Briefly describe what you felt when you placed your hands in the bowl of tepid water:

   ____

   ____

   ____

3. What did you feel when you touched items in the classroom with one warm hand and one cold hand?

   ____

   ____

   ____

Draw and label diagrams illustrating what happened when you put your hands in each bowl of water. Record the actual temperatures of the water on your diagram. Use arrows to indicate heat transfer.

Warm Water

Tepid Water

Cold Water

8 | Thermometers

Background Information for Teachers

In this lesson, students will make their own thermometers, and investigate other commonly used types of thermometers.

How does a thermometer work? What is different about water when it is close to freezing, or close to boiling? What is happening in the water? Robert Brown discovered the answers to these questions in 1827. He was observing pollen (too small to be seen with the naked eye) through a microscope. The pollen was in a solution of water. The pollen seemed to be moving even though the water appeared to be motionless. After thinking about this for some time, it became apparent to Brown that the particles of water were moving the pollen grains around. This provided the evidence that scientists were looking for to help them develop a theory of matter (all matter is made up of tiny particles, and the particles are in constant motion). The motion of particles of matter has come to be called *Brownian Motion.*

Thermometers make use of the fact that substances expand when they are heated, and contract when they cool. Most liquids, like the alcohol in a thermometer, expand (increase in volume) as their temperature rises, and contract (decrease in volume) as their temperature drops. In the centre of a thermometer there is a very narrow tube. As the alcohol in a thermometer expands it takes up more space and appears to travel up the tube. Conversely, as it contracts, it takes up less space and appears to travel down the tube. Alcohol in thermometers is often dyed red so that it is easier to see.

What makes the alcohol expand or contract? As the particles in a substance move around the bulb of the thermometer, there is an energy transfer between the particles of the substance and the glass of the thermometer casing. There is then a transfer of energy between the glass and the alcohol. This process continues until an equilibrium is reached between the substance, the glass of the thermometer casing, and the alcohol in the thermometer. If the average kinetic energy of the molecules in the substance is greater than that in the thermometer, (e.g., hot soup, hot air, hot stove element) there is a net transfer of energy to the alcohol. This causes the particles in the alcohol to move more quickly, thus stretching their bonds. The alcohol expands, rising up the centre tube of the thermometer, indicating a rise in temperature.

How do cold substances cause the alcohol to contract? As noted earlier, heat is energy that flows from a warmer object or substance to a cooler one. In this case, the relative warmth of the alcohol in the thermometer is transferred to the cooler substance. The particles in the alcohol slow down because heat energy has travelled to the cooler substance. This decrease in kinetic energy of the particles of alcohol causes it to contract.

Materials

- thermometers of various types (meat thermometer, candy thermometer, oral thermometer, outdoor thermometer, bimetallic strip thermometer, and so on.)
- small glass jars with lids
- translucent straws
- hammers and nails (Nails need to be the same diameter as the straws.)
- food colouring
- Plasticine or white glue
- bowls of warm water, cold water, and tepid water
- instruction sheet titled, "Constructing a Homemade Thermometer" (included. Make a photocopy for each student.) (2.8.1)

8

- graph paper
- coloured pencils
- thin permanent markers
- reference material on thermometers (also see Web Sites)

Safety Note: For safety reasons, no mercury thermometres should be used.

Activity: Part One

In this activity, students will create their own thermometers using a small jar, coloured water, and a straw. Provide each student with Activity Sheet A (2.8.2), a straw, a small jar with a lid, and either Plasticine or white glue. Have them follow the directions on the instruction sheet (2.8.1) to make their own thermometer.

Note: White glue will create a better seal than Plasticine between the lid and the straw, but requires at least 20 minutes to dry.

Once all students have made their own thermometer, divide the class into working groups, and provide each group with a bowl of ice water, tepid water, and warm water.

Note: Ensure that the level of the water in the basins does not exceed the height of the homemade thermometers.

Have the students place their thermometers in each basin as described on Activity Sheet A (2.8.2), and record their results on the chart provided.

Following this activity, challenge students to explain how their thermometers worked. As you listen to students' responses, focus on their observations of the liquid in the thermometer *expanding* when in contact with warm water and *contracting* when in contact with cold water. Explain that the particles in warm water have more *kinetic energy* (they are moving faster) than the particles in cold water. When the thermometers were placed in the

warm water basin, there was a transfer of energy (heat) from the warm water to the thermometer. As the particles in the thermometer gained energy, they began to move faster (increased kinetic energy) and moved farther from each other, causing the liquid to expand. As a result, the liquid in the thermometer was forced up the straw. In the same way, the particles of cold water had less kinetic energy than the particles in the thermometer. This resulted in a transfer of energy from the thermometer to the cold water. As the kinetic energy of the liquid in the thermometer decreased, the liquid contracted and was drawn back down the straw.

As students become aware of this concept (warm liquids expand, cool liquids contract), they should update their learning logs. The concepts learned in this lesson are closely related to understanding that all matter is made up of particles, and that the addition of heat energy causes the particles to speed up and stretch their bonds.

Activity Sheet A

Directions to students:

Use the chart to record what happens when you place your thermometer in cold, tepid, and warm water. Write a paragraph describing how your thermometer works (2.8.2).

Activity: Part Two

After the students have constructed their thermometers, discuss the pros and cons of the devices they made. Ask:

- How are these thermometers the same as commercially made thermometers?
- How are they different?
- Which would provide a more accurate reading of temperature?

Hands-On Science • Grade 7

Display several different types of thermometers. Discuss the properties that each has that make it suitable for its purpose. Focus on temperature range, accuracy, safety (would they want to use a mercury-filled glass thermometer in a baby's mouth?), availability, and suitability for specific tasks. For example, oral thermometers, used to measure body temperature, have a narrow temperature range and are very accurate. An outdoor thermometer, is not nearly as accurate, but has a much wider temperature range.

Divide the class into pairs of students, and provide each pair with a copy of Activity Sheet B (2.8.3). Have the students select a thermometer to research and present to the class.

Note: Several web sites included at the beginning of this unit have excellent information about a variety of thermometers.

Activity Sheet B

Note: This is a two-page activity sheet.

Directions to students:

Select a type of thermometer to research, answer the questions, and present your findings to the class (2.8.3).

Extensions

- Challenge students to use the design process to improve the home-made themometer that was constructed in class. Provide time for planning, constructing, and testing the thermometer.
- Demonstrate how a bimetallic strip bends in different directions depending on the temperature of the water it is put in. Challenge students to explain how it works.
- Have students examine thermographic pictures, such as thermoscans of humans showing heat transfer by radiation and thermograms of houses that indicate heat loss. These special photographs are taken with cameras that are sensitive to infrared rays and use colour to indicate areas of heat and cold. Generally speaking, the colours used to represent the heat spectrum range from the purples and blues, which indicate coldness, to reds, oranges, yellows, and whites, which indicate areas of great heat – white being the hottest. Areas that are at room temperature generally show up as greens and browns. For example, in an infrared photograph of the outside of a house, the heat energy lost around the windows and doors would show as shades of red; well-insulated walls would show as shades of blue. On a thermoscan of the human body, areas around the head would appear as white and yellow, whereas the legs would appear in mostly blue shades.

- Once students have examined such photographs, they can create self-portraits similar to thermoscans. Have them work in pairs to trace their bodes on mural paper, then colour in the outline with similar shading to the thermoscans examined.

Note: Emphasize that thermographs should be completely covered in colour. This will reinforce the concept that heat is all around us all the time, and everything has a temperature. This will also help to ensure that students take enough temperature readings.

- Students can display their collection of thermoscans as an attractive mural in the classroom or in another high-traffic area of the school.

Assessment Suggestion

Observe students as they construct their homemade thermometers. Focus on their ability to follow directions and use materials appropriately. Use the Anecdotal Record sheet on page 16 to record results.

Constructing a
Homemade Thermometer

To make a homemade thermometer, you will require the following supplies:

- small glass jar with a tight-fitting lid
- hammer
- nail
- drinking straw
- Plasticine or white glue
- water and a couple of drops of food colouring
- thin permanent marker

Follow these steps to construct your thermometer:

1. With the marker, draw horizontal lines on your straw. Make the lines about 1 cm apart for the entire length of the straw.

2. Make a hole in the lid of the jar the same size as the diameter of the straw. You can do this with a hammer and nail.

3. Fill the jar to the top with cold water. Add a couple of drops of food colouring so that the water can be seen easily.

4. Tightly screw on the lid of the jar.

5. Place the drinking straw through the hole in the lid so that it almost touches the bottom of the jar.

6. Seal the space between the straw and the jar lid with Plasticine or a bead of white glue so that no air can get in or out.

Investigation Directions

Place your thermometer in each basin of water, and wait for the thermometer to settle on a reading. Record the thermometer's reading in the chart below. Use the "Notes" column to describe what is happening.

	Thermometer Reading	Notes
Cold water		
Tepid water		
Warm water		

Explain how your thermometer works:

____

____

____

Date: _________________________   Name: _______________________________

Thermometers and Mechanisms That Make Use of Heat Sensors

(Circle the type of thermometer/mechanism you will research.)

Galileo Thermometer   Ear Thermometer   Oral Thermometer

Medical Thermometer   Candy Thermometer   Meat Thermometer

Infrared Camera   Outdoor Thermometer   Thermostat

Bimetallic Strip   Thermo-coupling

Remote-Controlled Thermometer

1. Describe what the thermometer/mechanism is used for.

2. Describe how the thermometer/mechanism works.

3. Draw and label a diagram.

Effects of Heating and Cooling on Volume

Background Information for Teachers

Heat is related to the motion of particles in a substance. Adding heat causes particles to move faster, stretching the bonds that hold the particles in place. Removing heat from a substance causes its particles to slow down. When particles have slowed down and are not straining at their bonds, the bonds become more effective in holding onto the particles. The net effect of this is that the particles are often drawn in closer (especially with liquids and gases), and the substance contracts.

This lesson is designed to demonstrate effects of a change in temperature on the volume of solids, liquids, and gases. Two activities in this lesson are demonstrations, given the caution required in performing them. The last is a take-home experiment that includes a challenge question for students to solve.

Safety Note: When conducting the demonstrations, model proper safety procedures. Use protective gloves or oven mitts to avoid burns.

Materials

- empty 2-litre pop bottles (one per group)
- large balloons (one per group)
- ball-and-ring apparatus
- bowl of water
- thermometer
- access to hot and cold running water
- electric kettle
- heat source (electric burner, hot plate)
- kitchen tongs
- chart paper
- markers
- protective gloves or oven mitts

Activity: Part One

This demonstration will illustrate the effect of heat on the volume of a solid. Heat up the water in the kettle so that it is freely boiling. Explain to the students that you will be using the steam from the kettle to help demonstrate the effect of heat on solids.

Pass around the ball-and-ring apparatus for students to examine. Have them demonstrate that the ball just barely passes through the centre of the ring. Ask:

- What do you think will happen if I heat the ball with the steam from the kettle?

Have students share their predictions and the reasons for them. Record these on chart paper. Now test their predictions by holding the ball in the steam. After ten seconds, try to pass the ball through the ring (the time necessary for this will vary with the size of the ball-and-ring apparatus). If the ball still passes through, continue heating and testing until the ball has expanded enough so that it no longer passes through the ring. Ask:

- Why do you think this happened?
- What did we do to the ball? (added heat)
- What is the ball made of? (metal)
- How does heat affect metal?

Record students' ideas on the chart paper. Ensure that they understand that heat caused the ball to expand. Guide the students to more specifically understand that the particles (or molecules) in the ball took on energy from the steam. The kinetic energy increased causing the particles in the ball to move faster, pulling at their bonds and causing the ball to expand. Now ask:

- What do you think would happen if both the ring and the ball were placed in the steam?
- Will the centre of the ring close in (expand inwards) or will the centre of the ring expand outwards, allowing the expanded ball to pass through?

▶

After sharing and recording predictions, place both the ring and the ball in the steam, and hold them there for at least one minute. When ready, complete the demonstration by passing the ball through the ring.

Now challenge the students to use both their eyes and ears for the next step in this demonstration. Use a heat source such as an electric burner to increase the temperature of the ball. While you heat the ball, have a student measure the temperature of the water in the bowl, and record this reading on chart paper. After at least one minute (times will vary), caution the students to listen and observe very carefully as you quickly plunge the hot metal ball into the water.

Have the students share their observations. They should see the water bubble and sputter and steam rising from the water, and hear a searing sound.

Have a student measure and record the temperature of the water again and, as a class, discuss any changes that have taken place. Students should be able to note that the water is notably warmer.

Challenge the students to explain what has happened in this investigation. Through your discussions with the students, lead them to understand that the heat that was transferred to the ball caused the molecules in the ball to begin moving faster, making the ball hotter. When the ball was plunged into the water, much of the energy in the molecules of the ball was transferred very quickly to the water. This transfer was so quick that the molecules of water immediately surrounding the ball vapourized (changed state from liquid to gas).

Activity: Part Two

Note: If access to sinks is limited, this investigation may be done as a centre activity for small groups, while the rest of the class completes another task.

This activity will demonstrate the effect of heat on the volume of a gas. Divide the class into working groups, and provide each group with one empty 2-litre pop bottle with a lid and one balloon. Provide students with a copy of Activity Sheet A (2.9.1) to complete as their group conducts each investigation.

First, have the groups half fill their pop bottle with hot tap water and screw the lid on tightly. Have them shake the bottle a few times, then remove the lid and hold the bottle upside down over a sink. As soon as the water has drained from the bottle, have the students quickly screw the lid back on. The bottle will begin to collapse almost immediately. Ask:

- What did you observe?
- Why do you think this happened?

Discuss that heat is being transferred from the air inside the pop bottle to the relatively colder air outside the bottle. The kinetic energy of the molecules in the air in the bottle is decreasing, and the air is contracting. Ask:

- What do you think might happen if you hold the bottle under cold water?

Have students share their predictions, then hold the bottle under cold running water to see if it collapses further.

Now have the groups remove the caps from their bottles and ensure that the bottles are no longer collapsed. Have the students blow up the balloon to stretch it, then place it over the neck of the pop bottle. Ask:

- What do you think will happen if you place the bottle under hot water?

Have the students share their predictions, then hold the bottle under hot running water.

Discuss their observations. The balloon should begin to inflate as energy is transferred from the hot water to the air inside the bottle. The kinetic energy of the air molecules is increased causing the air in the bottle to expand. Explain to the students that just as heat energy caused the ball in the last experiment to expand, heat can also cause gases to expand. Now ask:

- What do you think will happen if the bottle is held under cold running water?

Allow students to test their predictions. The students will immediately notice that the balloon has not only shrunk but, in some cases, been pulled into the neck of the bottle. The balloon may even seem to inflate inside the bottle.

Now challenge students to explain what has happened. Focus their thoughts on the temperature of the water and the molecules of air. Students should be able to explain that the energy (heat) of the air molecules was transferred to the cold water. With this sudden reduction of energy in the molecules of air, the bonds holding the air molecules contracted, pulling the molecules closer together. This resulted in a reduction in the volume of air.

Students should now update their Learning Logs with the understanding that heat can change the volume of solids and gases.

Activity Sheet A

Directions to students:

After each investigation, record your findings. Draw a sketch of what happened, and explain why it happened (2.9.1).

Activity: Part Three

This is a take-home activity for students. It will challenge them to think about the special properties of water. Give each student a copy of Activity Sheet B (2.9.2). Allow them to report their results during the next class.

Note: The answer to the Challenge Question (If liquids contract when they are cooled, why does water expand when it freezes?) is complex. For a complete answer, check out **www.science.ca** (click on "Ask a Scientist," then select the "Top 10" questions regarding the special properties of water).

Activity Sheet B

Note: This is a two-page activity sheet.

Directions to students:

Take the activity sheet home, and follow the instructions. Record your findings on the sheet, and bring it to your next class (2.9.2).

Pop Bottle Experiment

For each investigation, illustrate what happened, and explain why it happened.

The Question of Water

Materials:

- three equal-sized pop bottles with tight-fitting lids.
- water
- freezer
- permanent marker

Procedure:

1. Fill the first pop bottle with water until it is about 1/3 full. Tightly screw the cap back on the bottle. Mark the level of the water on the pop bottle using a permanent marker. Label this bottle "A."

2. Fill the second pop bottle with water until it is about 2/3 full. Tightly screw the cap back on the bottle. Mark the level of the water on the outside of the pop bottle using a permanent marker. Label this bottle "B."

3. Fill the third pop bottle with water until it is full. Tightly screw the cap back on the bottle. Label this bottle "C."

4. Place the bottles in a freezer overnight.

Hypothesis:

(Write down what you think will happen to each of the three bottle.)

Pop Bottle A (1/3 full of water)

____

Pop Bottle B (2/3 full of water)

____

Pop Bottle C (full of water)

____

Observations:

Draw diagrams of the pop bottles:

Before Freezing:	After Freezing:
Pop Bottle A	**Pop Bottle A**
Pop Bottle B	**Pop Bottle B**
Pop Bottle C	**Pop Bottle C**

Write a summary of your observations:

____

____

____

____

Challenge Question: If liquids contract because the loss of heat (energy) means that the particles of the liquid are pulled closer together, then why does water expand when it freezes?

You may wish to explain the answer to this question on your own, or you can do some research to find the answer. Record your response on the back of this sheet. Include diagrams to support your explanation.

10 | Changes of State

Background Information for Teachers

At this level, it is suggested that students focus on three states of matter; solids, liquids, and gases. In future science courses, the students will learn about colloids (e.g., gelatin), polymers (e.g., latex and rubber), and other forms of matter that blur the lines of solids, liquids, and gases.

Each state of matter has its own unique properties.

Solids: have a rigid shape and cannot flow like a liquid or gas. The particles of a solid vibrate in one spot because they are tightly held in place by their bonds.

Liquids: take the shape container that they are poured into, and they can flow. This means that the particles of a liquid can slide past one another and still be connected by the bonds holding the particles together. Due to the relatively weaker bonds, the particles of a liquid can move much more freely than those of a solid.

Gases: Like liquids, gases can flow and will take the shape of the container they are in, but gases are unique in that they expand to fill the container they are in. The spaces between the particles of a gas are quite large relative to the spaces between the particles of solids and liquids.

To help students (and teachers) understand the density of particles and magnitude of spaces present in solids, liquids, and gases, imagine the following:

There are three equal-sized elevators. Each elevator door represents a different state of matter (solid, liquid, and gas).

The three elevator doors open at the same time to reveal the number of people/particles in each state.

The "solid" elevator is crammed to the roof with people who all are the same size and look alike. They are all squirming, but none is able to move any real distance.

The "liquid" elevator is full of people who all look alike, but they can move freely around and past one another. As the door opens, they "flow" out of the elevator.

The "gas" elevator has only a few people in it, all of whom are jumping up and down, from the ceiling to the floor, and bouncing off the walls. As the door opens, they escape down the hall and drift off in different directions, bouncing off the walls, floor, and ceiling.

Solids, liquids, and gases can change their state if the required amount of heat (energy) is added or taken away from the particles of matter. Many students recognize this principle when they relate how water can transform from a solid (ice), to a liquid (water), to a gas (steam). They might also be able to explain that this change in state is a result of the addition of, or removal of, heat.

This change of state, if graphed, follows a definite curve, or progression. A graph of a change of state is called a *heating curve*. The flat sections of the graph, where the substance is melting or boiling, is called a *plateau*.

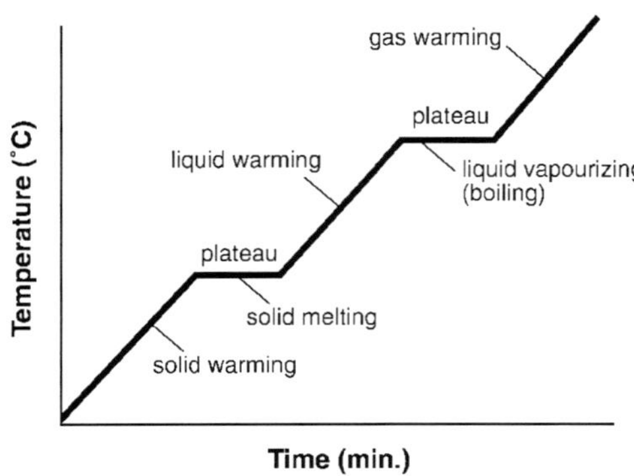

10

Materials

- hot plate
- large Pyrex beaker (or other heat safe)
- crushed ice
- thermometer
- protective gloves or oven mitts
- graph paper (included. Copy one sheet per student.) (2.10.2)
- dry ice (can be purchased from most welding and medical gases supply stores)
- plate (to display the dry ice)

Activity: Part One

For safety purposes, this investigation is best conducted as a demonstration. Fill the large Pyrex beaker with crushed ice. Place it on a hot plate, and position a thermometer so that it is suspended in the ice and does not touch the bottom of the beaker. Ask:

- What form of water is in the beaker? (ice)
- What state of matter if this? (solid)
- What is the *freezing point* of water? (0°C)

Hand out the Activity Sheet A (2.10.1), and read over the directions with the students. Take an initial temperature reading of the ice. Begin heating. Ask:

- What do you think will happen to the ice as it is heated?

- At what temperature do you think the ice will reach its melting point?

- At what temperature do you think the water will reach its boiling point?

As the ice melts and the water warms, take temperature readings at one-minute intervals. During this process, discuss the water's changes of state from solid to liquid to gas (*vapour*), as well as the concepts of *evaporation* and *condensation*.

Have students use the chart on the activity sheet to record the temperature readings.

Safety Note: For safety purposes, wear gloves, and be sure to avoid direct contact with the hot steam produced as the water heats up.

When the activity is completed, have the students graph the data. Discuss criteria for their graphs.

Explain to the students that during the time of the plateau, the temperature of the water is not rising, in spite of the additional heat being transferred into it from the hot plate. The added energy is being used to free the particles from their bonds: the energy is creating a change in state rather than increasing the temperature. There are two plateaux: one when the particles of ice are freed to become a liquid; one when the particles of water are freed to become a gas.

Activity Sheet

Directions to students:

Use the chart to record temperature readings (2.10.1). When all temperature readings have been recorded, graph your results (2.10.2).

Activity: Part Two

Sublimation (the change of state from a solid directly to a gas) can be easily observed with dry ice. Place the dry ice on a plate in the open air, and have students examine it. It will seem to steam and will quickly disappear. Discuss observations, and introduce the term *sublimation*.

Students should now be able to update their Learning Logs with their new understanding of the Particle Theory of Matter and how it relates to the concepts covered in these activities.

Extension

Have students research the uses of dry ice. Several other substances that occur as gases at room temperature have specific uses in their liquid state (e.g., liquid nitrogen, liquid oxygen). Have students research how these substances are made and what they are used for.

Assessment Suggestion

As a class, identify criteria for the students' graphs. For example:

- appropriate title
- accurate labels
- accurate presentation of data
- neatly constructed

List these criteria on the Rubric on page 19 and record results.

Change of State
and the Heating Curve

Directions:

- Use the chart below to record the temperature readings from the thermometer.
- Take readings at one-minute intervals.
- Stop recording the temperature when the water has been boiling for at least 4 minutes.
- Make sure to take a temperature reading of the steam that is produced by the boiling water.
- Following this investigation, graph your results.

Observations:

Time (minutes)	Temperature (°C)	Notes

Background Information for Teachers

Heat energy can move from one place to another in three different ways: conduction, convection, and radiation.

Conduction is heat transfer through solids. As the particles take on heat energy, they begin to vibrate faster. Their increased energy and motion causes the adjoining particles to move faster because they are held closely together by strong bonds. In this way, the energy applied to some of the particles of a solid is transferred (conducted) to other particles in the solid.

Convection is the transfer of heat energy in liquids and gases. This is different from conduction in that as the particles of a fluid are heated, they begin to move in what are known as *convection currents*.

Lava lamps are excellent examples of convection currents. The globs of wax and water near the light source at the bottom of the lamp become hot and, therefore, less dense. This is because the heat energy that they took on has caused their particles to spread out. Now that the wax and water particles are less dense (lighter), they begin to rise away from the heat source. As the warm wax and water rise, their extra heat energy is drawn off, and their particles become dense once again. This begins a cycle where lighter, warm fluid particles rise and are replaced from underneath by denser cooler fluids. The cycle repeats itself over and over.

Radiation is the transfer of heat energy via special waves (e.g., ultra violet, electromagnetic). This allows heat to be transferred through space where there are few, if any, particles of matter.

Another important concept is *heat capacity* or *thermal capacity*. This is a measure of how well a substance stores heat. The heat capacity of a material is the amount of heat required per unit increase in temperature. Thus, a substance with a high heat capacity, such as water, will not increase in temperature quickly with the application of heat. Conversely, a substance with a low thermal capacity, such as copper, will increase in temperature significantly with the application of the same amount of heat.

Materials

- soldering gun
- copper electrical wire (12 guage, 50 cm long)
- aluminum electrical wire (12 guage, 50 cm long)
- paper clips
- petroleum jelly
- pliers
- timing device (clock with second hand)
- graph paper (included) (2.11.1)
- hot plate
- cup hooks
- large glass beaker (Pyrex or other heat safe material)
- water
- floodlights (three is preferable; if doing this activity on a bright day go outside and use sunlight)
- black, green, and white construction paper
- three thermometers
- dark food colouring or nutmeg
- clock with second hand

Activity: Part One

Safety Note: For safety purposes, this investigation should be done as a demonstration, with student involvement as appropriate.

▶

Wrap one end of the copper wire around the tip of an unplugged soldering gun (3 or 4 times). Screw the cap hook into a wall or bulletin board. Attach the other end of the wire to the cup hook Use petroleum jelly to attach ten paper clips at 3 cm intervals along the length of the wire, as in the illustration below.

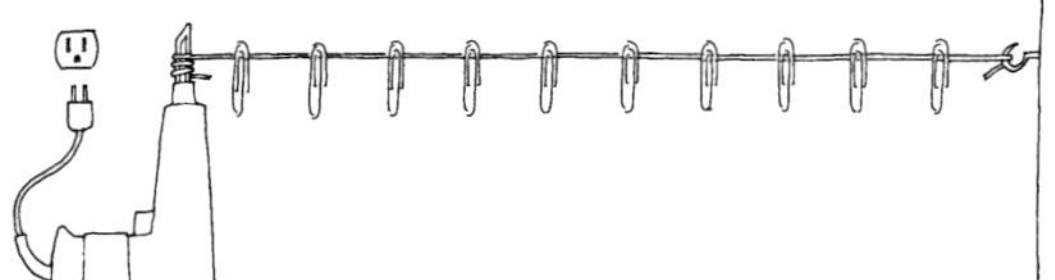

Once the apparatus is ready, ask:

- What do you think will happen if we plug in and turn on the soldering gun?

- Why will the paper clips fall off?

- Distribute Activity Sheet A (2.11.1) and review the directions with students.

Test the students' predictions by conducting the investigation. Plug in the soldering gun and have the students observe the heating of the wire, and record how long it takes for each paperclip to fall off. Introduce the term *conduction* during the process, and discuss the concept as it occurs. Have the students use the chart on Activity Sheet A to record results.

Using pliers, remove the copper wire from the soldering gun and cup hook. Wait several minutes for the gun's tip to cool, then wrap the aluminum wire 3 or 4 times around the tip of the soldering gun and attach the other end to the cup hook. Attach another ten paper clips with petroleum jelly at 3 cm intervals along the length of the wire. Ask:

- Do you think the paper clips will fall at the same rate from the aluminum wire as they did from the copper wire?

Test the students' predictions by repeating the experiment.

The students should have observed that the aluminium wire dropped its paper clips much faster than the copper wire.

Challenge the students to explain why different metals conduct heat differently. Hopefully the students will infer that the particles of copper are much more dense (closely packed together) than the particles of aluminum. This means that it takes more time to transfer the heat energy by conduction through the copper wire.

Provide students with the graph paper (2.11.4) and have them construct the graph according to the directions provided on Activity Sheet A.

Activity Sheet A

Note: This is a two-page activity sheet.

Directions to students:

Use the chart to record how long it takes for each paper clip to fall. Once the investigation is completed, use the graph paper provided to record the results (2.11.1 and 2.11.4).

Activity: Part Two

Note: This activity is best completed as a classroom demonstration.

Place a large beaker of water on a hot plate. Warm the water, but make sure that the water does not boil. (Warm water will maintain easily identifiable convection currents; boiling water will not.)

Have students observe closely as you carefully place several drops of dark food colouring into the water at the side of the container. Students will notice that the food colouring disperses in a downward swirl, only to reach the bottom of the beaker and continue upwards.

Challenge your students to explain what is happening. Encourage students to use terms such as *fluids, particles, heating,* and *cooling.* This demonstration may have to be repeated

11

several times to allow all students to observe it carefully.

After the students have tried to explain what is going on in the beaker, explain to them that this is a demonstration of heat transfer by *convection*. Heat is transferred from the hot plate to the beaker by conduction. Heat is transferred to the water at the bottom of the beaker by conduction. As the water at the bottom of the beaker warms, the molecules begin to move farther from each other, reducing the density of the warmed water. The warm, less dense water rises, and cooler, denser water flows into its place. The particles of food colouring are carried along with the convection currents.

Activity Sheet B

Directions to students:

Draw a diagram illustrating heat transfer by convection, and write a brief paragraph describing the demonstration (2.11.2).

Activity: Part Three

This investigation is a great outdoor activity if it is a warm, sunny day. Otherwise floodlights, such as the kind used during school stage productions, will work well.

Divide the class into working groups, and provide each group with copies of Activity Sheet C (2.11.3) and white construction paper. Review the directions provided on the activity sheet, and have the groups conduct the investigation.

Students should find that the temperature rose the fastest under the black paper and the slowest under the white paper. After students have had sufficient time to complete this activity, discuss the results they obtained. Ask:

- Did all of the groups obtain similar results?
- What were the general trends in the data?

Students will be able to point out that the black paper absorbed heat from a radiant source very well. White paper did not absorb much heat from a radiant source, and the green paper absorbed heat somewhere in between the black and white paper.

Challenge the students to explain why dark-coloured paper resulted in a greater heat gain through radiation than lighter colours. Dark colours (or the chemical pigments that result in dark colours) absorb more light energy than they reflect. Light colours (or the chemical pigments that result in light colours) reflect more light energy than they absorb.

Following this discussion, have students construct graphs of the data collected.

Have the students update their Learning Logs.

Activity Sheet C

Note: This is a three-page activity sheet.

Directions to students:

Use the chart to record your thermometer readings, answer the questions, and graph your results (2.11.3 and 2.11.4).

Extensions

- Have students investigate the insulating properties of various materials. One way to do this is to find or create similar-sized containers made from different materials (e.g., glass, metal, plastic, wood, Styrofoam). Put an equal amount of water in each container. Ensure that the temperature of the water in each container is the same at the beginning of the experiment. Place the containers of water in a basin of hot water (being careful that none of the hot water spills into the containers). Take temperature readings in each of the containers at regular intervals.

- Invite guest speakers such as engineers or architects to discuss challenges in designing structures that allow for expansion and contraction. What building materials withstand these stresses well? What materials (such as insulation) can minimise the effects of radiant heat on a structure?

- Have students research ocean currents as an example of large-scale convection currents.

Assessment Suggestion

Use the Individual Student Observation sheet on page 17 to record students' accuracy and attention to detail while they conduct the investigation in Activity: Part Three.

Heat Transfer by Conduction

Paper Clip #	Time it took for paperclips to fall from Copper Wire	Time it took for paperclips to fall from Aluminum Wire
1		
2		
3		
4		
5		
6		
7		
8		
9		
10		

Write a paragraph describing the results of this investigation.

____

____

____

____

Date: ___________________   Name: _______________________________

Heat Transfer by Convection

Draw a diagram illustrating how heat can be transferred by convection.

Write a brief description of the demonstration.

____

____

____

____

____

Heat Transfer by Radiation

Directions:

1. Place the white, green, and black construction paper next to each other in a sunny spot or under a floodlight.

2. Place a thermometer under each piece of paper so that you can read the temperature without removing the thermometer.

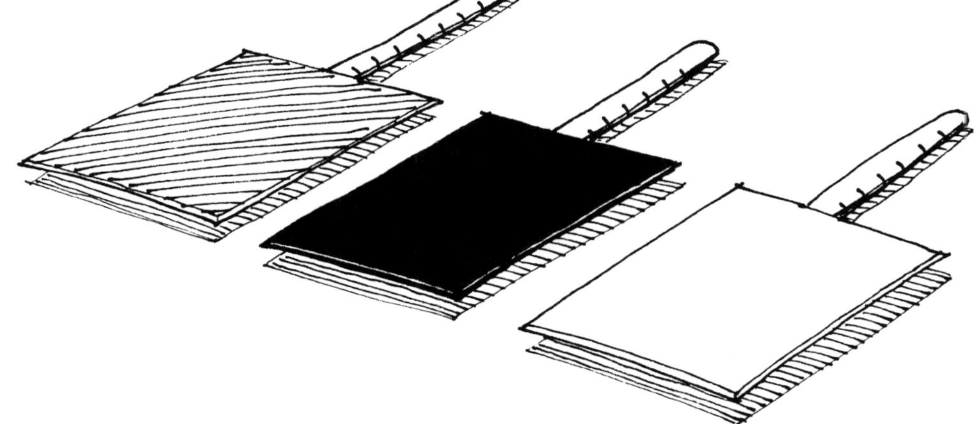

3. Observations: Record the thermometer reading for each
colour of paper at 30-second intervals.

Time	Green Paper Temperature °C	Black Paper Temperature °C	White Paper Temperature °C

4. Construct a broken line graph of the data you collected. Each
line on your graph will represent one of the paper colours.

5. Which colour of paper resulted in the most heat transferred
by radiation? The least?

____

____

____

6. How could the colour of a house affect heating/cooling costs?

____

____

____

12 | Producing Heat

Background Information for Teachers

By now, the students have observed demonstrations of heat and its properties. This lesson investigates the different methods of producing heat. There are four ways in which heat can be produced.

1. **Mechanical energy:** There are four types of mechanical energy:

   - friction (from surfaces rubbing against each other)
   - distortion (e.g., bending a paper clip out of shape)
   - compression (e.g., the air inside a bicycle tube heats up as more air is pumped into it)
   - percussion (e.g., pounding on a surface with a hammer)

2. **Chemical energy:** This is the energy that is released from molecules, as atomic bonds are broken.

3. **Electrical energy:** This can be turned into heat by forcing the electricity to travel through a material that resists the flow of electrons. A stove element is a familiar example of this. As the electrons move through the stove element, they begin to agitate the particles in the stove element. The particles begin to move faster, and energy is given off as heat.

4. **Nuclear energy:** This is the energy that is released when the very structure of individual atoms is either split apart (nuclear fission as in a Can-Du reactor) or joined together (nuclear fusion as in the Sun).

Note: In this lesson, students produce heat through some mechanical and chemical means. Although they will not be producing heat through electrical energy or nuclear energy, it is appropriate to discuss examples of each of these processes.

Materials

- plaster of Paris (craft type, not industrial)
- paper cups (not Styrofoam)
- hammers
- nails
- blocks of wood
- thermometers
- plastic film wrap
- large paper clips
- chart paper
- markers
- baby-food jars (or other small jars) with lids
- water
- disposable stir sticks

Activity: Part One: Mechanical Energy

In this activity, students will use friction, distortion, and percussion to produce heat energy.

1. Friction:

This example is very simple and is something most of your students will have done at one time or another. Ask your students to rub their hands vigorously together. Heat will be produced almost at once.

Explain that, in this example, heat is formed by *friction*. Record this term on chart paper, and discuss its meaning. Further explain that friction is a form of mechanical energy created by movement.

Brainstorm with your students other everyday examples of heat caused by friction. Some examples are rug-burn, car tires that heat up when moving quickly (if your students have watched any car racing, they will be familiar with this), and the heat from pistons moving in an engine.

Note: Discuss with students that heat is not always a desirable by-product of friction. Particularly in mechanical devices where metal surfaces rub together constantly, friction is usually reduced with the use of lubricants. The lubricants form a thin, liquid layer between the surfaces. As the particles in the liquid have far more freedom of movement than the particles in a solid, less friction (and, therefore, less heat) is produced.

2. Distortion:

Hand out to each student a large metal paper clip. Have the students make a straight piece of wire from each paper clip, and then challenge them to race you in bending the wire back and forth until it breaks. As they do this, explain that the molecules in the wire are being squeezed and pulled repeatedly, and this causes heat. Bending the wire produces enough heat so that the particles in the wire overcome the bond holding them in place and separate. Have the students feel the severed ends of the paper clip as soon as it breaks. They should notice that the ends of the paper clips are warm. Explain to students that this heat was produced by *distortion*, another form of mechanical energy. Distortion is the process of changing the shape of an object. Add this term to the chart paper, and discuss its meaning.

3. Percussion:

Supply students with metal hammers, nails, and blocks of wood. Make sure the nails are not long enough to extend through the blocks of wood. Have students feel the striking face of their hammer, noting its approximate temperature. Instruct students to hammer one or two nails into the wood and feel the striking face of their hammer again. The hammer should be noticeably warmer. Explain that this form of mechanical energy is called *percussion*. Add this term to the chart paper, and discuss its meaning.

4. Compression:

Compression is difficult to demonstrate in a classroom, but there are several everyday examples of heat caused by compression. Most notably, the back of a refrigerator or freezer gives off a great deal of heat because the compressor used to cool the inside of the unit heats up on the outside of the freezer. The compressor compresses the cooling fluid (giving off heat), then allows it to expand rapidly. The sudden decrease in pressure allows the gas to expand rapidly. Without added energy, the rapidly expanding gas decreases dramatically in temperature.

Activity: Part Two: Chemical Energy

Safety Note: Industrial paster of Paris can produce high heat, and particles can be dangerous if inhaled. Be sure to use the plaster of Paris used for crafts, and sold in craft stores.

By now the students have observed many examples of heat produced by chemical means (candles burning, for instance). Challenge the students to explain what happens when matter is burned. After sharing ideas, explain that when a substance is burned, molecular bonds are broken. When these bonds are broken, the energy that was held by them is released as heat. A burning log will produce much more heat than a cardboard box because the log has so much more mass (particles of matter). Burning matter is a form of *chemical energy*. Add this term to the chart.

Explain that chemical production of heat can also occur without burning. As certain chemicals react with each other, the molecular structure of the compounds may be changed as more stable compounds are formed. Excess energy from within broken molecular bonds may be given off as heat. For example, heat is released when plaster of Paris is mixed with water.

For this activity, each student will need a paper cup (not Styrofoam) half filled with plaster of Paris, another container filled with an equal amount of water, and a disposable stir stick. Have students feel the outside of the cup with plaster of Paris in it and note its relative temperature. Students should then carefully add the water to their plaster of Paris and stir the mixture. Every few minutes, have students feel the outside of their cups and note any change in temperature. It may take half an hour or more for a temperature peak to be reached in the plaster of Paris.

Note: You may wish to use a thermometer in one or more of the mixtures to provide quantitative results that complement the students' qualitative observations. If you do not mind sacrificing an inexpensive thermometer, you can place one directly into the mixture. Alternatively, if you have a thermometer or temperature probe that tapers to the end (some thermometers bulge at the bottom), you can wrap it in plastic film wrap to protect it.

Discuss students' observations during this investigation. Explain that plaster of Paris is, in essence, gypsum powder. It takes energy to remove the water from gypsum rock. That energy is stored as chemical energy in the powder until it is released in a chemical reaction when water is added, essentially forming gypsum rock.

Once the students have investigated and discussed heat produced by mechanical and chemical energy, have them complete Activity Sheet A (2.12.1).

Be sure to have students complete their Learning Logs with what they have learned from these investigations.

Activity Sheet A

Note: This is a two-page activity sheet.

Directions to students:

Draw a picture illustrating the production of heat from each of the four types of mechanical energy, and from chemical energy. Write a brief description of how the heat is produced in each example (2.12.1).

Activity Sheet B

This activity is a homework assignment. Provide students with Activity Sheet B (2.12.2). Have students share their answers during the next class.

Directions to students:

Find at least 15 devices in your home that use electrical energy to produce heat (wanted heat or unwanted heat). For each item indicate other forms of energy (if any) that are also produced by the device (2.12.2).

Extension

Have students conduct research to identify and describe how nuclear energy is transformed into heat energy.

Sources of Heat Energy

Draw a diagram illustrating each of the following sources of heat energy. Write a brief description of how the heat is produced.

Mechanical Energy: Friction

Mechanical Energy: Distortion

Mechanical Energy: Percussion

Mechanical Energy: Compression

Chemical Energy: Burning

Chemical Energy: Plaster of Paris

Home Electrical Survey

Find at least 15 devices in your home that use electrical energy to produce heat. Also note if there are other forms of energy produced by the device, such as motion, sound, and light.

	Electrical Device Producing Heat	Other Forms of Energy Produced From This Electrical Device
1		
2		
3		
4		
5		
6		
7		
8		
9		
10		
11		
12		
13		
14		
15		

13 | Design Challenge

Background Information for Teachers

The study of science is intricately interwoven with technology and society. This design challenge will engage students as they plan, build, and test a prototype of a cooler.

Safety Note: Be sure to consider safety factors during the design and construction process. For example, students should be supervised when using glue guns or other construction tools, and should wear safety goggles. Any fibreglass should be used only with protective gloves.

Materials

- materials for constructing coolers (collected by students)
- masking tape
- duct tape
- safety goggles
- glue, and low temperature glue guns
- Popsicles (5 per group)
- thermometers (one per group)
- scrap paper
- information sheet titled, "Design Challenge" (included. Make a copy for each student.) (2.13.1).

Activity

Hand out the information sheet (2.13.1) to all students. Review the instructions carefully to ensure that all students understand the goal of the challenge. Spend some time reviewing the basic concepts that have been presented in this unit, and take the time to answer any questions that are brought up by students.

Divide the class into working groups, and have them discuss their design ideas. Provide each group with plenty of scrap paper to work out their design ideas. When they have agreed on a final design, students should create a "blueprint"

on the activity sheet (2.13.2). The blueprint should be fully labelled indicating materials needed and proposed structure. Once you have approved the "blueprint," students may begin construction of their cooler. Allow a few days for the collection of required materials, and at least one full class for construction.

The testing phase of this challenge will need to begin three hours before your science class. Depending on the time of day that your science class is scheduled, you may need to ask students to gather before school or at lunchtime to begin the testing phase of the challenge.

Note: You will have to decide how long to let the challenge run based on your observations of how well the coolers have been constructed. Allow enough time for some melting to occur, but not so long that all of the Popsicles have melted into slush.

Place five Popsicles and one thermometer into each cooler at the beginning of the challenge. Make sure that the thermometer is not in direct contact with the Popsicles (you need a reading of the air temperature in the coolers, not the temperature of the still frozen Popsicle).

After the three-hour time period has passed, open the coolers one at a time, and record the air temperatures. The cooler with the lowest air temperature will be considered the most effective.

As your students enjoy their frozen treats, have the students in each group explain how they made their cooler and what changes they might make next time. Allow time for questions or constructive feedback from the other students.

13

Activity Sheet

Directions to students:

Once your group has finalized a design, record your design plans. Your blueprint should be fully labelled, and indicate materials needed and proposed structure. When your finished blueprint has been approved, begin construction (3.10.2).

Assessment Suggestions

- As students work together to design and construct their coolers, observe their ability to work together on this challenge. Use the Cooperative Skills Teacher Assessment sheet on page 21 to record results.

- Have students complete the Cooperative Skills Self-Assessment sheet on page 23 to reflect on their ability to work with their classmates.

End-of-Unit Assessment

Reflect on the tasks undertaken by each student throughout the unit to complete the End-of-Unit Assessment chart on page 26. Consider all assessment tools, investigations, and activities when identifying and commenting on individual student achievement.

Design Challenge

What is the problem?

■ It is a hot, sunny day, and you and four friends have decided to go to the beach. You have to bring the Popsicles and make sure that they are still frozen for eating in the afternoon.

■ You are to design, construct, and test a new prototype for a Popsicle cooler that will keep Popsicles frozen for three hours.

How big can the cooler be?

■ The cooler that you construct has to be large enough to hold five double Popsicles. Its outside dimensions should not be larger than a typical student backpack. The cooler needs to be easy to transport to the beach.

What materials can I use?

■ You are encouraged to use a variety of materials for constructing your prototype. Keep in mind the information you learned about insulators and conductors, and how these affect cooling and heating, as you gather materials.

Do I have to make a plan first?

■ Yes. This simple step will help you solve any unforeseen problems. It will also help you focus on the process for this design challenge.

■ You will be required to show your blueprint design sheet to your teacher for approval prior to beginning construction.

How long do the Popsicles have to stay cool?

■ You will place the frozen Popsicles in your prototype cooler, and leave them in the classroom at room temperature for three hours. If your cooler works well, you will still have a tasty frozen snack at the end of the challenge.

Is that all?

■ You must also be able to explain to your classmates the following:
Why you chose the materials you did.
What challenges you had to overcome in your design.
What you felt worked well and what could have worked better in this challenge.
What you would change next time.

Date: _______________________   Name: _______________________

____

____

Cooler Blueprint

Materials Required:

______________   ______________   ______________

______________   ______________   ______________

______________   ______________   ______________

______________   ______________   ______________

References for Teachers

Ford, Lenoard, A. *Chemical Magic.* New York: Dover Publications, 1993.

Gardner, Robert, and Kemer, Eric. *Science Projects About Temperature and Heat* Hillside, NJ: Enslow Publishers, 1994.

Herr, Norman, and Cunningham, James. *Hands-On Chemistry Activities with Real Life Applications, Volume 2.* West Nyack, NY: Center for Applied Research in Education, 1994.

Kovac, Jeffrey, and Sherwood, Donna. *Writing Across the Chemistry Curriculum: An Instructor's Handbook.* Upper Saddle River, NJ: Prentice Hall, 2001.

Kyn Barker. *Heat.* Don Mills, ON: Addison-Wesley, 2000.

Lauw, Darlene, and Cheng Puay, Lim. *Heat.* New York: Crabtree Publishing Co., 2002.

Lechtanski, Valerie. *Inquiry-Based Experiments in Chemistry.* Washington: American Chemical Society, 2000.

Tocci, Salvatore. *Experiments With Heat.* New York: Children's Press, 2002.

Wood. W. Robert. *Heat fundamentals : funtastic science activities for kids.* Philadelphia, PA: Chelsea House,1999

Forces and Structures

Books for Students

Berlow, Lawrence H. *Reference Guide to Famous Engineering Landmarks of the World: Bridges, Tunnels, Dams, Roads, and Other Structures*. Phoenix: Oryx Press, 1997.

Ching, Francis. *Building Construction Illustrated*. New York: Van Nostrand Reinhold/co Wiley, 1975.

Hoban, Tara. *Construction Zone*. New York: Greenwillow Books, 1997.

Hooker, Saralinda, and C. Ragus, and M. Salvadori. *The Art of Construction: Projects and Principles for Beginning Engineers and Architects*. Chicago: Chicago Review Press, 1990.

Isaacson, Philip M. *Round Buildings, Square Buildings, and Buildings That Wiggle Like a Fish*. New York: Knopf, 1988.

Kline, Michael P. and C. Johmann, E. Reith. *Bridges: Amazing Structures to Design, Build & Test (Kaleidoscope Kids)*. Charlotte, VT: Williamson Publishing, 1999.

Levy, Matthys, and K. Woest, M. Salvadori. *Why Buildings Fall Down: How Structures Fail*. New York: W.W. Norton, 2002.

Martin, George A. *Fences, Gates, and Bridges: A Practical Manual*. Chambersburg, PA: A. C. Hood , 1997.

National Geographic. *The Builders: Marvels of Engineering*. 1998.

Reichold, Klaus, and B. Graph. *Buildings That Changed the World*. Munich, NY: Prestel, 1999.

Salvadori, Mario G., and C. Ragus, S. Hooker. *Why Buildings Stand Up: The Strength of Architecture*. New York: W. Norton, 2002.

Scarre, Christopher, and C. Scarre. *The Seventy Wonders of the Ancient World: The Great Monuments and How They Were Built*. New York: Thames & Hudson, 1999.

Stevenson, Neil. *Architecture*. New York: DK Publishing, 1997.

Web Sites

- **www.pbs.org/wgbh/buildingbig/**

  Building Big is a PBS web site that deals with structures and construction. The site includes an online educators' guide, interactive challenges, and a glossary of terms. The site is well worth a visit before starting this unit.

- **www.pbs.org/wgbh/nova/bridge/**

  PBS/Nova – Build a Bridge. This site contains information on the basic support structures used for bridge building. There are also several short video clips including an excellent clip of the undulation of the Tacoma Narrows Bridge before its collapse in 1940 (click on "Build a Bridge," then "suspension bridges," scroll to the bottom to find the video links).

- **www.dot.state.oh.us/ preventivemaintenance/**

  Ohio Department of Transportation on-line bridge maintenance manual – although this site's primary purpose is to provide information about bridge maintenance, it contains a large amount of information about several different support structures used to construct bridges. It also contains an excellent glossary of bridge terms.

- **www.ce.ufl.edu/activities/trusslab/ trussndx.html**

  University of Florida, Civil Engineering Laboratory – Truss Bridge Laboratory. This site contains information about how to construct a truss bridge, as well as descriptions of a variety of truss designs.

- **www.pbs.org/wgbh/nova/wtc/**

  Nova companion web site for "Why the Towers Fell" video.

- **www.civl.port.ac.uk/comp_prog/ bridges1/BrooklynBridge.htm**

  Information about the Brooklyn Bridge.

- **www.goldengatebridge.org/research/ construction.html**

  Information about the Golden Gate Bridge.

- **www.civl.port.ac.uk/comp_prog/ bridges1/Storbaelt.htm**

  Information about the Storbaelt Bridge.

- **www.civl.port.ac.uk/comp_prog/ bridges1/SydneyHarbour.htm**

  Information about the Sydney Harbour Bridge.

- **www.icivilengineer.com/Landmarks/ Bridges/Akashi_Kaikyo/**

  Information about the Akashi Kaikyo Bridge.

- **www.confederationbridge.com**

  Detailed information and visuals of the Confederation Bridge that joins Prince Edward Island and New Brunswick.

- **www.telus.net/bigcelt/vancbc2.htm**

  Information about the design, construction, and features of Vancouver's Lion's Gate Bridge.

- **www.ambassadorbridge.com**

  This web site has information on the Ambassador Bridge that joins Windsor Ontario to Detroit Michigan.

- **www.peacebridge.com**

  This web site contains information about the Peace Bridge in Ontario.

- **www.cntower.ca**

  Information on Toronto's CN Tower, including field trip details and related learning resources.

- **www.winnipeg.ca/publicworks/majorprojects**

  This City of Winnipeg site provides information, blueprints, and photographs of recently constructed bridges, such as the Provencher, and Norwood Bridges.

- **www.Kraftconst.com/Bridges.html**

  This site is maintained by Kraft Construction Company, and provides photographs, costs, and design details on several Manitoba bridges.

- **www.scatliff.mb.ca/profile/bridge_architecture/bridge_architecture.html**

  This site provides photographs, design plans, and construction details on several bridges in Manitoba.

- **www.winnipeg411.com/photos/**

  This site has several photos of Winnipeg buildings and bridges. There are also links to other related topics.

- **http://canada.archiseek.com/manitoba**

  An excellent site with photographs and descriptions of buildings in Manitoba, with links to other provinces and countries architecture web sites.

Introduction

In this unit, students will become familiar with the basic principles of forces as they relate to natural and human-built structures. Through research and investigations, students will learn to recognize the internal and external forces that affect structural stability, as well as the methods and materials used to maximize strength when designing such structures. Within these designs, students will identify and compare various common shapes used to enhance the strength of each material used in construction.

During the unit, students will be very active as they discover and test the forces that pertain to structures. At times, the classroom may resemble an engineer's study or perhaps even a construction site. The hands-on experiences provided in this unit will facilitate students' learning about forces and structures.

Prior to teaching this unit, collect pictures of famous structures such as The Golden Gate Bridge, The Eiffel Tower, The Leaning Tower of Pisa, The Sears Tower, and The CN Tower. Also be sure to include pictures of local buildings and bridges.

Aside from the Internet, other good sources for these images and related information are engineering magazines, tourist pamphlets from travel agents, *Canadian Geographic*, *National Geographic*, Bill Nye videos, and videos produced by *Popular Mechanics for Kids*.

Science Vocabulary

Throughout this unit, teachers should use, and encourage students to use, vocabulary such as: *frame structure, shell structure, solid structure, centre of gravity, stability, compression, tension, shear, torsion, internal and external forces, structural stress, structural fatigue, structural failure, load, magnitude, point and plane of application*, and *efficiency*. Extension vocabulary is also presented in some lessons.

1 | Classifying Structures

Background Information for Teachers

A structure is designed to perform a specific function, whether it be a human-made structure like a house, chair, or bridge; or a natural structure such as a bird's nest, or a honeycomb. All structures are designed to resist the forces that act on them.

In this unit, students will investigate various types of structures. They will use the design process to test materials and structural plans, as they experiment with forces and loads acting on these structures.

Structures can be classified into three distinct categories; solid structures, frame structures, and shell structures.

Solid structures, or *mass structure* are those that are made of solid pieces of strong material. Castles, Stonehenge, and dams are examples of solid structures.

Frame structures are made of parts connected in a set arrangement. The Eiffel Tower, some bridges, electrical towers, and most house roof are frame structures.

Shell Structures are moulded into a shape that provides strength and stability. They rely on curves or arches to provide strength. A geodesic dome, which also incorporates features of a frame structure, a quinzee (snow cave), igloos, and a helmet are examples of shell structures.

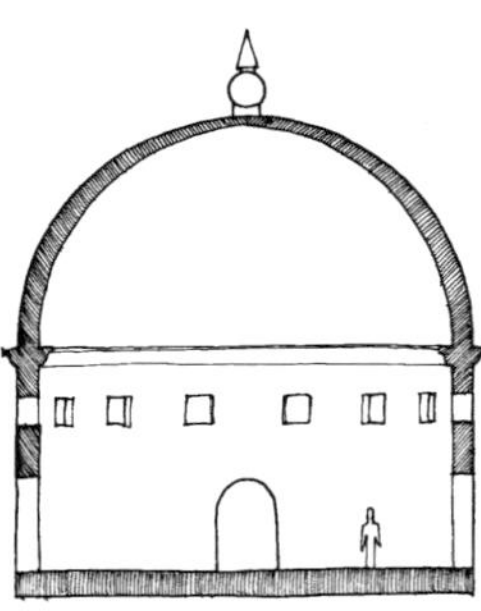

Materials

- pictures of solid, frame, and shell structures from magazines, calendars, and printed from computer sources
- various sports helmets
- egg cartons
- dominoes, tiles, or building blocks (non-interlocking)
- straws
- clipboards
- chart paper
- markers
- plastic drinking straws
- gram weights (one set for each working group of students)
- small paper plates
- desks
- masking tape

Activity: Part One

Introduce this activity by displaying pictures of the different structure types (human built and natural solid, frame, and shell structures). Ask:

- What are these objects?
- What do they have common?

- How are they different?
- How would you classify these pictures?

Discuss students' responses and, as a class, group the pictures according to students' suggestions.

Note: At this level, students should be familiar with the concept of structures from previous units on the topic "Everyday Structures," in Grade 1, "Stability," in Grade 3, and "Forces Acting on Structures and Mechanisms," in Grade 5.

Explain that each structure is classified based on its design, appearance, and purpose.

Introduce students to the three types of structures, using the following set of group activities.

Divide the class into working groups, and provide each student with a copy of Activity Sheet A (3.1.1) to be completed during the following investigations.

Shell Structure Activity:

Provide students with helmets and egg cartons. Have them examine the objects. Ask:

- What are these structures used for? (protection)
- What materials are used to make these structures?
- How do you think the structures are made?

Explain to the students that the helmets and egg cartons are examples of shell structures. Shell Structures are curved, hollow structures that provides strength and stability. Dome buildings, quinzees (snow caves), and kayaks are examples of shell structures.

Castle Activity:

Provide students with dominoes, tiles, or non-interlocking blocks. Have the groups construct a small castle with dominoes, tiles, or building blocks. After they have built their castles, ask:

- What will happen if you remove a block/tile/domino from the castle wall?

Have students record their prediction on Activity Sheet A (3.1.1), then test their prediction by taking one brick out of the wall. The stability of the structure depends on which brick is removed. If the brick is removed from near the top, the structure will not be affected. If the brick is removed from near the bottom of the structure, the whole structure may collapse. In both cases, the students will notice that the bricks are important to the overall stability of the structure. The removal of one brick may severely damage the integrity of the structure.

Explain to the class that their castles are examples of solid structures. Solid structures, or mass structures, are those that are made of solid pieces of strong material. Castles, igloos, and dams are examples of these structures.

Bridge Activity:

Provide each group with masking tape, plastic drinking straws, gram weights, and a small paper plate. Have the groups place two desks slightly apart to create a span just smaller than the length of their plastic straws, but wider than the paper plate. Have the groups use ten plastic straws to make a bridge between the two desks. Their bridges may be secured to the desks using tape.

Once the bridges have been constructed, explain to the class that the straws are the load-bearing portion, or the deck, while the desks act as the support pillars.

Have the students place a small paper plate on their bridge's deck, then place gram weights on the plate, and observe the effect. Next, have the students place another weight on the plate, and then observe the effect. Ask:

- How many grams do you think your bridge can support?

▶

Have the students record their predictions on the activity sheet (3.1.1). Have the groups test their bridges with increasingly heavier gram weights until the bridges collapse.

Once the collapse has occurred, ask:

■ Why did the straws bridge to collapse?

The students should respond that once the load became too heavy, the structure could not support it any more.

Explain to the class that their bridges are examples of frame structures. Frame structures are made of parts connected in a set arrangement. The Eiffel Tower, bridges, and most houses are frame structures. These structures require calculations regarding how much weight they can support.

Once students have completed Activity Sheet A provide them with Activity Sheet B (3.1.2) to identify and describe the three types of structures; shell, solid, and frame).

Activity Sheet A

Directions to students:

Use the activity sheet (3.1.1) to record your predictions and your observations during investigations.

Activity Sheet B

Directions to students:

Draw a labelled diagram of each type of structure. Be sure to provide a rationale for your example in the space provided.

Activity: Part Two

Explain to students that they are going to go on a walking tour around the community to observe different types of structures.

> **Note:** Select your route carefully to ensure that it will offer a variety of structures.

Provide the students with Activity Sheet C (3.1.3) and clipboards to use while on the field trip. While walking, discuss the design of the structures, the uses of various structures, and the materials used to make them. Also look for structures that use features of other types of structures. For example, most houses have a solid structure foundation (concrete), with a frame structure design above.

Activity Sheet C

Directions to students:

During the walking tour, identify examples of each type of structure. On the chart, record the name of the structure, its location, and any unique features.

Activity: Part Three

Have the students use their experiences and knowledge to determine a class definition of a structure by conducting a Think-Pair-Share activity. First, have each student write a definition based on what they have learned so far. Next, divide the class into pairs and have the students read and revise their definitions. Finally, have each pair share their definitions with the class. Record these on chart paper. Discuss ideas and determine a class definition.

Activity: Part Four

Activity Sheet D (3.1.4) is a glossary chart to be used throughout the unit. Make several copies of this sheet for each student to bind together as a booklet. Front and back covers can be added as well. As new terms are introduced, students can record these, provide definitions and examples, and draw diagrams. This may also include images from web sites, or other computer-based resources.

1

Note: Remember that a structure is designed to perform a specific function, and that all structures are designed to resist the forces that are expected to act on them. These ideas should be integrated into the class definition.

Students will find the glossary to be useful for review, study, and reference purposes throughout the unit.

Activity Sheet D

Directions to students:

As new vocabulary is introduced throughout this unit, record each term, and provide a definition, example, and diagram.

Extensions

- Have the students construct geodesic domes using commercial kits or toothpicks and miniature marshmallows.

- Have the students research examples of buildings and structures developed by different cultures. (e.g., pagoda, thatch hut, clay home, castle, pyramid, and so on)

- Examine and discuss traditional designs of indigenous people. (e.g., wigwam, tipi, longhouse, and igloo)

Activity Centre

Display the collection of pictures of structures used during the class. Encourage students to cut out pictures from magazines or newspapers to add to the display.

Assessment Suggestion

Observe students on the walking tour. Focus on their ability to identify and describe the different types of structures. Use the Anecdotal Record sheet on page 16 to record results.

Structures

1. a) What shape is the helmet? _________________________________

   b) What shape are the cups in the egg carton? _______________

   b) What kinds of structures are the helmet and egg carton? _________

2. What do you predict will happen if you remove a brick from the castle wall?

   ____

   ____

   b) What kind of structure is the castle? _____________________

3. a) How much mass (g) do you think your straw bridge can hold?

   ____

   b) Test your bridge and record the mass at which it collapsed. _______

   c) Draw labelled diagrams of what the straw bridge looked like before
       you added the load, and then after you added the load.

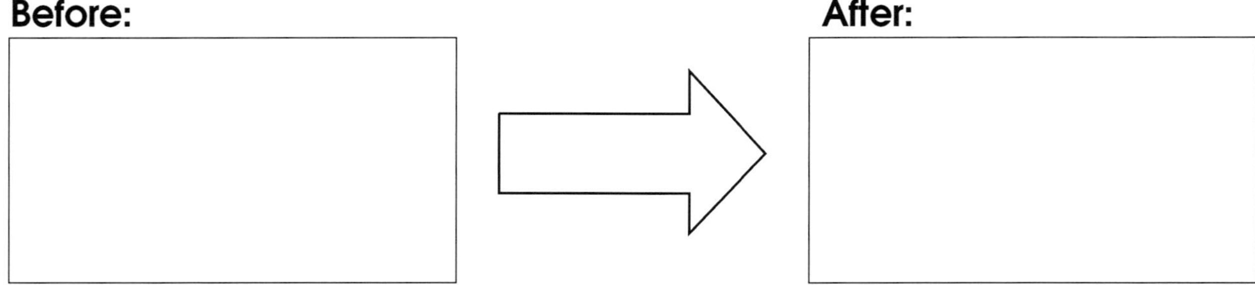

Before:

After:

   d) What kind of structure is the bridge? _____________________

   e) What would happen if a bridge could not support a fully loaded
   truck? How is this similar to the masses placed on the straws?

   ____

   ____

Date: ____________________ Name: ________________________________

Classifying Structures

Draw examples of a:

Solid Structure	Frame Structure	Shell Structure

These are SOLID STRUCTURES because:

____

____

____

These are FRAME STRUCTURES because:

____

____

____

These are SHELL STRUCTURES because:

____

____

____

Date: _______________________   Name: _______________________________

Structures Field Trip

Name of Structure	Location	Structure Type	Special Features and Uses

Name: ___________________________________

Unit Glossary

Term	Definition	Examples	Diagrams

2 Nature's Structures

Background Information for Teachers

Some of the most complex structures are naturally occurring and can be found all around us.

Plant leaves, for example, have evolved to have a main rib that extends from the base and supports the weight of leaf. From the main rib, other secondary ribs taper away towards the edge of the leaf. This lightweight, naturally occurring structure is mechanically sound and structurally efficient.

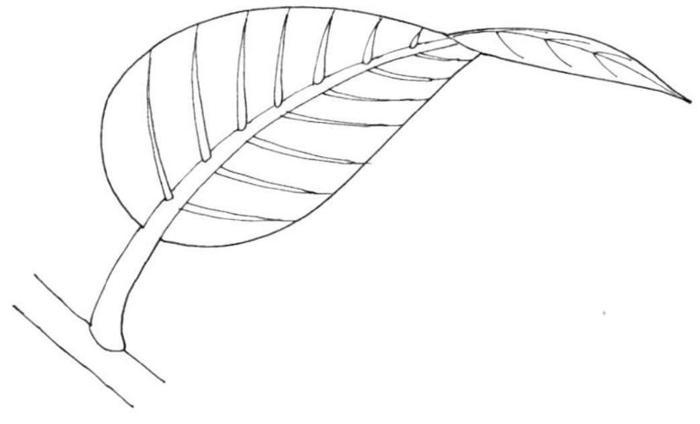

Another example of a naturally occurring structure is the compound eye of an insect, such as a fly.

All of the small parts of this a compound eye are held together by a geodesic dome-like structure on the outer surface of the eye. This structure is rigid and stable to support the cornea. This support allows the eye to function properly. Buckminister Fuller designed geodesic dome buildings, based on the structure of an insect's compound eye structure.

Animals construct structures for shelter (e.g., spider web, beaver dam). Honeybees use design maximization when they produce honeycombs. The honeycomb is designed to store the most honey possible within a minimal wall surface.

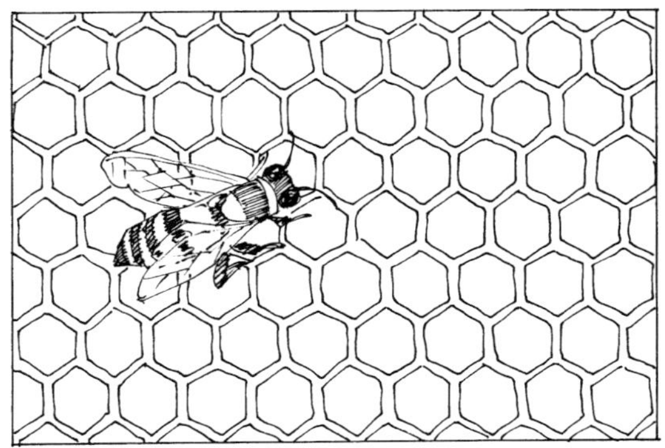

Many of nature's structures can be classified as shell, frame, or solid structures. For example:

Shell structures: wasp nest, cocoon, clam shell

Frame structure: skeleton, spider web, bird's nest

Solid structures: cave, beaver dam (built with solid pieces of strong material, trees)

Materials

- mural paper
- markers
- thumb tacks
- visuals and samples of a variety of nature's structures, such as:

- various plant leaves
- turtle shell
- blown up diagram of a fly's eye, or any compound eye
- honeycomb
- beaver dam diagram or model
- clam shells
- skeletons (models or visuals)
- wasp nest
- cocoon

Note: Senior school biology teachers, or university instructors, may have samples that can be borrowed for class use.

Activity

Display visuals and other examples of natural structures. As a class, discuss each item, focusing on the design. Use the Background Information for Teachers to support discussion and provide further detail.

Have the students reflect on the previous lesson on classifying structures. Ask:

- Do you see any similarities between nature's structures and the human-made shell, frame, and solid structures we studied?

Through discussion, have students identify similar features among natural and human-made structures.

Divide the class into pairs and provide each pair of students with an activity sheet (3.2.1). Have the students work together to brainstorm and classify structures found in nature. These can be recorded on the activity sheet. Also encourage the students to gather visuals that represent these structures.

Note: Provide time in class for students to begin this task, but also provide opportunities for computer and library research so that the students can expand their knowledge.

Have each pair of students present their findings to the class. As students provide examples, record a summative list of shell, solid, and frame structures found in nature. Also create a bulletin board display by having the students post their examples on mural paper. Classify the examples on mural paper divided in three sections that classify the images.

Activity Sheet

Directions to students:

Record examples of shell structures, frame structures, and solid structures found in nature.

Date: ______________________   **Name:** ______________________

Identifying and Classifying Nature's Structures

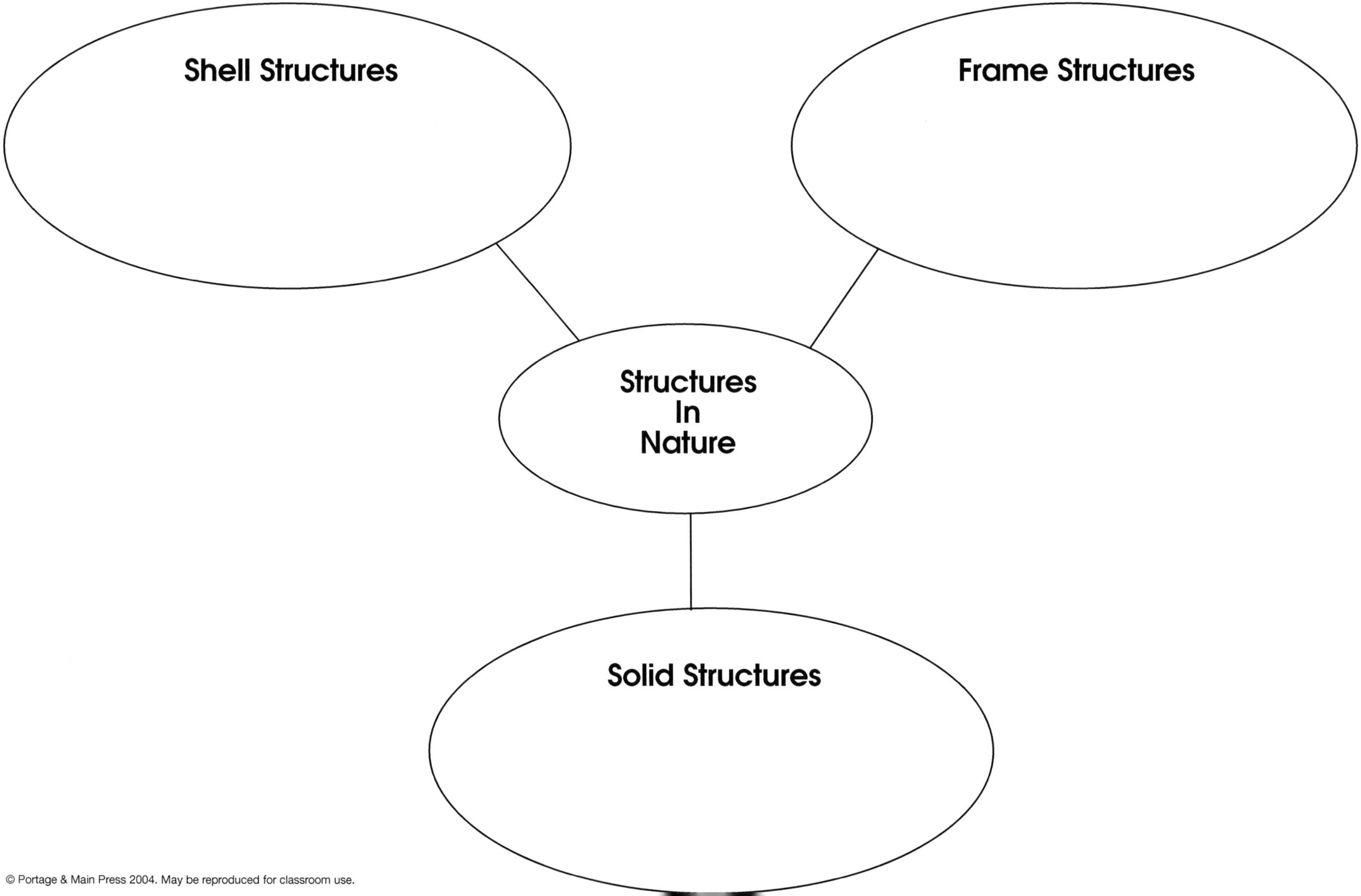

Shell Structures

Frame Structures

Structures
In
Nature

Solid Structures

3 | Centre of Gravity

Background Information for Teachers

Generally, when we refer to the force of *gravity*, we are referring to the *pull* or attraction that Earth exerts on an object. This force is responsible for the *weight* of bodies on Earth. Gravitational force acts between objects, depending not only on the *mass* of each object but on the distance between the objects. For example, there is greater gravitational force acting between Earth and an object sitting on its surface than there is between Earth and that same object at a great distance away. English physicist Isaac Newton developed the theory of Universal Gravitation; based on observations of planets and their orbits around the sun.

Gravity is not a constant value across the universe. In fact, the gravitational pull on the moon is only 1/6 of that on earth. This is because the mass of Earth is so much greater than the mass of the moon. The greater the mass of an object, the greater its gravitational pull.

All objects are attracted to Earth due to gravity. Every object is made up of small particles that are each pulled towards Earth with an equal force. Earth's pull on an object consists of equal, parallel forces, each acting on all the particles that make up the object. These forces form the *net force* known as the *force of gravity*. This force will act on the object through a point called the *centre of gravity*.

The position of the centre of gravity of a structure will affect the structure's *stability*. *Stability* refers to a structure's capacity to remain standing and undamaged when acted upon by forces. The stability of a structure depends on the types of materials, how they are used, and how the stucture's mass is distributed. For example, when building a tower out of blocks, the centre of gravity must remain within the area of the tower's *base of support* to allow the tower to remain standing. If the centre of gravity is outside the area of the tower's base, the structure will topple over.

Materials

- chart paper
- markers
- rulers
- overhead projector
- cardboard
- scissors
- golf clubs
- hockey sticks
- pennies
- tape
- metre sticks
- non-interlocking blocks e.g. planko blocks, Jenga, or dominoes (large quantity for building towers)
- illustration of the Leaning Tower of Pisa (included. Make an overhead copy of this sheet.) (3.3.4)

Activity: Part One

Divide the class into pairs, and provide each pair of students with Activity Sheet A (3.3.1), a ruler, cardboard, and scissors. Challenge the students to try to balance the ruler only one finger. While one partner does so, have the other identify where the finger was placed along the length of the ruler. Ask:

- Does the position of your finger relative to the length of the ruler matter?

- Why does it matter?

- Would the position of your finger be different if you were to balance the ruler on a paper towel roll instead of your finger?

Have the students place their finger towards one end of the ruler and observe what happens.

As a class, discuss students' understanding of gravity. During this discussion, use the Background Information for Teacher to provide explanations and answer questions. Ask:

- What force was pulling on the ends of the ruler? (gravitational force)

- How does gravity act? (it pulls objects toward the centre of the Earth)

- What would happen to all objects on Earth if there was no gravitational force?

- Where does is there less gravitational force? (outerspace, the moon's surface)

Have students continue investigating gravitational force by working with their partners to complete Activity Sheet A (3.3.1).

Note: Students will find that the ruler balances when they hold their finger halfway along its length. The centre of gravity for each object that they test will be at the centre of the object.

Activity Sheet A

Note: This is a two-page activity sheet.

Directions to students:

Use the activity sheet to record your investigations with gravitational force.

Activity: Part Two

Note: Before beginning this activity, make several unbalanced "teeter-totter" devices by taping a different number of pennies to each end of a ruler.

Divide the class into working groups. Provide each group with a golf club, a hockey stick, and a metre stick.

Have the groups examine the golf club. Ask:

- Do you think you could balance the golf club on your finger, in the same way you balanced the ruler? Why or why not?

- If you were able to do it, where do you think the balance point on the golf club would be? Why?

Have the students work together in their groups to investigate the centre of gravity of irregular objects. Provide them with Activity Sheet B (3.3.2), and have them record their results as they complete their investigations.

Note: The centre of gravity of these irregular objects will not be at the centre of the object, but will be closer to the object's heavier end. As such, the balancing of these objects will be more difficult than balancing the ruler.

When all groups have completed the investigations and activity sheet (3.3.2), review their results.

Activity Sheet B

Directions to students:

Complete the chart provided to explain the location of the centre of gravity of irregularly shaped and weighted objects. Select one object of your choice to include in this investigation.

Note: Students may select items found in the classroom, personal items, or items from home.

Activity: Part Three

This activity is intended to demonstrate that changes in the location of a structure's centre of gravity affect the structure's stability. Through an investigation of tower construction, students will learn that the wider the base of the tower, the taller the tower can be built.

Divide the class into working groups. Provide each group with blocks and a metre stick. Explain to students that they are going to investigate tower construction and stability.

Provide each group with Activity Sheet C (3.3.3). Have the students use the sheet to guide the investigation and to record their observations

This activity reinforces the concepts of stability and centre of gravity and the relationship between them. After the investigation, ask:

- Which towers were more stable, those with narrow bases or wide bases? (wide)

- Why do you think this is so? (the centre of gravity must be maintained within the area of the base, so if the base if larger, there is more stability).

- At what point did your narrow towers collapse? (when the centre of gravity was outside the base of the tower)

Encourage students to use the terms *stability* and *centre of gravity* during this discussion.

Apply this investigation to a real-life example. Display the overhead illustration of the Leaning Tower of Pisa (3.3.4). Ask:

- How does the leaning tower of Pisa stay standing, despite its obvious lean?

Encourage students to use their conceptual knowledge to explain this phenomenon. Explain that the reason the tower has not fallen over is because the centre of gravity still lies over the base of the structure.

Activity Sheet C

Directions to students:

Complete this activity sheet during the construction of your towers.

Extensions

- Leaning Tower of Pisa models are available to purchase at local stores or online. Students can also construct their own models using interlocking blocks.

- Research and discuss how concepts of stability, balance, and centre of gravity are used in sports. For example, in football, linemen use these concepts in their stance to help prevent opposing players from pushing them over. In volleyball, a player considers these concepts when preparing to bump the ball without losing balance. In gymnastics, the gymnast uses the concept to balance on her hands on the balance beam.

- Invite a guest speaker such as an athlete, or the physical education teacher into the classroom to discuss the diverse ways in which the concepts of stability, balance, and centre of gravity are used in sports.

Assessment Suggestions

Observe students as they work together in their groups in the tower construction competition. Focus specifically on each student's ability to work collaboratively with the group. Use the Cooperative Skills Teacher Assessment sheet on page 21 to record results.

Also have students complete a Cooperative Skills Self-Assessment sheet on page 23 to reflect on their ability to work together.

Date: ________________   Name: ________________

Centre of Gravity

1. Draw a labelled diagram to show where you had to place your finger to balance the ruler.

2. What force was pulling on the ends of the ruler?

____

3. Your finger, pushing up on the ruler, counteracted the pull of gravity only when the force of gravity was divided equally on either side of the ruler. Draw two diagrams to illustrate the forces when the ruler was balanced, and when the ruler was not balanced.

Balanced   **Not Balanced**

4. The balancing point you found with the ruler is called the centre of gravity. Draw a 10 cm circle on the cardboard provided and cut it out. If you were to try to balance this circle on your finger as you did with the ruler, predict where the centre of gravity would be. Draw a diagram in the space below.

Prediction: ____

____

Diagram:

Test your prediction. Record your observations.

____

____

5. Cut out other geometric shapes and test them for their centre of gravity. Draw a diagram of your results in the spaces below.

| Triangle | Square | Rectangle |

Centre of Gravity of Irregular Objects

Balance each of the following objects on your finger. Record your observations on the chart below.

Object	Diagram (Be sure to identify where the centre of gravity is located.)	Distance (cm) (from the centre of gravity to the left end of the object)	Distance (cm) (from the centre of gravity to the right end of the object)
Hockey Stick			
Golf Club			
Your Chosen Object			

Centre of Gravity and Tower Stability

Build a tower with one block as the base. Continue adding blocks one at a time. Build the tallest possible tower.

1. How did you need to position the blocks in order to maintain the stability of the tower?

____

2. How tall was your tower before it collapsed? ________________

3. Why did the tower collapse?

____

Use your own design to build the tallest tower you can.

Draw a diagram of your plan.

4. How tall was this tower before it collapsed? ________________

5. Did this tower have more or less stability than you first tower?

____

6. Why was this tower more stable?

____

____

The Leaning Tower of Pisa

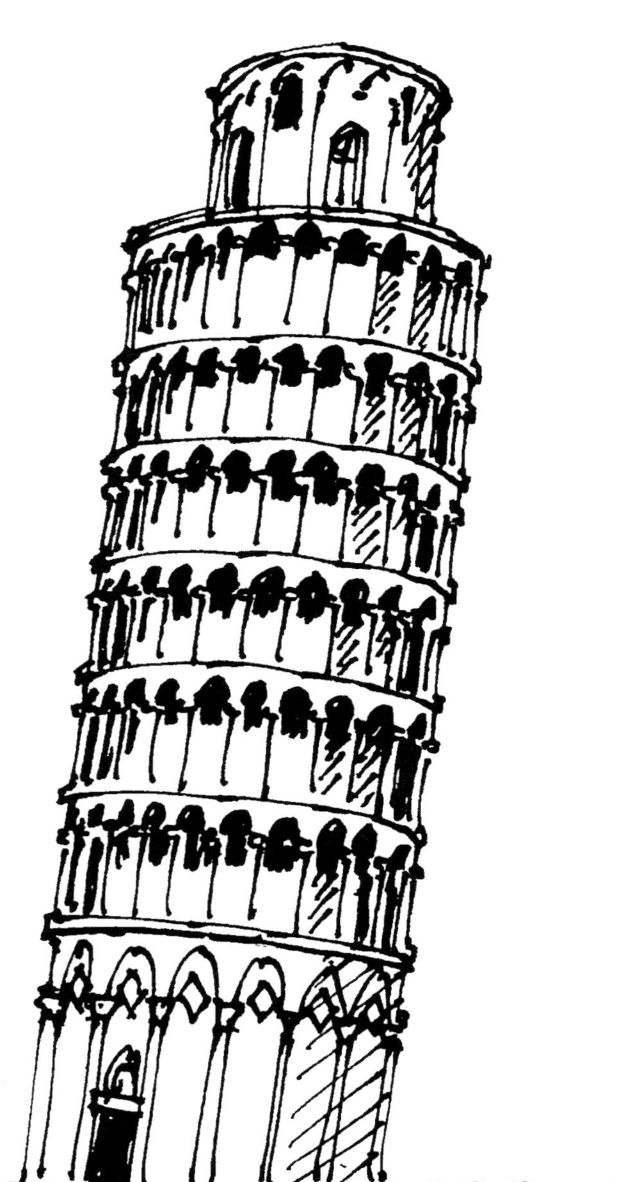

4 | Effects of Internal Forces

Background Information for Teachers

Force is the push or pull upon an object resulting from an object's *interaction* with another object. Whenever there is an interaction between two objects, there is a force upon each of the objects. When the interaction ceases, the two objects no longer experience the force. Forces only exist as a result of an interaction between objects.

This lesson focuses on several internal forces that act on structures:

Compression: the result of forces squeezing together

Tension: the pulling apart of a structure

Shear: the result of the forces acting in opposite directions of each other

Torsion: a twisting force

This lesson will introduce vectors. Vectors are arrows that are used to represent the direction and magnitude of a force. Each vector has two parts – a tip and a tail. The vector tip points in the direction of the force that is being applied. Vectors can be used in the following example:

A weak force is not enough to move the fridge. The vector is short.

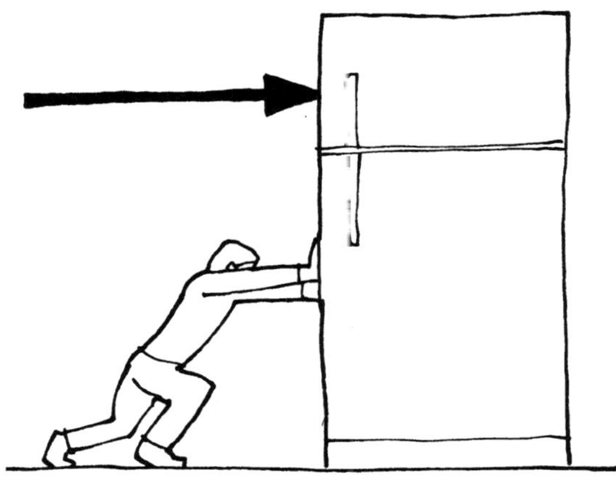

A stronger force is enough to move the fridge. The vector is longer.

Materials

- uncooked spaghetti
- safety goggles for each student
- chart paper
- markers
- metre sticks
- masking tape
- empty ice cream pails
- gram weights
- sheets of paper
- scissors
- container of water
- dish cloths
- elastic bands
- unsharpened pencils

Activity: Part One

Conduct the following demonstration to illustrate the terms tension and compression.

Safety Note: Be sure to use safety goggles during these activities.

▶

Take a handful of uncooked spaghetti and grip the strands between your hands. Start to flex the spaghetti. As you continue to flex the spaghetti, some of the strands will begin to snap. Ask:

- Where does the spaghetti start to snap first – the outer or inner strands, or both together?

Discuss this as students observe the demonstration. They will notice that the outer strands break first. Explain that these strands are being stretched or pulled apart by the force of tension. The strands on the inside are being squeezed or pushed together by the force of compression.

Record these terms on chart paper and, as a class, determine definitions for each. Introduce vectors as a means of representing the direction and strength of forces. Discuss ways in which these definitions can be represented using diagrams and force vectors, and include these with the definitions. For example:

Spaghetti Strands

Now provide each student with their own safety

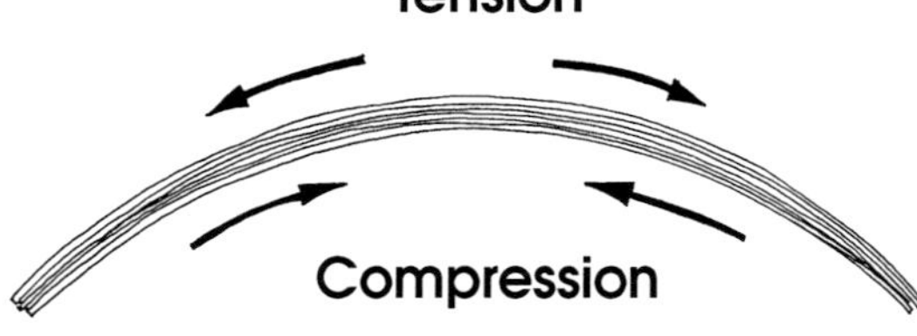

goggles and 5 or 6 strands of spaghetti. Have the students hold their spaghetti together tightly at both ends, then flex their spaghetti until it snaps. Encourage them to observe which strands snap first. Ask:

- Which strands were under tension?

- Which strands were under compression?

As a class, discuss other examples of compression and tension, such as:

Tension: stretching an elastic band, hanging clothes on a clothesline, blowing bubbles with gum

Compression: flattening cookie dough, making a snowball, chewing gum

Also discuss examples of tension and compression forces as they relate to built structures such as bridges.

Activity Sheet A

Directions for students:

Answer the questions related to tension and compression forces. Draw a diagram that has the forces clearly labelled (3.4.1).

Activity: Part Two

Divide the class into working groups and provide each group with a metre stick, an ice cream pail, masking tape, and gram weights. Have one student hold the meter stick on the edge of a table or desk, with 10 cm of the metre stick on the table and the remainder suspended freely in a horizontal position. Be sure that the metre stick is in a flat position, with the calibrations facing upward. Have another student hang the empty ice cream pail 20 cm from the end of the metre stick, and tape it in position. Have the other group members add weights and observe the metre stick. Ask:

- What happens to the shape of the meter stick as you add more weights? (the metre stick bends)

- Which part of the metre stick is experiencing the force of tension? (the top)

- Which part of the metre stick is experiencing a force of compression? (the underside)

Now have the groups hold the metre stick on its edge, so the graduations face towards the walls of the classroom. Have them place the empty ice pail 20 cm from the end of the metre stick and add weights in the same manner. Ask the students:

- What happens to the meter stick now? (less bending)

- How would you explain this difference?

Encourage the students to share their ideas. Explain that, in the first case when the meter stick was flat, there was perhaps .5 cm of wood to support the load or weights in the ice cream pail. By turning the meter stick on its edge, its strength was greater because of the increased thickness of the material used to support the load. The thicker the actual support the more structural strength it provides.

Record these new terms (load and strength) on chart paper and, as a class, determine working definitions. Also include examples and diagrams of each.

Activity Sheet B

Directions for students:

Answer the questions related to tension and compression forces in structures. Draw two diagrams of the meter sticks that have the forces clearly labelled (3.4.2).

Activity: Part Three

To demonstrate the force of shearing, provide each students with a piece of paper and scissors. First, have them tearing the paper in half, observing the forces that they use on the paper. Ask:

- What actions or forces acted on the paper? (opposite forces)

Explain to the class that this is an example of shear, which is the result of forces acting in opposite directions of one another. Now have the students examine the scissors and observe closely as they use the scissors to cut paper. Ask:

- How do the scissors use shear force? (the 2 blades move in opposite directions)

On chart paper, record the term shear and, as a class, determine a working definition. Include a diagram and any suggested examples.

Activity Sheet C

Directions for students:

Answer the questions related to shear forces (3.4.3).

Activity: Part Four

To demonstrate the force of torsion, soak a dishcloth in water and use a twisting motion to wring it out. Have the students describe the action you are using to remove the water from the cloth. Explain that this force is called torsion, which comes from the root word torque meaning "to twist or rotate."

On chart paper, record the term torsion and, as a class, determine a working definition. Include a diagram and suggested examples.

Note: Prior to distributing the elastic bands, it is a good idea to review safety precautions with the students. Indicate that the elastics are to be used for the investigation only, and should not be stretched or aimed at anyone, or anything. Be sure to collect all of the elastic bands after the activity is complete.

▶

Now provide students with an elastic band and unsharpened pencil. Have the students wrap one end of the elastic around their pencil while they hold the other end of the elastic. Have them twist the pencil several times to twist the elastic until it is taut. Ask:

- What do you think will happen when you release the pencil?

Have the students test their predictions by releasing their pencils (while still holding the elastic), and observing as the pencil spins and the elastic untwists. Explain that this is another working example of torsion, where the twisting force is applied to the elastic to make the pencil spin.

Review the definitions, examples, and diagrams of the four forces presented in this lesson (tension, compression, shear, and torsion). Explain to the class that these are examples of internal forces. Discuss this term and have students explain why it may be used to describe such forces.

Activity Sheet D

Directions to students:

Complete the activity sheet (3.4.4) to record you investigation with the force of torsion.

Extensions

- Broken bones are the result of a force applied to the bone such that it undergoes structural failure. Bones can be broken by compression force, or they may be broken as a result of torsion. Contact an orthopaedist (doctor who specializes in bone structure) to present to students.

- Chalk pieces can be used to demonstrate the breaking of bones. Striking a piece of chalk lightly with a hammer will result in a break, or a splinter.

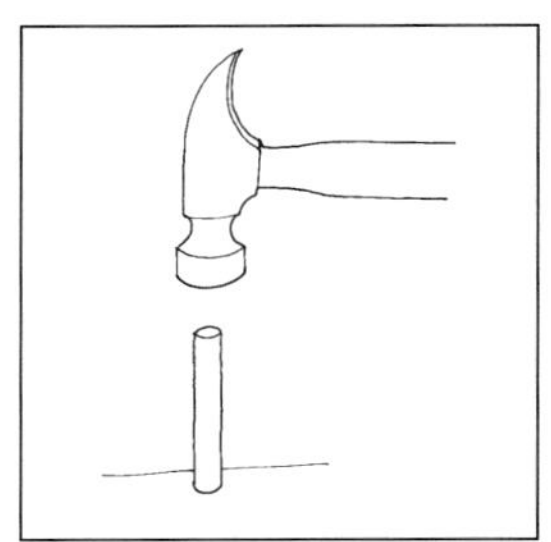 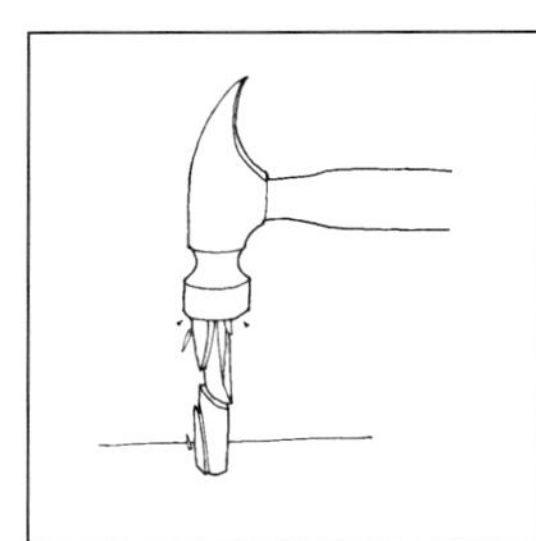

Twisting a piece of chalk will result in a spiral fracture.

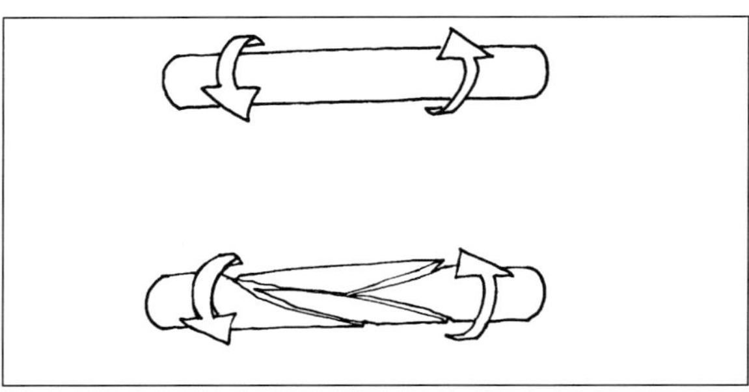

- Have the students investigate the use of torsion to build their own rubber band propelled vehicles. These can be designed and constructed by students or they may also be purchased as kits from toy and hobby stores.

Date: _______________________   Name: _______________________

Compression and Tension

Slowly bend the spaghetti strands until they begin to break.

Draw a diagram of the spaghetti. Label the top and bottom part of the bend, with arrows to show the direction of the forces acting within the spaghetti.

Write a brief description of what is happening.

____
____
____
____
____
____
____
____
____

Describe a real-life example of these forces at work:
Compression:

____

____

Tension:

____

____

Date: _________________________   Name: _______________________________

Compression and Tension
in Structures

Draw a labelled diagram with vector arrows to show the forces of compression and tension on the metre stick with the ice cream pail load.

Describe how the position of the metre stick affected the amount of bending that occurred. Why was this?

____

____

____

____

Shear Force

Draw labelled diagrams with vector arrows to show the force of shear. Describe each example.

Tearing paper

____

____

____

____

____

Cutting paper with scissors

____

____

____

____

____

Date: ______________________   Name: ______________________

Torsion

Describe the force of torsion:

____

____

____

An example of torsion is:

____

Draw a labelled diagram of the investigation with the elastic band and pencil. Include vector arrows.

Effects of External Forces on Structures

Background Information for Teachers

This lesson is based on the concept of *external forces*, and focuses on direction and magnitude of external forces like *gravity, friction, current*, and *buoyancy*.

For this lesson, it is necessary to be familiar with Newton's Laws of Motion.

Newton's first Law of Motion: Every object in a state of uniform motion tends to remain in that state of motion unless an external force is applied to it.

Newton's Second Law of Motion: The relationship between an object's mass, its acceleration, and the applied force is:

F = ma (Force = mass x acceleration)

Acceleration and force are vectors; in this law the direction of the force vector is the same as the direction of the acceleration vector.

Newton's Third Law of Motion: For every action there is an equal and opposite reaction. The third law is critical to understanding the balancing of forces.

The ability of a structure to withstand external forces is affected by its structural strength. With greater structural strength, the structure will be able to withstand external forces. The strength of a structure depends on the materials used and how the materials are arranged in a specific design. This lesson introduces students to the use of pairs of vector arrows to show balanced and unbalanced forces.

Materials

- overhead projector
- diagram titled, "The Effects of External Forces on Structures" (included. Make an overhead copy of this sheet) (3.5.1)
- non-permanent overhead pen
- diagram titled, "Force Vectors" (included. Copy and cut out the arrows) (3.5.3)
- scotch tape
- aquarium (or other similar large transparent container)
- water
- wind-up or battery-operated toy boat
- ruler
- pennies

Activity: Part One

Display the overhead diagram, "The Effects of External Forces on Structures" (3.5.1).

Focus on the diagram of the first house, without snow on its roof. Ask:

- How would we use arrows to indicate forces?

Demonstrate the use of vectors. Place a force vector, or arrow, pointing down indicating gravity, and a force vector pointing up for the force applied by the house itself. It is important to make the lengths of both force vectors the same. This shows that there is a balance of the forces.

Now look at the diagram of the second house, with snow on the roof. Ask:

- How would we use vectors to indicate forces?

Explain that although the snow adds extra weight to the roof, the structure is still able to balance this force and maintain its structural strength. As a result, the arrows are the same length to show that the forces are still balanced,

but both arrows are longer to show that the magnitude of the forces has increased. Draw the arrows as below:

Now display the diagram of the third house, with its roof collapsing under the weight of a larger amount of snow.

Ask:

- How would the vectors appear at the exact time that the roof collapsed?

- Would the arrows be the same length?

- Would the forces be balanced?

Explain that the force of gravity, in conjunction with the weight of the snow, causes the forces to become unbalanced. The snow force is greater than the possible supporting force of the structure. The house can no longer support this heavy load. As a result, the downward vector would be longer.

After the house collapses, the vector arrows are once again equal.

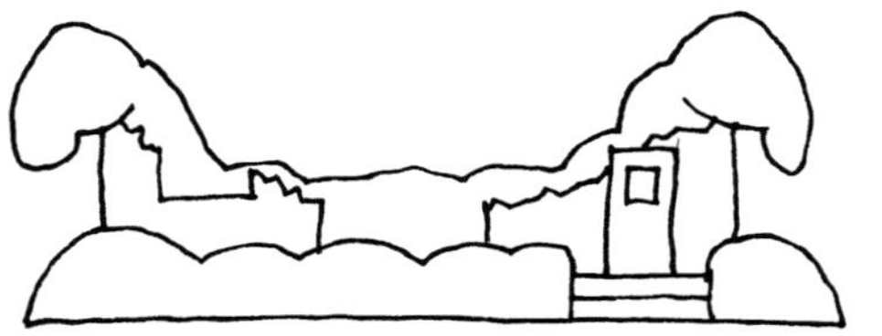

Have students complete Activity Sheet A (3.5.2).

Activity Sheet A

Directions for students:

In box A, draw a diagram of a house on a summer day. In box B, draw a diagram of the same house in the middle of winter when it is covered with snow. In box C, draw a diagram of the same house collapsed under the weight of a heavy snowfall. Include force vectors on both diagrams. Describe the differences between the diagrams.

Activity: Part Two

Fill the aquarium $2/3$ full with water. Place the toy boat in the water. Let it sit there for a moment. Tape the cut-out vector arrows on the side of the tank to represent gravity and buoyancy. The boat floats, which means that the gravity and the buoyancy forces are balanced, so the arrows you use should be the same length. This represents a scenario in which a boat would be sitting on a calm body of water. Ask:

- What would happen if there was a current in the water?

The responses will likely focus on the pushing of the boat backwards. When you are satisfied with the answers given by the students, place the "current" arrow on the outside of the aquarium, pointing towards the front of the boat. Water current is a force and requires a force vector to represent it. You can demonstrate current simply by pushing a ruler back and forth in the water. Ask:

- What would happen if you started the boat's motor?

The responses you will receive will note the forward motion of the boat. The motor "pushes" the boat. This force is called thrust. Take the "thrust" force vector and tape it on the fish tank

▶

5

pointing at the back of the boat. Wind up (or turn on) the boat and let it move around the tank to demonstrate the idea of thrust. The 'thrust arrow' is longer than the 'current' arrow, to represent a greater force that allows the boat to move forward against the current.

Distribute Activity Sheet B (3.5.4). This sheet requires the students to draw their own force vectors on the boat when the boat sinks under the added weight of too many passengers.

Once they have made their predictions, add pennies to the boat until it sinks. At this point, take the second, longer gravity vector arrow and attach it to the outside of the aquarium. The longer vector arrow signifies an increase in the magnitude of the force. The forces are unbalanced, so the boat sinks. The students will see this and can verify their work on Activity Sheet B (3.5.4).

Note: By adding enough pennies to the boat, you will accomplish two things. First, you will sink the boat; reminding students that the structure of the boat has a finite threshold where it will remain buoyant. Also, this incorporates the previous example with snow on the roof of the house. Too much snow, like too many pennies on the boat, will increase the force on the structure, causing it to collapse.

Activity Sheet B

Directions for students:

Complete the activity sheet (3.5.4) to record information about the effects of forces on floating boats.

Extension

- The extension activity sheet (3.5.5) provides an opportunity for students to draw their own examples that illustrate external forces. To help students open their minds to different examples, suggest that they consider what happens when:
  - someone drives onto a bridge in a truck that exceeds the bridge's weight restriction
  - leaves a patio umbrella open during a wind storm

The Effects of External Forces
On A House

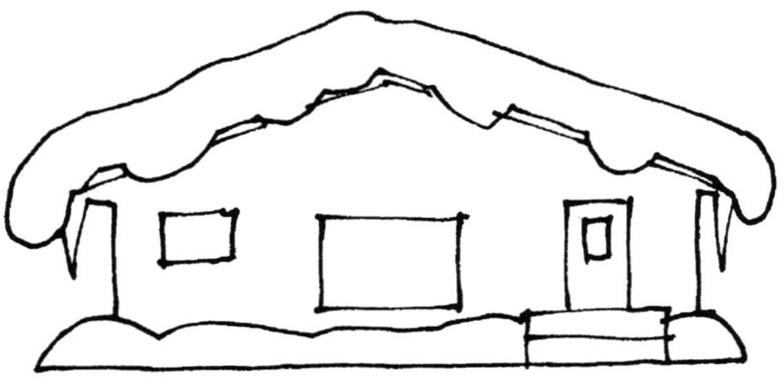

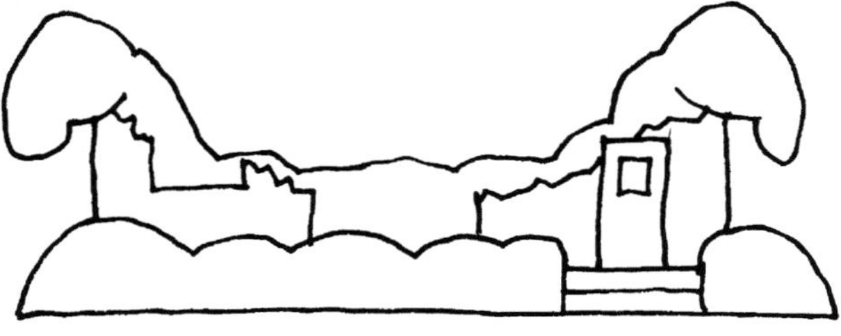

The Effects of External Forces on a House

A - House

B - Snow Covered House

C - Collapsing House

C - Collapsed House

Describe the differences between these diagrams, and explain your use of vector arrows.

____

____

____

Force Vectors

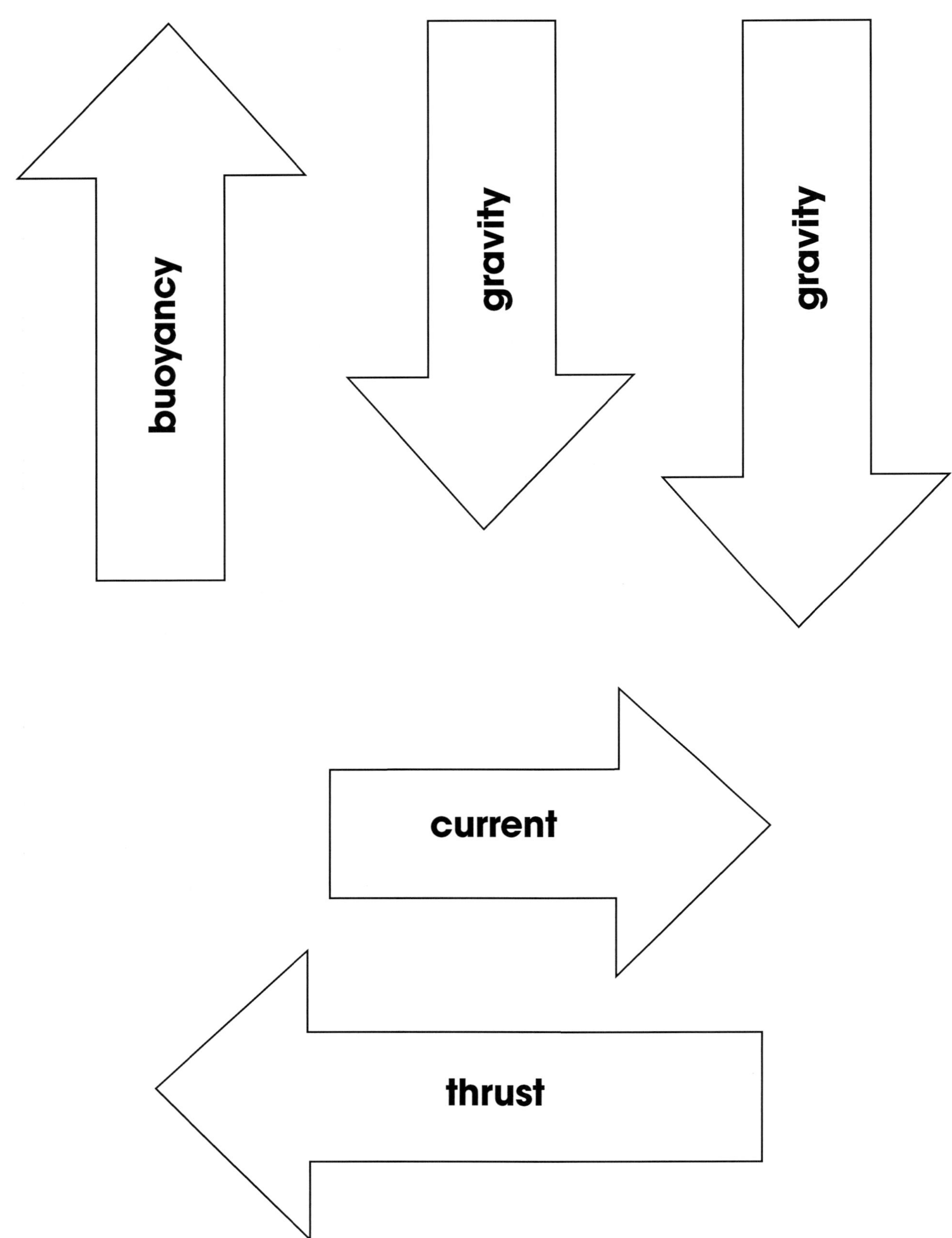

The Effects of External Forces
on a Boat

Draw a diagram of a boat with no passengers and label it with force vectors.

Draw a diagram of a boat sinking under the added weight of too many passengers, and label with force vectors.

Date: ______________________   Name: ______________________________

Effects of External Forces
on Structures

1. Draw a diagram and label it to show the external forces acting on a structure.

Balanced Forces:	Unbalanced Forces:

2. Describe this example:

____

____

____

____

____

6 | Stress, Fatigue, and Failure

Background Information for Teachers

This lesson is based on the NOVA website, "Building on Ground Zero." The site documents the collapse of the World Trade Center Towers after the terrorist attacks of September 11, 2001.

The website **http://www.pbs.org/wgbh/nova/wtc/** includes features such as a video preview, an article on the World Trade Center's engineering features, and an audio slide show detailing the events from impact to collapse of the towers.

Materials

- access to a computer, preferably with classroom display features (or have students work at computer stations)
- chart paper
- markers
- poster board
- sketch paper

Activity: Part One

Explore the website as a class, focusing on each feature and discussing related concepts. Consider the following sequence of studies:

- Watch the "Video Preview," and discuss students' perceptions and thoughts about the towers' collapse.

- Read and discuss the article "Towers of Innovation." Discuss the engineering and safety features of the World Trade Center.

- Watch the "Impact to Collapse" audio slide-show. Have students use Activity Sheet A (3.6.1) to create a storyboard depicting the events leading to the collapse of the towers.

Activity Sheet A

Directions to students:

Use the storyboard sheet to illustrate and describe the events leading to the collapse of the World Trade Center Towers (3.6.1).

Activity: Part Two

Explore the interactive demonstration "The Structure of Metal." Discuss possible explanations for the collapse of the towers. Ask:

- What internal and external forces were acting on the towers?

On chart paper, record the terms *structural stress, structural fatigue,* and *structural failure.* Challenge students to suggest definitions of each term. Use their ideas and other sources to determine accurate definitions. Record these on chart paper.

Activity: Part Three

Listen to the audio report "The Tallest Tower." In it, an engineer describes the features of a skyscraper in Shanghai. Compare the features of this building to those of the World Trade Center Towers.

Activity: Part Four

Divide the class into working groups. Provide the groups with sketch paper, poster board, and markers. Have students use the information gathered in this lesson to determine reasons for the collapse of the towers.

Have each group design a poster that presents the students' ideas. They can design their posters on sketch paper, present their rough drafts to you for feedback, then create their posters.

Have each group present its poster to the class, and discuss the ideas featured.

Extension

Have students investigate bridge collapses featured on the website<http://www.ketchum.org/bridgecollapse.html>. This website presents four different bridge disasters caused by structural stress, fatigue, and failure.

Have pairs of students select one disaster to research and present to the class. The extension activity sheet (3.6.2) provides guiding questions to compete the research.

Why the Towers Fell - A Story Board

<table>
<tr><td>1.</td><td>2.</td><td>3.</td></tr>
<tr><td>4.</td><td>5.</td><td>6.</td></tr>
</table>

Bridge Disasters

1. What is the name of the structure being researched?

   ____

2. Where was the structure located?

   ____

3. When was the structure built?

   ____

4. Draw a diagram of the structure prior to the disaster.

5. When did the disaster occur?

   ____

6. Explain what caused the disaster. Be sure to think about and describe the effects of internal and external forces.

   ____

   ____

7. Describe the impact of this disaster.

   ____

   ____

8. Lessons for the future: What was learned from this disaster?

   ____

   ____

   ____

7 | Investigating Beam Bridges

Background Information for Teachers

This lesson involves students conducting a preliminary investigation followed by a more comprehensive experiment to determine whether the magnitude of the weight needed to cause structural failure of a beam bridge differs at various points along the plane of the bridge. The purpose of this lesson is twofold - construct the bridge, and analyze it for points of stability and stress induced failure.

Bridges are of two general types: fixed and movable. Fixed bridges are usually classified by their basic shapes or components such as arches, trusses, beams, girders, and cables. This experiment uses fixed bridge design.

Movable bridges are more complex structures and have specialized mechanical operations for opening a portion of the bridge

For the purpose of this lesson, being familiar with a *beam bridge* is all that is necessary. Discussion about the other three main bridge shapes will be addressed in the next lesson.

A *beam*, or *girder bridge* is the most simple and inexpensive bridge to construct. In its most basic and simplistic form, the *beam bridge* is merely a horizontal beam that is supported by pillars. It can be as simple as a log crossing a river, or wood planks on a footbridge. Beam bridges are often short in length, and are designed to support a large array of loads. The difficulty in making a long beam bridge is the increased number of supporting pillars needed to support the structure. The beam itself must be strong enough to support its own weight, as well as the weight of any load applied to the bridge. Automobile traffic is a good example of such a load. When a load pushes down on the beam, the beam's top edge is compressed while the force of tension stretches the bottom edge.

On average, most beam bridges are less than 80 metres long. The longest beam bridge, the "Lake Ponchartrain Causeway" in Louisiana, is almost 38.4 km long and has chain links holding over 3,700 pieces together. In this activity, students will identify the relationship between beam bridge length and the number of supporting pillars needed.

Materials

- stack of books (recommend 6-10 books per working group)
- pennies
- 30 cm flexible plastic rulers
- small buckets with handles (these can be made from yogurt containers. Punch 3 holes in the sides to attach string or wire. A 3-hole handle will be more stable.)
- uncooked spaghettini (thinnest noodles)
- weights (washer, nuts, or other similar objects. If pennies are used, at least $10 worth will be required. Slightly heavier weights would reduce quantities required.)
- elastic bands
- graph paper (included. Make a copy for each student.) (3.7.3)

Activity: Part One

Divide the class into working groups and provide each group with a stack of books and a 30 cm flexible plastic ruler. Have the groups position the ruler with each end on top of a stack of books, with 5 cm of the ruler set on top of each stack. This apparatus is a simple model of a beam bridge. Explain that a beam bridge, or girder bridge is the most simple and inexpensive bridge to construct. In its most basic and simplistic form, the beam bridge is merely a horizontal beam that is supported by pillars. In this activity, the stacks of books represent the pillars, and the ruler represents the beam. The weight of the beam and anything on top of the

Hands-On Science • Grade 7

beam, pushes straight down on the support pillars. The beam itself must be strong enough to support its own weight, as well as the weight of any load applied to the bridge. Automobile traffic is a good example of such a load. When a load pushes down on the beam, the beam's top edge is compressed while the bottom edge is stretched by the force of tension.

With the ruler resting on the stacks of books, have the students hang the bucket from the mid-point of the bridge and begin adding pennies to the bucket. Ask:

- In what direction is the force being applied? (downward on the beam ruler)

- How is the addition of pennies affecting the beam bridge?

Explain that adding the pennies changes the magnitude of the force on the beam bridge. As the load increases, the magnitude of force increases. Record this term on chart paper, along with a working definition.

Have the groups keep track of the number of pennies needed for the ruler to begin bending, as well as the number of pennies needed for the entire ruler to give way and fall to the ground. What the students will observe is that it takes a few pennies to start the ruler bending, but it will take many more pennies to make the bridge collapse.

Now have the students push the books further apart, so that the ruler beam spans 25 cm between the book stacks. Ask:

- Do you think that the bridge will be more or less stable now? Why?

Have the groups test their predictions and observe that the increase in beam length will decrease the strength of the beam (ruler), causing is to buckle sooner and with a lighter load. Ask:

- Why did the ruler bend and collapse sooner when the length of the beam was increased?

Explain that although the beam was shorter in the first case, its strength was greater because the supporting pillars were closer together, giving the beam more support.

Have the students complete questions 1-3 on Activity Sheet A (3.7.1).

Activity: Part Two

With the same apparatus, focus students' attention to the point and plane of application of the force on the ruler beam bridge. Ask:

- In the last activity, where was the load positioned? (at the centre of the ruler)

Explain that this is the point of application of the force. Record this term on chart paper, along with a definition and diagram. Ask:

- Do you think that changing the position of the load will affect the structural strength of the beam?

Discuss students' responses, then have them test their predictions by investigating what happens when this point of application is modified. Have the groups place the bucket 5 cm from one of the pillars, and secure it in place with masking tape. Ask:

- Do you think the bridge will be more or less stable now?

Have the groups test their predictions by adding pennies until the beam collapses. Students will observe that the placement of load in terms of its location on the structure is a major contributor to structural fatigue, tension, and stress. Placement of the load closer to each supporting pillar increases the strength of the overall structure. The weakest point of a beam bridge is the middle.

▶

Now focus on the direction of the force. Ask:

- At what angle is the force being applied? (at a right angle, directly down on the beam in a vertical manner)

Explain that this is referred to as the plane of application. Record this term and, as a class, determine a working definition. Include a diagram and examples.

Have the students complete Activity Sheet A (3.7.1).

Activity Sheet A

Directions to students:

Use the activity sheet to record information about the beam bridge that you construct.

Activity: Part Three

In this activity, students will use the experimental procedure to investigate beam bridges. Divide the class into working groups and provide each group with Activity Sheet B (3.7.2), uncooked spaghettini, elastic bands, a small bucket, and weights. Explain the task as follows:

1. Construct a simple spaghettini beam bridge by bundling 10 pieces of spaghettini with an elastic.
2. Position the bridge so that it spans 2 desks, with 5 cm of beam supported on each pillar.
3. Measure the length of the bridge, then hang the bucket at the mid-point on the bridge.
4. Add weights to the bucket until the bridge collapses.
5. Build another identical bridge. Hang the bucket 5 cm from one pillar. Add weights until the bridge collapses.
6. Continue building bridges and testing them to find the strongest and weakest points along the beam. Hang the bucket at each 5 cm intervals along the beam.

Focus students' attention on the activity sheet. In their groups, have them discuss the Purpose of the experiment and formulate a question to record on the sheet. Next, have the students discuss their Hypotheses and record them. The Materials and Method sections of the sheet can also be completed prior to conducting the experiment.

Provide plenty of time for the groups to experiment and complete the activity sheet. Following the investigation, have each group share their Results, Conclusions, and Applications.

Note: The conclusion should explain the relationship between the magnitude of weight and point of application, as well as identify the strongest and weakest points along the plane of the bridge.

Finally, have students graph the results of their experiment, using the graph paper included with this lesson (3.7.3). Review the criteria of a correct graph prior to conducting this activity:

- appropriate title
- labelled axes
- accurate calibrations
- clear data presentation

As an alternative, have students create computer-generated graphs of their results.

Activity Sheet B

Directions for students:

Use the activity sheet to record the spaghettini beam bridge experiment (3.7.2).

Extension

- Have students construct beam bridges from other materials such as craft foam, styrofoam strips, balsa wood, wooden skewers, straws, or twigs. They can then investigate the effects of changes in the magnitude, and position of loads.

Assessment Suggestion

Assess students' graphs using the criteria
discussed in Activity: Part Two. List these criteria
on the Rubric on page 19, and record results.

Date: _________________   **Name:** _____________________________

Beam Bridges

1. What is a beam bridge?

____

____

2. Diagram your beam bridge model.

3. When the bucket was placed in the centre of the beam, how many pennies did it take before the beam collapsed?

____

4. When the bucket was placed at one end of the beam, how many pennies did it take before the beam collapsed?

____

5. What is the relationship between the position of the load and the distance from the supporting pillars?

____

____

____

Beam Bridge Experiment

Purpose: ____

____

Hypothesis: ____

____

Materials: ____

____

Method: ____

____

____

____

____

Results: ____

____

____

____

Conclusion: ____

____

____

Application: ____

____

____

____

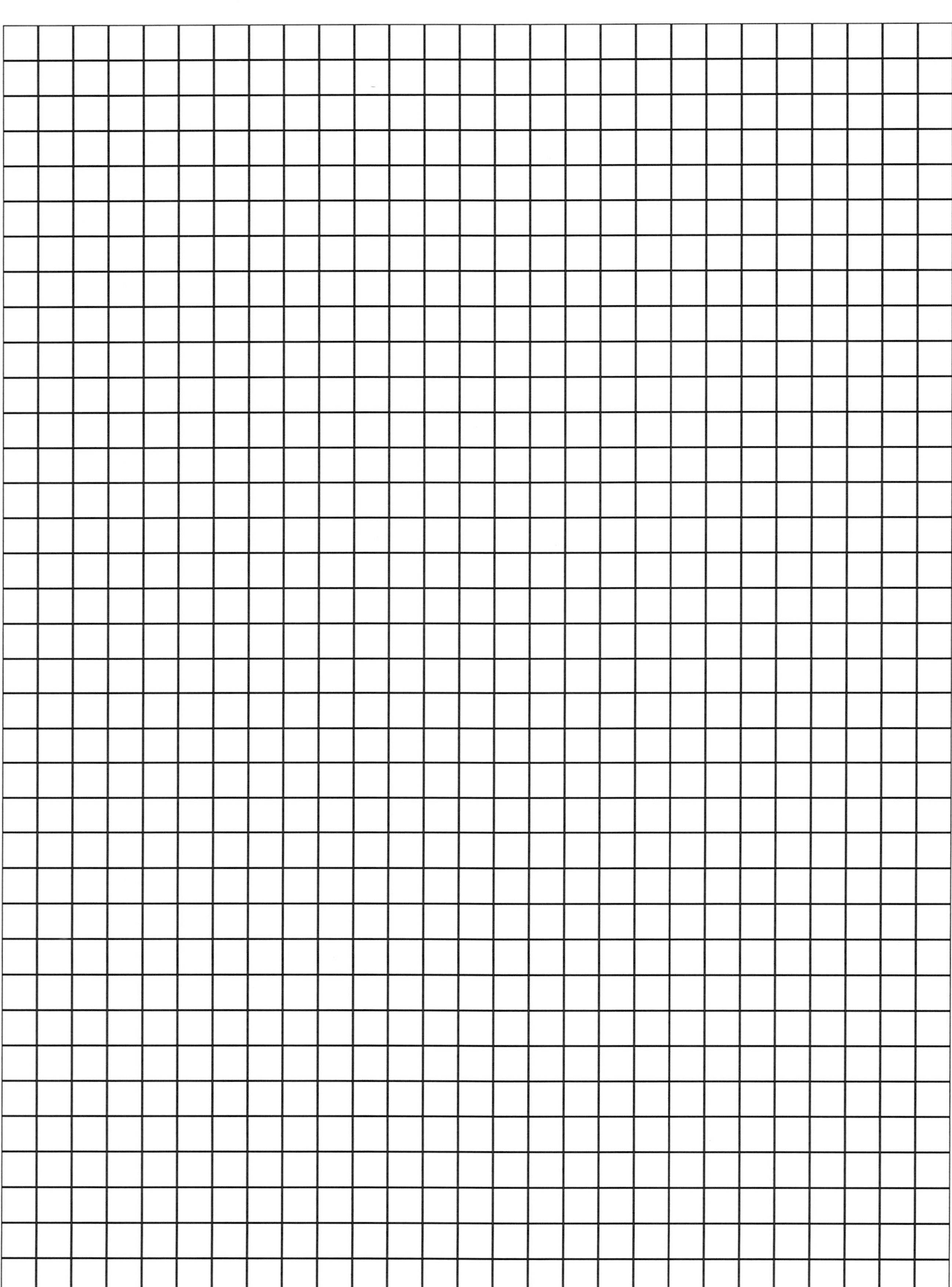

Types of Bridges – Structural Forms and Components

Background Information for Teachers

This lesson introduces the students to the different types of supports used for different structures. In the previous lesson, the students learned about a *beam bridge*. Beam bridges have at least two support *pillars* – one at each end of the bridge. This lesson allows you to identify the other types of supports – including *arches, trusses and struts, suspension,* and *cables*. Below is a brief description of each type of support structure.

Beam bridges consist of a beam or girder spanning the gap between two pillars.

This is a simple diagram of a pillar-supported *beam bridge*.

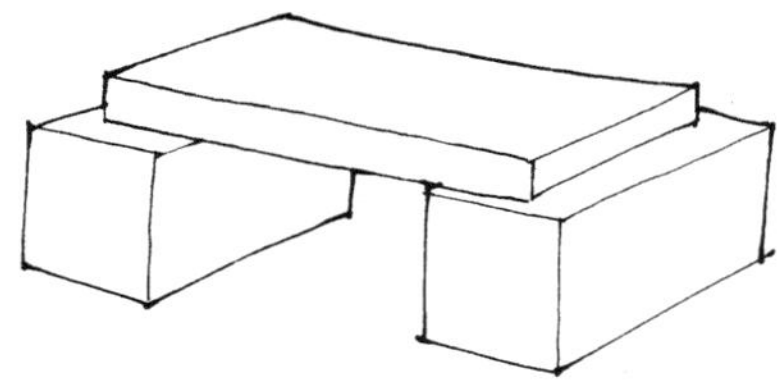

This is a diagram of the forces acting on a *beam bridge*.

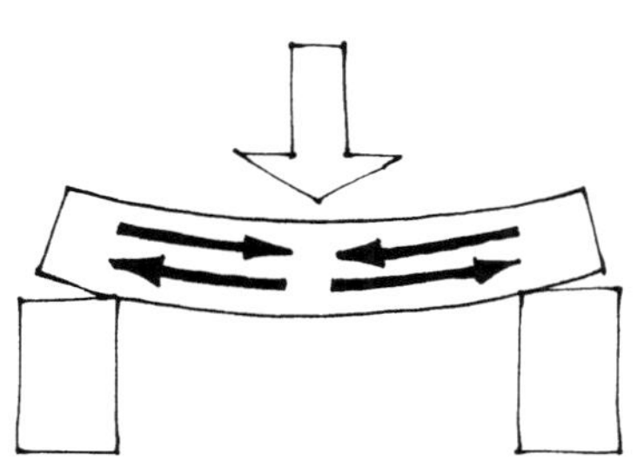

Some examples of beam bridges are:

- Confederation Bridge, linking Prince Edward Island and New Brunswick (Although the Confederation Bridge also incorporates some arches, it is primarily a beam bridge.)

- Lake Ponchartrain Causeway, Louisiana.

Arches: Arches are among the oldest forms of structural support. Unlike the straight pillars that support a beam bridge, arches are curved. The arch carries the weight outward along the curve to the supports at each end, called abutments. The abutments carry the load and stop the bottom of the bridge from spreading out.

This is a simple diagram of an arch supported bridge.

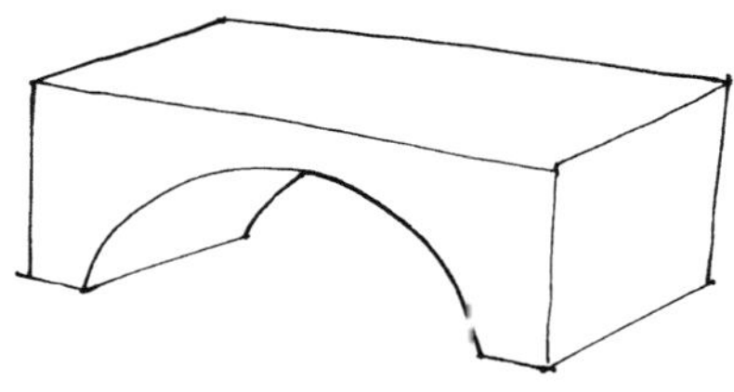

The arrows represent the forces present on an arch supported bridge.

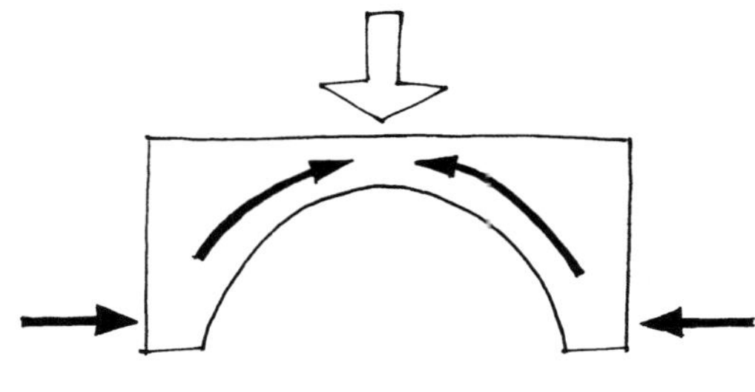

Some examples of arch bridges are:

- Garabit Viaduct, Massif Central, France
- Iron Bridge, Shropshire, England

Trusses and Struts: A *truss bridge* is similar to a beam bridge, but is much stronger. A truss is a structure composed of *members* connected together to form a rigid framework. A *member* is a load-carrying component of the structure. Most truss-supports consist of members interconnected in triangles. A *strut* is the structural member that connects the two main trusses together on a *truss bridge*. The struts work together with the overall lateral structural supports to resist lateral loads, such as those caused by wind. The trusses and struts themselves are straight, rigid pieces of material. This type of support prevents the twisting or swaying that both arch and beam bridges can experience under great stress (e.g., high wind, and earthquakes). A strut is a member of the framework that resists compression forces. A *tie* is a member of framework that resists being stretched (tension).

This is a simple diagram of a *truss bridge*.

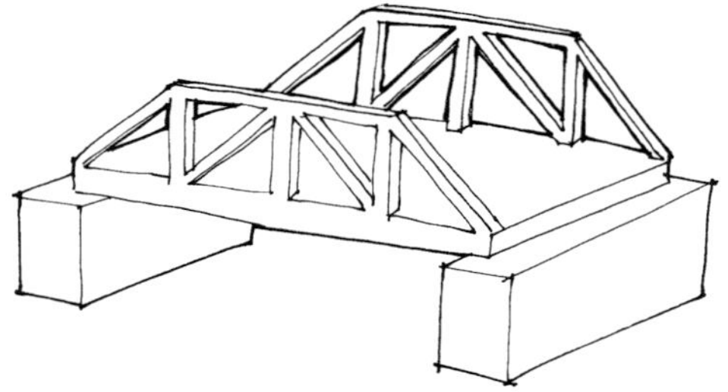

The arrows indicate the forces associated with this type of bridge.

Some examples of truss bridges are:

- Firth of Forth Bridge, Scotland
- Quebec Bridge over the St. Lawrence River

Suspension: This type of support holds the structure in place from above. The bridge is suspended from huge cables that extend from one end of the bridge to the other. The cables pass over high towers placed immediately above the pillars and are secured at either end of the bridge at points called *anchorages*. Suspension bridges can be quite long. Unlike load bearing pillars or arches, the cables carry most of the weight of the bridge. The anchorages are usually imbedded in either solid rock or massive concrete blocks. Inside the anchorages, the cables are spread over a large area to evenly distribute the load, and to prevent the cables from breaking free.

This is a diagram of a suspension bridge:

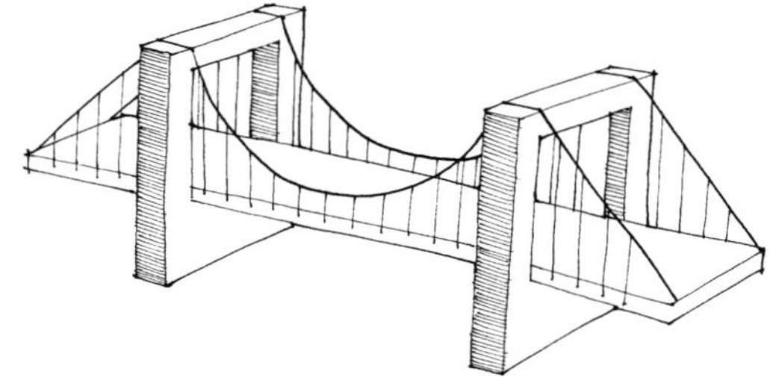

The arrows indicate the forces associated with this type of bridge.

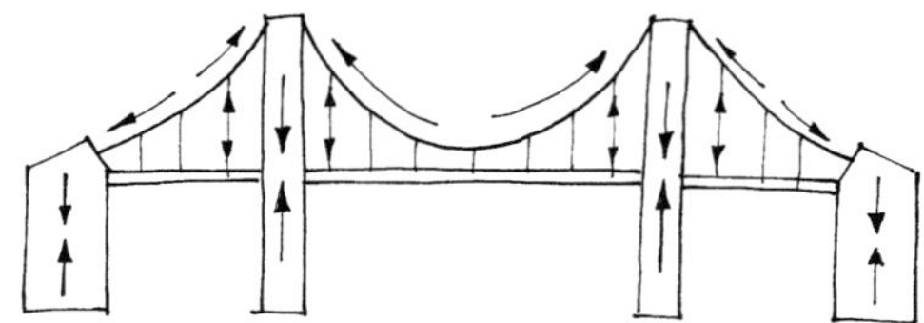

Some examples of suspension bridges are:

- Lion's Gate Bridge, Vancouver
- Golden Gate Bridge, San Francisco

8

Materials

- cardboard
- scissors
- books or other heavy objects
- tongue depressors
- butterfly fasteners
- hammer
- nails
- thread
- string
- rope
- variety of pictures of bridges
- photocopied pictures of bridges (cut these sheets in half to show only one half of the bridge structures)
- art paper
- sketching pencils
- glue

Activity: Part One

Divide the class into working groups and provide each group with cardboard, scissors, and several books. Have the students cut a piece of cardboard roughly 3 cm wide and 30 cm long.

Have the students gently bend this strip into a curve or arch, and place it on the desk so it resembles an arch.

Next, have the groups gently press down on the top of the arch. Ask?

- What happened to the arch? (ends move apart as the curve moves downward)

- What is this an example of? (compression)

Now, have the students place piles of books at each end of the curved cardboard arch. Instruct them to gently press down again on the top of the arch, and observe what happens.

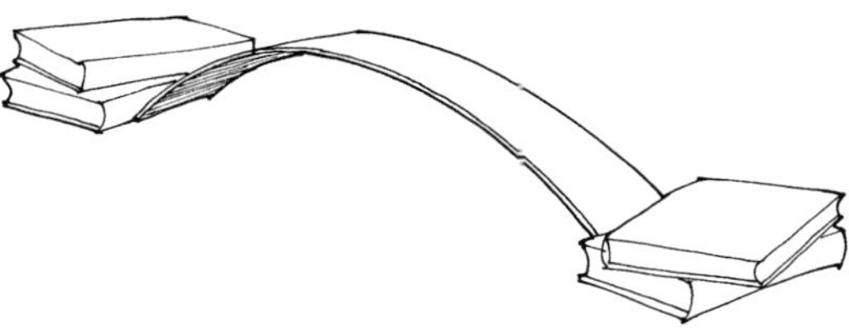

Explain that the arch can support more weight now that the ends are anchored in place with the piles of books. This is a model of an arch supported bridge. The books act as abutments at each end of the bridge structure and prevents the arch from spreading or f attening out. Each part of the arch support is under compression when there is load on the structure. Engineers and bridge designers select materials that can remain strong under pressure. The Romans used stone to make arch suport. Today, steel and pre-stressed concrete are used.

As a class, discuss any arch supports with which the students are familiar. Challenge the students to look for examples of arch supports in their local community, and in pictures of structures throughout this unit.

Have the students record their observations on the first section of the activity sheet (3.8.1).

Activity: Part Two

This demonstration illustrates the basics of truss support. Make a small hole in each end of the two toungue depressors, using a hammer and nail. Attach the tongue depressors together at one end using a butterfly fastener. At the other ends of the two tongue depressors, tie a piece of thread to each. (Alternately, cut notches on the outside edges at the botom of each tongue depressor, and tie the thread around.) Pull the tongue depressors apart gently, until the thread is taut. This is a model of a three-member truss.

▶

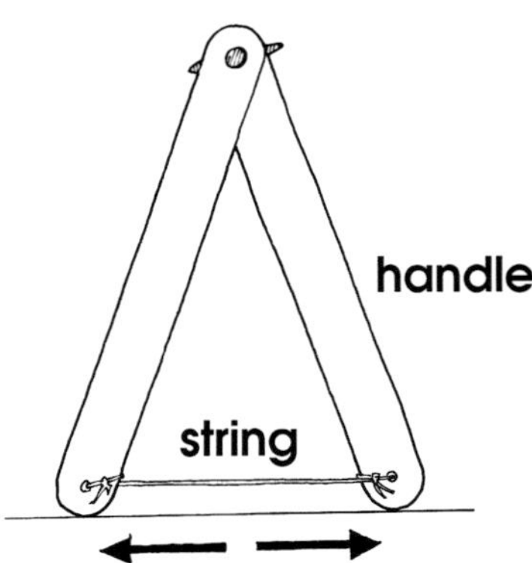

Display the model truss for the class, and explain that a *truss* is a structure composed of *members* that are connected together to form a framework. In this case, each tongue depressor and the thread are members, and carry the weight of the components of the structure. Most trusses consist of members that are interconnected in triangles.

Hold the model truss upright, with the thread component resting on a table top. With your finger, press down on the centre hinge, on the top of the truss. Ask:

- What happens to the string as I press down?

Explain that you are applying a *load* to the truss. The *load* is the force applied to the structure. As the load is applied, the string experiences tension, and the hinge experiences compression, as noted in the diagram below.

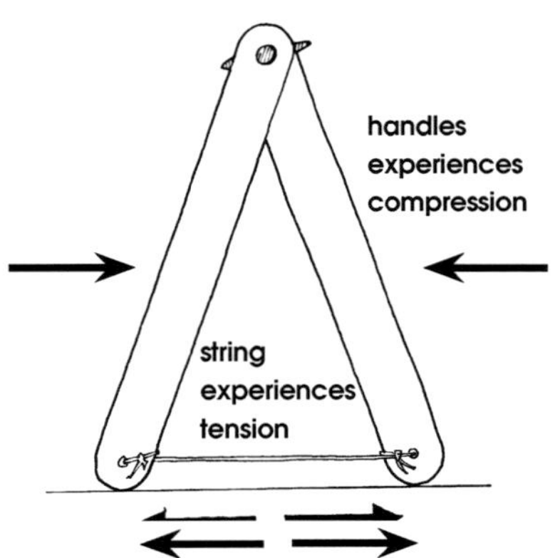

Now apply a heavy load on the truss by pushing very hard on the top. By pushing hard enough, you will break the string. This is because the total internal force caused by compression and tension is greater than the strength of the structure. Structural failure occurs at this point. In this case, the string breaks.

As a class, discuss students' familiarity with trusses. Ask:

- Have you seen a truss?
- Where are they commonly used? (bridges, house roofs)

Challenge students to identify trusses within structures in the local community, and in pictures of structures studied throughout this unit.

Have the students record their observations on the second section of the activity sheet.

Activity: Part Three

Once again, divide the class into working groups. Provide the groups with several identically shaped books, string, and scissors. Have them follow these instructions:

1. Take two identical books and tie loops around the top of each and stand them upright.

2. Tie a third string (35-40 cm long) between each of the loops so that it hangs loosely between the books.

3. Place the books standing upwards on the desk about 30 cm apart.

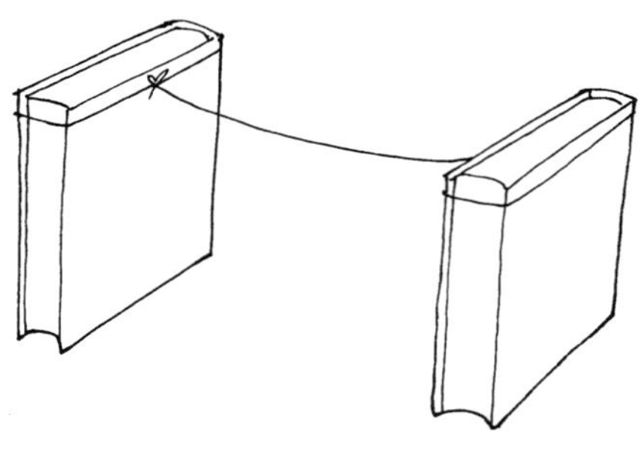

8

Once all groups have their books set up, ask:

- What do you think will happen if you press down on the string?

- Why do you think this will happen?

Have the groups test their predictions and discuss their results. The structures are unstable and the books will collapse inward.

Now have the students follow these instructions:

1. Stand the books upright.

2. Drape a piece of string across the middle of the upright books. Place a stack of heavy books on each end of the string to hold it in place. You may find that you have to tie a few knots in each ends of the string, or tie pencils to the ends of the string to keep them from slipping out from under the stacks of books).

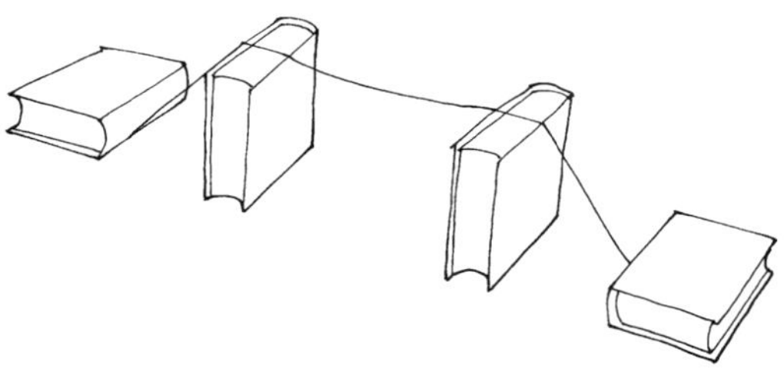

Have the groups predict what will happen if they press on the centre of the string. Have them test their predictions and discuss the results.

Students will notice that the stacks of books that secure the strings help to stabilize the bridge. Explain that this is an example of a suspension-supported structure. On a suspension bridge, cables pass over high towers above the pillars, and are then secured at either end at points called anchorages. On the model made in class, the stack of books at either end of the string acted as anchorages.

Discuss students' familiarity with suspension bridges. Challenge them to identify examples in their local community and in pictures of structures studied throughout the unit.

Have students record their observations on the third section of the activity sheet (3.8.1).

Activity Sheet

Note: This is a two-page activity sheet.

Directions for students:

Use this activity sheet to record your work and the predictions you make about the structural support demonstrations.

Activity: Part Four

Discuss symmetry as it pertains to bridge design. Students will be familiar with this concept from studies in mathematics, but the term should be discussed for review purposes.

Display a variety of pictures of bridges for students to examine. Ask:

- How are the bridges balanced, or symmetrical?

- Are both ends of the bridges the same?

- Are both sides of the bridge the same?

- What would happen if a bridge was not designed in a symmetrical way?

Discuss the importance of symmetry in maintaining stability in bridge structures.

As a follow-up to this discussion, provide each student with a picture showing only half a bridge. Have them glue the pictures onto art paper, and challenge them to use their understanding of symmetry to complete a sketch of the missing half of the bridge.

Display the drawing/pictures in the classroom. Use this opportunity to discuss the structural supports of each bridge displayed. Identify examples of beam bridges, arch supports, suspension supports, and cable-stayed supports.

Activity Centre

Provide a large variety of pictures of bridges (photographs, illustrations, printed pictures from web sites, and so on). Challenge students to identify and classify the bridges according to the structures, shapes, and types of supports used. Display the sorted pictures on a bulletin board. Challenge students to add to the display as they locate new pictures.

Extensions

- Have students research the Tacoma Narrows Bridge in Puget Sound, Washington. In November of 1940, four months after construction was completed, the bridge collapsed as a result of the forces created by 42 mile per hour winds. This caused great shock in the engineering community, as the bridge was supposed to have been designed to withstand winds of 120 miles per hour. Nicknamed "Galloping Gertie", the bridge oscillated both horizontally and vertically. Downloadable video of the oscillation and the eventual collapse can be found at the PBS/Nova site for "Building Bridges" **http://www.pbs.org/wgbh/nova/bridge/**.

- Have students research the arch designs used by the Romans and compare them to the arch supports used today. Students will find that the Romans used stone arrangements to create an arch support, whereas today steel and pre-stressed concrete is used. Diagrams of famous arch based structures are valuable to show to the class.

- Have students log on to **http://www.pbs.org/wgbh/nova/bridge/build.html**. The site contains thorough descriptions of different bridge types. Have students go through the steps identified on the web site.

Bridge Supports

Part One: Arch Support

Draw diagrams of each arch support as it is pressed down with the force from your finger.

Arch support
with no abutments

Arch support with
books as abutments

What difference do the abutments make in this type of structural support?

____

____

Part Two: Truss Support

Draw the compression and tension force vectors experienced
by the truss model.

Why did the thread break?

____

____

____

____

____

____

____

____

Part Three: Suspension Support

Explain why the books did not collapse after the anchorages
were put in place.

Diagram

Explanation:

____

____

____

____

____

____

____

____

9 Designing, Constructing, and Testing Bridges

Materials

- tape
- straws
- straight pins
- small paper plates
- gram weights

Activity

In this activity your students will have an opportunity to apply what they have learned about force vectors and support structures in building a bridge. The objective of this experiment is to build the strongest bridge possible, within specific guidelines.

Note: This lesson may take several class periods to design, construct, and test bridges.

Divide the class into working groups and provide each group with the activity sheet (3.9.1). Have the students review and discuss the sheet, and allow time for them to brainstorm and evaluate different bridge designs that they could construct using the materials given. They should than select on design, plan it, and predict its load-bearing ability. Once the groups have completed their plans, they may begin construction and testing their bridges.

Once all bridges have been built, have each group present their bridge design to the class. Encourage the groups to describe the support structures they used and provide a rationale for why they chose that structure.

Once presentations are complete, test each structure to see how much weight it will bear before structural failure occurs. As these structures represent bridges, the weight should be applied to the top of the deck, not suspended from it. Place a small paper plate on top of each bridge deck and add gram weights until the structure collapses.

Once all bridges have been tested, discuss the various bridge designs and the diversity in load-bearing ability. Allow the groups an opportunity to discuss modifications and improvements to their bridge that would increase its structural strength.

Activity Sheet

Note: This is a two-page activity sheet.

Directions to students:

Use the activity sheet (3.9.1) to record the design process of building your bridge.

Extension

- Take photographs of each bridge and display them in the classroom and throughout the school. If you have a digital camera or scanner, consider displaying these pictures on your class/school web site.

Assessment Suggestion

Conference with students individually. Have them present their bridge design and describe the forces that acted upon it. Also have them explain what could be made to improve the stability and strength of the bridge. Use the Individual Student Observation sheet on page 17 to record results.

The Design Process - Bridge Testing

The Challenge:

- Your group may only use a maximum of 18 straws, and 18 pins. You may bend the pins and cut the straws but no other material may be used.

- The bridge must be at least 7.5 cm wide and span a distance of at least 25 cm. This is longer than one straw.

- The bridge will be tested to determine its load-bearing ability.

Our Bridge Design:

1. Predict the load (in grams) that your bridge will bear before it collapses.

____ grams

2. Construct the bridge and present your design to the class.

3. Test your bridge. Record the load at structural failure.

____ grams

4. **What would you do to improve your design if you could build and test another bridge?**

____

____

____

____

5. **Draw a plan for your improved bridge design.**

10 | Increasing Strength of Materials

Background Information for Teachers

In order to construct a stable structure, designers must understand strengths and weaknesses of structural shapes. They must also recognize the physical strengths of and limits of the materials used for construction. This lesson explores different solid materials to determine strength and elastic properties.

Elastic force is the force in deformed (stretched) matter that allows it to return to its original shape.

Flexibility is the material's ability to bend and move without distortion or damage.

Strength is a measure of how much load a structure can sustain. This is measured by the amount of force a structure can withstand before failure occurs.

Materials

- paper (recycled photocopy paper)
- pennies
- tape
- glue
- books
- metre sticks
- information sheet titled, "Tower of Power Contest Rules and Instructions" (included. Make a copy for each group of students.) (3.10.2)
- straws
- small metal paper clips
- small paper plates

Activity: Part One

This activity provides illustrates that construction materials can be manipulated to provide added structural strength. Students will fold paper to create corrugations that provide extra rigidity, and allow the paper to bear a greater load.

Divide the class into working groups, and provide each group with Activity Sheet A (3.10.1), sheets of paper, and a stack of books. Have them make a beam bridge from a flat piece of paper, and a stack of books. Instruct students that they may not fold their paper and should simply lay the flat paper across two piles of books. Once the bridges are constructed, have students measure the span of their bridges. Have them add pennies to the bridge deck until the structure fails. Be sure to remind the students to count the number pennies they used to cause the collapse of the bridge. Have students record their results on Activity Sheet A (3.10.1).

Now ask students to build another beam bridge with the same span as the first one. They should use the same sheet of paper for the bridge deck. However, this time the paper should be folded back and forth (corrugated). Have students place the folded paper across on the stacked books. Have them add pennies to the folded bridge deck until structural failure occurs. Have students record their results on Activity Sheet A (3.10.1).

Students should find that it will take a greater number of pennies to cause structural failure of the second bridge.

Allow students to design and build a third bridge of the same span as the first two, but with a new piece of paper. This time allow the students to fold or manipulate the paper in any way they choose to form the bridge deck. Also allow them to use small amounts of tape or glue to hold joints together. Have them add pennies to the new bridge deck until structural failure occurs. Have students draw a diagram of their new design on Activity Sheet A (3.10.1), and describe the results of their investigations.

10

Activity Sheet A

Note: This is a two-page activity sheet.

Directions for students:

Complete the activity sheet (3.10.1) with details of your investigation of materials for bridge design and support.

Activity: Part Two

The purpose of this activity is to explore and investigate the effects of shape, materials, and balance in building a tower made of drinking straws. Students will be challenged to build a tower that is strong enough to hold the largest number of pennies before it collapses. This activity is a method for readdressing some of the concepts learned earlier in the unit and applying them to understanding material and structural strength.

Divide the class into working groups. Provide each group with the Tower of Power Contest Rules and Instructions Sheet (3.10.2), a metre stick, pennies, scissors, 50 straws, 120 small paper clips, and a paper plate.

Explain to the groups that they will be constructing towers using straws and paper clips. They will test the strength of their towers by placing a paper plate on top of the tower and adding pennies to the plate. The construction will be conducted in three phases as outlined on the Tower of Power Contest Rules and Instructions sheet (3.10.2). Review this sheet in detail with students.

Once the groups have constructed their towers and are ready to test them, provide each student with a copy of Activity Sheet B (3.10.3) to complete in the testing process.

Note: When this activity is complete, have the groups keep their towers as they will be needed for Lesson 11.

Activity Sheet B

Note: This is a two-page activity sheet.

Directions for students:

Use the activity sheet (3.10.3) to answer questions about the Tower of Power you have designed, constructed, and tested.

Extensions

- Have students investigate other methods for increasing the strength of materials. For example, the process of lamination of adjacent members can be demonstrated with wooden or bamboo skewers. Construct a beam bridge using a bundle of bamboo sticks that are held together with an elastic band, and supported on two stacks books. Construct a second beam bridge with the same number of bamboo sticks. Modify this beam by dipping the bundle of sticks in glue. The glue not only binds the bamboo sticks together, but also laminates the outer surface and provides the beam with much more rigidity. Lamination will increase the load the beam will be able to support. Have students observe, compare, and test the strength of the two bridges.

- Have students research the design and construction of famous tall buildings, such as Toronto's CN Tower, Calgary's Husky Tower, New York's Empire State Building, Chicago's Sears Tower. Have them use the activity sheet (3.10.4) to record their findings.

Materials and Bridge Strength

1. In the space below, draw a diagram of your first bridge made with a flat piece of paper.

How wide is the bridge? ____

What is the span (length) of your bridge? ____________________________

How many pennies did it take to cause structural failure? ______

2. Draw a diagram of your second bridge made with the folded piece of paper.

How many pennies did it take to cause structural failure? ______

Why was the bridge stronger after you folded the paper for the bridge deck?

____

____

3. Draw a diagram of your third bridge made with your own design.

Describe the changes you made to your design and explain why you thought these changes would make your bridge stronger. Did your design changes work? How many pennies did it take to cause structural failure of this new bridge?

____

____

____

____

____

____

____

____

____

Tower of Power Contest Rules and Instructions

Step 1:

❑ Design and build a Tower of Power using 15 straws and paper clips, but no other materials. Your Tower of Power can be any shape, but it must be able to support a paper plate on the top. When your 15-straw Tower of Power stands upright on its own, stop building.

Step 2:

❑ Place the paper plate on top of the tower. Gently place 20 pennies onto the paper plate. As you add this load, examine the tower's stability and look for weak spots.

❑ Draw a diagram of your 15-straw Tower of Power on the activity sheet Answer question 1.

❑ Something to think about: Could the weak spots make the tower collapse if there was more weight added?

Step 3:

❑ Remove the paper plate.

❑ Identify one weak spot on the tower. What modification could your team make in an effort to strengthen the weak spot?

❑ *Remember:* Anything you could change on your Tower of Power is a variable worth investigating. In the space provided, make a list of possible changes that might improve your tower.

❑ Some variables you may consider are:

Shape: What shape is the strongest in terms of structural support?

Strength: Can you join or fold anything to increase the tower's strength?

Length of straws: Should some straws be longer? Should some straws be shorter?

Joints: Is there another method to connect the straws together?

Locations of strong beams: Should the strongest beams be near the top or bottom of the Tower of Power?

Size of base: What effect would changing the size of the foundation have on your tower?

Step 4:

❑ It is now time to make a change to the Tower of Power. Choose one variable from the list that you made on the activity sheet, and make this change on the tower. Make only one change at a time.

❑ Place the paper plate on your tower to test the change you just made. Add 20 pennies to the paper plate, and note any changes to your tower's stability. Record your results on the activity sheet.

Step 5:

❑ Continue to build your tower by adding another 15 straws. Perform a stability and strength test by placing the paper plate on top of the tower and adding 20 pennies to the plate.

❑ Draw a diagram of your 30-straw Tower of Power in the space provided on the activity sheet.

❑ Identify and change a weak spot to make it stronger. Record this change in question 6.

Step 6:

❑ Add the last 20 straws to your Tower of Power. Repeat the strength and stability test by adding the paper plate on top of the tower and adding 20 pennies to the plate.

❑ Make final changes to the your Tower to improve the strength, shape, and height.

Final Assessment

❑ Complete the following on the activity sheet.

❑ Name your tower.

❑ Measure and record the height of your tower.

❑ Gently add one penny at a time to the paper plate until the structure collapses. How many pennies can the Tower of Power support before structural failure occurs?

❑ Write a paragraph listing the features that made your Tower of Power strong and stable. Be sure to explain how each feature helped strengthen the tower's weak points.

❑ Describe your tower's weak points. What finally made the tower collapse?

Date: _________________________   **Name:** _____________________________

Tower of Power Contest

Draw a diagram of your 15-straw Tower of Power in the space below.

1. Where, if anywhere, does you Tower of Power sag or bend?

   ____

2. What are the possible changes your team can make to improve your Tower of Power?

   ____

   ____

3. Which variable did you change?

   ____

4. Why is it important to only make one change at a time?

   ____

5. Test the tower again. Did the change make a difference to your Tower of Power's stability? If yes, describe the difference.

   ____

   ____

Draw a diagram of your 30-straw Tower of Power in the space below.

6. What change did your team make to the 30-straw Tower of Power to strengthen a weak spot?

____

____

7. Complete the 50-straw Tower of Power

Our Tower of Power is called ___________________________

The height of our Tower of Power is ___________________________

How many pennies did the Tower of Power hold before it collapsed? __________

What features made your Tower of Power strong?

____

____

____

Describe your tower's weak points. What made it finally collapse?

____

____

____

Date: ________________________   **Name:** ________________________________

Famous Tall Buildings

Name and location of the building:

____

Diagram of the building:

Who designed the building? ____

When was the building constructed? ________________________________

Unique features and interested facts about the building:

____

____

____

____

11 | Structural Efficiency

Background Information for Teachers

For the following lesson, you must be familiar with the following equation:

$$\text{Structural Efficiency} = \frac{\text{Maximum Mass}}{\text{Mass of Structure}}$$

Students will use this balculation to determine the structural efficiency of various structures.

Materials

- Bridges and Towers of Power constructed in Lesson 10
- chart paper
- markers
- balance scales and weights (or electronic scales if available)
- pennies
- calculators
- Information sheet titled, "Toothpick Bridge Competition Rules and Guidelines" (included. Make a copy of this sheet for each group of students.) (3.11.2)
- toothpicks
- warm-glue guns
- stacks of books
- 2.5 cm wide x 10 cm long wood block (cut from a wooden ruler or wood shim)

Activity: Part One

This activity requires students to have the bridges and Tower of Power that they constructed in Lesson 10. On chart paper, record the equation for structural efficiency as noted in the Background Information for Teachers. Ask:

- How could you use this equation to determine the structura efficiency of your bridges and towers?

Have the students weigh their structures and record the mass. Next, have students weigh the number of pennies necessary to cause structural failure in each structure. From these values, have students calculate the structural efficiency of their structures and record them on Activity Sheet A (3.11.1).

As a class, share results and discuss the variation in structural efficiency among the bridges and towers.

Activity Sheet A

Directions for students:

Use the activity sheet to record calculations of structural efficiency (3.11.1).

Activity: Part Two

The purpose of this activity s to have students construct a 15 cm toothpick bridge that will be assessed on two criteria. The two criteria are:

1. The structural efficiency cf the bridge.

2. The total cost value. For this variable, you may use the following guidelines.

Each toothpick used costs 10 cents

Glue costs a flat fee of $2.00

Note: Glue adds weight, which decreases the structural efficiency value

The cost value will be calculated as follows:

$$\text{Total Cost Value} = \frac{\text{Cost of supplies}}{\text{Load capacity}}$$

▶

Divide the class into working groups and provide each group with the Toothpick Bridge Competition Rules and Guidelines (3.11.2). As a class review the criteria for constructing, testing, and evaluating the toothpick bridges.

Have students complete Activity Sheet B (3.11.3) while working on their bridge. When complete, test all bridges and discuss results. When assessing the designs, focus on the structural efficiency and cost value of each bridge.

Activity Sheet B

Directions for students:

Use the activity sheet to record information about the toothpick bridge contest (3.11.3).

Calculating Structural Efficiency

Calculate the structural efficiency of your bridge and Tower of Power. Be sure to show all your work.

Remember:

Structural Efficiency = $\dfrac{\text{Maximum Mass}}{\text{Mass of Structure}}$

A. Beam Bridge # 1

The structural efficiency is ________________________________.

B. Beam Bridge # 2

The structural efficiency is ________________________________.

C. Beam Bridge # 3

The structural efficiency is ________________________________.

D. Tower of Power

The structural efficiency is ________________________________.

Toothpick Bridge Competition Rules and Guidelines

Construction details:

The width of the bridge may not exceed 5 cm.

The length of the bridge may not exceed 25 cm.

The bridge deck must support a 2.5 cm x 12 cm x 2 cm block.

The bridge must be constructed entirely of toothpicks.

Glue may be used only at the joints of the wood members.

The mass of the bridge must not exceed 20 grams.

Competition details:

1. The mass of the bridge will be determined before testing.
2. The bridge will be tested using a 2.5 cm x 12 cm x 2 cm wood block.
3. The bridge deck will be placed between two stacks of books that are the same height. These act as abutments. The bridge span must be 15 cm.
4. The group will begin to add free masses to the bridge deck until the bridge collapses.
5. The group will calculate the load capacity.
6. Groups will calculate structural efficiency and cost value.

Criteria:

1. Calculate the structural efficiency of your bridge using the following equation:

$$\text{Structural Efficiency} = \frac{\text{Maximum Mass}}{\text{Mass of Structure}}$$

2. Assess the cost of your bridge. Each toothpick costs 10 cents. Glue costs a $2.00.
3. Assess the cost value of your bridge using the following equation:

$$\text{Total Cost Value} = \frac{\text{Cost of supplies}}{\text{Load capacity}}$$

Date: _________________________   Name: _________________________

Bridge Design

Diagram of your bridge upon completion

Length of bridge: _____________   Width of bridge: _____________

Mass of bridge: _____________

Number of
toothpicks used: _____________ Total cost of toothpicks: _____________

Cost of glue: $2.00   Total cost for supplies: _____________

Cost Value: _____________

Load capacity: _____________

Structural efficiency: _____________

12 Researching and Evaluating Bridge Designs

Materials

- Information sheet titled, "Researching Bridges" (included. Make a copy for each student.) (3.12.1)
- reference material on bridges
- access to computers and Internet
- wall map of the world
- student atlases
- chart paper

Activity: Part One

In this activity, students will research the construction and specifications of existing bridges. Some examples include:

Akashi Kaikyo Bridge
Ambassador Bridge
Brooklyn Bridge
Confederation Bridge
Golden Gate Bridge
Lion's Gate Bridge
Peace Bridge
Storbaelt Bridge
Sydney Harbour Bridge

Also consider including bridges in and around your local community, such as the Provencher Paired Bridges or the Norwood Bridge in Winnipeg.

Divide the class into working groups, and provide all students with the information sheet titled, "Researching Bridges" (4.12.1). Review the sheet as a class. Explain that each group will select a bridge to research, and will plan an oral presentation about the bridge.

Have each working group choose a different bridge. Provide access to print resources as well as Internet web sites such as:

www.confederationbridge.com
for information about the confederation bridge joining Prince Edward Island and New Brunswick.

www.telus.net/bjgcelt/vancbc2.htm for information about the Lion's Gate Bridge in Vancouver.

www.civl.port.ac.uk/comp_prog/bridges1/ BrooklynBridge.htm for information on the Brooklyn Bridge in New York.

www.goldengatebridge.org/research/ construction.html for information on the Golden Gate Bridge in San Francisco.

www.civl.port.ac.uk/comp_prog/bridges1/ Storbaelt.htm for information on the for Storbaelt Bridge in Denmark.

www.civl.port.ac.uk/comp_prog/bridges1/ SydneyHarbour.htm for information on the Sydney Harbour Bridge in Sydney, Australia.

www.icivilengineer.com/Landmarks/Bridges/ Akashi_Kaikyo/ for information on the Akashi Kaikyo Bridge in Japan.

www.ambassadorbridge.com/ for information about the Ambassador Bridge in Ontario.

www.peacebridge.com/ for information about the Peace Bridge in Ontario.

www.winnipeg.ca/publicworks/majorprojects This City of Winnipeg site provides information, blueprints, and photographs of recently constructed bridges, such as the Provencher Paired, and Norwood Bridges.

Note: Groups may wish to divide the tasks/ questions among group members. Ensure, however, that all students participate in the oral presentations.

Activity: Part Two

Display a wall map of the world. Explain to the class that they are going to use their knowledge of bridges to design a bridge for a new location. Provide students with the activity sheet (3.12.2). As a class, use the wall map to identify possible

12

locations of some bridges. Discuss some of the features of the geographical locations of the bridges, and determine the reasons these bridges should be built.

Have students work independently to complete the activity sheet. They may use print resources, Internet sites, and student atlases to help them complete the task.

Provide an opportunity for students to share their solutions with the class. Discuss and evaluate the types of bridges suggested for each location

The following solutions are appropriate:

Location 1 - A 1500 m span across Great Slave Lake where there is large ship travel.

Solution: A suspension bridge can support the length needed to allow for a shipping channel.

Location 2 - A 40 m span across the trans-Canada highway near Winnipeg.

Solution: A beam bridge would work well because of the relatively short span, and minimal support needed.

Location 3 - A 300 m span across Welland Canal where barge traffic is heavy.

Solution: A cable-stayed bridge would allow a large enough span to allow for barge traffic.

Location 4 - A 200 m span across a canyon gorge near Fraser, B.C.

Solution: An arch bridge could be built into the rock eliminating the need for towers or pillars.

Activity Sheet

Note: This is a two-page activity sheet.

Directions for students:

Use the activity sheet to record your bridge design (3.12.2).

Extension

■ Focus on the construction of the famous bridges researched in this lesson. Discuss the cost of bridge construction, including the energy used in the building process. Have students share their research findings. As a class, brainstorm the types of energy used in bridge construction and use (e.g., gasoline, hydro-electricity, and so on).

Assessment Suggestion

As a class, determine criteria for the oral presentations on the bridge research. For example:

■ Team members all participated in research.

■ Presentation was supported by visuals.

■ Presenters used clear speaking voices.

■ Answered questions clearly.

List the criteria on the Rubric on page 19 and record results during oral presentations.

Date: ___________________________   **Name:** _________________________________

Researching Bridges

1. Select one bridge to research.

2. Draw a labelled diagram of the bridge.

3. Consider the following questions as you do your research and plan your presentation.

   - Where is the bridge located (geographically)?

   - What type of bridge is it?

   - What materials is the bridge made of?

   - How was the bridge constructed?

   - When did construction on the bridge begin and end?

   - What is the span of the bridge?

   - How many car lanes are there on the bridge?

   - Does the bridge have a pedestrian walkway?

   - Can people ride their bicycles over the bridge?

   - What colour is the bridge?

   - How is the bridge lit?

   - Is there a toll to cross the bridge?

   - What is the bridge's load capacity?

   - What is the bridge's mass?

   - What is the estimate of the bridge's structural efficiency?

   - Are there any interesting facts about the bridge that make it stand out from other bridges?

Bridge Design

Select one of these four locations:

- 1500 metre span across Great Slave Lake where large ships travel.

- 40 metre span across the trans-Canada highway near Winnipeg.

- 300 metre span across Welland Canal where barge traffic is heavy.

- 200 metre span across a canyon gorge near Fraser, B.C.

Select one of these four bridge types:

Beam Bridge

Arch Bridge

Suspension Bridge

Cable-Stayed Bridge

The location is:

____

The bridge type you think best fits this location:

____

The reason(s) for your decision:

____

____

____

____

Draw a diagram of your bridge design:

What materials would you use in constructing this bridge?

____

____

List the names and locations of other bridges of the same type.

____

____

____

13 | Product Research and Design

Background Information for Teachers

In this lesson, students will research the design and construction of play structures. Collect catalogues from companies that build play structures, and check out the web sites for local businesses. Also consider having sales representatives from these companies speak to the students about how the play structures are researched, designed, costed out, and constructed.

Materials

- catalogues from companies that build play structures
- access to computers and Internet sites
- access to a variety of play structure sites in the local community

Activity: Part One

Take the students outside to view the school's play structure (or a structure at a nearby school or community park). Have the students examine and describe the structure, focusing on the overall shape, parts (slide, monkey bars, swings, poles), and surroundings.

- What is the purpose of the play structure?
- What materials is it made of?
- How do you think it was built?
- Which part of the structure was constructed first? (surface/foundation)
- How do you think it was constructed?
- Do you think this is a safe structure to play on? Give examples that support your opinion.
- Would this structure ever need to be replaced? Why?
- How would you dispose of the structure if it were to be replaced?

Discuss the 'life story' of a play structure; from initial preparation of the area, through the construction of the play structure, to the structure's disposal and replacement.

Have students complete Activity Sheet A (3.13.1) while observing the play structure

Activity Sheet A

Directions to students:

Follow the directions on the sheet to record your observations of the play structure.

Activity: Part Two

Take a walking tour around the local community to examine a variety of play structures. At each site, discuss the features of the structures. Draw comparisons in structure, design, and age of the play structures.

During this lesson, discuss how play structures have changed over time (e.g., materials used, types of design). Early play structures were often made of wooden beams. More recent play structures tend to have rubber coatings over metal frames, with several moulded plastic components. Challenge students to explain why these changes may have occurred.

Note: Ideas for new products are the result of research and experience with past products. In the case of play structures, safety concerns and durability research have resulted in changes in the materials used and designs of these structures.

Activity: Part Three

If possible, have a play structure sales representative speak to the class about how play structures are designed and constructed. Also have the guest speaker provide information on product research, marketing, and building costs.

Activity: Part Four

Focus students' attention on the diagrams they drew of the play structure. Ask:

- How could this play structure be improved?
- What could be added to better meet children's play needs?
- How do you think people go about planning a new play structure?

Divide the class into working groups and provide each group with Activity Sheet B (3.13.2). Have them use catalogues and Internet sites to research play structure designs and costs.

Activity Sheet B

Note: This is a two-page activity sheet.

Directions to students:

Conduct research to gather information on play structure designs and companies.

Extensions

- Have students work in groups to build a model play area. Encourage them to design their structures to scale, and include all elements of the areas (e.g., play structures, tree, seating areas, garbage cans, water fountains, sand boxes, and green spaces). This project could culminate with a presentation to a local city councillor to share ideas on what students see as important recreational elements in their local community.

- Have students look at other products to determine how they are researched, tested, designed, and constructed. Focus on products that have changed significantly over time, e.g. automobiles, telephones, computers, golf clubs.

Assessment Suggestion

Have students complete the Student Self-Assessment sheet on page 22 to reflect on their learning about structure design and production.

End-of-Unit Assessment

Reflect on the tasks undertaken by each student throughout the unit to complete the End-of-Unit Assessment chart on page 26. Consider all assessment tools, investigation, and activities when identifying, and commenting on, individual student achievement.

Play Structure Design

Draw a diagram of the play structure:

List the materials used in the construction of the play structure:

Surface and foundation materials:

____

____

____

Play structure materials:

____

____

____

Product Research

Imagine that you are part of a parent council group that has been given the responsibility. of researching, designing, and projecting the costs for the replacement of the school's play structure. Use catalogues and web sites to conduct your research.

1. Look through catalogues and on web sites to view play structure components. List the features that your group would like to include in your play structure.

2. Draw a diagram of a play structure that include all of the components listed above.

3. Children love to play on swings. Select three companies that sell swings. Complete the chart.

Company	Swings Model	Positive Features	Negative Features

4. Choose the company that will build your play structure. Explain why you chose this company.

____

____

____

____

References for Teachers

Andrews, W.A., T.J.E. Wolfe and J.L. Elix. *Physical Science: An Introductory Study*. Scarborough, ON: Prentice-Hall, Ltd. 1978.

Hawkes, Nigel. *Structures and Buildings*. New York: Twenty-First Century Books, 1994.

www.education-world.com/index.shtml

http://ericic.syr.edu

http://educationindex.com/index/html

www.ocup.org

http://tqd.advanced.org/3616/physics/index.html

www2.edu.gov.mb.ca/ks4/cur/science/found/5-8.asp

http://ist05.ma.psu.edu/~rwk6/intro.html

www.oecta.on.ca/curriculum/currindex.htm

bridgecontest.usma.edu/manual.htm

Unit 4
Earth's Crust

Books for Students

Bain, Iain. *Mountains and Earth Movements.* England: Wayland, 1984.

Clifford, Nick. *Incredible Earth.* Toronto: Stoddart, 1994.

Decker, R., and B. Decker, *Volcanoes.* San Francisco: W.H. Freeman & Company, 1981.

Dixon, Dougal, and Raymond L. Bernor, ed. *The Practical Geologist.* New York: Simon & Schuster, 1992.

Fodor, R. V. *What Does a Geologist Do?* New York: Dodd, Mead & Co.,1977.

Gallant, Roy A., and Christopher J. Schuberth. *Discovering Rocks and Minerals: A Nature Guide to Their Collection and Identification.* New York: Natural History Press, 1987.

Hall, Cally. *Gem Stones.* Toronto: Stoddart, 1994.

Oldershaw, Cally. *Atlas of Geology and Landforms.* New York: Franklin Watts, 2001.

Oliver, Ray. *Rocks & Fossils.* London: Hamlyn, 1993.

Parker, Steve. *The Practical Paleontologist.* New York: Simon & Schuster, 1990.

Pollock, Steve. *The Atlas of Endangered Resources.* New York: Belitha Press, 1995.

Sutherland, Lin. *Earthquakes and Volcanoes.* New York: Weldon Owen Production, 2000.

Symes, Dr. R. F. *Rocks & Minerals.* Toronto: Stoddart, 1997.

Web Sites

- **www.pbs.org/wgbh/aso/tryit/**

  Click on "Mountain Maker Earth Shaker" to use the interactive models of plate tectonics. This informative site gives detailed background into scientific discovery, scientists, and basics of earth sciences.

- **www.geography.learnontheinternet. co.uk/topics/structureofearth.htm#plate**

  This geography site provides a map of Earth's plates, diagrams of faults, and information about earthquakes and volcanoes.

- **http://kids.earth.nasa.gov**

  Click on "Land," then scroll down to "Continental Drift and Plate Tectonics" to play games, take a quiz, and use the interactive map. This site also contains information on evidence supporting Continental Drift, NASA's role in satellite investigation, and why Continental Drift is important to "Me."

- **www.fi.edu/earth/earth.html**

  This site is filled with information, outstanding links, and teacher information about plate tectonics, earthquakes, and volcanoes.

- **http://pubs.usgs.gov/publications/text/ dynamic.html**

  "This Dynamic Earth: The Story of Plate Tectonics" provides detailed information and amazing graphics to explain the formation and changes in Earth's crust.

- **www.quia.com/customs/514main.html**

  A fun site with four games that challenge students' knowledge about Earth's crust.

- **www.neic.cr.usgs.gov**

  The National Earthquake Information Center's site provides teachers and students with information about earthquakes in North America and around the world. Check out the EQ Facts & Lists, Hazards & Preparedness, Science & Technology.

- **www.eqnet.org**

  The EarthQuake Information NETwork provides up-to-date information and the most recent statistics on earthquakes around the world. Read reports and new releases, and learn about relief efforts for the people affected by earthquakes.

- **http://volcano.und.nodak.edu/**

  The University of North Dakota provides up-to-date information on volcanoes, locations, satellite maps, teacher information, kids stuff, in an exciting and in-depth site.

- **http://geology.csupomona.edu/alert**

  Click on "minerals," "igneous," "meta," or "sed. thin" exercises and find detailed information, pictures, and information on identifying and classifying rocks and minerals.

- **www.fi.edu/fellows/payton/rocks/ index2.html**

  This "Rock Hounds" site provides information about rocks and minerals. You will find lesson plans, activities, animations, pictures, and details about igneous, metamorphic, and sedimentary rocks.

- **www.em.gov.bc.ca/mining/Geolsurv/ Publications/InfoCirc/Ic1987-5/intro.htm**

  The British Columbia Ministry of Energy & Mines provides information, pictures, diagrams, and clues to classifying rocks.

- **www.fe.doe.gov/education**

  "Fossil Fuels Future" gives the history and technological development of coal, oil, and gas resources. This is a well-organized introduction to the fuels we use most, and presents information on how to use the technology so that these fuels will be sustainable in the future.

- **http://agcwww.bio.ns.ca**

  This Natural Resources of Canada site brings a team of specialists in marine and petroleum geology, geophysics, geochemistry, and geotechnology to provide information about Canada's coastal and offshore land masses. Click on "Government & Geoscience" to learn about natural resources.

- **www.nrcan-rncan.gc.ca/kids/index_e.html**

  Click on "Nature and the Environment" and "Minerals and Metals at Home" to find information on how to start a mine, hidden treasures, mining facts, careers in the mining industry, and much more. This Government of Canada web site is fun and informative.

- **http://mmsd1.mms.nrcan.gc.ca/mmsd/ facts/default_e.asp**

  This Natural Resources Canada web site has interactive maps and detailed information about geologic resources in Canada.

- **http://soils.usda.gov**

  The United States Department of Agriculture developed this easy-to-use and extensive site about soils. If you are a geographer, soil scientist, land use manager, teacher, or student, you will find scientific information about the formation and conservation of soil.

- **www.wtamu.edu/~.gov/is/kids**

  "Dr. Dirt", a professor of plants, soils, and environmental sciences answers questions, provides information, and gives great ideas for experiments about soil. A fun site for students and teachers.

- **www.mininglife.com**

  This site has information on mining in Canada.

- **www.mining.ca**

  This web site offers information on mining in Canada.

- **http://homepages.which.net/~fred.moor. index.htm**

  Click on "World of Soil" to find out about soil formation, care, ph and acidity, and plant food.

- **www.earthscienceworld.org/careers/**

  This site explains the careers available for geoscientists: where they work, salary outlooks, and contact information about job opportunities. You will also find "Geoscientist Profiles" and a guide to university departments of geosciences in Canada and the United States.

- **www.geosociety.org**

  Geological Society of America. Click on the link for "Education and Teacher Resources."

- **http://vulcan.wr.usgs.gov**

  This is the home page for the Cascades Volcano Observatory.

- **www.sciencenorth.ca**

  This Sudbury, Ontario, site has good educational resources for mining.

- **www.seismo.nrcan.gc.ca**

  The Natural Resources Canada site provides an opportunity for students to examine maps of Canada that display seismic activity.

- **www.gov.mb.ca/itm/mrd/minerals/ convention/**

  This is a Government of Manitoba web site with information on the province's mining industry.

Recommended Videos

- **Plate Tectonics: Our Restless Planet**

This video explains the changes of the planet due to volcanic eruptions, earthquakes, sea floor spreading, subduction zones and mountains pushing up. The theory of Pangea and how the continents have positioned themselves is depicted. (15 min Grades 5 – 10, 1999)

(Classroom Video - #107 1500 Hartley Ave, Coquitlam, BC V3K 7A1
Toll Free Phone: 800 665 4121)

- **Volcanoes (Junior): What causes volcanes**

This video is a compilation of the best volcanic footage from around the world with clear explanations of causes and volcanic types. Plate tectonics is the underlying theme for this presentation. (22 min Grades 4 – 7, 1985)

Classroom Video - #107 1500 Hartley Ave, Coquitlam, BC V3K 7A1
Toll Free Phone: 800 665 4121

- **Plate Tectonics**

Concepts and terminology discussed include: continental drift, Pangea, Gondwanaland, seafloor spreading, tectonic plates, plate boundaries, divergent boundaries, convergent boundaries, mountain building, folding and faulting, and landforms. (20 min Grades 5 – 9, 2003)

MacIntyre Media Inc. 1-800-565-3036

- **Volcanoes and Earthquakes**

Concepts and terminology discussed include: molten rock, magma, lava, cindercone, shield volcano, composite volcano, cladera, Ring of Fire, earthquake, seismic waves, seismograph, and Richter Scale. (20 min Grades 5 – 9, 2003)

MacIntyre Media Inc. 1-800-565-3036

- **Forces Shaping the Earth**

Concepts and terminology discussed include: erosion, deposition, mass movement, creep, slump, landslide, alluvial fan, delta, stream erosion, wave erosion, ice erosion, glaciers, glacial deposits, wind erosion, and wind deposits. (20 min Grades 5 – 9, 2003)

MacIntyre Media Inc. 1-800-565-3036

- **Weathering and Soils**

Concepts and terminology discussed include: mechanical weathering, chemical weathering, oxidation, carbonation, soil formation, soil texture, horizons, soil type, soil profile, leaching, subsoil, soil conservation, and groundwater. (20 min Grades 5 – 9, 2003)

MacIntyre Media Inc. 1-800-565-3036

- **Minerals and their Properties**

Major mineral groups and basic mineral crystal systems are discussed. The effect of the chemical structure on the properties of minerals is shown using colourful animation of atoms and ions. Terminology included in this video: inorganic, lustre, streak, colour, cleavage and fracture, specific gravity, hardness, Mohs scale, ore, metals, gemstone. (20 min Grades 5 – 9, 2001)

MacIntyre Media Inc. 1-800-565-3036

- **Rocks and the Rock Cycle**

This video introduces three types of rocks – igneous, metamorphic and sedimentary. The rock cycle is illustrated with animation. Terms and concepts explained in the video include: rock cycle, igneous, metamorphic, sedimentary, texture, and mineral composition. (20 min Grades 5 – 9, 2001)

MacIntyre Media Inc. 1-800-565-3036

▶

■ **Igneous and Metamorphic rocks**

The formation of igneous rocks is explained using animation. Important terminology and concepts conveyed in this video include: extrusive rock, intrusive rock, lava, laccolith, pluton, contact metamorphism, regional metamorphism, foliated, and parent rock. (20 min Grades 5 – 9, 2001)

MacIntyre Media Inc. 1-800-565-3036

■ **Sedimentary Rocks**

In this program the classification system and features of sedimentary rocks is outlined. This video investigates sedimentary rock and the formation of fossils. Terminology and concepts discussed in this video include: clastic rock, organic rock, chemical rock, sediment, ripple marks, concretions, geodes, compaction, cementation, precipitates, evaporated, petrifaction, trace fossils, index fossils, unconformity, fault, extrusion. (20 min Grades 5 – 9, 2001)

MacIntyre Media Inc. 1-800-565-3036

Introduction

In this unit, students will investigate Earth's crust. They will develop an understanding of the structure of our planet and how that structure affects the continents, the landscape, and how it impacts on human populations. Through research and study, students will discover why earthquakes occur, how mountains form and volcanoes erupt, how rocks and minerals are created and change, and where soil comes from. Students will also learn about the environmental impacts of mining Earth's surface.

Prior to teaching this unit, collect a large quantity of rocks and minerals. Also encourage students to bring items from home that will add to the study of rocks, minerals, and geology.

Note: Rock and mineral collections can also be obtained through geological societies, local departments of mines and natural resources, and science suppliers.

Display books about earthquakes, volcanoes, mountains, rocks, minerals, soil, and mining. See Books for Students for suggestions.

Collect pictures from magazines, tourism publications, and calendars of different mountains, rivers, volcanoes, and other landscapes from around the world.

Plan any related field trips well in advance, and contact guest speakers from the geology field to talk about rocks and minerals, gems, rock collecting, volcanoes, earthquakes, mining, or other topics relating to Earth's crust.

Science Vocabulary

Throughout this unit, teachers should use, and encourage students to use, vocabulary such as: *crust, mantle, outer core, inner core, magma, lava, crystallization, lithification, sedimentation, igneous rock, metamorphic rock, weathering* (physical, biological and chemical), *erosion, rock cycle, fossil fuel, geothermal energy, continental drift theory*, and *theory of plate tectonics*.

1 | The Continental Drift

Background Information for Teachers

Geology is the study of planet Earth. Scientists who study Earth are called *geologists*, or *geoscientists*. By studying the history of Earth and the Solar System, geologists try to understand how the earth was formed, how old it is, and how it has changed over time. These scientists look at rocks in order to understand how rock was made and how landscapes change.

Plate tectonics is the movement and interactions of the lithospheric plates (the outer layer of Earth, which contains the crust and upper part of the mantle). Scientists work together to answer questions about the continental drift. Continental movements have been investigated by paleontologists, climatologists, oceanographers, ecologists, biologists, geologists, and geophysicists. The end result has been a greater knowledge of Earth and the changes that can be recognized in the climate, landforms, and life forms.

Materials

- chart paper
- markers
- wall map of the world
- globe
- story titled, "Alfred Wegener's Continental Clues" (included. Make a copy for each student.) (4.1.2)
- overhead projector
- diagram titled, "Fossil Remains" (included. Make an overhead transparency.) (4.1.3)
- pencil crayons
- scissors
- glue sticks
- construction paper

Activity: Part One: Continental Drift

Introduce the unit by challenging the students to present what they know about the structure of Earth. Provide students with a copy of Activity Sheet A (4.1.1), and have them complete the first two columns. Following this task, have students share their ideas and answer questions about Earth's crust.

Display a large map of the world and a globe at the front of the class. Ask:

- Have people always thought Earth was round?
- What are some reasons why people used to think Earth was flat?
- How do we know that Earth is round?
- What do we know about the earth's shape and structure?
- Has Earth always looked the way it does today?
- What type of scientists study Earth's formation?

Discuss the terms *geology* and *geologist* with the students, and create a class definition for each term. Record these on the chart paper. Ask:

- Why is the study of geology important?

Provide each student with a copy of the story (4.1.2). As a class, read paragraphs one and two, and discuss the information presented. On the overhead, display the diagram titled, "Fossil Remains" (4.1.3). Continue to read the story together, and discuss the work of Alfred Wegener. Ask:

Hands-On Science • Grade 7

- What is a meteorologist?
- How do you think Alfred Wegener felt when no one believed him?
- Why would he keep working on his theory if no one believed him?
- What does this tell us about scientific research?

Note: Throughout the unit, have students complete the third column of their KWL chart as they gain understanding and are able to answer the questions they recorded in the second column.

Activity Sheet A

Directions to students:

On the KWL chart, record your ideas and questions about Earth's crust. As you learn the answers to your questions, complete the third column of the chart (4.1.1).

Activity: Part Two: Continental Puzzle

Divide the class into working groups. Distribute Activity Sheet B (4.1.4). Have students cut out the continent shapes and try to fit them together to make the shape of Pangea. Ask:

- Why do the edges of the continents not match up perfectly?
- Do you think the theory of continental drift is a realistic theory?

Activity Sheet B

Directions to students:

Colour each continent a different colour. Cut out the shapes and try to fit the pieces together to make the shape of Pangea. Glue the pieces onto construction paper, and add a title to your completed puzzle (4.1.4).

Activity Sheet C

Note: Provide each student with several copies of the three-point-approach chart, for new vocabulary (4.1.5). Students may want to bind the sheets together and add a title page.

Directions to students:

Throughout the unit, identify new terms related to your study of Earth's crust. Record terms, definitions, examples, and diagrams (4.1.5).

Extension

Research the discoveries of Harry Hess, J. Tuzo Wilson, and Arthur Holmes, and find out what they contributed to our knowledge and understanding of Earth's crust.

Assessment Suggestion

Observe students as they complete the continental drift puzzle. Focus on their ability to solve problems. Use the Anecdotal Record sheet on page 16 to record results.

Date: ___________________   **Name:** ___________________________

KWL

What I know about Earth	What I want to know about Earth	What I learned about Earth

Alfred Wegener's Continental Clues

When looking at a map of the world, it is not difficult to see that some of the continents look as if they could fit together like pieces of a giant puzzle. Alfred Wegener (1880-1930), a German meteorologist, saw this connection and found that if he included the continental shelves (the part of each continent that is covered by shallow ocean water), the fit of the puzzle was even better. He believed that millions of years ago all of the continents were joined together. He named this super-continent Pangaea, which is Greek for "all the land." At some point, Pangea split and began to move apart, settling into the continents that we know today. His theory was called "continental drift."

Alfred Wegener found several other clues to support his theory. In places where the shape of the continents matched up, for example, between Brazil and part of Africa, the sequence in the layers of rocks (sandstone, shale, coal) also matched. He also observed that the same types of fossil remains of plants and animals, including dinosaurs, were found on different continents, even though they are separated by vast distances.

The weakest part of Wegener's argument was his explanation of why and how the continents moved. He suggested that the rotation of Earth and the gravitational pull of the moon caused the movement. Thirty years after Wegener's death, scientists found evidence of the sea floor spreading, which was undeniable proof that Earth's crust does split and move, and carries the continents with it. At this point, Alfred Wegener's theory and his life's work were finally substantiated.

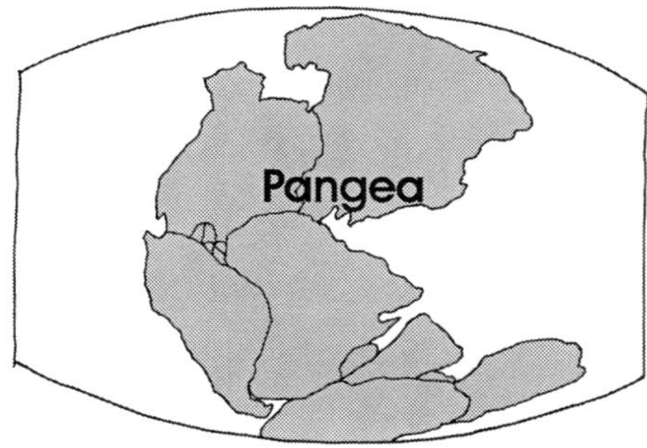

200 million years ago

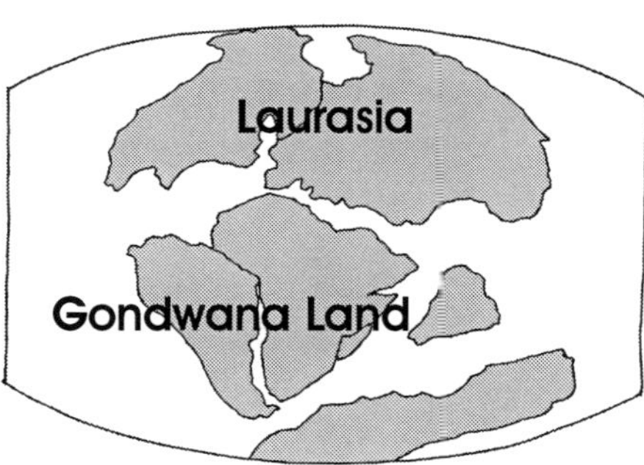

140 million years ago

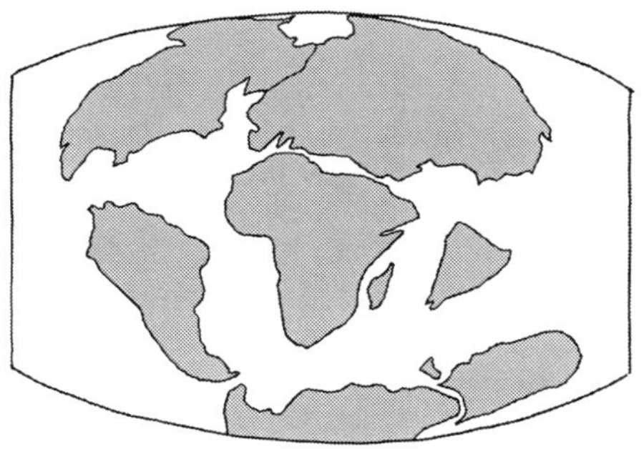

65 million years ago

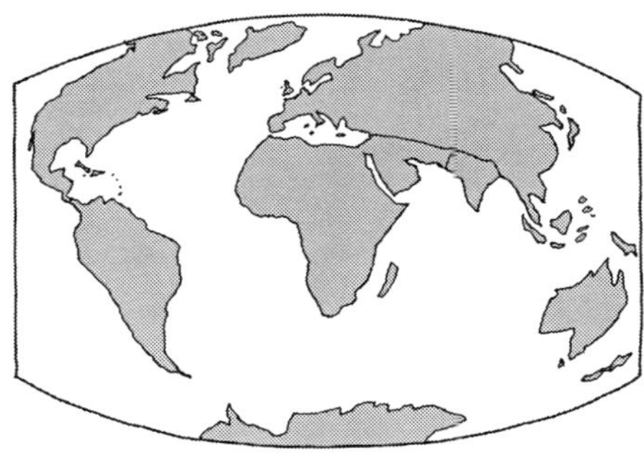

Present day

Fossil Remains

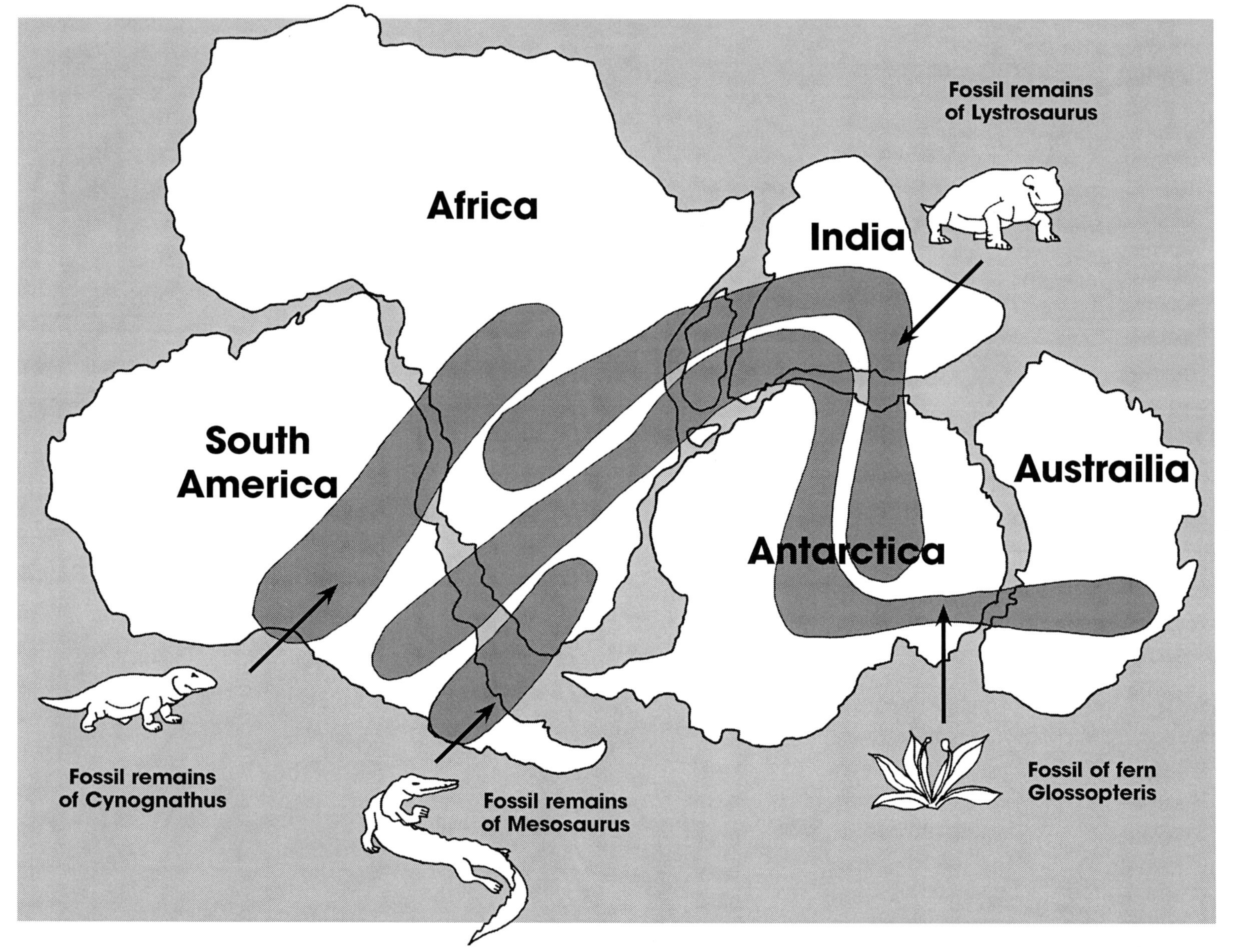

Three-Point-Approach

Definition	Term	Diagram
	Examples	
Definition	**Term**	**Diagram**
	Examples	
Definition	**Term**	**Diagram**
	Examples	

Background Information for Teachers

Crust: Earth's hard outer shell. The crust is thickest beneath the land masses (up to 70 km) and thinnest under the oceans (6 – 11 km).

Mantle: The layer beneath the crust that makes up more than three-quarters of Earth's volume (25900 km thick). The mantle is solid, but the upper part is soft – like asphalt on a hot day. It is in this weaker upper area where convection currents and some melting occur.

Molten Outer Core: Made up of iron and nickel. The outer core is 2000 km thick.

Solid Inner Core: Made up of iron and nickel. It is 2740 km thick and has a temperature of 4000°C. The enormous pressure at the centre of the planet is strong enough to turn the liquid metals of the inner core into solids.

Materials

- information sheet titled, "Technology and Plate Tectonics" (included. Make a copy for each student.) (4.2.1)
- map titled, "Earth's Tectonic Plates" (included. Make an overhead transparency of this sheet.) (4.2.2)
- wall map of the world
- coloured pencils
- overhead projector
- paper towels
- hard-boiled eggs (one for each student)
- plastic knives

Activity: Part One: Technological Advances and Discovery

Provide students with a copy of the information sheet titled, "Technology and Plate Tectonics" (4.2.1). Read the information together and discuss the technologies that have led to new discoveries about the movement of the continents. Display the overhead map of Earth's tectonic plates (4.2.2). Ask:

- What is happening to the ocean floor?
- How does the continual recycling of the ocean floor affect the continents?

Activity: Part Two: Tectonic Plates

Display the wall map of the world. Provide each student with a paper towel, a hard-boiled egg, and pencil crayons. Have students imagine that the egg is Earth. Challenge the students to draw the earth's continents on the egg. Allow students time to complete this task.

Explain to the students that, unlike an egg's shell, scientists have discovered that Earth is split into sections that are called *plates*. Have the students make large cracks on the shell of the egg by gently tapping it on their desks. Allow the students time to observe the egg's shell after it is cracked. Ask:

- How is a cracked shell different from a smooth shell?
- How might it be compared to Earth's tectonic plates?
- What might have caused cracking of Earth's surface?

Have students set their egg on the paper towel. Provide students with Activity Sheet A (4.2.3). Explain that Earth is made of several different layers. Use the Background Information for Teachers to describe these layers. Have students label their diagrams during this discussion.

Draw the students' attention back to the egg. Distribute a plastic knife to each student. Demonstrate how to cut the egg vertically, down to approximately the middle. Then cut the egg horizontally through to the vertical cut. Remove the wedge of egg. Have the students repeat the process. Provide students with Activity Sheet B (4.2.4). Have them draw diagrams and record

their discoveries about the similarities and differences between Earth and an egg.

Activity Sheet A

Directions to students:

Label the parts of the Earth, and write a brief description for each. Colour the diagram (4.2.3).

Activity Sheet B

Directions to students:

Draw, and label a diagram of the egg showing its layers. Draw, and label a diagram of the earth showing its layers. Answer the questions (4.2.4).

Extensions

- Have students research the discovery of hydrothermal vents on the ocean floor, the life forms that live around these vents, and the submersible equipment used to study the vents.

- Have the students research other scientists who have made discoveries about the ocean; for instance, Jacques Cousteau or Dr. Sylvia Earle.

- Show the video *Ocean Exploration*, by Bill Nye, to provide more information about oceanography and exploration.

Assessment Suggestion

Observe students as they conduct the investigation of the earth. Focus specifically on each student's ability to compare and contrast Earth with an egg. Use the Individual Student Observations sheet on page 17 to record the results.

Technology and Tectonic Plates

Discoveries, through experimentation and observation, are the foundations of knowledge and technological advances. Such is the case with research of Earth's oceans and continents. One of the first major discoveries were those of the scientists aboard The British H.M.S. Challenger expedition. The expedition lasted from 1872 to 1875. The ship sailed 111, 000 kilometres, measuring ocean depth and characteristics of the ocean floor throughout its journey. The results of this expedition showed that an extensive north to south ridge ran down the middle of the Atlantic Ocean between the Americas and Europe and Africa. Frank Taylor analyzed the data more than thirty years later, in 1908. He proposed that the ridge was evidence that the continents had been pulled apart by tremendous forces.

In the 1950s, two British geophysicists, Fred Vine and Drummond Matthew, discovered that the ocean floor was made up of younger rock than that of the continents. Using deep-sea drilling technology, Vine and Matthew were able to analyze core samples. They found that the oldest oceanic crust is less than 200 million years old. Continental rocks, on the other hand, were tested and found to be up to 4.1 billion years old. One important question remained: Where had the old ocean floor gone?

With the introduction of computers in the 1960s, a greater understanding of the ocean floor emerged. It was discovered that the youngest ocean floor is in the middle of the Atlantic and the oldest is at the edges, proving that the sea floor is spreading. Sonar imaging used echo sounding to map the ocean floor. Later, remote-controlled submarines recorded data in depths of 6000 metres. Today, satellites are able to detect minute movements on the earth. The new technology used to study the earth shows that continents and oceans are made of over 15 different tectonic plates. The boundaries of the plates are found mainly in the ocean. In some areas the plates are being forced apart, while other plates are being forced down, back into the centre of the earth. The movement of tectonic plates proves that the continents are moving and helps explain the volcanic eruptions and earthquakes that affect our world.

Sonar Imaging

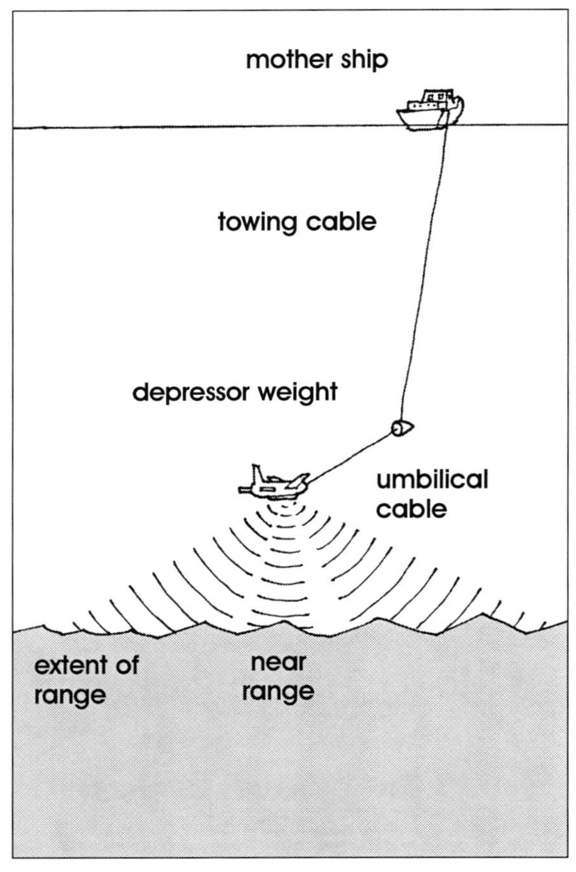

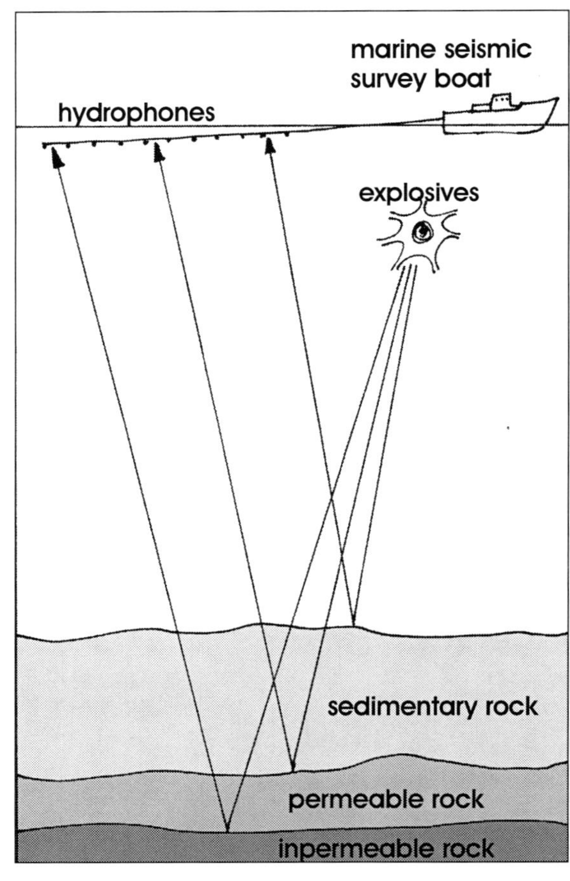

Earth's Tectonic Plates

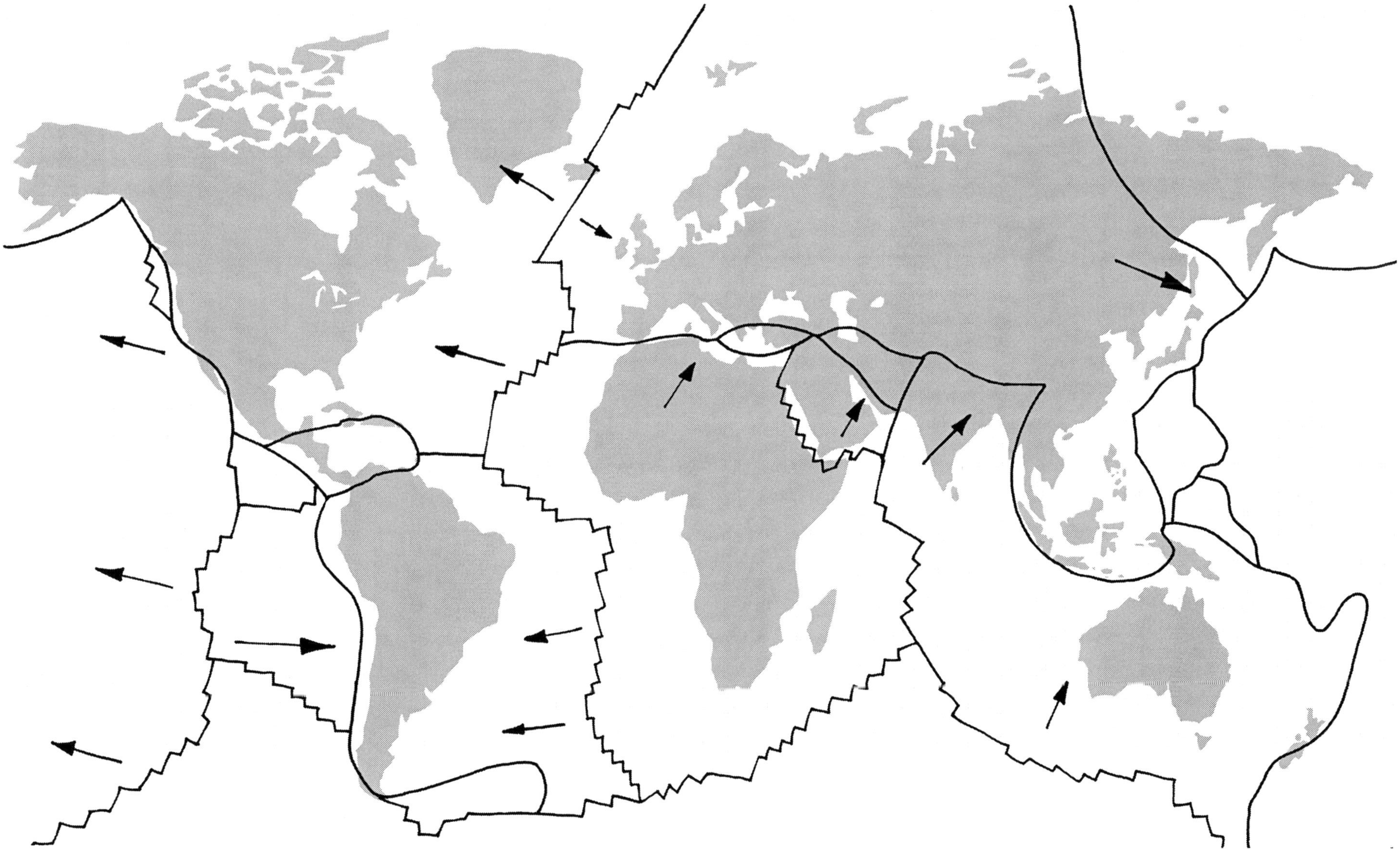

Earth's Structure

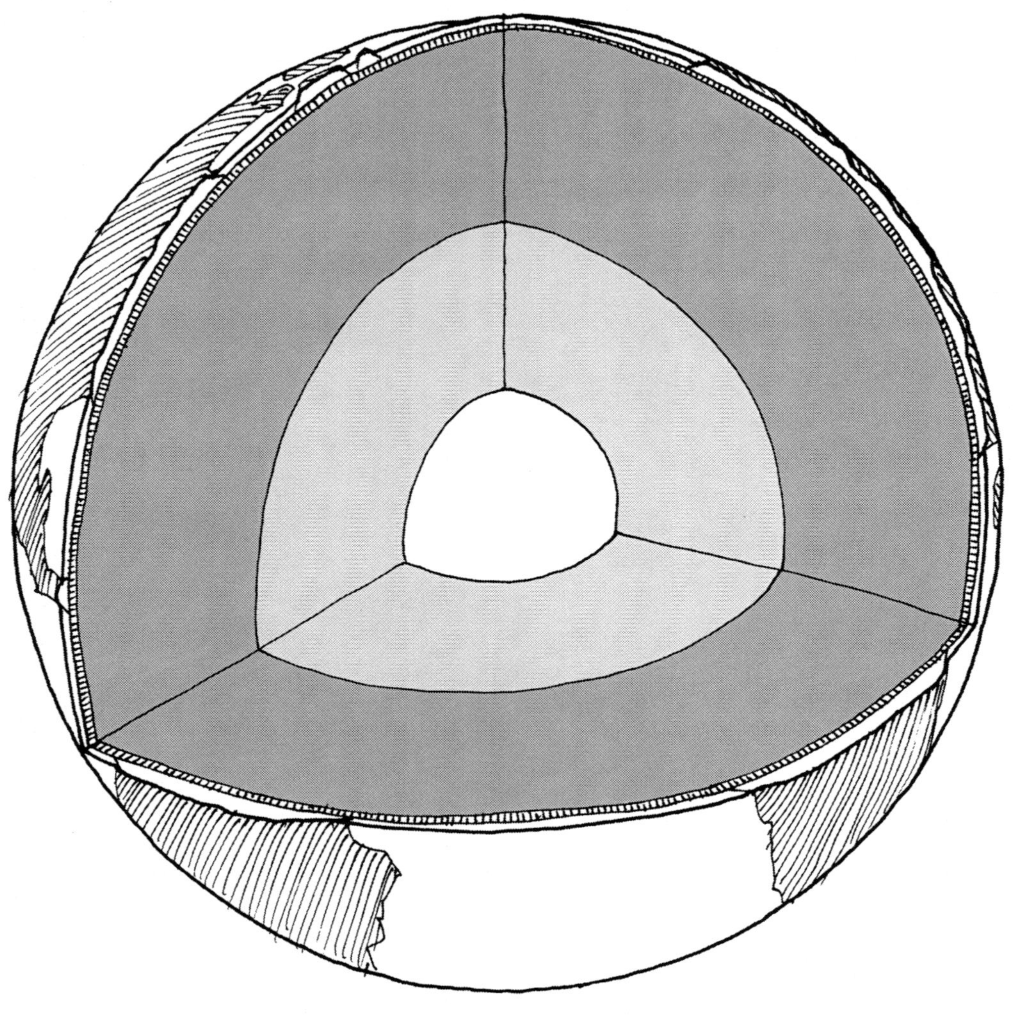

Crust: ____

Mantle: ____

Outer core: ____

Inner core: ____

Date: ___________________   **Name:** ___________________________

Diagram of Earth

Diagram of an Egg

How are the structures of Earth and an egg similar?

____

____

____

____

How are the structures of Earth and an egg different?

____

____

____

____

3 | Earth's Changing Surface

Background Information for Teachers

Earth's tectonic plates are constantly moving, though this movement occurs at a very slow rate of several centimetres each year. This movement is caused when hot, molten rock is forced up from deep in the mantle, toward Earth's crust. The hot, molten rock is more buoyant than the solid rock around it, so it rises upward through the mantle. At higher levels, it spreads out and cools, which makes it heavier, causing it to sink as it spreads out. This process is called a *convection current*.

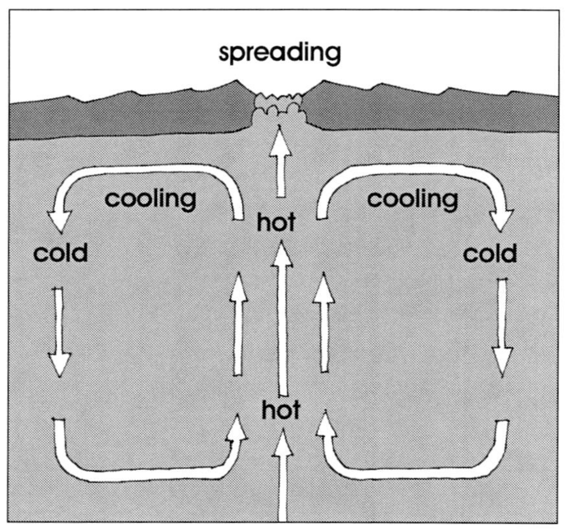

The enormous force of the convection currents splits Earth's crust apart. Where the magma reaches the surface, several things occur. As new crust is formed and plates are pushed apart, mountain ranges are created on the ocean floor. The continental crust is lighter than the oceanic crust, and even though the continental crust is thicker, it "floats" as the top layer above the mantle. Some of the tectonic plates are oceanic crust only, and some are both ocean crust and continental crust.

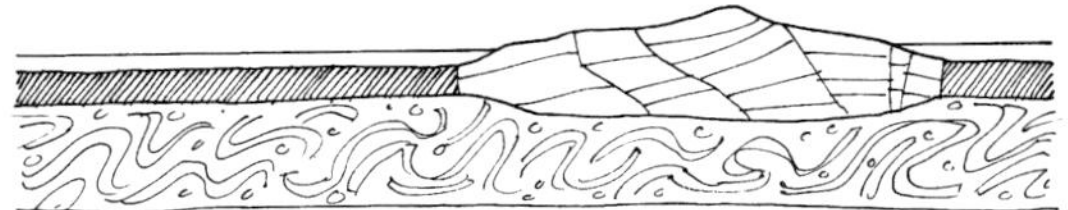

As plates separate from one another at one boundary, they collide at other boundaries. Where this happens, the thick dense oceanic crust slides beneath the edges of the other plate.

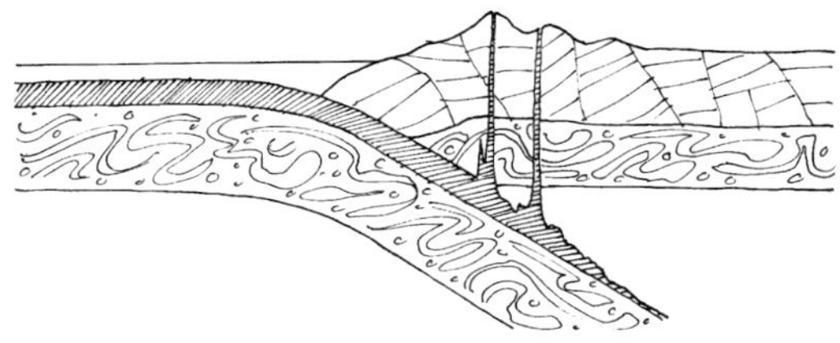

As the slab is pushed down, it heats up and then melts, producing buoyant magma that rises and creates volcanoes. The area where this transformation occurs is called the *subduction zone*. The process of subduction can also form deep ocean trenches at the point where an ocean plate is forced below a continental plate. This cycle of plate movement is ongoing and continually reshapes Earth's crust.

There are three kinds of boundaries between tectonic plates. First, when two plates are forced apart, magma rises between them, cools, and creates new crust. This type of plate boundary is called a *constructive margin*. Second, if one thinner plate is forced under a thicker plate, the thinner plate is transformed back into magma. This type of plate boundary is called a *destructive margin*. And last, when two plates slide past each other they neither create nor destroy crust. This type of plate boundary is called a *conservative margin*. The grinding movement at a conservative margin, however, often results in earthquakes.

3

Materials

- hot water and ice water (For safety purposes, ensure that the hot water is not hot enough to cause burns. Pour the hot water into one container and cold water into another. Place ice cubes in the container of cold water to keep the water cold.)
- clear 2-litre pop bottles
- food colouring
- index cards
- masking tape
- marker
- diagram titled, "Convection Currents" (included. Make an overhead transparency of this sheet.) (4.3.2)
- overhead projector
- diagram titled, "Spreading Ridge" (included. Make an overhead transparency of this sheet.) (4.3.3)
- diagram titled, "Geothermal Station" (included. Make an overhead transparency of this sheet.) (4.3.5)
- hot plate
- kettle
- water

Activity: Part One: Convection Currents

Explain to the student that they are going to investigate the motion of fluid at different temperatures. Divide the class into working groups and provide each group with 4 pop bottles, masking tape, index cards, markers, and hot and cold water. Distribute Activity Sheet A (4.3.1) for students to use to record their observations.

Conduct the investigation as follows:

1. Fill two of the pop bottles with cold tap water until there is no air left in the bottle. Label one bottle A1 and the other B1.

2. Add a few drops of food colouring to A1.

3. Fill two of the pop bottles with hot tap water until there is no air left in the bottle. Label one bottle A2 and the other B2.

4. Add a few drops of food colouring to B2.

5. Place an index card over the opening of A2, turn the bottle over, and place A2 on top of A1. Place an index card over the opening of B1, and place B1 on top of B2.

6. Carefully slide the index cards from between the bottles, and observe what happens.

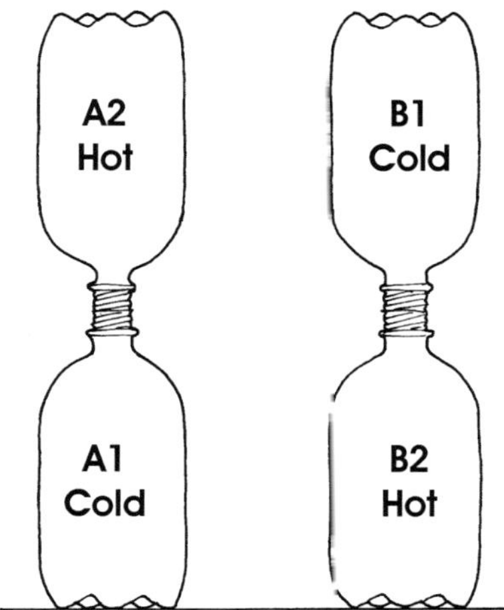

Have the students closely observe the movement and flow of the water and use the activity sheet to record their observations. Ask:

- What happens to the hot water when it comes in contact with the cold water?
- What does this tell you about how hot and cold temperatures affect the movement of liquids?

Display the diagram titled, "Convection Current" on the overhead (4.3.2). Use the Background Information for Teachers as a guide to discuss and explain the effects of convection currents on Earth's crust. Ask:

- How does the experiment compare to the magma inside Earth?

- How do the convection currents affect the tectonic plates?

Activity Sheet A

Directions to students:

Draw diagrams to show your observations of the movements of hot water and cold water. Also complete the extension question about the movement of magma (4.3.1).

Activity: Part Two

Display the diagram titled, "Spreading Ridge" (4.3.3) on the overhead. Explain the effect of convection currents on the tectonic plates. Use the Background Information for Teachers as a guide. As a class, discuss the diagram. Ask:

- What features on Earth's crust does the movement in the plates create?
- Why does subduction occur along the boundary between ocean and continental plates? (ocean plates are much thinner and denser than continental plates)

Focus now on the three types of plate boundaries. Again, use the Background Information for Teachers to describe this phenomenon, as students conduct a hands-on demonstration.

Explain to the students that that they are going to use their hands and bodies to demonstrate the three different types of plate boundaries and the force that they produce. Have the students stand close together, in two lines. Have each student make a fist with each hand and place their knuckles together so their elbows are out to the side. The students' elbows should be touching the elbows of their neighbours.

Have the students imagine that their fists are two tectonic plates, and their elbows are the outer edges of these two plates. For a constructive margin, ask the students to slowly pull their fists apart. Ask:

- What would take the place of the space between the two plates moving apart? (magma rises between them, then cools to create new crust)

For a destructive margin, ask the students to place their fists together again and push them together. As the pressure builds between the fists, ask them to push one fist harder than the other, and allow one fist to slide over the other. Have them push the "strong" fist over the "weaker" fist, until the "stronger" fist is at the elbow of the other arm. Ask:

- Why would one plate be forced over the other? (one plate is thicker than the other)
- What happens to the thinner plate? (turns back into magma)

For a conservative margin, ask the students to place their fists together again and slide them back and forth, rubbing their knuckles together. Ask:

- Is new plate created or old plate destroyed? (no)
- What happens to the two plates as they rub past each other? (grinding motion)
- What might be the result of the friction between this type of movement between two plates? (earthquakes)

Activity Sheet B

Directions to students:

Describe the three types of tectonic plate boundaries (4.3.4).

3

Activity: Part Three: Geothermal Energy

Review the structure of Earth. Ask:

- How is the temperature of the earth's core different from the crust?
- What is a *hot spring*?
- Has anyone been to a hot spring?
- What do you think makes the water in a hot spring so hot?

Explain to the students that heat from Earth's core warms water that is trapped in Earth's crust to form hot springs.

Display the diagram titled, "Geothermal Station" (4.3.5). Explain to the students that heat from magma in the crust and upper mantle also heats water that is trapped below the surface. (This energy can be tapped and used to produce electricity and to heat homes.)

Turn on the hot plate and begin heating the water. Have students observe closely as the hot plate heats the water and steam begins to rise. Ask:

- What happens to the water as it is heated?
- How is steam produced?
- Why is the force of the steam so strong?
- How is this similar to heated water coming up from the mantle?
- Is this type of energy a renewable resource?
- Is this a reliable source of energy?
- Would you use this type of energy if it was available?

Discuss this investigation, then provide each student with a copy of Activity Sheet C (4.3.6) to complete.

Activity Sheet C

Directions to students:

Draw, and label a diagram of the demonstration heating water. Complete all questions on the activity sheet (4.3.6).

Extensions

- To further demonstrate convection currents, display a lava lamp and discuss how it works. The movement inside the lamp is caused by heat, as convection currents. As an alternative, use a hot plate and transparent cookware to heat a layered mixture of Jell-O, oats, and Jell-O. Observe the movement as the mixture is heated:

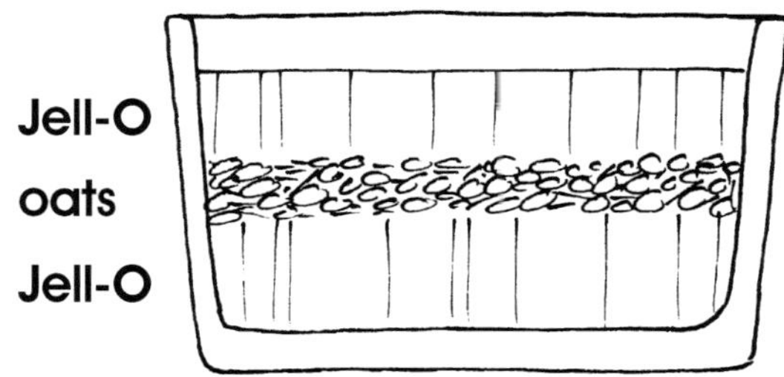

- The deepest ocean trench in the world is the Mariana Trench in the Pacific Ocean. It is 11,033 metres deep, which means it could swallow the tallest mountain on land, Mount Everest. Have the students research this and other ocean trenches for discoveries from the deepest parts of the ocean.

Assessment Suggestions

- Observe the groups as they investigate convection currents. Focus specifically on their ability to work together to complete the task. Use the Cooperative Skills Teacher Assessment sheet on page 21 to record results.
- Have students complete a Cooperative Skills Self-Assessment sheet on page 23 to reflect on their ability to work together.

Convection Currents:
Movement of Fluids at Different Temperatures

Observations of the pop bottle investigation:

_______________________________   _______________________________

_______________________________   _______________________________

_______________________________   _______________________________

_______________________________   _______________________________

Molten magma is like water. What do you think happens when hot magma rises toward the crust and cools? Explain the reasons for your answer based on your observations from this investigation.

____

____

____

____

Convection Currents

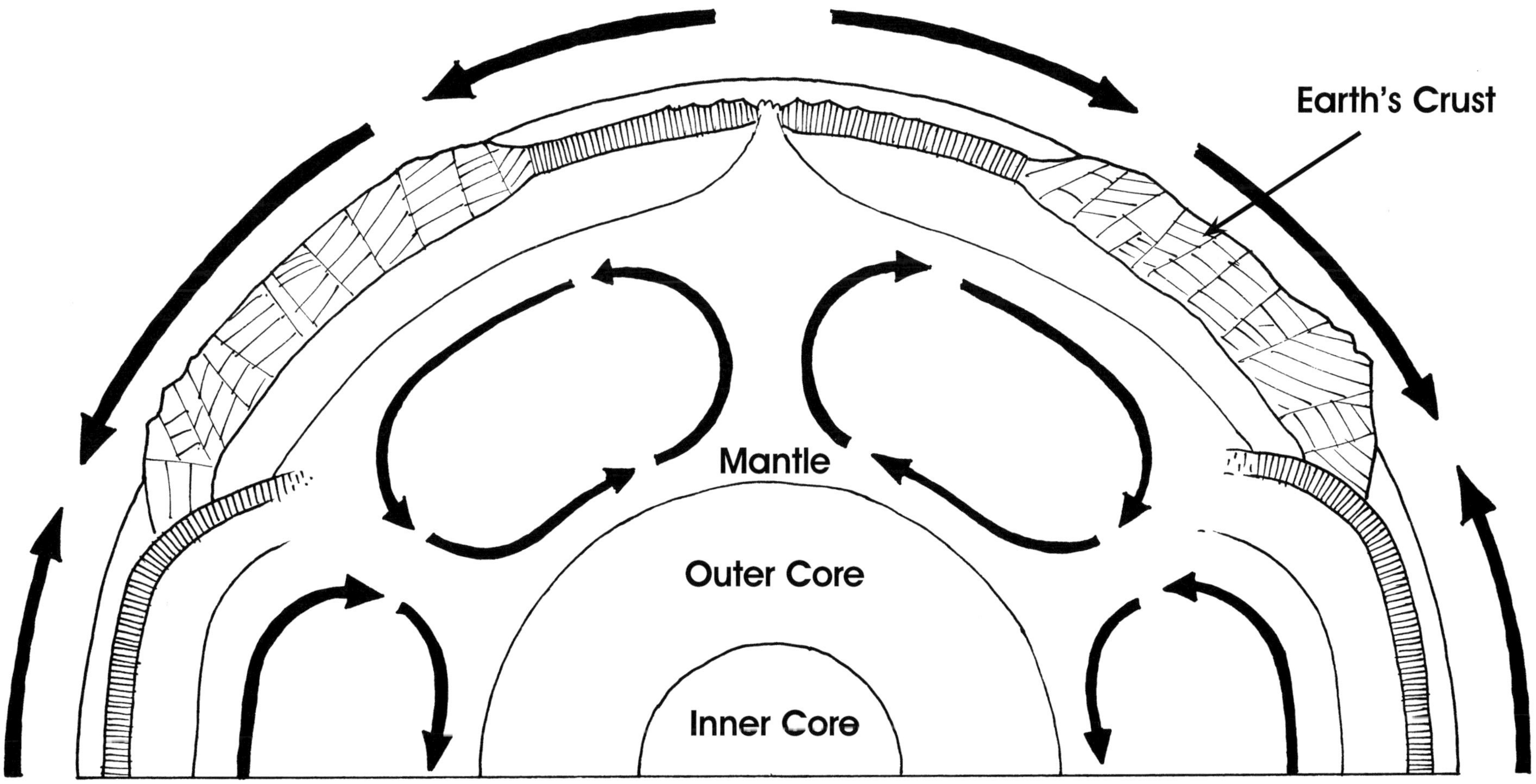

Spreading Ridge

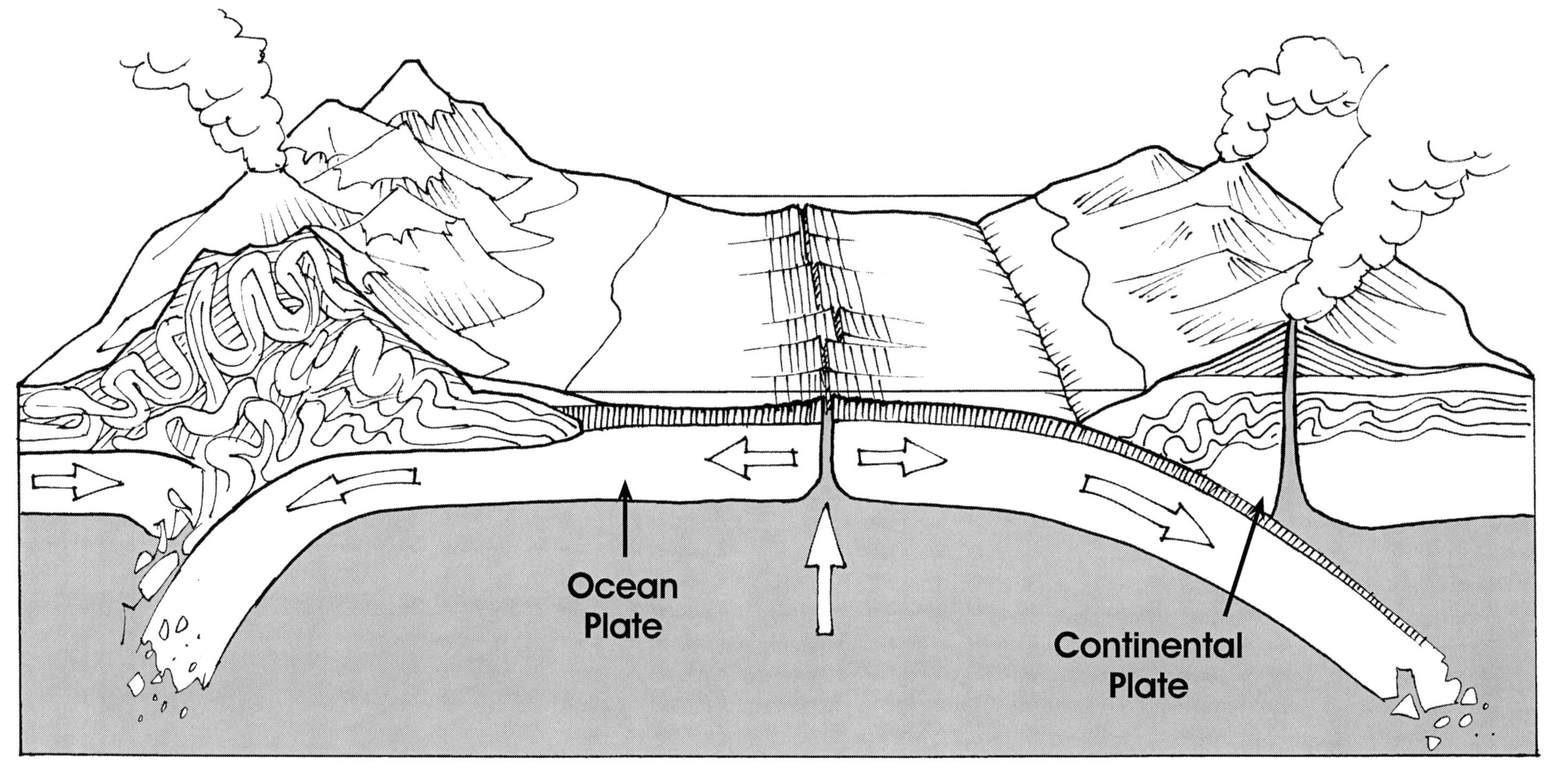

Tectonic Plate Movement

Constructive Margin

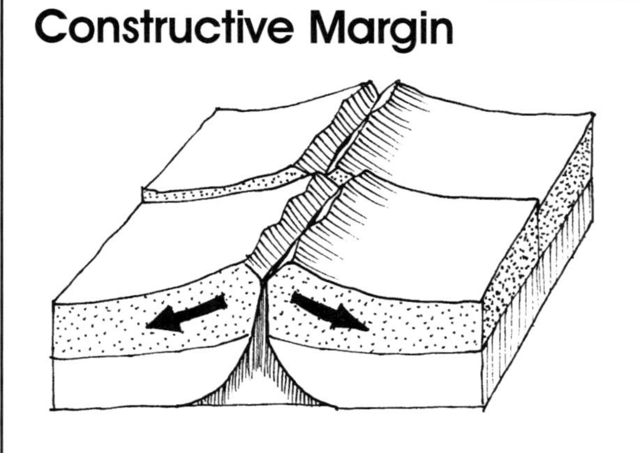

Description of Margin: _______________

____

____

____

Description of Force: _______________

____

____

____

Destructive Margin

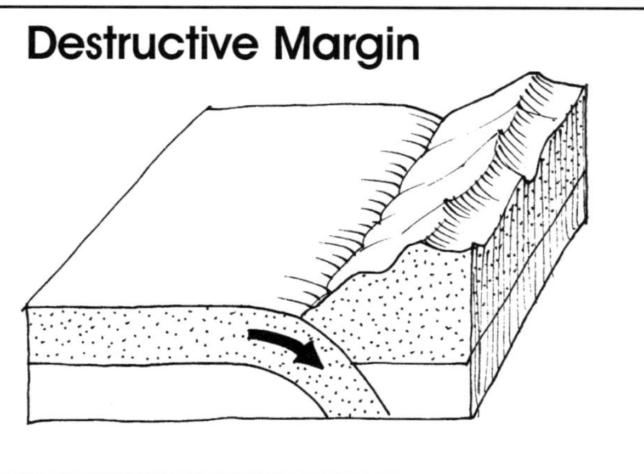

Description of Margin: _______________

____

____

____

Description of Force: _______________

____

____

____

Conservative Margin

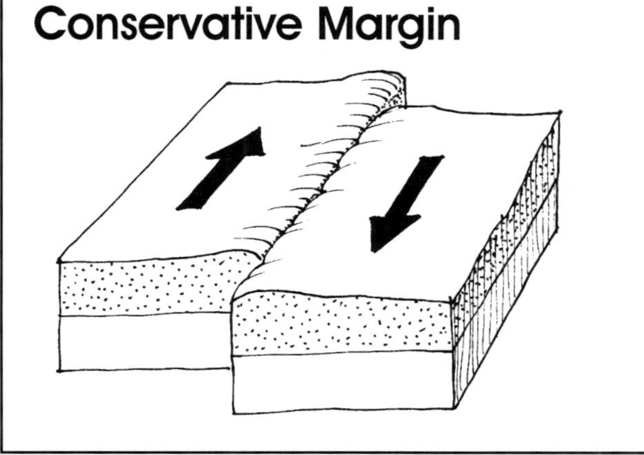

Description of Margin: _______________

____

____

____

Description of Force: _______________

____

____

____

Geothermal Station

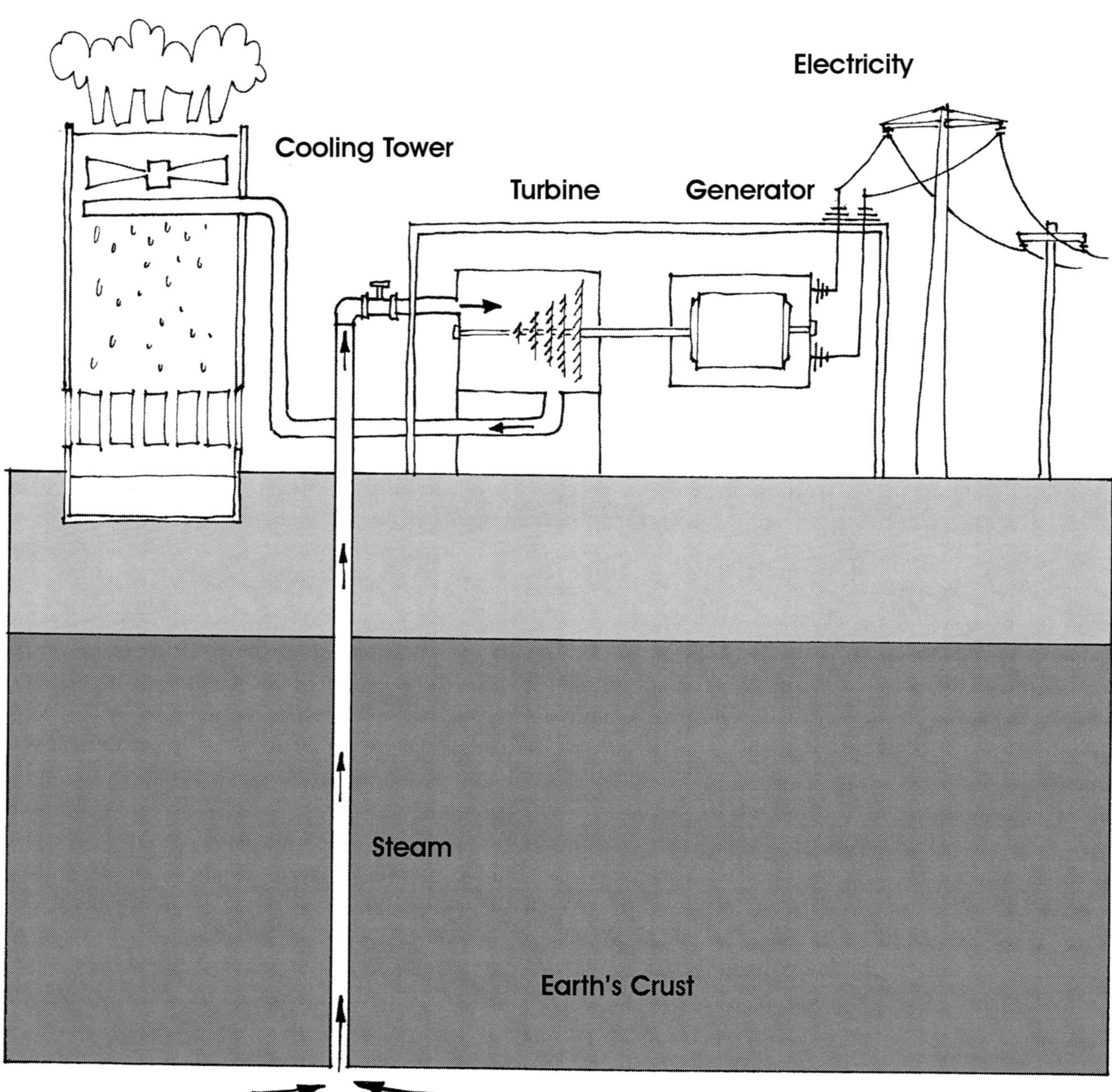

Geothermal Energy

Explain how the experiment is similar to a geothermal installation.

____

____

____

____

____

How does geothermal electricity compare to hydroelectricity in terms of environmental impact and power capacity?

____

____

____

____

____

4 | Mountain Formation

Background Information for Teachers

Most mountain ranges occur along past or present tectonic plate boundaries. As the plates pull apart or push against one another, three basic processes cause mountains to form: folding, faulting, or volcanism. Some mountains stand alone. However, most mountains are joined together in a line, or *series*. A series of mountains together is called a *range*, and several ranges of mountains are referred to as a *chain*.

Mountains form in several ways: (1) by folding when two plates push against one another, and the rocks that are being compressed buckle and fold, (2) by faulting when the earth's crust cracks and the rocks on either side slide up or down, past one another, and (3) by volcanism when magma rises from deeper rocks and erupts or extrudes at Earth's surface. (Volcanic mountains are discussed in detail in lesson 6.)

Materials

- overhead projector
- map titled "Earth's Tectonic Plates" (included with lesson 2) (4.2.2)
- diagram titled, "Earth's Major Mountain Ranges" (included. Make an overhead transparency of this sheet.) (4.4.1)
- student atlases
- information sheet titled, "Earth's Major Mountain Ranges: Answer Key" (included. Make an overhead transparency of this sheet.) (4.4.3)
- diagram titled, "Mountain Types" (included. Make an overhead transparency of this sheet.) (4.4.4)
- 4 colours of modelling clay (enough for each student)
- plastic knives
- rolling pins

Activity: Part One: Mountain Locations

Display the diagram titled, "Earth's Tectonic Plates" from lesson 2 (4.2.2) on the overhead. Explain to the students that the majority of mountains are found along the boundaries of tectonic plates. To illustrate this, place the map titled, "Earth's Major Mountain Ranges" (4.4.1) overtop the map titled, "Earth's Tectonic Plates" (4.2.2). Ask:

- Why are most mountain ranges and plate boundaries in the same location?

Discuss students' ideas and concepts in detail, using the Background Information for Teachers to explain why mountains form along boundaries of the tectonic plates.

Divide the class into working groups. Distribute atlases to each group, along with Activity Sheet A (4.4.2). Have the students use their atlases to identify the twenty major mountain ranges of the world.

Once the groups have finished, display the information sheet titled, "Earth's Major Mountain Ranges: Answer Key" (4.4.3), and have students check their results.

Activity Sheet A

Directions to students:

Using the atlas, locate the topographical maps of the continents. Complete the map titled, "Find Earth's Major Mountain Ranges" by identifying and labelling the twenty major mountain ranges on the different continents of the world (4.4.2).

Activity: Part Two: Mountain Types

Display the diagram titled "Mountain Types" (4.4.4). Using the Background Information for Teachers, explain and discuss the different mountain types.

4

Divide the class into working groups. Provide each group with four colours of modelling clay, rolling pins, plastic knives.

Have the students make a rectangle shape from each colour of modelling clay, and pile the clay layers on top of one another. Have the students flatten the clay with a rolling pin. Ask the students to imagine that the layered clay is part of Earth's crust.

Leave the diagrams of mountain types on the overhead for reference during this activity. Explain to the students that they are going to create two different mountain types using the modelling clay. Provide the following instructions:

1. To create a fold mountain, lay the clay on a smooth surface, and put one hand on either side of the clay. Slowly push your hands and the clay together until the clay bends and folds.

Ask:

- What do your hands that are pressing the clay together represent?
- What happens when two thick pieces of Earth's crust are pushed together?

2. To create a fault mountain, make a diagonal cut through the middle of the clay with a plastic knife.

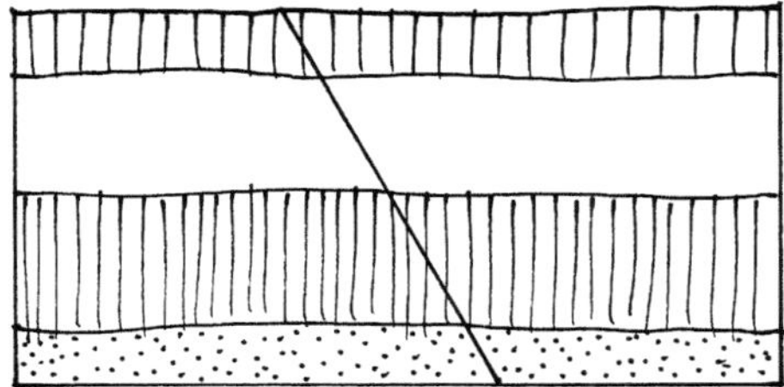

Place one hand on either side of the clay, and slowly push the pieces together.

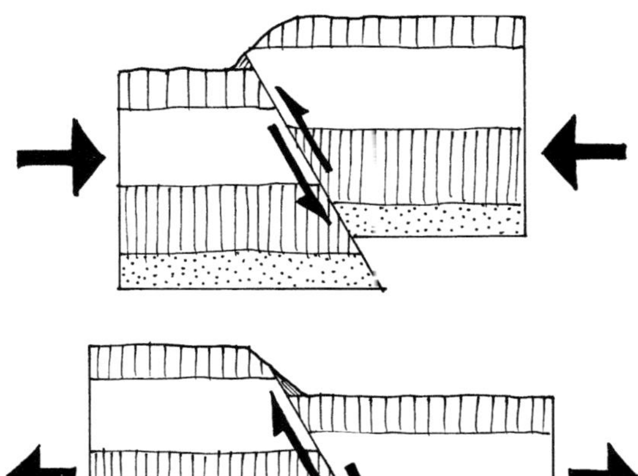

Ask:

- What happens to the two pieces of clay?
- Why might one layer of crust push over top another piece?

Now, place one hand on either side of the clay and slowly pull the pieces apart.

Ask:

- What happens to the pieces of clay?
- Why might one layer of crust pull away from another?

As a conclusion to the activity provide students with Activity Sheet B.

Activity Sheet B

Directions to students:

Draw a diagram showing how folding and faulting can create mountains, as demonstrated with the modeling clay. Indicate the direction of the tectonic movement with arrows. Describe the causes of the mountain formation (4.4.5).

▶

Extensions

- Have students research one of the 20 major mountain ranges and present their findings. Students can search for information about the type, height, age, people who have climbed the mountain, and so on.

- Examine pictures of different types of mountains. Have students identify them as fold, fault, or volcanic mountain types.

Earth's Major Mountain Ranges

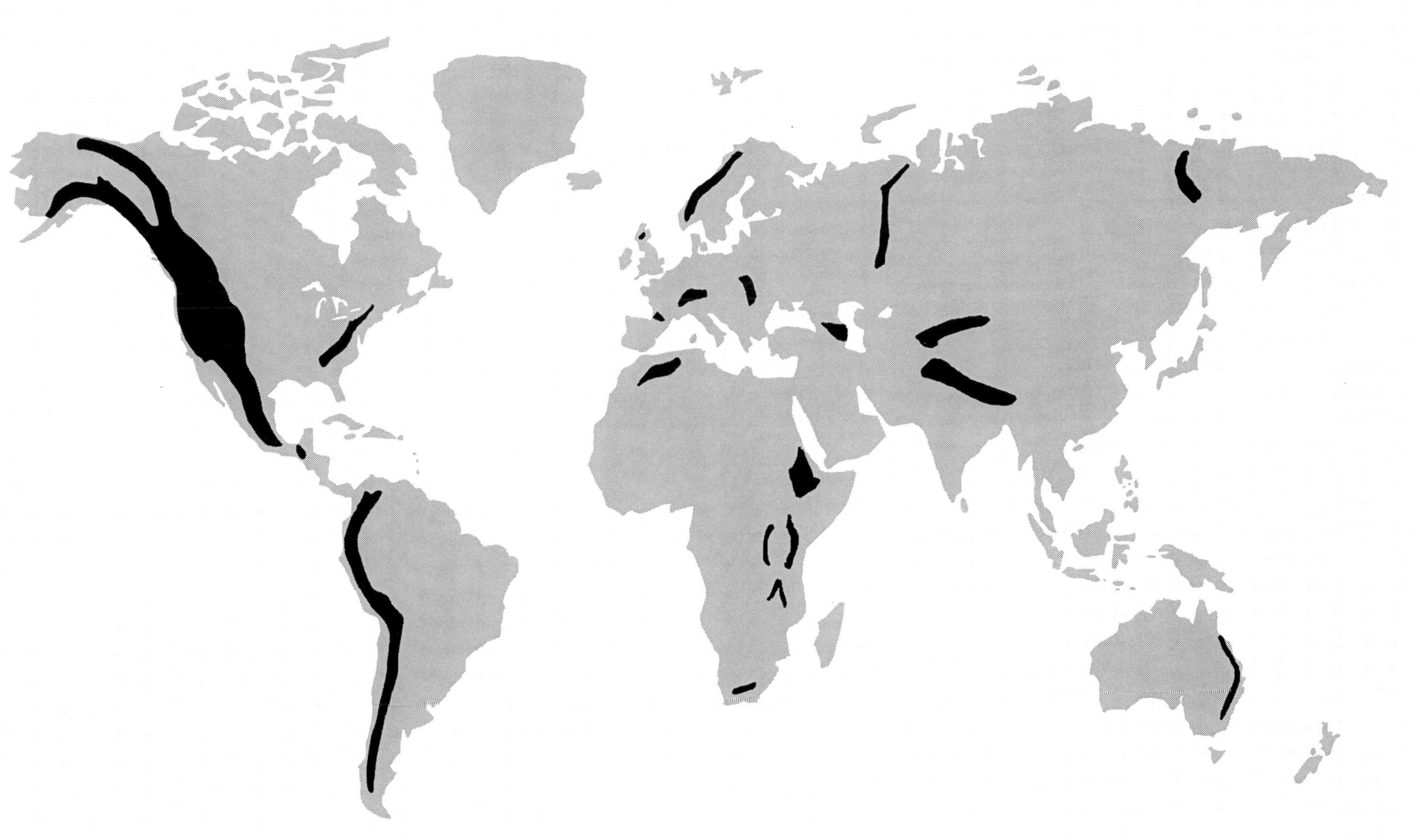

Date: _______________________   Name: _______________________

Find Earth's Major Mountain Ranges

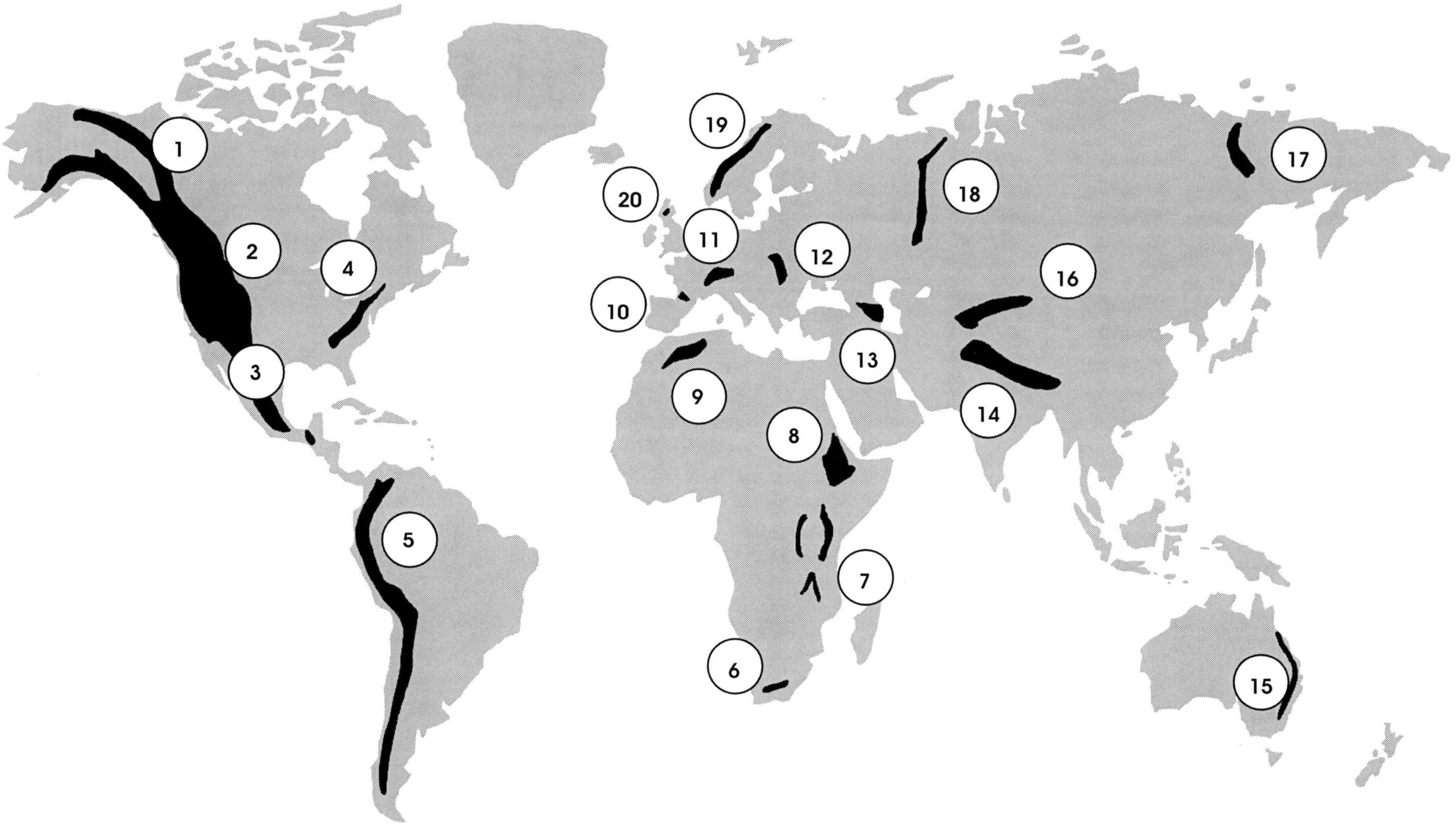

Earth's Major Mountain Ranges: Answer Key

1. Mackenzie Mountains
2. Rocky Mountains
3. Sierra Madre
4. Appalachians
5. Andes
6. Drakensberg Mountains
7. East African Rift Valley
8. Ethiopian Highlands
9. Atlas Mountains
10. Pyrenees
11. Alps
12. Carpathian Mountains
13. Caucasus Mountains
14. Himalayas
15. Great Dividing Range
16. Tien Shan
17. Verkhoyansk Range
18. Urals Mountains
19. Scandinavian Highlands
20. Scottish Highlands

Mountain Types

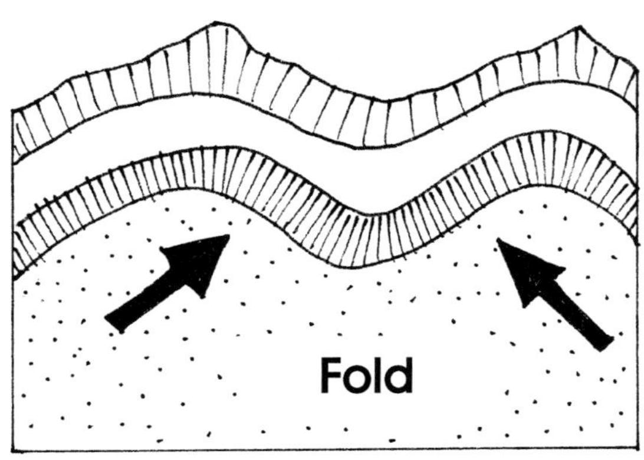

Mountain type

Fold

Cause of formation

Layers of rock buckle and fold when pushed together. The upfolds form the mountains and valleys.

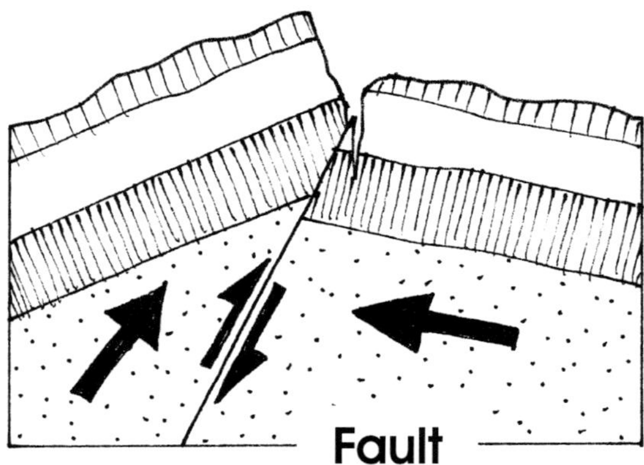

Mountain type

Fault

Cause of formation

The mountain is formed when layers of rock on one side of a fault crack and are pushed upward.

Mountain Building

Mountain type

____

Cause of formation

____

____

____

Mountain type

____

Cause of formation

____

____

____

5 | Earthquakes

Background Information for Teachers

Earthquakes occur in the same areas as Earth's mountain ranges. Because mountains are formed on the boundaries of plates, these rocks are unstable and prone to earthquakes. Earthquakes that occur in the ocean are found along underwater chains of volcanic mountains.

Earthquakes are sudden, violent movements deep in Earth's crust. The constant movement along the plate boundaries creates an enormous buildup of pressure. Although rock can absorb the pressure over hundreds, or thousands, of years, eventually the rock snaps apart under the stress. When this occurs, energy is released as shock waves, radiating from the *focus* or hypocentre. The hypocentre is the exact point where rock first cracks and moves. The point on Earth's crust directly above the hypocentre is called the epicentre. If the hypocentre is deep in Earth's crust, the tremors will be mild. However, if the hypocentre is close to the surface (or shallow), the tremors at Earth's crust will be more pronounced.

Shock waves occur as two types of seismic waves: primary (P) waves and secondary (S) waves. P-waves are the first to be detected by seismic monitoring stations. These waves collide into one another, stretching and squeezing the rock as they travel through Earth. P-waves can pass through solid rock, volcanic lava, water, and air, and travel twice as fast as S-waves. S -waves are slower and move the rock up and down, and from side to side. Unlike P-waves, S-waves cannot travel through liquid and, therefore, are not always detected.

The seismic waves that reach the top of Earth's crust are called *surface waves*. These waves do the most damage because they produce severe ground movements. The first movement that is detected is at the epicentre and may only last for 30–60 seconds, but continued movement or *aftershocks* may occur as the disrupted rock settles back into place.

Damage on the earth's surface from an earthquake can take the form of crumbling buildings, fires (from broken gas lines), earth fractures, landslides, and tsunamis. *Tsunamis* are gigantic sea waves caused by earthquakes, landslides, or volcanic eruptions on the seabed.

Since earthquakes can cause considerable damage to people and property, seismologists, (scientists who study earthquakes) attempt to learn as much as they can in order to be better equipped to predict tremors. Seismometers or seismographs record and measure seismic waves and determine the strength and duration of earthquakes. Often, earthquakes are measured on the Richter scale. This numbering system measures the magnitude of an earthquake. Each number on the Richter scale represents a 10-times increase in the ground movement as recorded on a seismometer.

In order to better protect people and property from the effects of earthquakes, engineers and architects attempt to design buildings that will better withstand substantial earthquakes. Cities located along certain fault lines, such as Vancouver and San Francisco, experience regular earthquakes. Many of the buildings are designed and built to withstand large tremors.

Materials

- overhead projector
- map titled, "Major Earthquake Locations" (included. Make an overhead transparency of this sheet.) (4.5.1)
- map titled, "Earth's Tectonic Plates" (included in lesson 2) (4.2.2)
- diagram titled, "An Earthquake" (included. Make an overhead transparency of this sheet.) (4.5.2)

- small blanket
- sand
- rubber mallets
- metre sticks
- large jar with a lid
- weights/rocks
- large sheets of white paper (e.g., chart paper or white mural paper)
- diagram titled, "Earthquake Destruction" (included. Make an overheard transparency of this sheet.) (4.5.4)
- information sheet titled, "The Destructive Power of Earthquakes" (included. Make a copy for each student.) (4.5.5)
- statistics chart titled, "Significant Earthquakes" (included. Make a copy for each pair of students.) (4.5.6)
- student atlases (one per pair)
- reference material on earthquakes
- access to the Internet

Activity: Part One: Shock Waves

Begin by determining students' background knowledge of earthquakes. Ask:

- What is an earthquake?
- Has anyone ever experienced an earthquake? Where? How did it make you feel?
- Where do earthquakes occur?

Display the map titled, "Major Earthquake Locations" (4.5.1). Ask:

- Do the locations of where earthquakes occur remind you of other patterns we have studied?

Place the map titled, "Earth's Tectonic Plates" (4.2.2) overtop of the map titled, "Major Earthquake Locations" (4.5.1). Ask:

- Why do earthquakes occur in the same places as the plate boundaries?

Display the diagram titled, "An Earthquake" (4.5.2). Use the Background Information for Teachers as a guide to explain the terms and process. Provide an opportunity for students to ask questions, clarify ideas, and describe an earthquake in their own words.

Now explain to the students that scientists who study earthquakes are called *seismologists*. For the next investigation, have the students to imagine that they are seismologists.

Explain that earthquakes produce surface waves. These waves cause a ripple effect on Earth's crust. Demonstrate a surface wave with the blanket. Hold the blanket on an edge and shake it like you would shake a sheet to smooth it out on a bed. Ask students to watch the ripples of the blanket. Ask:

- What happens to the size of the ripples along the blanket?
- Why does the size of ripples change?
- If the blanket were Earth's crust, where would the most damage occur? Why?

Divide the class into working groups. Provide each group with sand, a rubber mallet, and a metre stick. Have the students pour a small amount of sand onto the desk. Ask:

- What do you think will happen if you strike the desk with the mallet right next to the sand?
- What will happen to the sand when you strike the desk 20 or 30 cm away from the edge?

Discuss students ideas, then let them test their predictions. Ask:

- How is this activity like an earthquake?

Explain to the students that the sand represents Earth's surface and the mallet is like shock waves at the epicentre. Have the students conduct the activity again, closely observing the sand as they strike the mallet at different distances from the pile. Ask:

- What happens to the sand the farther away it is from the shock wave created by the mallet?
- What happens on the earth's surface when the earthquake's epicentre is close by? Farther away?
- How is the sand similar to seismic waves?

Discuss students' ideas and observations, then have them complete Activity Sheet A (4.5.3).

Activity Sheet A

Directions to students:

Draw a diagram of the sand and mallet investigation, then answer the questions on Activity Sheet A (4.5.3).

Activity: Part Two: Seismic Readings

Explain to the students that a seismometer records vibrations made by earthquakes. A seismogram is the visual measurement of seismic waves. In this investigation, students will make their own seismometer and then create a seismogram.

Divide the class into working groups. Provide each group with masking tape, a pencil, a large sheet of white paper, and a lidded jar filled with weights or rocks. Have the students place the sheet of paper on a desk and position the jar at one end of the paper. Have them attach a pencil to the side of the jar with tape so that the point of the pencil points down and just touches the paper. Have the students test their apparatus by slowly pulling the paper out from under the jar. The pencil should make a straight line on the paper.

***

Note: One student should monitor the jar to ensure that it does not tip. Stress that the students should not touch the jar unless it is going to fall over.

***

To conduct the investigation, have one student continuously pull the paper while another student gently shakes the desk from side to side to create P-waves. Then have them shake the desk a little more slowly, but harder, to create S-waves. Finally, have the student slowly jolt the desk from side to side to create even bigger, longer squiggles that will represent surface waves.

Once the groups have completed this investigation, discuss their results. Ask:

- How did the movement of the desk change the pencil line?
- Which lines on your paper represent S-waves? P-waves? Surface waves?

On their "seismograms", have the students draw brackets around the three different types of waves and label them as *P*, *S*, or *surface waves*. Have students compare and discuss their results. Ask:

- Why would recording and studying Earth's tremors be useful to seismologists?

Activity: Part Three: Earthquake Destruction

Display the diagram titled, "Earthquake Destruction" (4.5.4). Ask:

- What difference does the depth of the hypocentre make on surface waves?
- How might this impact on the degree of damage or destruction caused by an earthquake?

Have the students examine the third diagram on the sheet titled, "Tsunami" (4.5.4). Explain that a tsunami (a Japanese word) is a giant, destructive wave that can occur as a result of an earthquake below sea level. As the waves travel toward shallower water, they "pile up" on one another, forming increasingly higher, breaking waves.

Provide each student with a copy of the information sheet titled, "The Destructive Power

5

of Earthquakes" (4.5.5). Read, and discuss the information on the charts. Ask:

- Why are minor earthquakes more common than major earthquakes?
- How can an earthquake cause loss of life?
- What causes landslides and fires during an earthquake?

Divide the class into pairs of students. Provide each pair with the statistics chart titled, "Significant Earthquakes" (4.5.6), an atlas, and Activity Sheets B and C (4.5.7, 4.5.8). Have the students study the statistics, complete the map, and answer the questions.

Activity Sheet B

Directions to students:

Using the atlas, locate the sites of earthquakes on the world map. Colour in each country/area. Complete the legend (4.5.7).

Activity Sheet C

Directions to students:

Use the statistic chart and your completed world map on Activity Sheet B (4.5.7) to help you answer the questions (4.5.8).

Activity: Part Four:
Preparing for Earthquakes

Explain that because of the destructive nature of earthquakes, engineers and architects try to design buildings that will withstand earthquakes, and governments protect people living in earthquake zones by creating city plans and using safety measures that will save lives. Provide students with an opportunity to search print and electronic resources to gather and record data on past and present earthquakes, as well as information on quake-proof buildings and safety procedures during tremors. Have them use Activity Sheet D (4.5.9) to record their findings.

Once the activity has been completed, have the students share the information they gathered.

Activity Sheet D

Directions to students:

Use reference materials to answer the questions (4.5.9).

Activity: Part Five:
The Canadian Connection

Provide an opportunity for students to learn about seismic activity in Canada. Begin with a discussion to access the students' prior knowledge. Ask:

- Has there ever been an earthquake in Canada?
- Are earthquakes a common occurrence in our community?
- Have there been destructive earthquakes in Canada?

Provide an opportunity for students to examine maps of Canada that display seismic activity. Such maps are available on the Natural Resources Canada web site **www.seismo.nrcan.gc.ca** . Students can use the database to create maps that show the location and magnitude of all earthquakes in Canada since the sixteenth century.

Allow students time to examine and print out some maps. Discuss their findings. Ask:

- Where have most earthquakes occurred in Canada?
- What areas of Canada have experienced the fewest earthquakes?
- Where in Canada was the earthquake with the greatest magnitude?
- Why do you think there have been more major earthquakes in British Columbia than in central Canada?

▶

5

Display the overhead map titled, "Earth's Plate Tectonics" (from lesson 2). As a class, discuss the location of the plate boundaries in Canada, and relate this to the location of earthquakes across the country.

Extensions

- Liquefaction Experiment: Liquefaction is the process by which sediment or soil is transformed into a fluid mass because of an earthquake. To provide an example of this phenomenon, fill a pail with sand. Set a brick on top of the sand vertically and shake the pail. The brick may shake but will not fall over. Now pour enough water into the pail so that it is level with the sand. Again, shake the pail and the brick will sink into the sand. Liquefaction is often the reason buildings are damaged or destroyed, because soft loose ground becomes unstable during an earthquake.

- Chinese scientist Chang Heng built the first instrument for measuring earthquakes in the second century A.D. Later, in 1856, Luigi Palmieri invented the first seismograph. Since then many other scientific tools have been invented such as the creepmeter, the magnetometer, and Global Positioning Systems (GPS). Research these and other scientific equipment used for measuring earthquakes. Have students present their findings to the class.

- There are many videos available about the history and effects of earthquakes. Book a video about earthquakes from your local library, and view with your students and discuss.

- The San Andreas Fault is a conservative margin fault in the state of California. Because major quakes in this area are a certainty, considerable study takes place in this earthquake zone. Have students research the major earthquakes in this area, create a model of the fault, locate pictures, and develop a safety-and-rescue plan that may save lives in a future earthquake.

- Japan has 1,500 active faults and has had more than 400 major earthquakes in the last 1,000 years. The Japanese have been recording earthquake data for over 2,000 years because there are so many earthquakes, volcanic eruptions, and tsunamis that affect the inhabitants of the country of islands. Have the students research the ancient Japanese legends about earthquakes and tsunamis, and the latest Japanese technology.

Assessment Suggestion

Observe the students as they investigate and test their quake-proof structures. Focus specifically on the students' ability to follow instructions, record results, develop new strategies, and draw conclusions. Use the Anecdotal Record sheet on page 16 to record results.

Major Earthquake Locations

An Earthquake

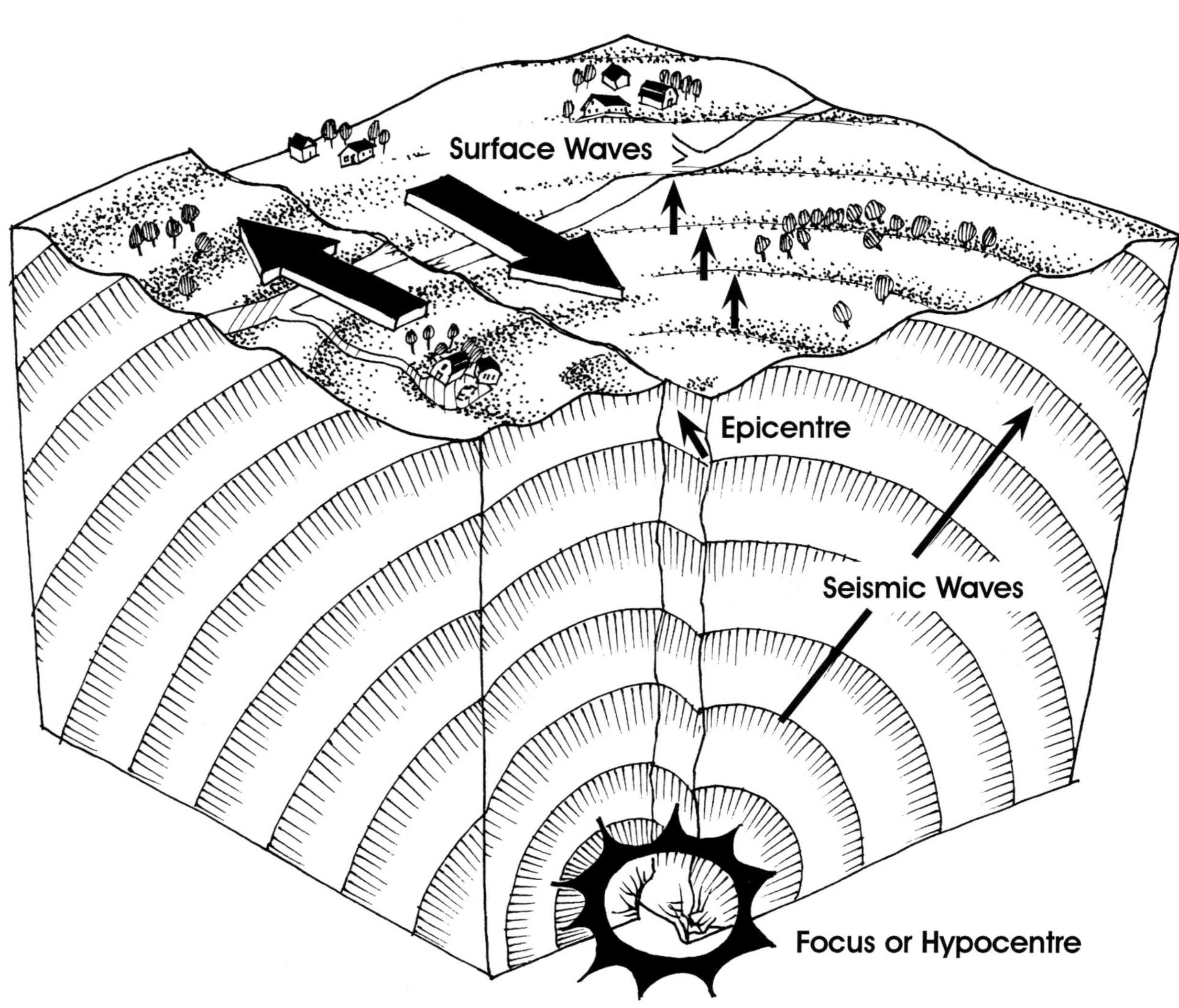

Investigating Earthquakes

4.5.3 – 341

Diagram of sand and mallet investigation.

1. How is this activity like an earthquake?

____

____

2. What does the sand represent?

____

3. What does the mallet represent?

____

4. What does the "jumping sand" represent?

____

5. What happens to sand that is farthest away from the shock wave created by the mallet?

____

6. What happens to Earth's surface if the epicentre of an earthquake is close to the surface? Farther away?

____

Earthquake Destruction

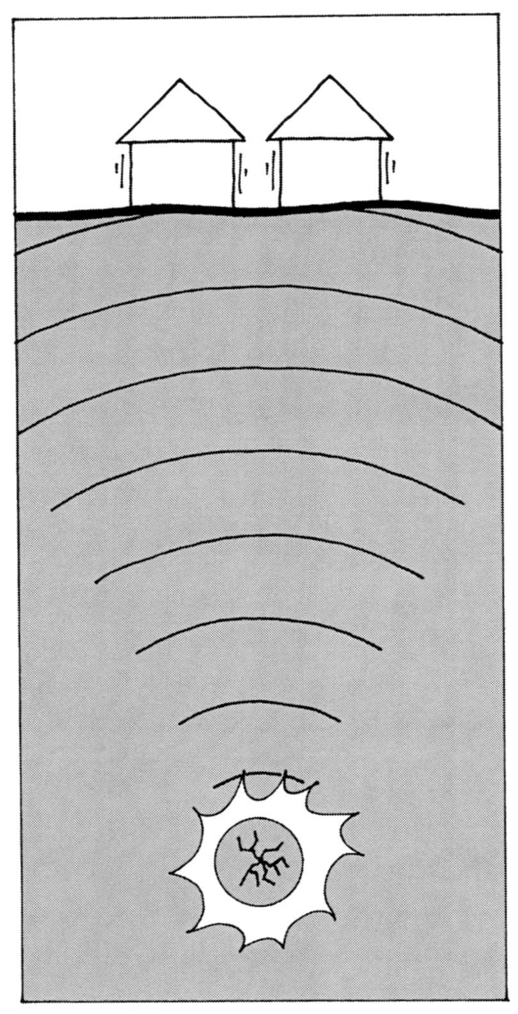

Tsunami

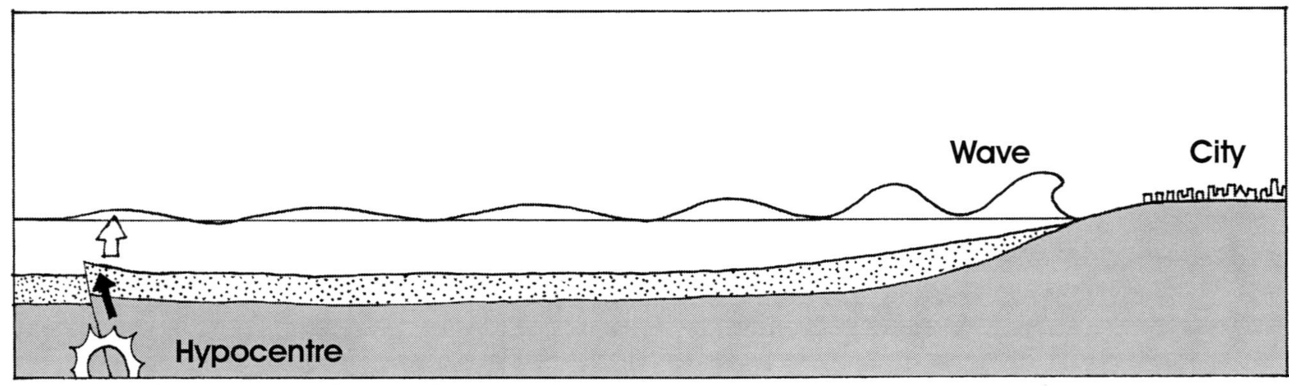

The Destructive Power of Earthquakes

The Richter Scale:

In 1935, seismologist Charles F. Richter developed a numbering system that measures the strength of earthquakes. Each increasing number on the Richter scale represents a 10-times increase in the ground movement recorded on a seismometer.

Magnitude	Description	Average per year	Intensity near epicenter
0-1.9	-	700,000	Recorded but not felt
2-2.9	-	300,000	Recorded but not felt
3-3.9	Minor	40,000	Felt by some
4-4.9	Light	6,200	Felt by many
5-5.9	Moderate	800	Slight damage
6-6.9	Strong	120	Damaging
7-7.9	Major	18	Destructive
8+	Great	1 every 20 years	Devastating

Some of the most destructive known earthquakes on record (50,000 or more deaths)

Date	Location	Deaths	Magnitude	Comments
Aug. 9, 1138	Aleppo Syria	230,000		
Jan. 23. 1556	Shansi China	830,000		
Nov. 1, 1755	Lisbon Portugal	70,000	8.7	Great tsunami
Dec. 28, 1908	Messian Italy	70,000-100,000	7.5	Tsunami
Dec. 16, 1920	Gansu China	200,000	8.6	Major earth fractures and landslides
Sept. 1, 1923	Kwanto Japan	143,000	8.3	
May 22, 1927	Xining China	200,000	8.6	Major earth fractures and landslides
May 30, 1935	Quetta Pakistan	30,000-60,000	7.5	Quetta almost completely destroyed
Jan. 27, 1976	Tangshan China	255,000 (official) 655,000 (estimate)	8.0	

*Source: http://neic.usgs.gov.neis/eqlist/eqsmode.html

Significant Earthquakes

January – March 2002

Date	Magnitude	Location
January 2, 2002	7.2	Vanuatu Islands
January 3, 2002	6.2	Afghanistan
January 3, 2002	6.6	Vanuatu Islands
January 9, 2002	5.3	Tajikistan
January 10, 2002	6.7	North Coast of New Guinea
January 17, 2002	4.7	Democratic Republic of Congo
January 19, 2002	4.6	Rwanda
January 20, 2002	5.1	Democratic Republic of Congo
January 21, 2002	4.6	Democratic Republic of Congo
January 21, 2002	5.1	Democratic Republic of Congo
January 21, 2002	4.7	Democratic Republic of Congo
January 21, 2002	4.6	Turkey
January 22, 2002	6.2	Crete
January 22, 2002	5.2	Democratic Republic of Congo
February 3, 2002	6.5	Western Turkey
February 3, 2002	4.9	Tajikistan
February 5, 2002	6.6	Papua New Guinea
February 17, 2002	5.4	Iran
February 20, 2002	4.9	Poland
March 3, 2002	7.4	Afghanistan
March 5, 2002	7.5	Philippines
March 25, 2002	6.1	Afghanistan
March 27, 2002	5.6	Afghanistan
March 28, 2002	6.5	Chile-Bolivia Border
March 31, 2002	7.1	Taiwan

(From USGS Earthquake Hazards Program)

Date: _______________________   Name: _______________________

Location of Significant Earthquakes
Jan – Mar 2002

Looking at Earthquake Statistics

Which country had the most significant earthquakes from January to March, 2002?

____

Why do you think that these countries experienced more significant earthquakes than other countries?

____

____

What patterns have you discovered about earthquakes from studying these statistics?

____

____

From studying these statistics, make prediction about when, where, and in what magnitude earthquakes will occur in the future.

____

____

Preparing for Earthquakes

1. List the locations and dates of three major earthquakes.

____

____

____

2. What changes were made to the infrastructure of cities where the earthquakes occurred?

____

____

____

3. How are buildings made to minimize damage from earthquakes? What are some examples?

____

____

____

4. List some safety procedures people should follow during an earthquake.

____

____

____

6 | Volcanoes

Background Information for Teachers

Magma is molten rock that exists inside the earth. Once the magma erupts at Earth's surface, the molten rock is called *lava*. A volcanic mountain is formed when erupting lava and ash settle and, over time, build up and form layers making a mountain. There are many volcanoes on Earth's surface. Like earthquakes, most volcanoes are located near tectonic plate boundaries. The plates are either being pulled apart, allowing molten rock to rise through the fractures (constructive plate boundary), or one plate is being pushed beneath another plate along a subduction zone (destructive plate boundary). As the plate is being subducted, it gets pulled deeper and deeper, until heat and pressure cause the slab to start melting. The magma is hotter, more fluid, and more buoyant, and tends to rise and collect in magma chambers in the earth's subsurface. Eventually, pressure and heat cause the magma to push out along fractures. Since volcanoes form above the deep, subducting slab, they are not located exactly at the plate boundary but down slope from it.

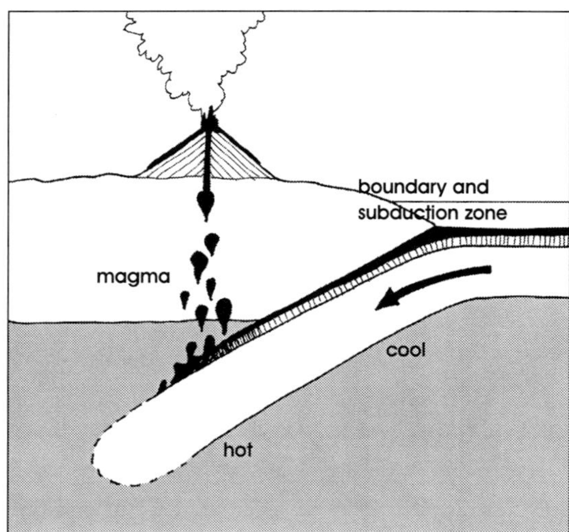

Volcanoes are classified into three categories:

Active: a volcano that is erupting

Dormant: a volcano that has not erupted for a long period of time but occasionally shows signs of activity. This may include releasing steam or lava bubbling at the surface.

Extinct: a volcano in which no activity has occurred for thousands of years

At present, there are approximately 1,500 active and dormant volcanoes on the surface of the earth and under the sea. The active volcanoes may erupt for a short time (hours), or they may erupt for many years. A large number of volcanoes lie in a belt that circles the Pacific Ocean. This belt is often referred to as the *Ring of Fire*.

Materials

- diagram titled, "A Volcano" (included. Make an overhead transparency of this sheet.) (4.6.2)
- overhead projector
- map titled, "The World's Volcanoes" (included. Make an overhead transparency of this sheet.) (4.6.3)
- information sheet titled, "Types of Volcanic Eruptions" (included. Make a copy for each student.) (4.6.4)
- map titled, "Earth's Tectonic Plates" (included in lesson 2) (4.2.2)
- videos about volcano
- safety glasses
- plastic film containers
- measuring spoons
- baking soda
- red wine vinegar
- liquid soap

▶

6

Activity: Part One

Introduce the lesson by challenging the students to present what they already know about volcanoes. Provide students with Activity Sheet A (4.6.1), and ask them to draw a diagram of a volcano and label its parts, using their prior knowledge.

Once the students have completed their diagrams, display the overhead diagram titled, "A Volcano" (4.6.2). Have students compare it to their own diagrams and modify their drawings accordingly. Ask:

- What is the difference between magma and lava?
- Why do volcanoes occur and erupt?

Discuss students' ideas, and use the Background Information for Teachers to answer these questions.

Now display the map titled, "The World's Volcanoes" (4.6.3). Have students closely examine the map and discuss the patterns they see when they look at the locations of the volcanoes.

Again, place the map titled, "Earth's Tectonic Plates" (4.2.2) over top of the map, "The World's Volcanoes." Ask:

- Do you see any relationship between the location of volcanoes and the tectonic plates?
- Do you see any relationship between the location of volcanoes and the location of earthquakes?
- Why is the understanding of plate tectonics so important?

Explain that, like earthquakes, volcanoes are located along the tectonic plate boundaries where subduction creates an intense heating of Earth's crust.

Provide each student with the information sheet titled, "Types of Volcanic Eruptions" (4.6.4). Read, and discuss the information. Ask:

- Which type of eruption would be the most dangerous?
- What type of injuries might people experience if they are too close to a volcano when it erupts?
- Which type of eruption would be the least dangerous?

Activity Sheet A

Directions to students:

Draw a diagram of a volcano and label all its parts (4.6.1).

Activity: Part Two: Volcanic Eruption

Explain to the students that volcanoes have a dramatic effect on Earth's crust. Volcanoes are responsible for mountain building and the creation of islands but also for the destruction of cities. As a class, watch a video that depicts the action of volcanoes. Discuss the movie, focusing on mountain building and the effects volcanoes have on Earth's crust and the people who live in volcanic areas.

Now explain to the students that they will be viewing a recreation of two different types of volcanic eruptions – one under low pressure and one under high pressure. This investigation will recreate the action of a volcano during an eruption.

Safety Note: For safety purposes, this investigation should be conducted as a demonstration, and is best done outdoors. Safety glasses are recommended for both the teacher and the student observers.

Provide students with Activity Sheet B (4.6.5). Explain that for the first trial, you are going to pour 1.25 ml of baking soda into the film container, add a few drops of liquid soap, then fill the container with red wine vinegar. Ask:

- What do you think will happen when I do this?

Have students record their predictions on the activity sheet. Test the students' predictions by conducting the activity, have them observe the steps, and record their observations on the activity sheet chart. Discuss the students' observation, and encourage them to explain the reaction.

Now explain to the class that, for the second trial, you will repeat the steps, but after the red wine vinegar has been added, you will quickly put the lid back on the film container. Ask:

- What do you think will happen this time?

Safety Note: The explosion of the lid is quite intense. Ensure the students are at least 3 metres away from the film container and wearing safety glasses.

Again, have students record their predictions on the activity sheet, stand back and observe, then record their observations on the activity sheet chart.

As a class, discuss the experiment and the student's recorded information. Ask:

- How is gas created in this experiment? (chemical reaction)
- What causes the explosive power in trial 2 of the experiment?
- How does this compare to an actual volcano?
- How is gas created inside a volcano? (heat)

Focus students' attention on the third column of their activity sheet charts. Display the overhead information sheet titled, "Types of Volcanic Eruptions" (4.6.4). Ask:

- What type of volcano do you think each demonstration attempted to recreate?

Discuss the five types of volcanoes and the two demonstration. Have the students complete the chart with their ideas.

Activity Sheet B

Direction to students:

Before you begin each trial, make a prediction about what you think will happen. Record the results of the trial, and then suggest the type of volcano the trial has attempted to recreate (4.6.5).

Activity: Part Three: The Canadian Connection

Discuss students' knowledge of volcanic activity in Canada. Ask:

- Where do volcanoes usually occur?
- Are there any active volcanoes in Canada?
- Are there any volcanoes of any kind in Canada?

Access the school's computer lab and have students use the web site **www.nrcan.gc.ca/ gsc/pacific/vancouver/volcanoes** to learn about volcanoes in Canada. The site also provides ideas for further activities and research.

Extensions

- The eruption of Tambora, Indonesia, in 1815, was the largest volcanic eruption ever recorded. Approximately 10,000 people died and the aftereffects caused worldwide problems. Ask students to research this and other famous volcanoes. Others include:
- August 24, C.E. 79: Mount Vesuvius erupted in Pompeii
    - August 28, 1883: Krakatau, Indonesia
    - June 10, 1886: Tarawera, New Zealand

6

- May 8, 1902: Mound Pelee, Marinique
- May 18, 1980: Mount St. Helens
- April 5, 1982: Galunggung, Indonesia
- January 8, 1983: Kilauea, Hawaii
- June 15, 1991: Mount Pinatubo, Philippines

- Iceland is often called "the land of ice and fire." This is because Iceland is located on a hot spot and also on the Mid-Atlantic Ridge, which is a seafloor spreading zone. Research this unique island for its volcanic activity, hot springs, and flooding.

Explain that not all mountains are formed at plate boundaries. Hot spots are very old regions of very high heat flow in Earth's mantle. Hot spots occur in the middle of tectonic plates. As the tectonic plate moves slowly across the hot spot, the heat causes the rocks to melt, and a volcano forms. The islands of Hawaii are located over hot spots in the Pacific Ocean. Measured from the seafloor to peak, hot-spot volcano Mauna Loa, on the island of Hawaii, is the world's tallest mountain. It is over 9 km high. Yellowstone Park's Old Faithful in the United States is also above a hot spot.

To recreate a model of a hot spot, take a large piece of cardboard and punch a line of 4–5 holes in it. Have one student hold the cardboard on one end and another student hold a tube of toothpaste under the first hole and squeeze gently. As the student continues to squeeze the toothpaste, have the other student slowly move the cardboard so the other holes pass over the tube.

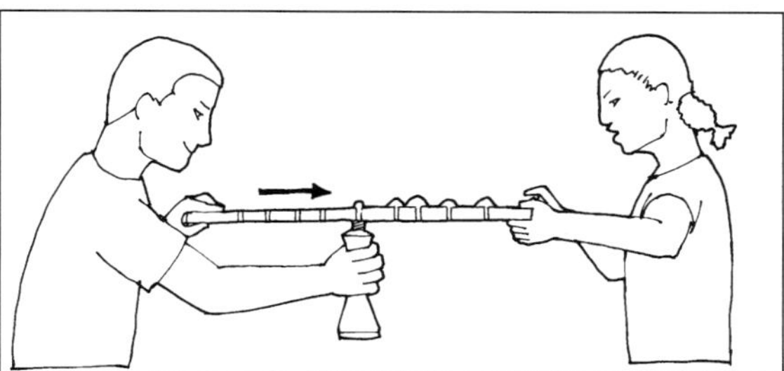

The blobs of toothpaste that appear on the cardboard are similar to hot spot volcanoes. The toothpaste is squeezed through the holes just like magma bursts through a tectonic plate.

- Have students use the extension activity sheet (4.6.6) to do further research on the volcanic activity in Hawaii. This is a two-page activity sheet.

- Have students research evidence of volcanoes elsewhere in the Solar System, such as the enormous volcano on Mars. Venus also shows evidence of volcanic activity.

- Have students research Canadian geophysicist J. Tuzo Wilson, who was pivotal in advancing the plate-tectonic theory through his research on hot spots and transform boundaries. See web site **http://pubs.usgc.gov/publications/text/Wilson.html**.

Assessment Suggestion

Have students complete a Student Self-Assessment sheet on page 22 to reflect on what they have learned about volcanoes.

Diagram of a Volcano

A Volcano

Ash cloud
Lava erupts through the crater
Hot lava flow
Lava rises through central vent
Side vent
Extinct magma chamber

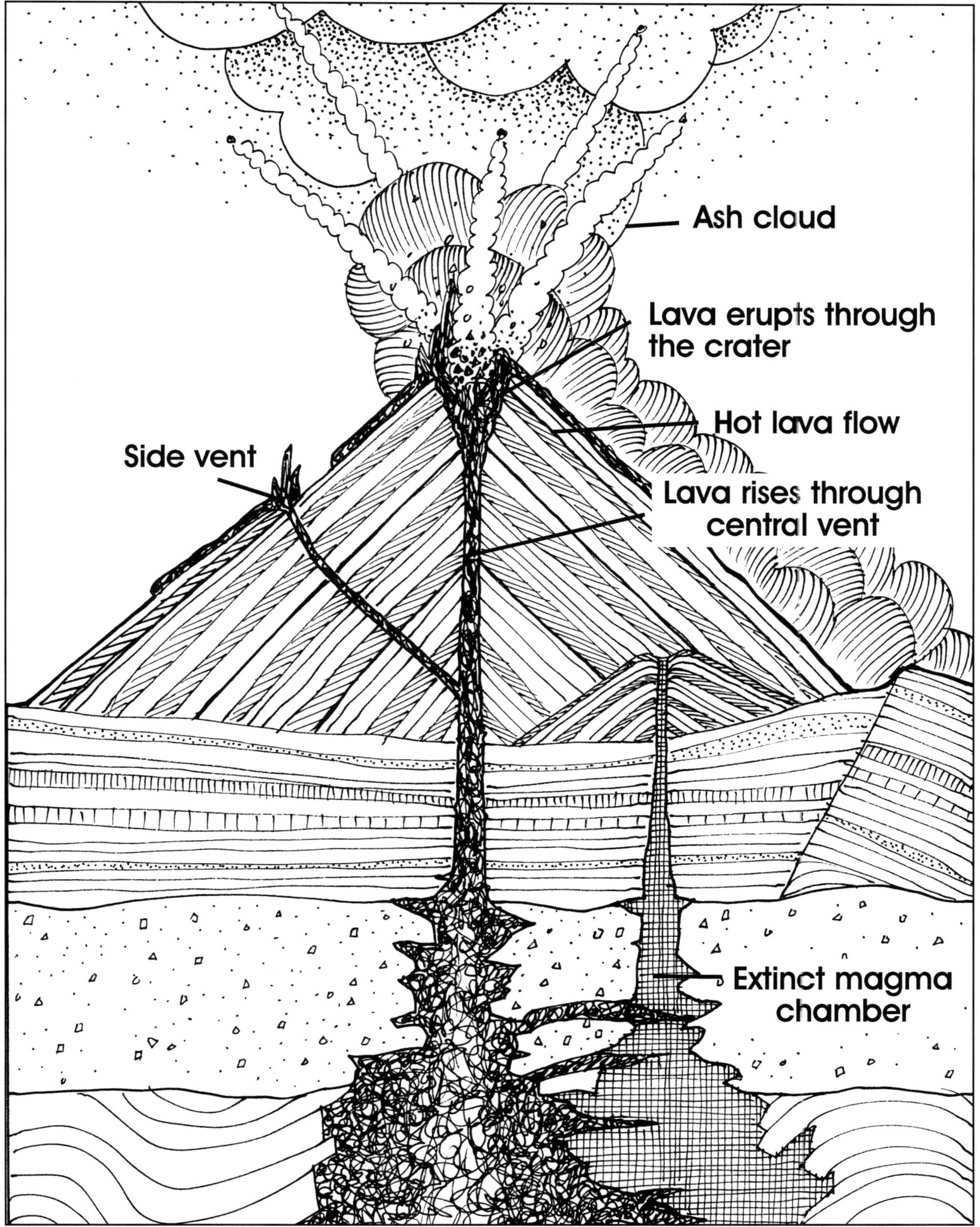

The World's Volcanoes

Types of Volcanic Eruptions

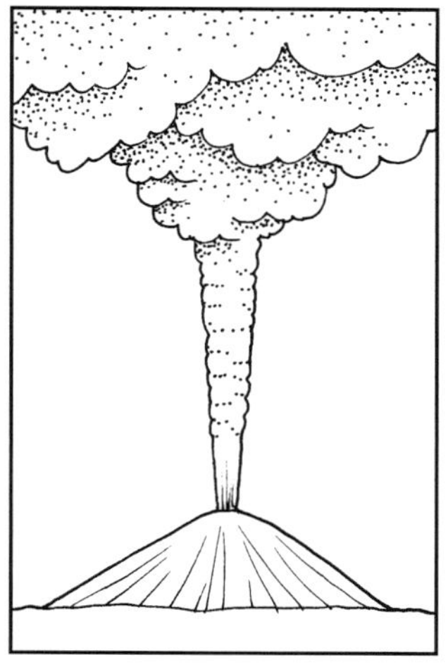

Plinian: a high-pressure explosion inside the mountain sends ash up to 30 km high when the magma chamber is emptied.

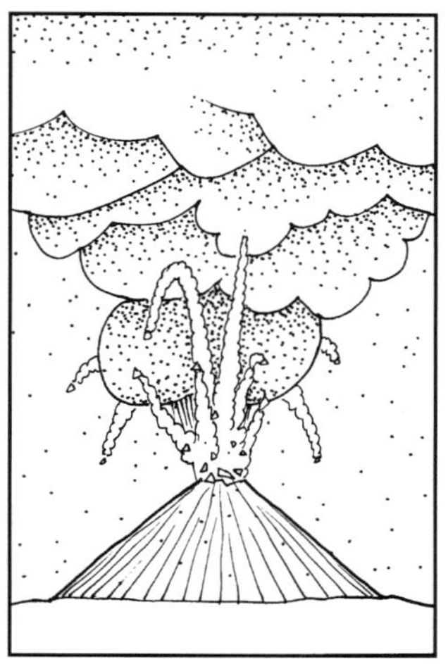

Vulcanian: a high-pressure explosion sends hot lava bombs and rocks high into the sky. This blast occurs because gas builds up under a layer of lava.

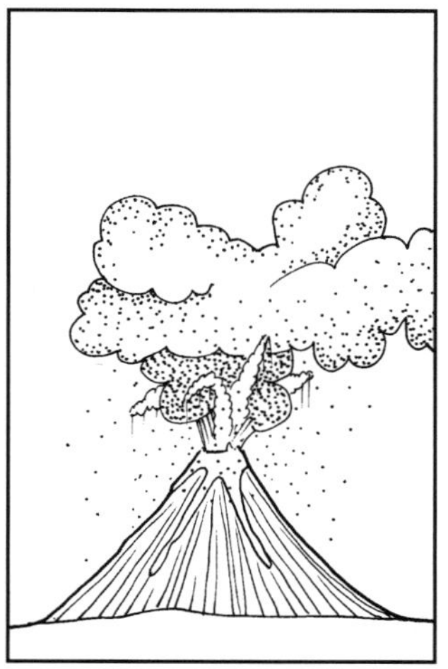

Strombolian: periodic low-pressure eruptions spew lava mixed with gas, rock, and ash into the air. This type of eruption creates tall cones.

Peléean: a low-pressure explosion of lava mixed with gas causes a pyroclastic flow (a torrent of hot lava, ash, and gas) like an avalanche down the mountain. The rising gases form an ash cloud above the flow.

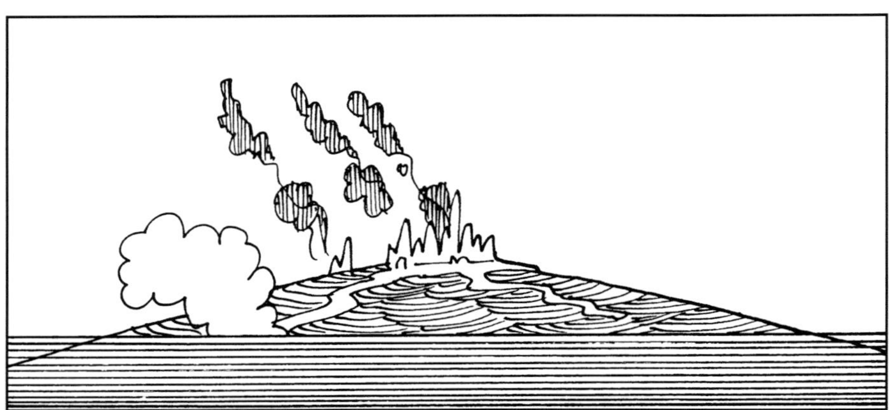

Hawaiian: a low-pressure eruption creates large lava flows that run from large craters, vents, or fissures. This type of eruption creates low shield volcanoes.

Date: ___________________________   **Name:** _______________________________

Volcanic Eruptions

4.6.5 – 357

Volcanic Trial	Prediction	Results	Type of Volcano Recreated
Trial #1 Lid Off			
Trial #2 Lid On			

Underwater Mountains

There are many mountains on Earth, both on the land and under the sea. Mountain chains under the sea were created from volcanic lava that poured out from huge cracks in the tectonic plates, then rose up above the surface of the water.

Mountains that rise up so high that they can be seen above sea level form islands. The Hawaiian Islands are the tips of volcanoes caused by hot spots in the Pacific Ocean.

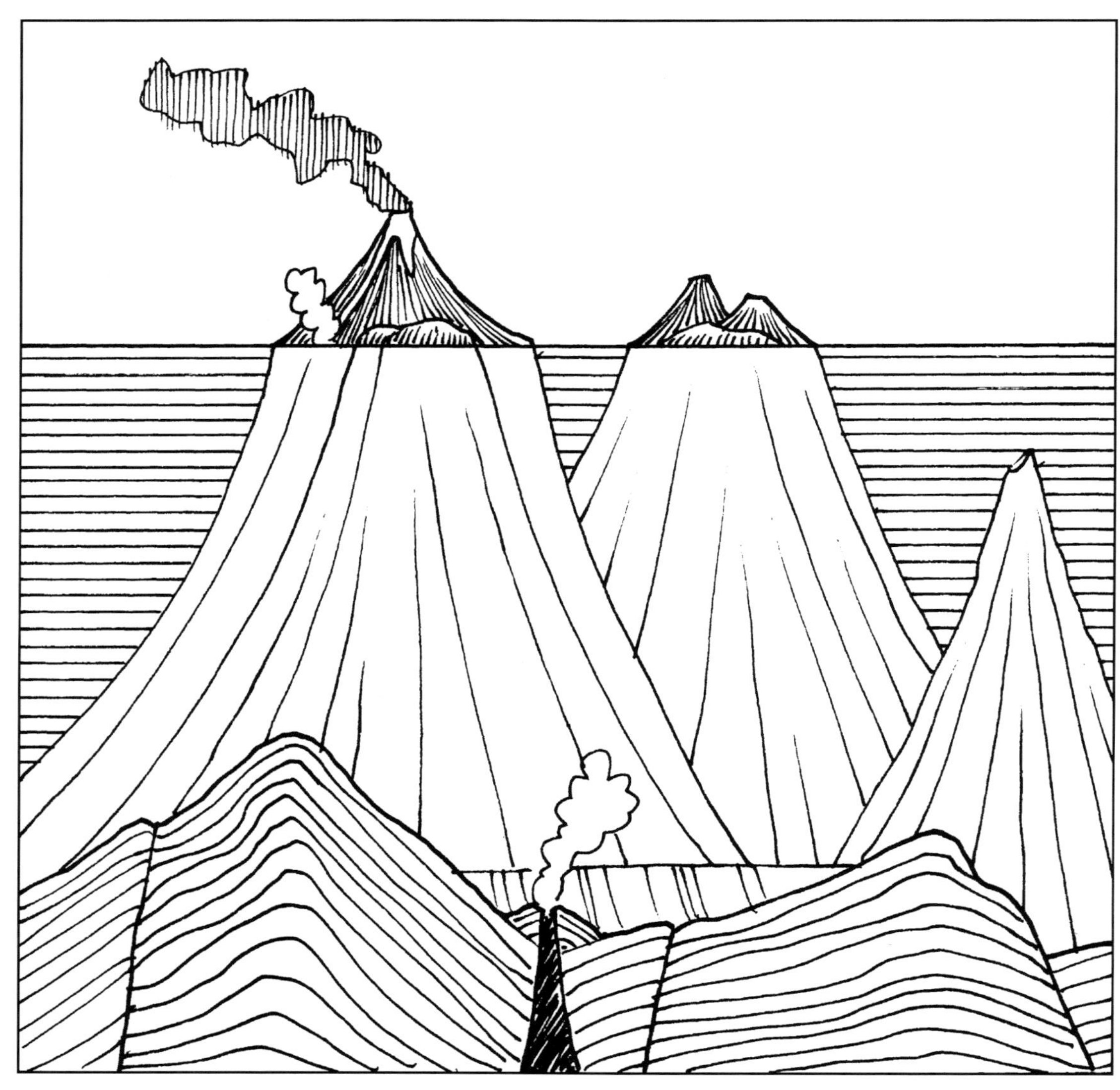

1. Identify the names of the Hawaiian Islands.

____

____

____

____

2. Are any volcanoes in the Hawaiian islands still active?
   If so, which ones?

____

____

____

____

3. How do these active volcanoes affect the inhabitants
   of these islands?

____

____

____

____

7 | Rocks and the Rock Cycle

Background Information for Teachers

Rocks are made up of one or more minerals. Minerals are naturally occurring solids with a specific chemical composition and a regular, ordered (geometric) arrangement of atoms: they have a specific crystalline structure. Table salt is a mineral (NaCl), and so is ice. The individual mineral crystals in a rock may be large enough to see with the naked eye (e.g., a piece of mica in a granite rock), but in many cases the individual crystals are so small they can only be seen under magnification. There are more than 3,500 different types of minerals, but less than 100 of them are common rock-forming minerals.

Rocks, and the minerals that form rocks, undergo a constant process of change in Earth's crust due to movement of the plates and weathering. New crust is created at spreading centres (e.g., oceanic ridges) and along subduction zones, where igneous and metamorphic rocks are formed. Wind, water, chemical processes, heating, and freezing continually wear the crust down. The products of this erosion make sedimentary rocks. This continuous cycle of change and rearranging is called the *rock cycle*.

There are three types of rock:

Igneous rock: When magma cools and hardens, either above or below ground level, it is called *igneous rock*. Igneous rock is made up entirely of mineral crystals.

Extrusive igneous rock (above Earth's surface) cools quickly, therefore, the individual crystals are small and cannot be seen without magnification. Extrusive (volcanic) rocks are typically smooth and evenly coloured. Examples include basalt and pumice. Some types of lava cool so quickly that crystals do not have time to form at all, and the resulting rock is a volcanic glass called *obsidian*.

Intrusive igneous rock (below Earth's surface) cools very slowly, which allows the crystals to grow large. Granite, with its large crystals, is a common intrusive igneous rock.

Metamorphic rock: Metamorphic rock forms when pre-existing rock is subjected to very high pressure and high temperatures. In some cases, this causes the minerals in the rock to transform (metamorphose) into different minerals (e.g., clay turning into garnet). In some cases, the same minerals exist, but their size and shape change (e.g., the tiny calcite crystals in limestone enlarge to form the metamorphic equivalent, marble). In Earth's crust, most metamorphic rocks are formed at destructive plate boundaries, where slabs of rock in subduction zones are heated, compressed, and folded as they are slowly pushed under the over-riding plate. Metamorphism is a very slow process and takes millions of years.

Sedimentary rock: All types of rock exposed at Earth's surface undergo weathering. Sediment is created eventually settles in lakes or oceans. As more sediment is deposited, the layers become compacted and form sedimentary rock. This process is called *lithification*. The *strata*, or layers, in the rock represent changes in the environment as the sedimentary rock was formed. Some examples are sandstone, limestone, and shale. Fossils are found in sedimentary rock. Sedimentary rock is usually soft and, compared to igneous and metamorphic rock erodes easily.

Note: Students will have some prior knowledge of this topic from their grade four unit "Rocks, Minerals, and Erosion." As a springboard to this lesson, assess students' prior knowledge. If you find that students have little conceptual knowledge of this topic, consider reviewing key ideas by conducting some of the activities from *Hands-On Science, Grade Four*.

7

Materials

- overhead projector
- diagram titled, "The Rock Cycle" (included. Make an overhead transparencyof this sheet.) (4.7.1)
- samples of the three rock types
- magnifying lenses
- information sheet titled, "Types of Rock" (included. Make a copy for each student.) (4.7.2)
- chart paper
- markers
- scissors
- poster paper
- markers
- landscape pictures of sedimentary strata (from magazines such as *Canadian Geographic, National Geographic*)
- glass jar
- sand
- shells
- stones or gravel
- leaves or twigs
- soil or peat moss
- samples of mineral crystals (quartz, halite, calcite)
- alum
- 2 small glass jars or Pyrex beakers
- sewing thread (1 m)
- cooking pot
- metal spoon
- hot plate, or similar apparatus
- water
- magnifying glass

Activity: Part One: Types of Rock

Divide the class into working groups, and provide each group with one of the rock samples, chart paper, a marker, and a magnifying lens. Have the students examine the rock carefully and record a list of descriptors on chart paper. Encourage the students to use their senses of sight and touch to describe the rock.

When all groups have developed an extensive list of descriptive words, have them share their charts with the class. Discuss students' background knowledge of rocks and minerals. Ask:

- What is a rock?
- How are rocks formed?
- What types of rocks can you name?
- What is the difference between a rock and a mineral?

As students provide answers, clarify their ideas using the Background Information for Teachers. Display the overhead diagram titled, "The Rock Cycle" (4.7.1). Read the information presented, and discuss the diagram. Explain to the students that rocks and minerals are constantly being formed on Earth, and that this process is called the *rock cycle*. Ask:

- How are rocks formed?
- How are volcanoes responsible for rock formation?
- How do heat and pressure affect rock?
- How is erosion responsible for rock formation?
- What are the three classifications of rock?

As students answer the questions, use the Background Information for Teachers to provide details and explanations. Use the diagram titled, "The Rock Cycle" (4.7.1) to discuss the process of rock formation, and encourage students to use the diagram to explain this cycle in their own words.

7

Now provide students with the information sheet titled, "Types of Rock" (4.7.2). Read through the sheet as a class, and discuss the formation of these rocks. During this discussion refer to the diagram titled, "The Rock Cycle" (4.7.1) to explain the process of rock formation.

Provide each student with Activity Sheet A (4.7.3), and have them complete the chart.

Activity Sheet A

Directions to students:

Complete the chart (4.7.3).

Activity: Part Two

Divide the class into working groups. Provide each group with scissors and Activity Sheet B (4.7.4). Have the groups cut out the sentence strips from the activity sheet, read them, and use them to describe the rock cycle.

Now challenge the students to use the sentence strips to create a cycle, concept web, flow chart, or other graphic organizer that depicts the rock cycle. Provide each group with poster paper, pencil crayons, markers, and glue. Have students use their prior knowledge of rock and mineral formation, and the sentence strips to create a poster of the rock cycle.

Provide plenty of the class time for this project. Have each group present their poster and display the posters in the classroom.

Activity Sheet B

Directions to students:

Cut out the sentence strips describing the different stages in the rock cycle (4.7.4). Use the sentences to create a cycle, concept web, flow chart, or other graphic organizer that explains the rock cycle. Provide arrows and diagrams to make your information clear. You may also add additional words to the diagram.

Activity: Part Three: Sedimentary Rock and Stratification

Display landscape pictures of sedimentary strata from magazines and books. Explain, and discuss the strata using the Background Information for Teachers. Ask:

- How are the layers in the rock formed?
- Why are the different layers evident?
- What might the different layers tell us about what happened on Earth at a particular time?

Explain to the students that they are going to create their own strata of sedimentary rock. Divide the class into working groups. Provide each group with Activity Sheet C (4.7.5), a glass jar, sand, shells, stones or gravel, leaves and twigs, and soil or peat moss.

Challenge the students to create their own strata by layering the material samples in the jar. Have the students create five layers and compact or firmly pack each layer to represent the lithification process. Have them then complete the diagram on the activity sheet (4.7.5).

Ask the students to imagine that they are geologists: Their strata represent a core sample of sedimentary rock they are to explain how each layer was formed. Have the students present their sediment strata to the class.

Activity Sheet C

Directions to students:

Once you have completed the layering in the jar, draw a diagram of your strata. Explain the formation of each layer by describing what might have happened on Earth at the time each layer was formed (4.7.5).

7

Activity: Part Four: Crystals

Divide the class into pairs of students, and provide each pair with a magnifier and crystal sample. Have the students examine and discuss the shape and structure of the crystals.

Now explain to the students that you will be demonstrating how crystals are formed. Provide each student with a copy of Activity Sheet D (4.7.6), and ask them to pay close attention to the demonstration.

Note: This experiment will have the best results if it is completed over two days.

1. Pour 500 ml of water and 112 g of alum into the cooking pot. Heat, stirring gently, until all of the alum is dissolved.
2. Pour 3 cm of the solution into a clean jar, uncovered, and set aside. Do not disturb the jar. Within an hour, small crystals will begin to form at the bottom of the jar. (Keep the remainder of the solution in the covered pot.)
3. Once the alum crystals have formed seeds approximately 1 cm in diameter, remove two of them from the jar. Tie one end of a piece of thread around a crystal and the other end around a pencil. Repeat this process for the other crystal. Place each crystal in its own clean jar suspended by the pencil.

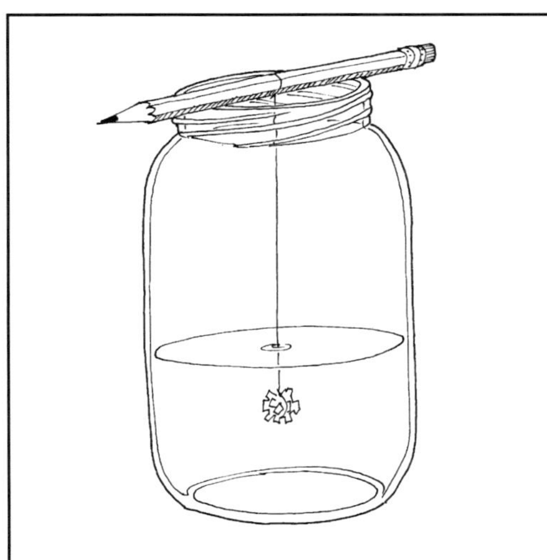

4. Take the remainder of the solution in the pot and pour enough into each jar to cover the crystal. (If crystals have formed in the solution in the pot, you will need to reheat the solution. Let this solution cool to room temperature before pouring it into the jars with the seed crystals. If the hot solution is poured over the seeds they will dissolve.)
5. Place one of the jars in a bowl of ice water and the other in a place at room temperature where it will not be disturbed.

After several hours (you may want to leave them overnight), have the student compare the crystals. Ask:

- What effect does the colder temperature have on the formation of crystals?
- Why does this occur?
- How does this compare to the formation of minerals?
- How do these crystals compare to the sample crystals we examined?

Activity Sheet D

Directions to students:

Draw a diagram of each jar on the activity sheet, and complete all of the questions (4.7.6).

Extensions

- Have the students write the geological history of their strata. Students could depict floods, shipwrecks, landslides, and so on. This paper can be written as a story or a geological document. Students may want an opportunity to share their stories with the class.

- Create other crystals by using salt or sugar. Compare and contrast these crystals with the alum.

- Examine different types of crystals found in the home. Some examples are white sugar, brown sugar, table salt, sea salt, or other salts. Examine these samples under a magnifying glass or microscope, and compare the different structures of the crystals.

- Real pure gemstones, such as rubies and emeralds, are rare and expensive. These factors have contributed to the development of artificial crystals that resemble the more precious stones. Research how the replicas are made and used.

The Rock Cycle

Through a combination of heat, pressure, and transportation, rocks move in a continuous cycle of change. As igneous rock is forced up to the surface of Earth's crust, it erupts from a volcano, where it is then exposed to weathering. Over long periods of time the rock is worn down and deposited in lakes or oceans. It becomes sedimentary rock. The sedimentary rock is sometimes exposed to heat and pressure and it then becomes metamorphic rock. Sometimes, rock is pushed back below Earth's crust, where it melts into magma. The rock cycle starts over again.

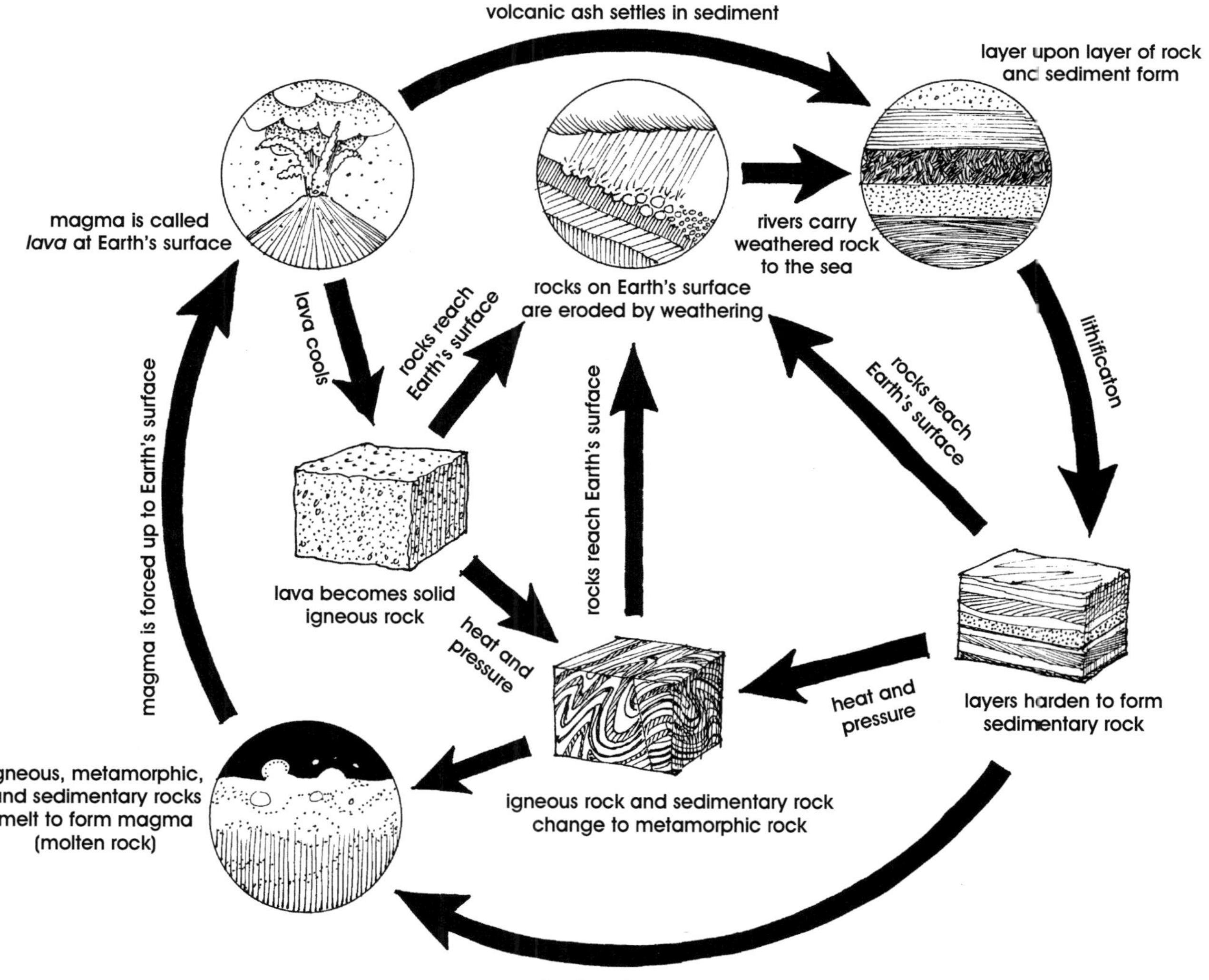

Types of Rock

Igneous rock: When magma – either above or below ground level – cools and hardens, it is called *igneous rock*. Igneous rock is made up entirely of mineral crystals. Extrusive igneous rock – formed above Earth's surface – cools quickly. The crystals are small and packed closely together. The rock is usually smooth and evenly coloured. Intrusive igneous rock – formed below the Earth's surface – cools very slowly, which allows the crystals to grow large. Granite is the most common example of intrusive rock. Obsidian, felsite, and pumice are other examples.

Metamorphic rock: Rock that has changed due to massive pressure and extremely high temperatures is called *metamorphic rock*. Most metamorphic rock is created deep in Earth's crust, as rocks are folded and compressed beneath other rocks. The pressure and heat cause the crystals to realign or recrystallize. Examples are marble (from limestone), slate (from shale), and gneiss (from granite). Metamorphism is a very slow process that takes millions of years.

Sedimentary rock: Over time, exposed igneous or metamorphic rocks undergo weathering. The sediment created eventually settles in lakes or oceans. As more sediment is deposited, the layers become compacted, forming *sedimentary rock*. This process is called *lithification*. Some examples of sedimentary rock are sandstone, limestone, and shale. Fossils are found in sedimentary rock. Sedimentary rock is usually soft and easily eroded in comparison to igneous and metamorphic rocks.

Rock Types

Name	Formation	Characteristics	Examples
1.			
2.			
3.			

The Rock Cycle Sentence Strips

Magma is forced up to Earth's surface as lava from volcanoes, which becomes solid igneous rock.

Igneous rock can also be formed when magma cools under the surface (example: granite).

Rocks on Earth's surface are eroded by weathering.

Rivers carry weathered rock fragments to the sea.

Sedimentary rock is formed when rock fragments settle and, over time, harden into rock. This process is called *lithification*. (example: limestone).

Igneous and sedimentary rocks are forced into Earth's crust through the movement of the plates. The heat and pressure of this movement cause the minerals in the rocks to change. The result is metamorphic rock (example: marble).

Igneous, sedimentary, and metamorphic rocks can be forced so far below Earth's crust that they melt and become magma once again.

The rock cycle begins again when magma is forced, by volcanic activity up to Earth's surface as lava.

Date: ___________________   **Name:** ___________________________
_
_   ___________________________
_
_   ___________________________
_
_   ___________________________

Sedimentary Rock and Stratification

Layer #1

Layer #2

Layer #3

Layer #4

Layer #5

Possible explanation for the formation of the strata:

____

____

____

____

Crystal Formation

Diagram of jar at room temperature

Describe the contents

____

____

____

____

____

____

Diagram of jar with ice water

Describe the contents

____

____

____

____

____

____

Explain how crystals are affected by temperature.

____

____

____

____

Classifying Minerals and Rocks

Background Information for Teachers

Classifying and identifying rocks and minerals are done by observing and testing their physical properties. Geologists use the following tests to identify minerals:

Hardness:

- measure on a scale of 1-10
- tested by scratching the mineral with a fingernail, penny, glass, and steel nail (the mineral must be scratched in the order shown)
- use Mohs' Hardness Scale to determine hardness

Mohs' Hardness Scale	
1 (softest) to 10 (hardest)	
Hardness	**Mineral**
1	Talc
2	Gypsum
3	Calcite
4	Flourite
5	Apatite
6	Orthoclase
7	Quartz
8	Topaz
9	Corundum
10	Diamond

- may wish to use a magnifying glass to see the surface more clearly to check for scratches

Streak Colour:

- use an unglazed tile called a streak plate
- rub corner of mineral on tile several times to see if it leaves a colour (Note: Some streak colours will be different from the colour of the mineral.)
- if mineral is harder than the streak plate, it will not leave a streak colour
- may wish to use a magnifying glass to find out the exact colour of the streak

Lustre:

- describe the surface appearance of a mineral as glassy, metallic, dull, or shiny

Texture:

- describe the feel of the surface of a mineral as rough, smooth, soapy, or bumpy

Colour:

- describe the colour of the mineral

Note: Some minerals are different colours, e.g., pink and white quartz, while others are always the same colour.

Materials

- set of 6 mineral specimens, numbered from 1 to 6 (small pieces of masking tape can be used for labelling)
- magnifying lenses
- hardness kit: penny, glass (tape three edges of small mirrors or glass pieces), galvanized steel nail
- overhead transparency of Activity Sheet A (4.8.1)
- overhead projector
- unglazed tile (streak tile)
- collection of rock and mineral samples
- collection of books, field guides, and identification charts on rocks and minerals

Activity: Part One: Classifying Minerals

Activity

Divide the class into working groups and provide each group with a set of six minerals. Have the students examine and compare the minerals. Ask:

- How are the minerals the same?
- How are they different?

▶

Explain to the students that minerals have certain properties or characteristics that enable us to identify them. On chart paper, record the five properties that will be tested (colour, lustre, texture, streak colour, and hardness). Ask the students to give suggestions on how each mineral could be tested for each property.

Once you have reviewed each of the properties used to identify the minerals, provide each group with an activity sheet and review the chart using the overhead sample. Focus first on colour. Have the students examine mineral sample #1 and describe the colour of the mineral. Have them record the colour on the chart. Now have the groups do the same for each mineral sample, deciding on one colour that best describes each mineral.

Review the term *lustre* as a way of describing the shininess of a mineral. Introduce the four descriptive terms used to describe lustre (*glassy, metallic, dull,* and *shiny*). Have the students examine the minerals and select one of the four terms that best describes each of the minerals and record this on the activity sheet.

Review the term *texture* and introduce the four descriptors (*rough, smooth, soapy,* and *bumpy*). Have the students manipulate the minerals and select one of the four terms that best describes each mineral's texture. Record this on the activity sheet.

Provide each group with an unglazed tile. Explain that streak colour is determined by rubbing a mineral on the tile to see what colour is left on the tile. Have the students test the minerals for streak colour and record the colour left on the tile for each mineral.

Note: If the minerals are harder than the tile, a streak will not be visible. In this case, students should record "no streak" on the chart.

For testing hardness, provide the students with a penny, glass, and a nail. Have them first test a mineral for hardness by trying to scratch it with their fingernail. Then try the penny, the glass, and the steel nail in that order. Have them examine the mineral each time with a magnifying glass to see if a scratch is left on the mineral. They should then check off each object that left a scratch on the mineral.

Note: Mohs' Hardness Scale will not be used at this stage to test hardness.

Once the students have completed their description of the six mineral specimens, challenge them to use a mineral resource guide to identify the minerals.

Activity Sheet A

Directions to students:

Test the properties of the six mineral specimens. Use a mineral resource guide to help identify each mineral (4.8.1).

Activity: Part Two: Designing Field Guides

Divide the class into working groups. Provide each group with several rocks and mineral samples, along with different books, field guides, and identification charts of rocks and minerals. Have groups discuss the variety of ways in which information is presented about classifying, identifying, and describing rocks and minerals. Also have them use the resources to identify their rock and mineral samples.

8

Explain to the students that they will be creating their own field guides for identifying rocks and minerals. Have each group create one field guide that can be photocopied for each member. Ask:

- What is a field guide used for?
- What type of information does a field guide give the reader?
- What would you need to know in order to identify rocks you find?
- Are pictures and diagrams necessary?
- How should a field guide be organized for easy identification?

Provide each group with Activity Sheet B (4.8.2). Allow the groups time to research, organize, and construct their field guides. Once the field guides are completed, have the groups present their books to the class and discuss what they have learned.

Activity Sheet B

Direction to students:

Read and follow all of the instructions carefully, and divide the tasks among the members in your group. Be creative in terms of layout and design, and remember the purpose of the field guide (4.8.2).

Extensions

- Introduce a simplified version of Mohs' Hardness Scale (below) and have students use this scale to test minerals.

Mohs' Hardness Scale	
1 (softest) to 10 (hardest)	
Minerals scratched by:	**Are the hardness of:**
fingernail	2.5 or less
penny	3 or less
glass	5.5 or less
steel nail	6.5 or less
none of the above	greater than 6.5

- Have students repeat the experiment using different minerals.

- Have students develop riddles about different minerals based on their identified properties. For example, "I am light grey with a little bit of white. I feel smooth, almost like soap. I am dull and can be scratched by a fingernail. Who am I?" (Answer: talc)

- Invite a geologist to speak to the class about rocks and minerals. This is also an opportunity for the speaker to review the guidebooks.

- Challenge the students to bring in rocks and minerals from home and attempt to identify them using their guidebooks.

- Some types of rocks are hardwearing and make good building materials. For example, tyndall stone, a type of limestone, is quarried in Manitoba and used in many of the province's buildings (e.g., the Manitoba Legislature). Have students visit an area where there are a number of stone buildings. In pairs or small groups, challenge the students to identify the types of rocks used in the construction. Use the extension activity sheets to complete this assignment (4.8.3 and 4.8.4).

- Gem stones are beautiful and interesting. Have the students choose a favourite gem stone, or their birthstone, and research its characteristics. The students can then present their discoveries to the class.

- Plan a class trip to a local quarry. The Stonewall Quarries, for example, has an excellent school program, with a grade appropriate curriculum focus. Stonewall is a source of limestone in Manitoba.

Classifying Minerals

Mineral	Colour	Lustre	Texture	Streak Colour	Hardness	Name of Mineral
#1					fingernail____ penny _______ glass _______ steel nail____	
#2					fingernail____ penny _______ glass _______ steel nail____	
#3					fingernail____ penny _______ glass _______ steel nail____	
#4					fingernail____ penny _______ glass _______ steel nail____	
#5					fingernail____ penny _______ glass _______ steel nail____	
#6					fingernail____ penny _______ glass _______ steel nail____	

Designing a Field Guide
for Rocks and Minerals

Work together in your group to create a field guide. You may choose to divide some of the tasks among group members.

1. Choose a minimum of 8 rocks and 8 minerals to describe in your guide.

2. For each rock include:
    a. picture
    b. classification (rock type)
    c. mineral content
    d. description of appearance
    e. unique characteristics
    f. locations found (You may choose to include a small map.)
    g. uses

3. For each mineral include:
    a. picture
    b. description of appearance
    c. unique characteristics
    d. locations found (You may choose to include a small map.)
    e. uses

4. Write a brief introduction to the guide (e.g., its intended audience and purpose).

5. Create a table of contents.

6. Create a front and back cover for your field guide. (Include a title, authors' biographies, and a back cover description.)

Building Materials: Stone Identification

Look at the overall appearance of the stone in the buidling.
Pay attention to the colour, texture, and structure.

Does the stone look evenly coloured with an even texture?

Yes | No

Yes: Look at the grains up close. Do you see fossil (shells, plants or skeletons)?

Yes | No

No: Do you see streaks or clouds of colour in a mostly white stone?

Yes | No

No: Are grains rounded like sand on a beach? → Yes

No: Look at the grains up close. Do you see a mixture of colours (black, grey, red, white, or pink)?

No | Yes

Limestone	Sandstone	Marble	Granite

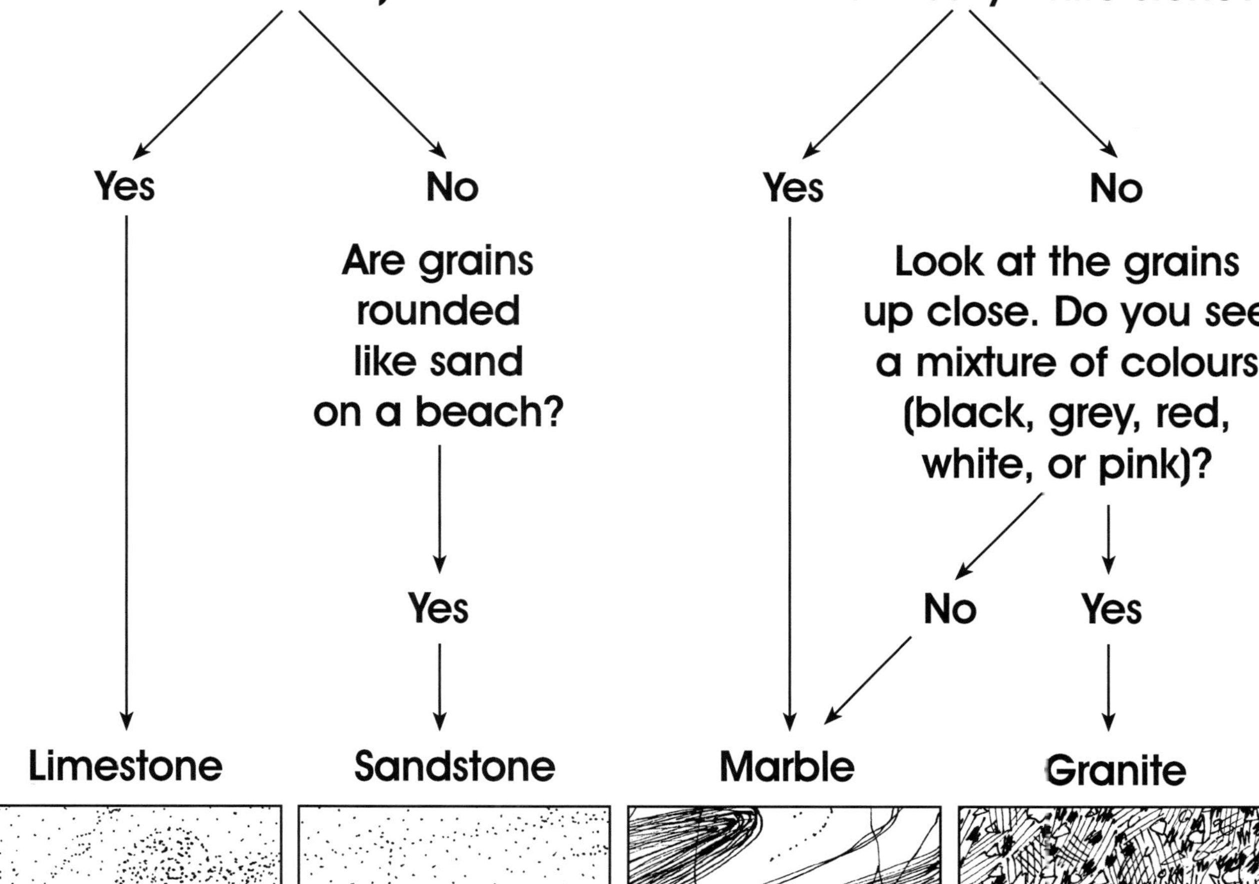
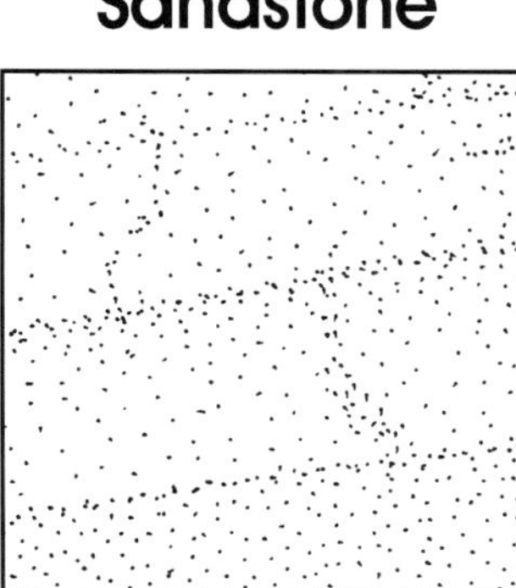
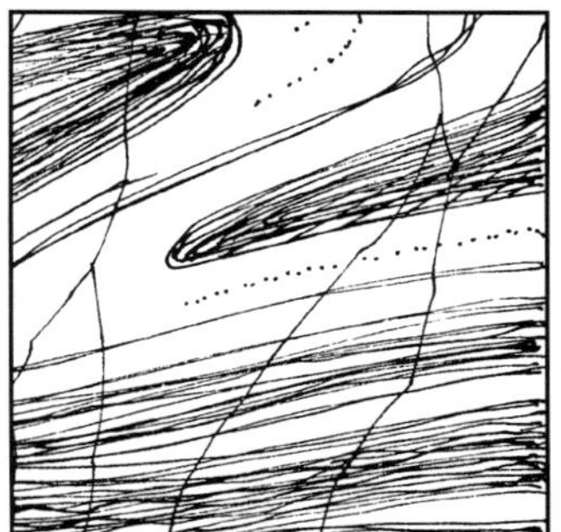
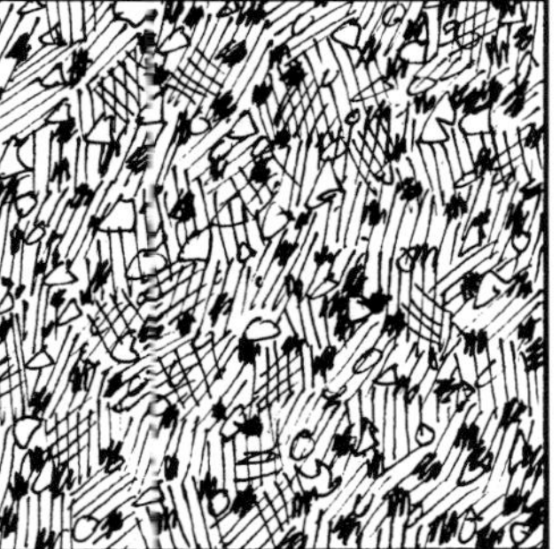

Date: ___________________   Name: ___________________

Examining Stone Buildings

Building Name	Unique Features	Characteristics of the stone (colour, texture, structures)	Stone Identification

9 | Erosion and the Landscape

Background Information for Teachers

Weathering is the process by which rocks are broken down on Earth's surface by rainwater, wind, heat, and cold. Erosion is the wearing away of the surface of the earth. Eroded rock eventually gets carried away in the form of rock fragments and is deposited as sediment. Unlike volcanoes or earthquakes that can produce sudden changes in the landscape, erosion is a very slow and steady process of change. Its results, however, can be just as dramatic.

Materials

- pictures of the Grand Canyon, Niagara Falls, or other major landforms created or affected by erosion
- overhead projector
- diagram titled, "Erosion" (included. Make an overhead transparency of these sheets.) (4.9.1)
- pieces of limestone
- vinegar
- glass beakers
- reference books on landforms, both local and worldwide
- materials for constructing landform models (identified and gathered by students)

Activity: Part One

Assess students' prior knowledge of rock formation and erosion. Show them pictures of the Grand Canyon, Niagara Falls, and/or other major landforms that erode. Ask:

- How was this landform created?
- What other types of landforms are created by erosion?

Display the overhead diagrams titled, "Erosion" (4.9.1). Ask:

- How is water or rainwater an agent of erosion?
- How do changing temperatures affect rock?
- What happens to water that settles into cracks of rocks when it freezes?
- How does wind contribute to weathering?
- What happens to eroded material? Where is it deposited?
- What type of rock does eroded sediment turn into?

Explain to the students that chemicals can also cause erosion. When carbon dioxide from the air mixes with rainwater, it forms a weak acid that dissolves certain types of rocks. Limestone is an example of rock affected by weak acid solutions.

Divide the class into working groups. Provide each group with three pieces of limestone, vinegar, and a glass beaker. Have the students place one piece of limestone in the beaker and pour the vinegar over top so it is covering the rock. The second piece of limestone will be the test constant. Ask:

- What kind of liquid is vinegar? (acid)
- How is vinegar similar to rainwater? (both have an acidic content)
- What do you think will happen to the limestone covered in vinegar?

Test the students' predictions by leaving the limestone in the vinegar for at least two hours. After removing the rock, have the students compare it to the test constant. Have them record their findings on Activity Sheet A (4.9.2), and discuss the results.

Note: Limestone is made of a mineral – calcite – that is soluble in acidic solutions. This explains the effects of the vinegar on the limestone.

▶

Activity Sheet A

Directions to students:

Compare and contrast the limestone that was soaked in vinegar to the piece that was not soaked. Complete the questions (4.9.2).

Activity: Part Two

Explain to the students that they will be creating a model of a landform. They will also research the geological history and formation of the landform and how weathering and erosion are connected to its formation. Some local examples are:

- Lake Agassiz
- Belais Moraine
- Manitoba Escarpment
- Red River Valley
- The Forks
- Grand Beach
- Carberry Sand Hills

Note: Students may also choose to study other well-known landforms in other regions of Canada and the world, such as:
• Great Lakes • Niagara Escarpment • Niagara Falls
• Grand Canyon • South Dakota Badlands
• River Islands of Attawapiskat River
• Muskeg and Ponds in the Hudson's Bay Lowlands
• Coastal Sand Dunes, Pinery Provincial Park, Eastern Shore of Lake Huron

To model this activity, discuss the Grand Canyon. Display pictures of this landform again. Ask:

- How do you think the Grand Canyon was formed?
- Where would you find information about this?
- How could you construct a model of the Grand Canyon?
- What materials would you use?

As a class, identify criteria for assessing this project. Record the criteria on chart paper for students to refer to throughout the research and construction process.

Provide each student with a copy of Activity Sheet B (4.9.3). Have them research their landform, create a model, and present their work to the class.

Activity Sheet B

Directions to students:

Follow the steps to complete your Landform Project (4.9.3).

Extensions

- Due to climate, freezing and thawing is an important erosion process in Canada. Have students investigate the effects of freezing and thawing by placing pieces of limestone and chalk in a plastic container of water and freezing it. Once the water is in solid state, thaw it at room temperature and examine the limestone and chalk.

- Have the students research acid rain and its affect on buildings, statues, and monuments around the world.

- Glaciers have a major impact on Earth's crust as they progress and recede during ice ages. Have students research the effects of glaciers on the landscape and identify local and national landforms that were formed by glaciers during the last ice age.

Assessment Suggestion

As a class, identify criteria for the landform research/model project. For example:

- provides detailed information on the formation of the landform
- identifies and gathers all materials required
- is an accurate model
- is clearly presented

List these criteria on the Rubric on page 19, and record results during presentations.

Erosion

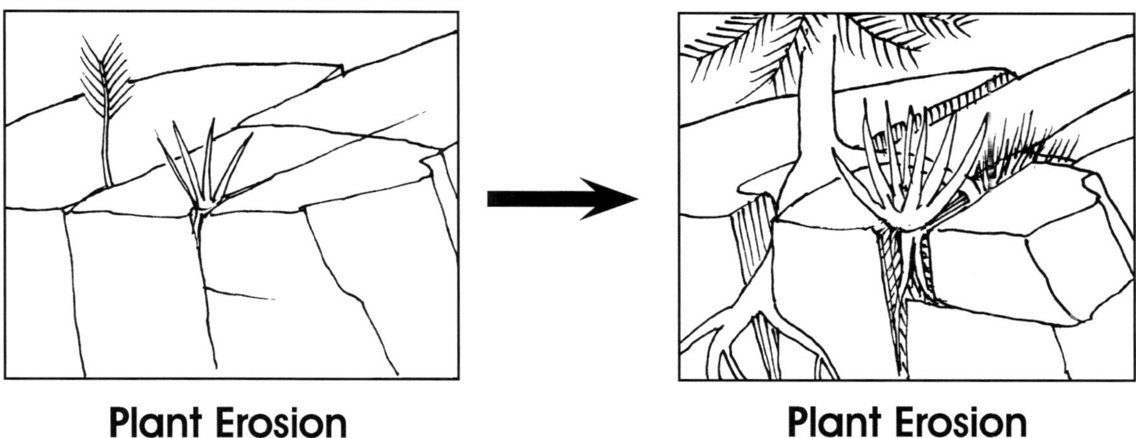

Plant Erosion   **Plant Erosion**

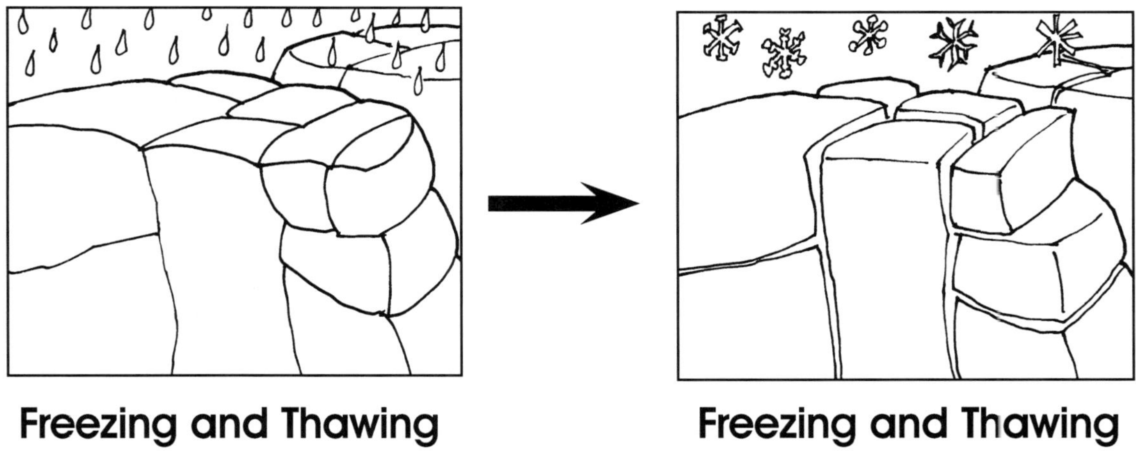

Freezing and Thawing   **Freezing and Thawing**

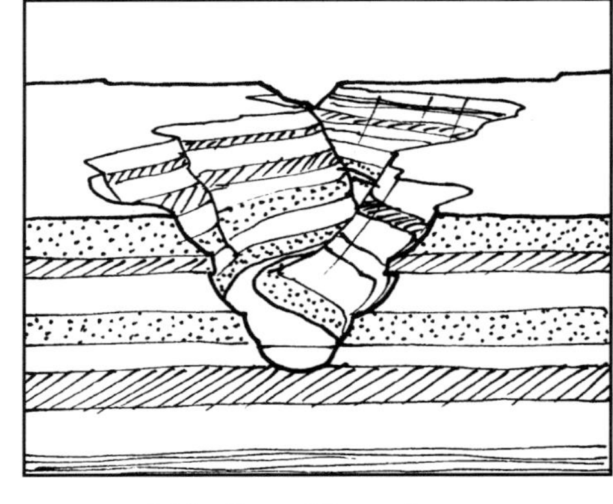

Water Erosion

Water Erosion

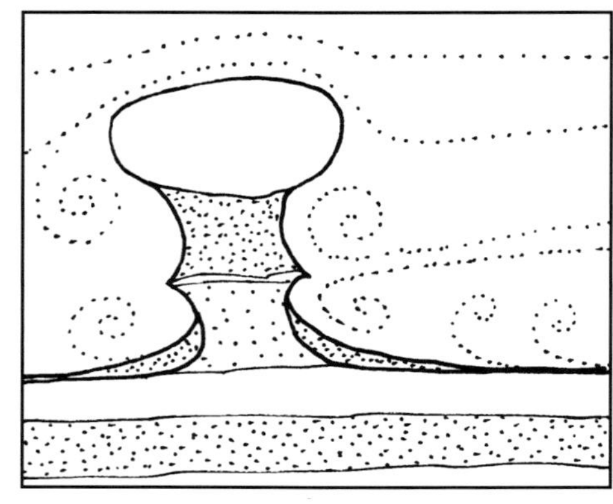

Wind Erosion

Heat and Cold

Heat and Cold

Heat and Cold

Life of a Mountain

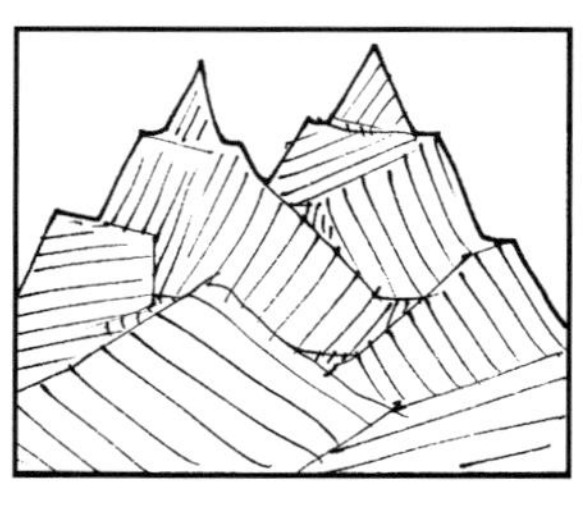

Young Mountain
Range

Wearing Away

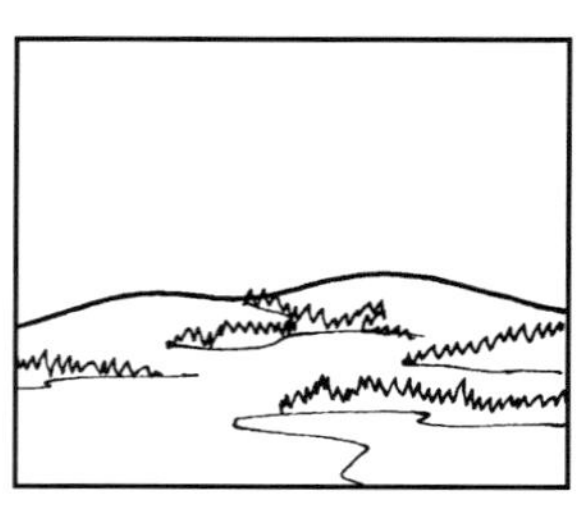

Old Mountain
Range

Chemical Erosion and Limestone

Describe the texture and structure of the limestone soaked in vinegar.	Describe the texture and structure of the limestone that was not soaked in vinegar.

How does rain affect a limestone building over time?

____

____

____

How does acid rain affect limestone buildings?

____

____

____

What are some solutions to the acid rain problem?

____

____

____

Date: _________________________   Name: _________________________________

Landform Project

Landform: ____

Location: ____

Complete the following steps:

1. Research your landform's geological formation, past, present, and future. Write a one-page description of the formation.

2. Design a model of the landform. Draw a diagram of your model.

3. Identify the materials required to build your model.

______________________   ______________________   ______________________

______________________   ______________________   ______________________

______________________   ______________________   ______________________

4. Construct your model.

5. Present your research and landform model to the class.

10 | Soil

Background Information for Teachers

A resource is anything in a natural environment that is useful to humans. Soil is a vital resource that is used in the daily lives of people and many other living things. For people and animals, the direct or indirect consumption of energy from plants grown in soil is what sustains life.

The process by which soil is created is a lengthy one. The process begins with weathering and erosion. Weathered rock accumulates on top of solid bedrock and forms layers in varying stages of eroded material. These layers build up to form the *regolith* – the layer of rock and rock fragments that cover most of Earth's surface. When seeds are deposited and plants begin to take root, the making of soil begins. The process of rock becoming soil is very slow and complex. It may take tens of thousands of years for soil to develop, yet it can be eroded and depleted in as short a time as a decade. On average, it takes 500 years to create 2.5 cm of topsoil.

Soil Profile: A cross section of soil from the surface down to the bedrock is called a *soil profile*. The layers that make up the profile are called *horizons*. The number and thickness of horizons vary with soil type. (See 4.10.1.)

Humus: The humus contains living organic material such as plant roots, animals, insects, worms, microorganisms, and organic chemicals along with decaying remains.

Topsoil: Topsoil is rich dark soil that contains the decomposed organic matter.

Subsoil: Subsoil has little organic material, but contains chemical elements that have been leached (washed down) from the layers above it.

Weathered Bedrock: Weathered bedrock is an infertile layer of rock fragments.

Bedrock: Bedrock is the lowest layer of solid rock.

Soil type is determined by climate, vegetation, topography, and the nature of the rock in a certain areas. The four basic soil types, formed in different climates, are:

- temperate forests: fertile, has an even brown surface layer, significant rainfall
- temperate grasslands: most fertile, deep layer of topsoil, dark brown to black in colour, adequate rainfall
- dry climate: infertile, little organic matter, light coloured, very dry
- tropical rainforest: thin fertile layer, red or yellow soil colour, clay layer below is infertile, heavy rainfall, becomes infertile if cleared

Materials

- samples of different types of soil
- magnifying lenses
- tweezers
- plastic spoons
- chart paper
- markers
- overhead projector
- information sheet titled, 'The Formation of Soil" (included. Make a copy for each student.) (4.10.1)
- information sheet titled, "Types of Soil" (included. Make a copy for each student.) (4.10.3)
- 1-litre clear plastic pop bottles
- scissors
- hammers
- nails
- glass beakers
- small stones
- pebbles

- sand
- clay
- topsoil
- organic material (grass, leaves, small sticks)
- water
- large measuring cups
- masking tape
- food colouring
- stopwatch
- information sheet titled, "Soil Depletion Factors" (included. Make a copy for each student.) (4.10.5)

Activity: Part One: The Nature of Soil

Divide the class into working groups, and provide each group with a different soil sample. Have the groups use magnifiers, tweezers, and spoons to examine the sample and record their observations on chart paper. Encourage the groups to be as detailed as possible in describing their soil sample.

Once all groups have completed the task, display the observations on chart paper around the classroom. Ask:

- What words describe the appearance of the soil samples? The texture? The smell?
- What words describe the composition of the soil samples?
- How do the descriptions of the different soil samples vary?
- Can you match the descriptions on the chart paper to the different soil samples?

Allow students time to examine the various samples and match the descriptions to the samples. Ask:

- Why are these soil samples different?
- How is soil formed?

Distribute the information sheet titled, "The Formation of Soil" (4.10.1). Read the paragraph, and discuss the process of terminology. Focus on the soil profile diagram. Use the Background Information for Teachers to explain and discuss the different layers. Ask:

- Which layers are of most value to plants?

Have the students complete Activity Sheet A (4.10.2) to reflect on their learning.

Activity Sheet A

Directions to students:

Complete the sentences using the terms at the top of the sheet (4.10.2).

Activity: Part Two: Characteristics of Soil

Now discuss the importance of soil as a resource. Ask:

- What is a *natural resource*?
- Does soil fit the description of a natural resource?
- How is soil important to all living things?
- Can all types of soil grow food?
- What kind of soil is better for agricultural production?
- What kind of soil is not suitable for agricultural production?

Distribute the information sheet titled, "Types of Soil" (4.10.3). Read through it as a class, and discuss the information and diagrams. Ask:

- What type of soil do we have in our community?
- How do people try to improve soil for plant growth?
- What does soil need in order to make it fertile?
- What happens to soil if it is compacted?

- Why are worms, insects, and bacteria good for soil?
- Why is soil drainage important?
- What are some differences in the ways sand, clay, and black soils drain?

Now explain to the students that they will be conducting an investigation to observe the characteristics of different soil profiles.

Divide the class into working groups, and provide students with Activity Sheet B (4.10.4), along with four 1-litre plastic pop bottles, scissors, a hammer and nail, four glass beakers, small stones, pebbles, sand, soil, organic material, water, a large measuring cup, masking tape, felt marker, food colouring, a plastic spoon, and a stopwatch. Have the students follow the directions provided to investigate soil profiles.

Following this investigation, discuss the results. Ask:

- Why is it important to understand the characteristics of soil?
- Which soil profile had the best water retention? Why?
- Why is water retention important?
- What could be done to increase or decrease the water retention in soils?

Discuss the graphs constructed by each group. Focus on the required elements of a graph:

- title
- labelled axes
- accurately calibrated markings on axes
- accurately presented data

Activity Sheet B

Note: This is a two-page activity sheet.

Directions to students:

Follow the directions for investigating soil profiles. Complete the chart (4.10.4). Use the graph paper provided to graph your results (4.10.5).

Activity: Part Three: Soil Conservation

Explain to the students that because soil is such a valuable resource it needs to be protected and conserved. Distribute the information sheet titled, "Soil Depletion Factors" (4.10.6). Discuss the factors and diagrams. Ask:

- Which factors are natural?
- Which factors are caused by humans?
- How does soil depletion affect the agri-food industry?
- What would happen in an area that lost all of its topsoil?
- How does contamination contribute to depletion of soil?
- How does overuse contribute to depletion of soil?
- Should homes be built on productive agricultural land?

Divide the class into working groups. Explain that they will be responsible for researching a strategy for soil conservation. Distribute Activity Sheet C (4.10.7), and read through it as a class. Ensure that students understand the task.

Provide a variety of resources on soil and soil conservation for students to use as they work on this sheet.

Activity Sheet C

Note: This is a two-page activity sheet.

Directions to students:

Identify and describe the soil conservation issue. Explain, and draw a diagram of your solution (4.10.7).

Extensions

- Take a field trip to a local nursery or greenhouse, and discuss the composition of different types of soils used to grow different types of plants.

- Iceland is a prime example of soil depletion due to the introduction of animals and the process of deforestation. Have the students research soil depletion and conservation in areas such as Iceland, the Sahara Desert, and tropical rainforests.

- Invite a speaker from a soil conservation organization, local university, or college to speak on issues and initiatives about soil in your community.

The Formation of Soil

The process by which soil is created is a lengthy and complex one. It begins with weathering and erosion. Weathered rock accumulates on top of solid bedrock and forms layers of rock in varying stages of eroded material. These layers build up to form the *regolith* (the layer of rock and rock fragments that cover most of Earth's surface). When seeds are deposited, and plants begin to take root, the making of soil begins. On average, it takes 500 years to create 2.5 cm of topsoil.

A Soil Profile

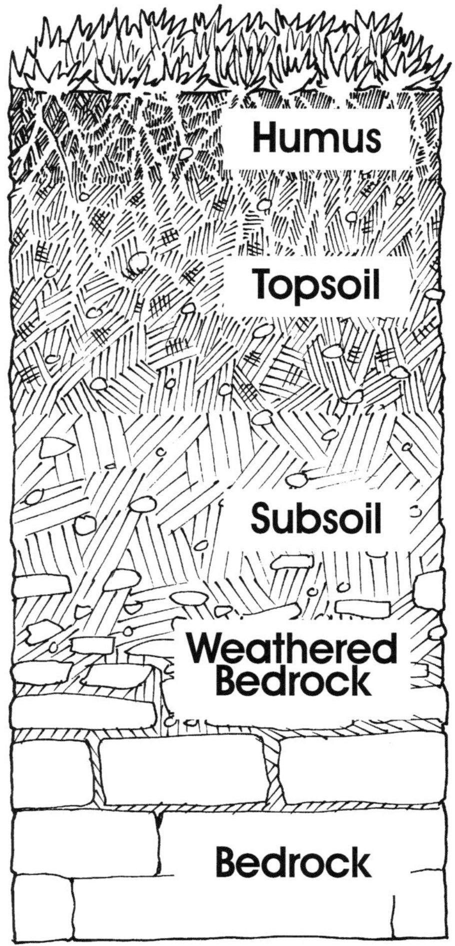

Understanding Soil

subsoil	bedrock	topsoil	profile
humus	weathered bedrock		regolith

It takes hundreds of years for soil to form. Erosion forms weathered rock that builds up in layers of rock fragments to form ____________________ that covers most of Earth's surface.

A cross section of the layers of soil is called a ________________.

The bottom layer of a soil profile is solid ________________.

Above this layer is an infertile layer of ________________________

____.

The top layer, ____________________, contains living plant roots, animals, and decaying material.

The fertile ____________________ is rich in humus.

The ____________________ is rich in minerals, but has little organic material.

Types of Soil

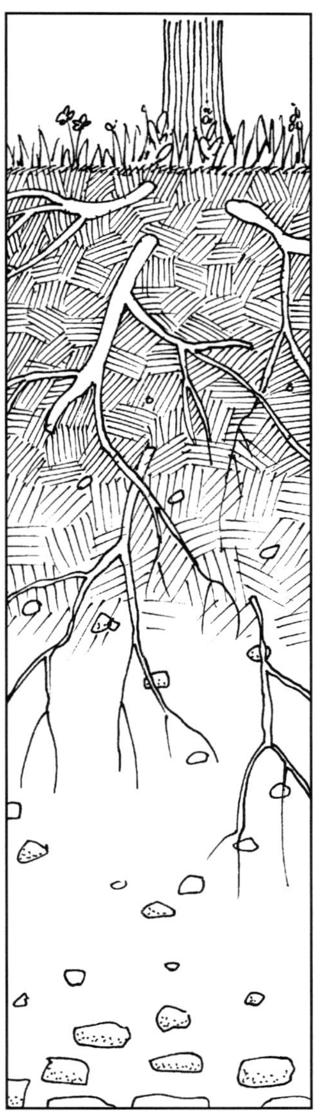

Temperate Forest

The soil is fertile in a temperate forest. The wet seasons of Europe have helped to establish forests with even brown surface soil.

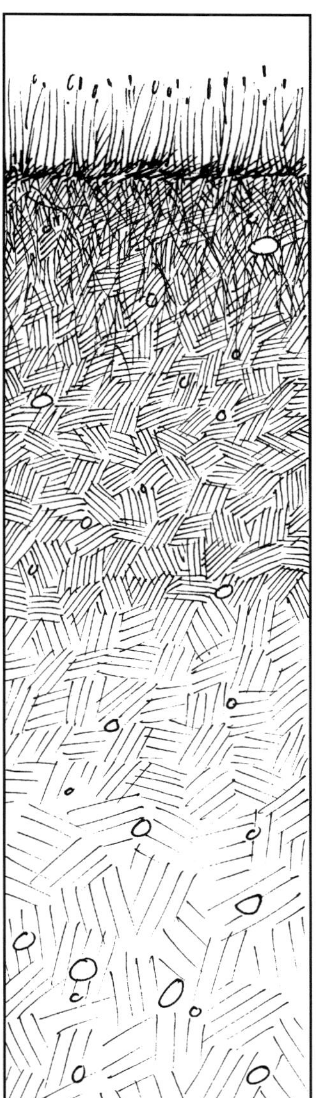

Temperate Grasslands

Temperate grasslands produce dark very fertile soil. It can be found on the North American prairie and in South America, Asia, Europe, Africa, and India.

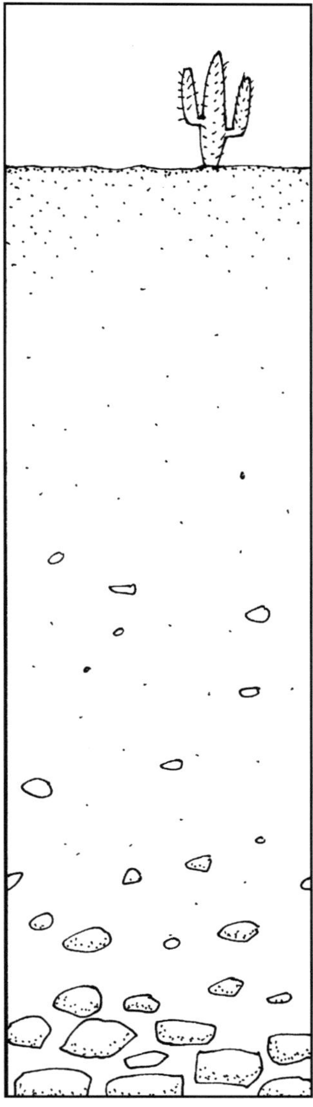

Dry Climate

Dry climates produce desert soil and contain little, if any, organic matter. Plants and trees will only survive if they are close to or surrounding an oasis.

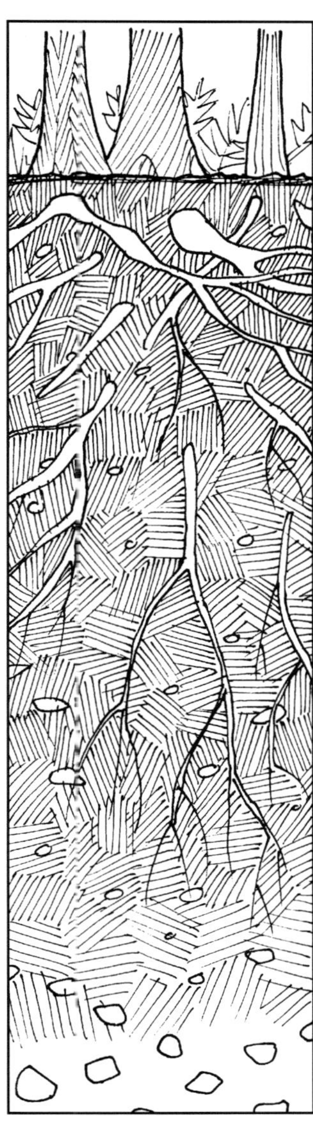

Wet Tropical Rainforest

The humus in a tropical rainforest is thin (up to 10 meters), but very fertile. The layers directly below the humus is clay, and is infertile. Clearing a tropical rainforest of all trees and vegetation will render the soil infertile.

Date: _______________________   **Name:** _______________________

Investigating Soil Profiles

Directions:

1. Cut the tops off the 4 pop bottles.

2. Using the hammer and nail, make 4 holes in the bottoms of the pop bottles.

3. Label the bottles as follows:
    A: Sandy soil is *A*.
    B: Clay soil is *B*.
    C: Prairie soil is *C*.
    D: Temperate forest soil is *D*.

4. Layer the bottles with an equal amount of small stones (representing bedrock) and pebbles (representing subsoil), leaving a 5 cm margin at the top of each bottle.

5. Fill the remainder of bottle *A* with sand.

6. Fill the remainder of bottle *B* with clay, and pack it lightly.

7. Fill the remainder of bottle *C* with a layer of topsoil and then with a layer of grass.

8. Fill the remainder of bottle *D* with a layer of topsoil, a layer of leaves, and a layer of small sticks.

9. Fill a large measuring cup with 500 ml of water. Add food colouring to the water.

10. Hold the bottle *A* over a beaker. Pour 125 ml of the coloured water into the bottle. Using the stopwatch, measure the length of time it takes for the water to flow through the soil profile and into the glass beaker. Repeat this process for the remaining soil profiles.

11. Measure the amount of water collected in the glass beakers for each of the soil profiles.

12. Record your results on the chart.

Investigating Soil Profiles

Bottle	Soil Profile Description	Length of Time for Water to Flow Through (seconds)	Amount of Water Collected in Beaker (ml)	Observations
A				
B				
C				
D				

Conclusions:

____

____

____

____

____

Soil Depletion Factors

Deforestation

Water Erosion

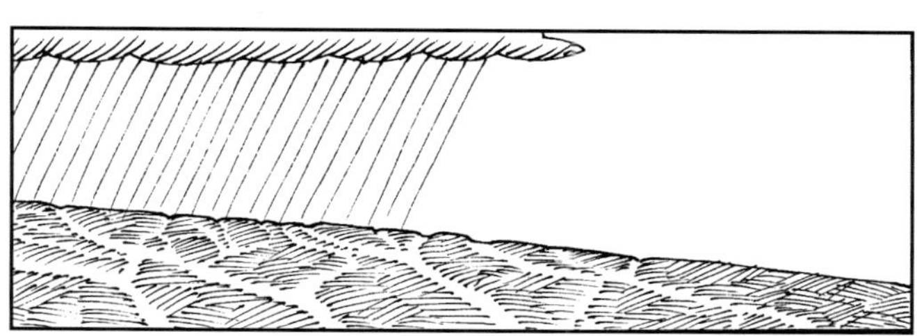

Wind Erosion

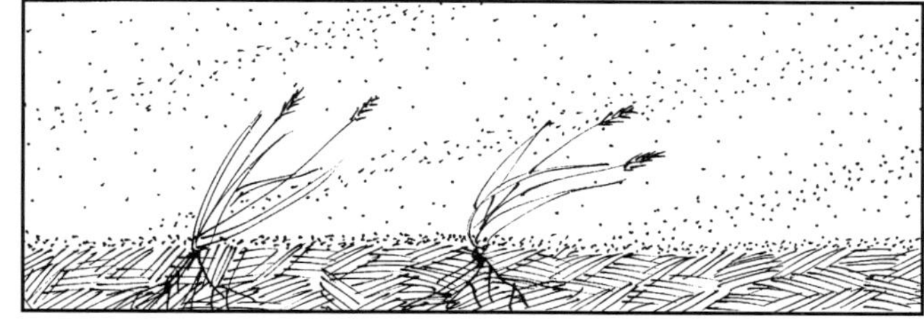

Cultivation

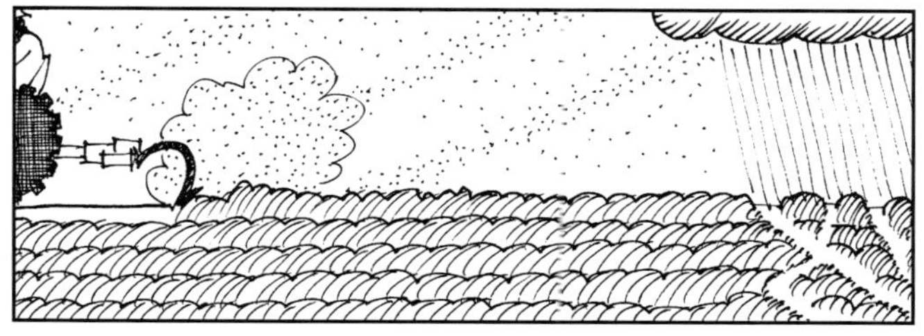

Contamination

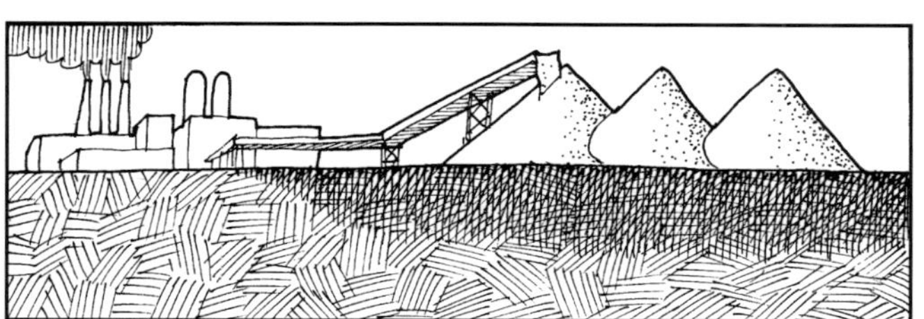

Urbanization

Soil Conservation

Imagine that you are a soil scientist, and you are trying to help conserve and improve soil for farming in different regions of the world. Choose one of the following scenarios (circle your selection):

A. Location: a mountainous region
   Problem: rains cause mudslides and soil to run down into the valleys

B. Location: a flat, treeless prairie
   Problem: wind storms blow away exposed topsoil

C. Location: dry sandy soil
   Problem: low productivity

D. Location: tropical rain forest
   Problem: clearing the forest causes a high degree of erosion due to heavy rainfall

E. Location: boggy marsh land
   Problem: root rot of crops, fungi and disease, low productivity

Your tasks:

1. State the soil conservation problem in your own words.

   ____

   ____

   ____

   ____

2. Draw a labelled diagram of the region on the back of this sheet, depicting the problem.

3. Describe your solution, and explain how it will conserve soil in
   the region.

____

____

____

____

____

____

4. Draw and label a diagram that shows how your solution will
   conserve soil.

11 | Resources and their Extraction

Background Information for Teachers

Metal: a chemical element that is usually solid at room temperature, conducts heat and electricity, and has a shiny appearance

Ore: a mineral that contains large quantities of metal

Alloy: a mixture of two or more metals that is melted, mixed, then cooled until it is solid

Leaching: when traces of minerals are dissolved from a rock by a liquid

Materials

- overhead projector
- information sheet titled, "Resource Extraction" (included. Make a copy for each student.) (4.11.1)
- diagram titled, "Seismic Testing" (included. Make an overhead transparency of this sheet.) (4.11.2)
- diagram titled, "Types of Mines" (included. Make an overhead transparency of this sheet.) (4.11.3)
- diagram titled, "Shallow Water Dredging and Deep Sea Mining" (included. Make an overhead transparency of this sheet.) (4.11.4)
- diagram titled, "Offshore Oil Well" (included. Make an overhead transparency of this sheet.) (4.11.5)
- reference material on minerals, metals, ores, and mining
- samples of copper or iron metallic ore
- hammers
- small towels or cloths
- funnels
- coffee filters
- vinegar
- glass beakers
- measuring cups with spout
- chart paper
- markers

Activity: Part One: Rock and Mineral Resources

Explain to the students that they have looked at soil as a resource, but there are many other natural resources. Ask:

- What types of natural resources are found in Earth's crust?
- What are they used for?

Brainstorm a list of natural resources, and record these on chart paper. Focus on natural resources that are extracted from Earth's crust through mining. Ask:

- Which natural resources are mined?
- How are they extracted from Earth?

Provide each student with a copy of the information sheet titled, "Resource Extraction" (4.11.1). Read, and discuss the information with the students.

Display the overhead diagrams titled, "Seismic Testing for Minerals" (4.11.2), "Types of Mines" (4.11.3), "Shallow Water Dredging and Deep Sea Mining" (4.11.4), and "Off Shore Oil Rigs" (4.11.5). Have students examine the diagrams carefully to determine the processes of each mining technique.

Provide each student with Activity Sheet A (4.11.6), and reference material about minerals, metals, and ores. Have the students use the reference material to complete the sheet.

Activity Sheet A

Directions to students:

Complete the chart to describe minerals, metals, and ore (4.11.6).

Activity: Part Two: Resource Extraction

Explain to the students that metals and minerals are usually contained in rocks and must be extracted. One way of extracting metals is called *leaching*.

Divide the class into working groups. Provide each group with a 100 g of copper or iron ore, a hammer, cloth, funnel, coffee filter, 250 mL of vinegar, a glass beaker, a measuring cup, and Activity Sheet B (4.11.7).

Have the groups wrap their sample inside the cloth and break it into small pieces using the hammer.

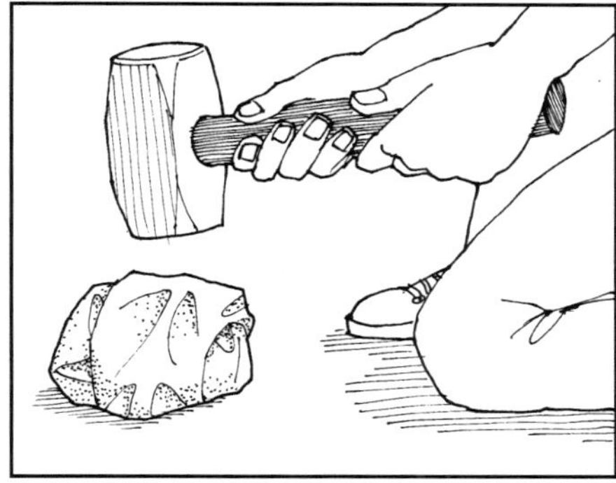

Next have the students place the coffee filter in the funnel and pour in the mineral fragments, while supporting the funnel over the beaker. Ask:

- What do you think will happen when the vinegar is filtered through the metallic ore?

Have the students record their predictions on the activity sheet.

Now have the students add the vinegar (leaching solution). As the liquid drains into the beaker, have the students note the colour of the vinegar. When the liquid has stopped dripping, pour it into the measuring cup and again into the funnel. The students may have to repeat this process two or three times.

Discuss the investigation. Ask:

- How successful was the extraction?
- What could be changed to increase the amount of metal extracted?
- How would the metal be removed from the solution?

Activity Sheet B

Directions to students:

Complete the sheet as you investigate leaching (4.11.7).

Extension

As a class, discuss what it might be like to work in a mine. Ask students to imagine that they are working as miners in mines, far from home. Have them write letters to their families describing their experiences.

Assessment Suggestion

Observe the groups as they investigate leaching ores. Focus on their ability to describe the process and draw conclusions. Use the Anecdotal Record sheet on page 16 to record results.

Resource Extraction

Much of what we need in order to produce food and clothing comes from the surface of Earth's crust. Many other materials we need to build such things as roads, buildings, bridges, and automobiles are found underground and must be mined.

The extraction or removal of these materials is complex and expensive. Before removal even begins, there are many years of exploration, research, development, and construction. Initially, people found minerals that were *outcrops* on Earth's surface. Today, scientists use elaborate technology to locate minerals that are far below the surface. The technology includes drilling core samples, seismic testing, and satellite imaging. Rocks have different characteristics and properties, which enable different kinds of equipment to pinpoint their locations. Some examples include:

- A magnetometer, which measures Earth's magnetic field to locate iron-ore, or nickel.
- A gravimeter is used to locate minerals that are light or heavy.
- A Geiger counter measures the radiation emitted from certain rocks (such as uranium ores).

Within Earth's crust, the location or depth of a mineral or material helps determine the type of mining technique used. If minerals such as coal, ore, or copper are found close to the surface (less than 300 m deep), an open pit or strip mine can be used. Drift mines are used if deposits are found in layers exposed on a hillside. If the location of the mineral or material is deep in the ground, a shaft mine must be used. Deep mining is the most expensive type of mining. Shafts and tunnels must be dug, water pumped out, the air ventilated, and workers, equipment, and the mined material must be moved safely. Shaft mines are generally dug to a maximum depth of 1800 m, but some diamond mines can be 3 km or more deep.

Minerals and other deposits can also be extracted from rivers, lakes, and oceans. Shallow-water dredging and deep-sea mining yield materials such as sand, gravel, tin, and manganese. Offshore wells are used to extract oil and natural gas. As land-based minerals become increasingly scarce, offshore reserves will become more valuable.

The environmental impact of mining is significant. Open pit mines scour the landscape, wastewater from deep shaft mines can be toxic, and deep-sea drilling can lead to water pollution. Mining practices have changed dramatically in the last several decades to address safety, sustainability, and restoration of the environment.

Seismic Testing for Minerals

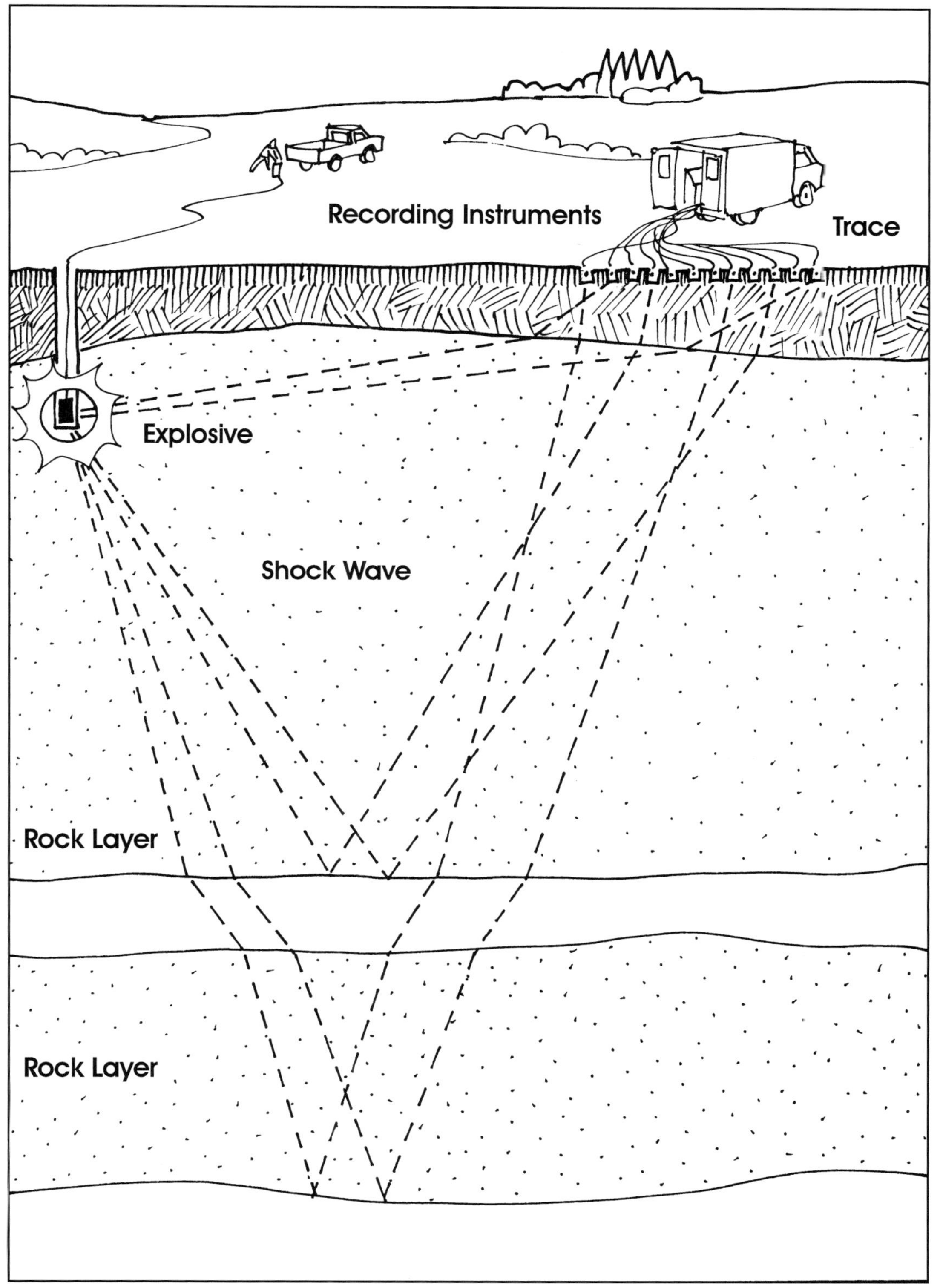

Types of Mines

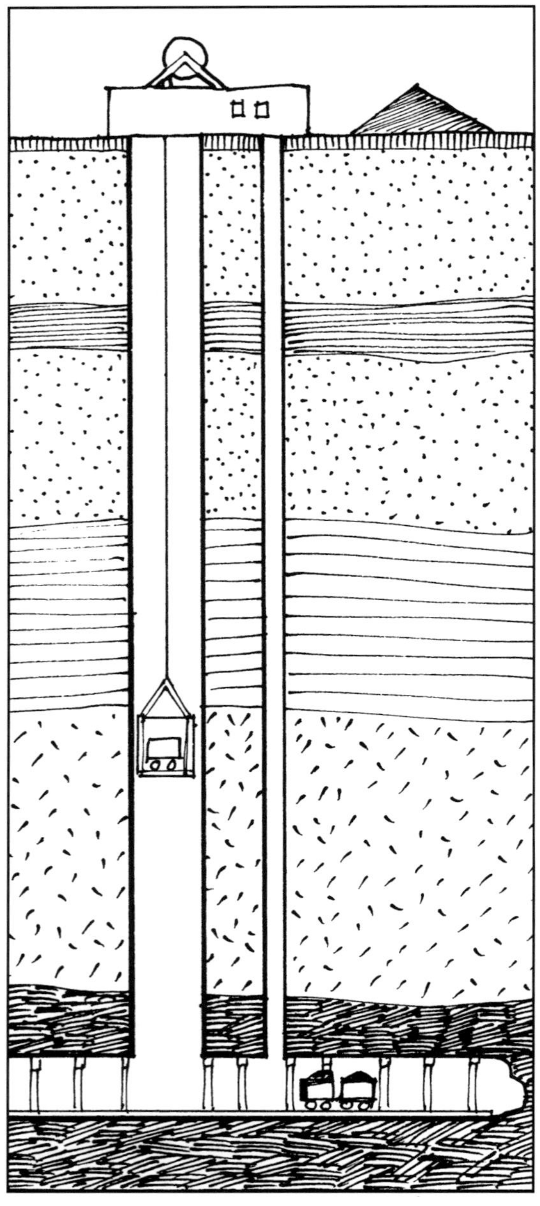

Shaft Mine

Drift Mine

Open Pit Mine

Shallow-Water Dredging

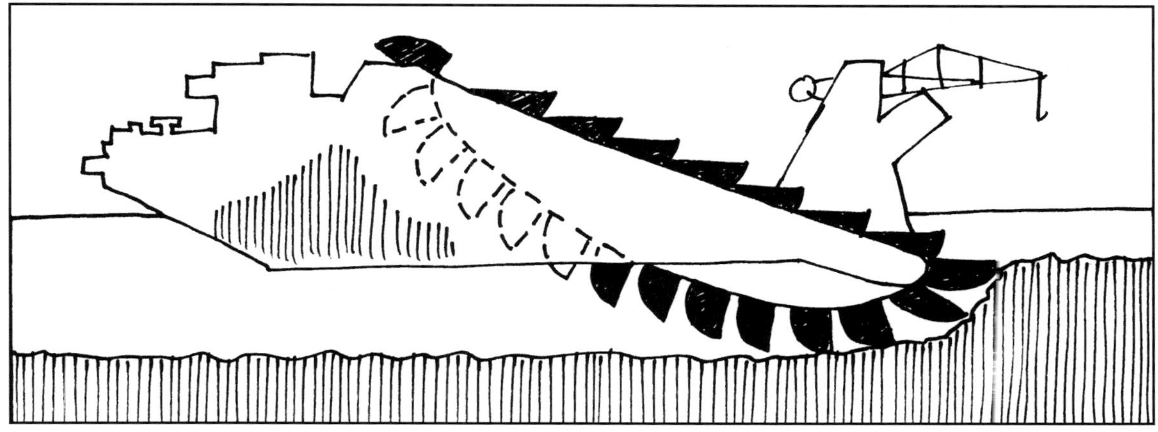

Deep-Sea Mining

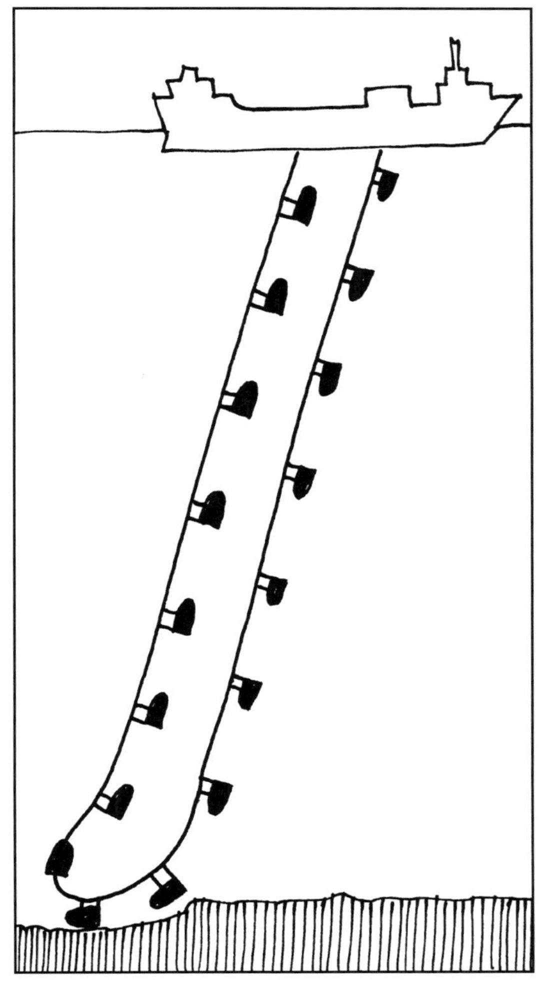

Dredging

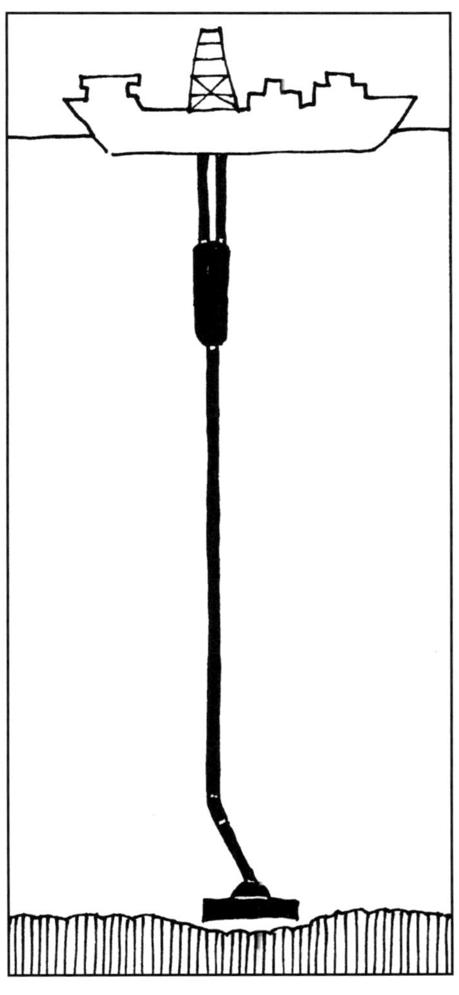

Suction

Offshore Oil Well

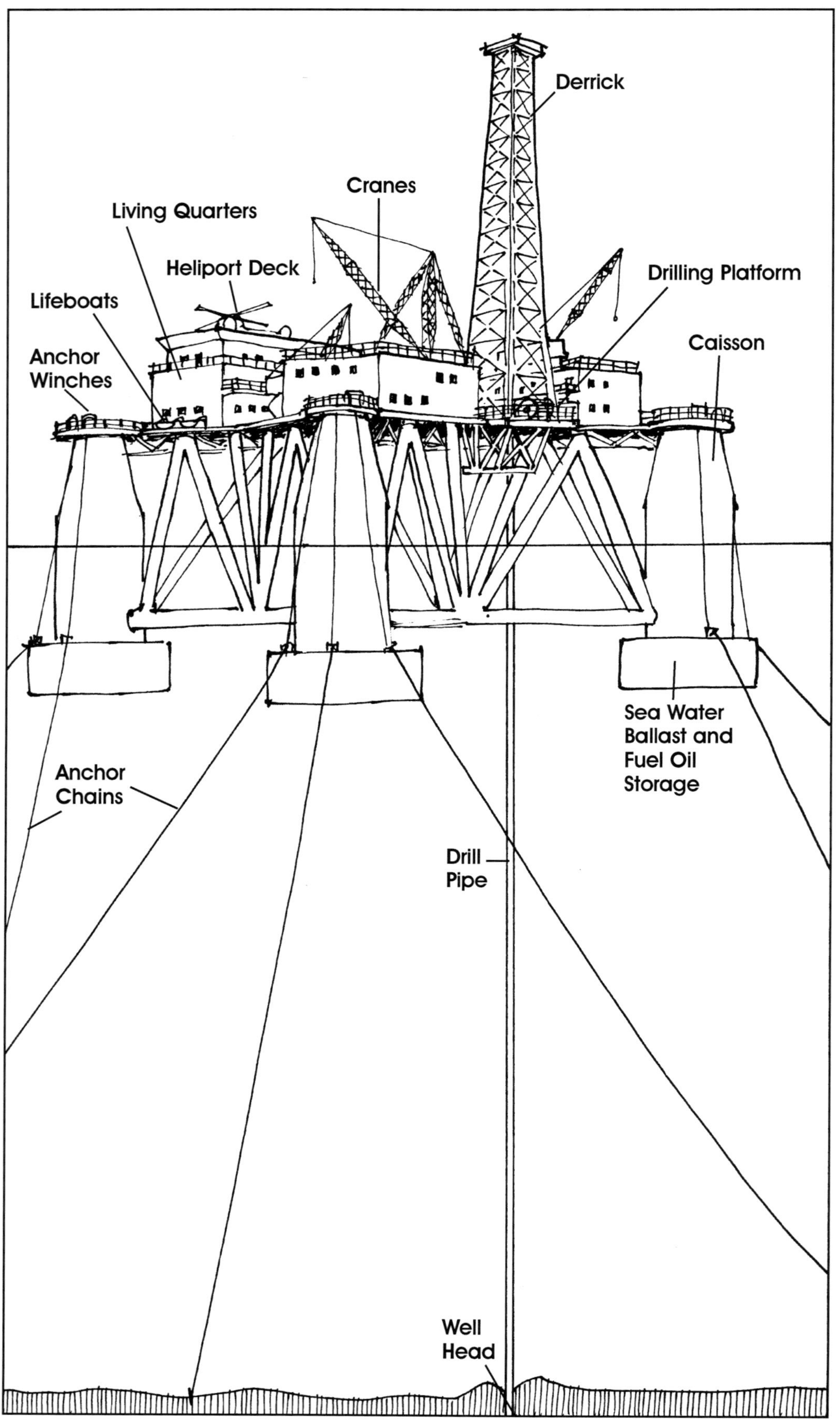

From Earth's Crust to You

Mineral Name	Ore Metal	Uses	Mining Method
Bauxite	Aluminum		
Rutile	Titanium		
Hematite	Iron Ore		
Bornite	Copper		
Sphalerite	Zinc Ore		
Galena	Lead Ore		
Cinnabar	Mercury		
Platinum	Platinum		
Gold	Gold		
Silver	Silver		

Date: ________________________   **Name:** ______________________________

Leaching Ores

Predict what will happen when the vinegar is filtered through the metallic ore.

____

____

Draw, and label a diagram of this investigation.

Observations:

____

____

____

What does the coloured vinegar indicate about its contents?

____

____

____

12 | Geological Resources

Background Information for Teachers

Canada is one of the largest exporters of rock and mineral products in the world. There are hundreds of mines across the country that extract coal, copper, potash, gold, iron ore, nickel, silver, uranium, zinc, and other rock products. We use these products in our every day lives, and the mining industry is vital to the Canadian economy.

Mining is a valuable primary resource in Manitoba, averaging $1 billion a year and employing approximately 3,000 people directly, and 10,000 people indirectly. Billions of years ago volcanoes erupted at the bottom of ancient seabeds and laid down deposits now known as greenstone belts. The mining resources we use today are found within these belts. The principle metals mined in Manitoba are nickel, copper, zinc, and gold, but specialty metals such as tantalum and cesium are also extracted. In addition to these metals, industrial minerals such as gypsum, salt, granite, limestone, peat, lime, sand, and gravel are also plentiful in Manitoba.

With the exception of the Tanco Mine, in Lac du Bonnet, the major sources of mined products in Manitoba are found in the north. Thompson, Flin Flon, Snow Lake, and Leaf Rapids are all mining centres in the province. There is considerable potential for future development. Diamond exploration, for example, has increased in the eastern and central regions of Manitoba.

Fossil fuels, such as coal, oil (crude petroleum), and natural gas were formed millions of years ago. Fossil fuels are the most widely used energy resources in the world. Fossil fuels are used for heating and cooling buildings, motorized transportation (cars, airplanes, and so on), and electricity.

Note: Students will likely have some background knowledge of fossil fuels from the grade six unit of Electricity, in which nonrenewable sources of energy are studied.

Materials

- student atlases
- map of Canada (included. Make a copy for each pair of students.) (4.12.1)
- map of Manitoba (included. Make a copy for each pair of students.) (4.12.2)
- reference materials on mining in Canada
- access to computer lab
- access to web sites with information about mining in Canada and Manitoba (see Web Sites)

Note: The site **http://mmsd1.mms.nrcan.gc.ca/ mmsd/facts/default_e.asp** can be used in Activity Part One to complete the map of Canada. This site provides maps of metal and nonmetal mines, and fossil fuel deposits in Canada. Students can also use atlases and other reference materials to complete the assigned task. Other related web sites and books that students can use for research on mining in Manitoba are listed at the beginning of this unit.

Activity

Note: This lesson requires access to a computer lab for research and web site use.

Divide the class into pairs, and provide each pair of students with an atlas and web site address. Have the students access the web site pages titled "Metal Mines," "Nonmetal Mines," and "Interactive Maps" to identify mined products in Canada and find the mine locations. Students may also use the atlas to locate metals and nonmetals mined in Canada.

Briefly discuss the geological resources in Canada. Ask:

- Which are examples of Canada's metal resources?

- Which are examples of nonmetal resources?

Now focus on fossil fuels. Ask:

- What is a fossil fuel? (a resource used for energy)
- What are examples of fossil fuels? (coal, oil, natural gas)
- Do the web site maps indicate where these resources are found in Canada?

Discuss the uses and locations of fossil fuel deposits in Canada.

Now provide the pairs with a map of Canada, (4.12.1)and have them plot the locations of two metal mines, two nonmetal mines, and two fossil fuel deposits (coal, oil, or natural gas). Students should create a legend on the map with symbols for each mine or deposit they locate.

Once the pairs have completed this task, ask:

Why are these resources important to Canada – to Manitoba?

What would a geologist's role be in the mining industry?

Explain to the students that they are going to research rock and mineral products that are mined in Manitoba. Using web sites and other reference materials, have each pair of students select a resource that is mined in Manitoba, then locate a mine on a map and research its operations.

Provide each pair with the map of Manitoba (4.12.2) and the four-page research guide (4.12.3). Review the research guide with the class:

1. Research Checklist - Review the requirements of the assignment
2. Interview – Review the interview process and etiquette
   - Phone or email the general manager or contact person at the mine.
   - Review the questions that will be asked.
   - Create additional questions that will be asked.
   - Remember to speak politely.
   - Take notes in point form during the interview.
   - Remember to thank the person for their time.
3. Keeping Our Research on Track
   - The chart should be completed on a regular basis.
   - Information should be recorded neatly and in detail.
4. Information Gathering
   - Gather information and make notes in point form.
   - Resources should be recorded at the bottom of the page, using the correct format. Provide students with sample bibliography format.

Also explain that each pair of students will present their research to the class. Discuss and brainstorm some interesting ways that research can be presented to the class (e.g., PowerPoint presentations, role-playing, project backboards, story boards, posters or murals, and so on).

Provide plenty of time for students to gather information, conduct interviews, display their research, and present to the class.

Activity Sheet

Note: This is a four-page research guide. Make multiple copies of the fourth page for students to use for taking notes during their research.

Direction to students:

Use the four-page research guide to plan your research (4.12.3).

Assessment Suggestion

As a class, identify the necessary criteria for the research projects. For example:

- completed all aspects of the project (including activity sheets)
- work is neatly presented
- detailed information on the resource and mine is inlcuded
- used various resources

List these criteria on the Rubric on page 19. Record results as the students present their projects.

Canada

YUKON
Whitehorse
NORTHWEST TERRITORIES
Yellowknife
NUNAVUT
BRITISH COLUMBIA
Victoria
ALBERTA
Edmonton
SASKATCHEWAN
Regina
MANITOBA
Winnipeg
ONTARIO
QUEBEC
Quebec City
NEW FOUNDLAND AND LABRADOR
St. John's
PEI
Charlottetown
Fredericton
NOVA SCOTIA
Halifax
NEW BRUNSWICK
Ottawa
Toronto
N
E
S
W
Legend

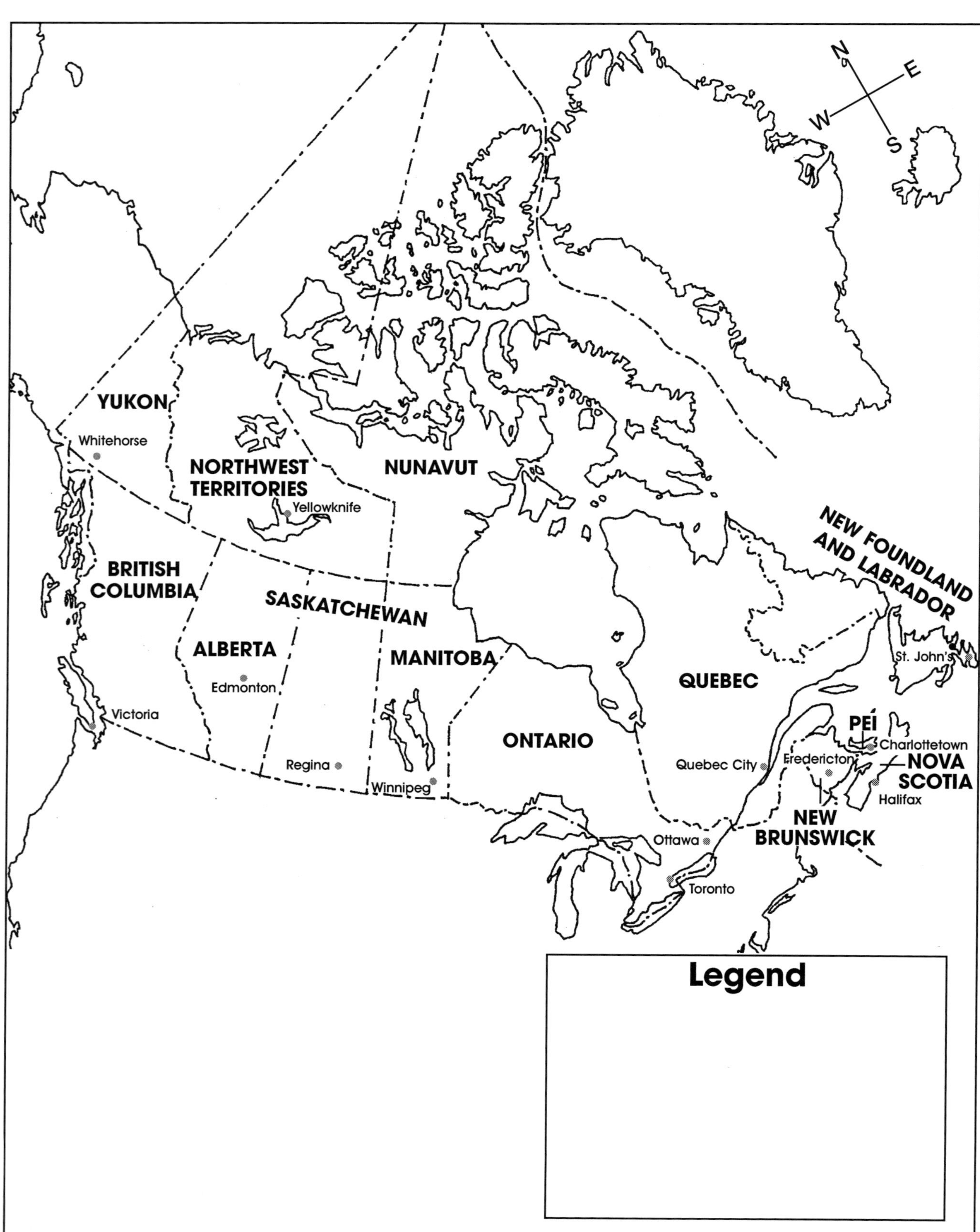

Manitoba

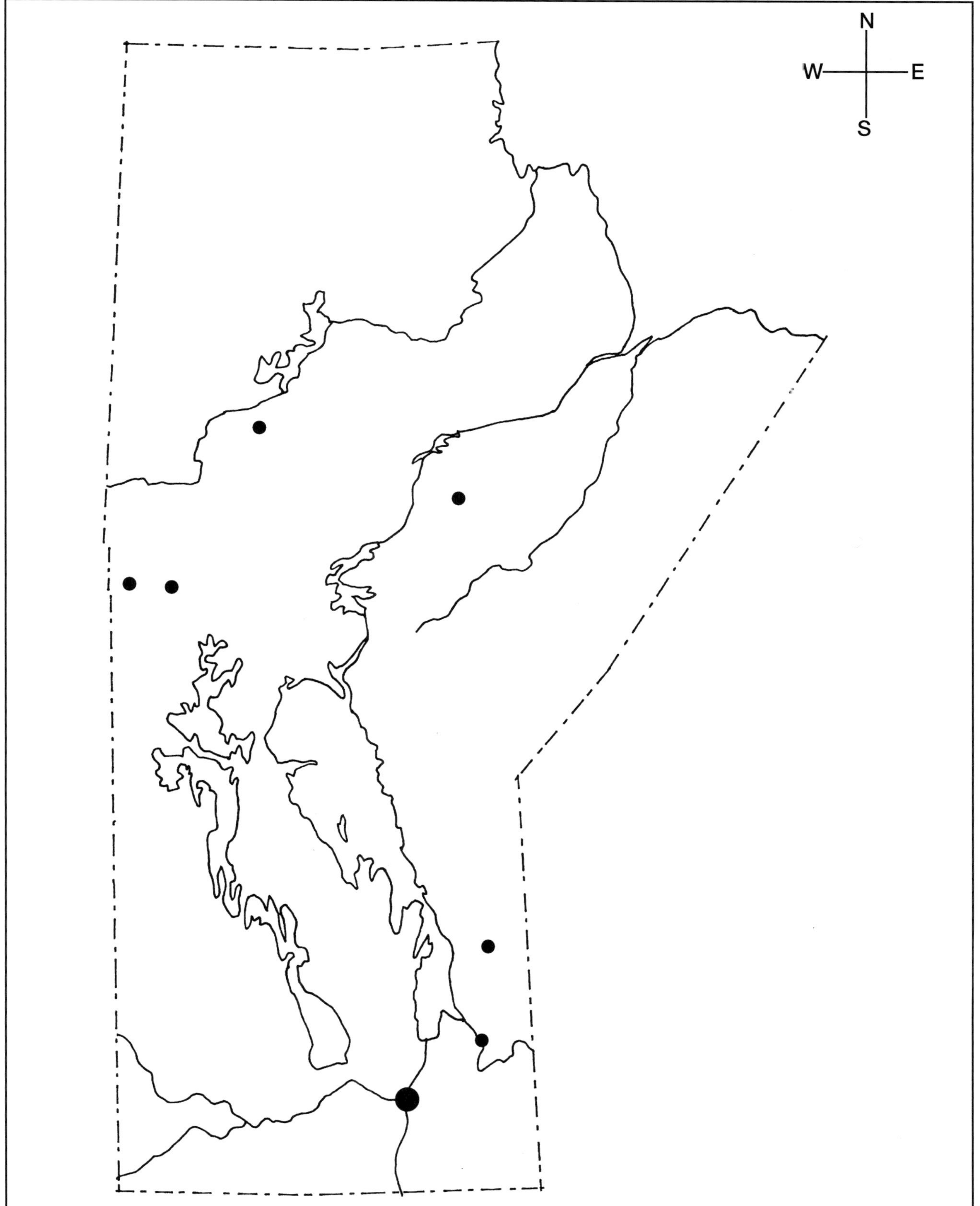

Date: _______________________   **Name:** _________________________________

____

Research Checklist

Research Topic: _______________________________

1. Choose a resource mined in Manitoba. ☐

2. Describe the resource and its uses. ☐

3. Locate a mine on the map of Manitoba. ☐

4. Provide information about the mine and the mining operation. ☐

5. Describe how the resource is processed and, if possible, how it is recycled. ☐

6. Interview ☐

7. Time-management record (Keeping Our Research on Track) ☐

8. Rough notes (Information Gathering) ☐

Date: _________________________   Name: _____________________________

____

Interview

Name of Person Interviewed: _________________________________
Mining Company: _________________________________

Questions	Answers
1. How many people are employed at the mine? Are they from the local area?	
2.	
3. How important is the mine to the economy of the local area?	
4.	
5. What environmental standards are in place to protect the surrounding area?	
6.	
7. What is the life span of the mine? How long will it be in operation?	
8.	

*Remember to speak politely and thank the person for their time.

Name: _______________________________

____

Keeping Our Research on Track
Time-Management Record

Research Topic: _______________________________

Date	Length of Time	What We Accomplished

Date: _______________   Name: _____________________
____

Information Gathering

Research Topic: _______________________________

Resources Used:

13 | Mining and the Environment

Background Information for Teachers

In Manitoba mining has both positive and negative implications for society. It provides needed products (metals), jobs for workers, and contributes to the province's economy. Mining also has some far-reaching implications for the health and sustainability of the natural environment. Sustainable development focuses on balancing society, the economy, and the environment so that natural resources can be used now and sustained for future generations.

Materials

- diagram titled, "Sustainable Development" (included. Make an overhead transparency of this sheet.) (4.13.2)
- chart paper
- markers
- overhead projector
- information sheet titled, "Mining Scenario" (included. Make a copy for each student.) (4.13.3)
- information sheet titled, "Advocacy Group Descriptions" (included. Make a copy, and provide each group with one description.) (4.13.4)

Activity: Part One: Land Use

As a class, discuss the students' understanding of how humans use land. Ask:

- What do we use land for?

Record students' ideas on chart paper. Focus on each land use. Ask:

- What type of impact does this use have on the land?

Provide each student with Activity Sheet A (4.13.1). Have students work in pairs to discuss each land use, the impact of land uses, and solutions.

Once students have completed this task, have them share their ideas.

Display the diagram titled, "Sustainable Development" (4.13.2). Ask:

- What does sustainable development mean?
- Why is sustainable development important?
- Why is sustainable development difficult to achieve?

Activity Sheet

Directions to students:

Complete the chart (4.13.1).

Activity: Part Two: The Mining Debate

Explain to the students that there are often many sides to how land could, or should, be used. Divide the class into four groups. Provide all groups with the Mining Scenario (4.13.3), and have them read it over together.

Next provide the groups with the Advocacy Group Descriptions (4.13.4). Groups should not share their advocacy information with any other group.

Explain to the students that they are going to conduct a mock town hall meeting to discuss the building of a new mine. Each advocacy group will play a role at the meeting. The president of the mining company will run the meeting. The mining company's board of directors will be responsible for presenting its plan to the other groups and answering questions that arise.

The other advocacy groups will ask questions and raise their group's concerns. They will also present solutions and alternatives for issues that concern them.

13

Provide class time for students to assign roles and plan their agenda for the town hall meeting. They may wish to incorporate costumes and relevant props (signs, posters, brochures, overheads, and so on).

Conduct the town hall meeting. Allow each advocacy group to present at the meeting, ask questions, and discuss issues.

Following the town hall meeting, discuss the process. Ask:

- Were you able to understand or sympathize with the perspectives of the other groups?
- Were their opinions and concerns valid?
- Why is it important for communities to hold these types of meetings?

Extensions

- Have the students research the Internet and newspapers for articles about mining in Manitoba and relate to the discussion about sustainable development.

- The Sierra Club, Greenpeace, and World Wildlife Fund are just some of the environmental groups that consider issues regarding land use. Have students research an environmental group, and discover the part the group plays in creating sustainable development.

- Have students research how mined materials and by-products of mining are recycled or reused.

Assessment Suggestion

Have students complete the Student Self-Assessment sheet on page 22 to reflect on their learning about mining and environmental issues.

End-of-Unit Assessment

Reflect on the tasks undertaken by each student throughout the unit to complete the End-of-Unit Assessment chart on page 26. Consider all assessment tools, investigations, and activities when identifying and commenting on individual student achievement.

Date: _______________________   Name: _____________________________

Land Use and Environmental Impact

Land Use	Positive Impact	Negative Impact	Solutions
Residential Homes			
Farmland			
Land Fill			
Open Pit Mine			
Park			
Railway Tracks			
Logging Road			
Golf Course			
Manufacturing Plant			

Sustainable Development

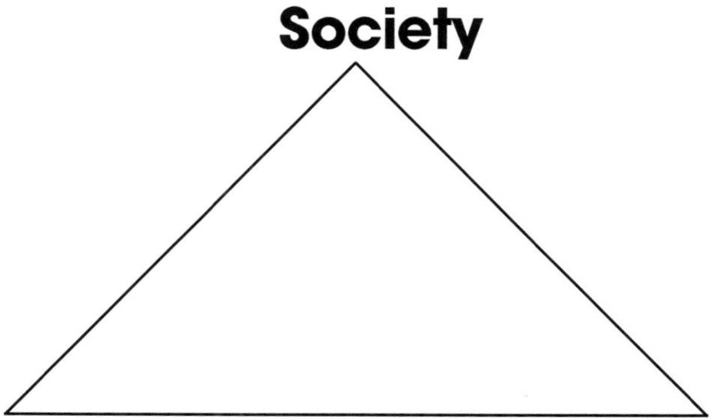

Sustainable Development of Minerals and Metals

When talking about minerals and metals, sustainable development incorporates the following elements:

- finding, extracting, producing, adding value to, using, re-using, recycling, and when necessary, disposing of mineral and metal products in the most efficient, competitive, and environmentally responsible manner possible, using best practices
- respecting the needs and values of all resource users and considering those needs and values in government decision making
- maintaining or enhancing the quality of life and the environment for present and future generations
- securing the involvement and participation of stakeholders, individuals, and communities in decision making

(Minerals and Metals: Towards a Sustainable Future, Government of Canada, 2000)

Mining Scenario

Proposed Mine Site: Northeastern Manitoba
Type of Mine: Shaft, 2 km in depth
Discharge: Two mining ponds = 30 million litres
No. of Employees: 100
Potential Revenue: $120 million per year

After ten years of exploration, feasibility studies, and development, the Great North Mining Company proposes to begin construction of a shaft mine. The mine location is presently a forested area and situated 2 km from the town of Bolder and 12 km from the town of Gravelstone. It is on the border of Timberlake Provincial Forest.

The development of the mine will involve building roads into the area, clearing 20 hectares of forest, and creating two mining ponds to contain the mining discharge. The mining company will be responsible for all development of the mine.

Members of the Great North Mining Company will be presenting a proposal for the mine site to the citizens of Bolder and Gravelstone to discuss the following issues:

1. Employment of local residents

2. Local business involvement

3. Wildlife management and environmental impact

4. Increased traffic and noise pollution

All interested parties are welcome to come and discuss these issues and ask questions.

Advocacy Group Descriptions

Great North Mining Company

The Great North Mining Company has been operating in Manitoba for 70 years, and is a main employer in the province. The company has a track record of employing people from the local area and keeping their employees informed and involved in the company. The past environmental record has been fair and is improving. The Great North Mining Company has invested 200 million dollars thus far, and it has high hopes for the mine. The mine has a potential life span of 30–45 years.

Environmental Group

The environmental group is concerned about the future survival of the forest and the water supply in the region. There is also a threatened population of moose in the area. The group feels that the development of the mine will decrease habitat of the moose and further impact the survival of the moose population. The mine will also have a detrimental impact on the adjacent parkland and the species of animals that live there. Although the mining company has a fair environmental record, it has not always looked out for the interest of the environment.

Bolder and Gravelstone Citizens (Pro)

This group involves 50% of the townspeople of Bolder and Gravelstone. With the slowing economy, jobs and further economic development of the area is welcome. The increase in jobs will provide more stability for the community, increase the tax base to support local schools and the hospital, and increase support for local business such as grocery stores, hotels, and banks.

Bolder and Gravelstone Citizens (Con)

This group involves 50% of the townspeople of Bolder and Gravelstone. These townspeople believe the development of the mine will increase traffic and pollution in the area. This will have a negative impact on the health of the local residents and cause a decrease in the number of tourists that value this environmentally pristine area.

References for Teachers

Decker, R, and Decker, B. *Volcanoes*. San Francisco: W.H. Freeman and Company, 1981.

Friedl, Alfred. *Teaching Science to Children: An Inquiry Approach*. Toronto: McGraw-Hill College Division, 1996.

Government of Canada. *Minerals and Metals: "Towards a Sustainable Future,"* Monograph No.10. Ottawa: Government of Canada, 2000.

Lawson, Jennifer. *Hands-On Science: Grade Four*. Winnipeg: Portage and Main Press, 2000.

Levenson, Elaine. *Teaching Children About Science*. New York: Tab Books, 1994.

______. *Teaching Children About Life and Earth Sciences: Activities Every Teacher and Parent Can Use*. New York: McGraw-Hill, 1994.

Pinet, Michele, Alain Korkos, and Fay Greenbaum. *Be Your Own Rock and Mineral Expert*. New York: Sterling, 1997.

Ricciuti, Edward R., and Margaret W. Carruthers. *National Audubon Society First Field Guide: Rocks and Minerals*. New York: Scholastic Canada, 1998.

Ticotsky, Alan. *Who Says You Can't Teach Science?* Toronto: Pearson, 1999.

Wyler, Rose. *Science Fun With Mud and Dirt*. New York: Simon & Schuster, 1986.